Cambridge Studies in Islamic Civilization

The rise and rule of Tamerlane

Cambridge Studies in Islamic Civilization

Titles in this series

ANDREW M. WATSON
Agricultural innovation in the early Islamic world
The diffusion of crops and farming techniques, 700–1100

ELIAS N. SAAD
Social history of Timbuktu
The role of Muslim scholars and notables, 1400–1900

G. H. A. JUYNBOLL
Muslim tradition
Studies in chronology, provenance and authorship of early Hadith

B. F. MUSALLAM
Sex and society in Islam
Birth control before the nineteenth century

SURAIYA FAROQHI
Towns and townsmen of Ottoman Anatolia
Trade, crafts and food production in an urban setting 1520–1650

NABIL A. SALEH
Unlawful gain and legitimate profit in Islamic Law
Riba, gharar and Islamic banking

SURAIYA FAROQHI
Men of modest substance
House owners and house property in seventeenth century Ankara and Kayseri

PATRICIA CRONE
Roman, provincial and Islamic law
The origins of the Islamic patronate

STEFAN SPERL
Mannerism in Arabic poetry
A structural analysis of selected texts, 3rd century AH/9th century AD–5th century AH/11th century AD

BEATRICE MANZ FORBES
The rise and rule of Tamerlane

AMNON COHEN
Economic life in Ottoman Jerusalem

The rise and rule of Tamerlane

BEATRICE FORBES MANZ
TUFTS UNIVERSITY

The right of the University of Cambridge to print and sell all manner of books was granted by Henry VIII in 1534. The University has printed and published continuously since 1584.

Cambridge University Press
Cambridge
New York Port Chester Melbourne Sydney

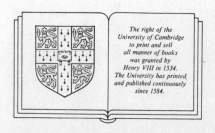

Published by the Press Syndicate of the University of Cambridge
The Pitt Building, Trumpington Street, Cambridge CB2 1RP
40 West 20th Street, New York, NY 10011, USA
10 Stamford Road, Oakleigh, Melbourne 3166, Australia

First published 1989
Reprinted 1990
First paperback edition 1991

Printed in Great Britain at the University Press, Cambridge

British Library cataloguing in publication data

Manz, Beatrice Forbes
The rise and rule of Tamerlane. –
(Cambridge studies in Islamic civilization).
1. Mongol Empire. Tamerlane
I. Title
950'.2'0924

Library of Congress cataloguing in publication data

Manz, Beatrice Forbes
The rise and rule of Tamerlane.
(Cambridge studies in Islamic civilization)
Bibliography.
Includes index.
1. Timur, 1336–1405. 2. Asia – History.
3. Conquerors – Asia – Biography. I. Title. II. Series.
DS23.M28 1989 950'.2'0924 [B] 88–25679

ISBN 0 521 34595 2 hardback
ISBN 0 521 40614 5 paperback

WD

Dedicated to my parents,
William Hathaway Forbes and Anne Pappenheimer Forbes
with love and gratitude

Contents

Maps

Acknowledgements

The first person I must mention is no longer here to receive my thanks. Professor Joseph Fletcher gave me invaluable help and encouragement throughout the early stages of this work, taking time even to proofread my dissertation during his fatal illness. I owe a great deal also to Professor Omeljan Pritsak who gave me valuable criticism and suggestions on my work, through many years of development.

I want likewise to thank Professor John E. Woods who has been unstinting of his time, insight and erudition in support of this and other projects. Numerous other scholars have also given me help with this work; I want particularly to thank Professors Edward Keenan, Rudi Lindner, Isenbike Togan, Thomas Allsen, David Morgan, and Lynda Schaffer for their very useful suggestions. My research assistant, Hamid Sardar-Afkhami, has ably assisted me with the final revisions. In addition, I owe very considerable gratitude to the many terminal watchers of the Harvard Computer Services who have helped me to master an unfamiliar medium.

I was able to spend a year abroad collecting materials on a Fulbright-Hays and International Research and Exchanges Board Fellowship. In the Soviet Union I have received assistance from the Institutes of Eastern Studies in Leningrad and Tashkent, and the Institute of History in Dushanbe. I want in particular to thank O. F. Akimushkin and other members of the Leningrad Institute for their help and advice. A generous fellowship from the Giles Whiting Foundation made it possible to spend a year working on my dissertation free from outside responsibilities. In the revision of the work I have been aided by fellowships from the American Council of Learned Societies, the Russian Research Center and the Center for Middle Eastern Studies at Harvard, and by research assistance from Tufts University.

I want to record my gratitude to my husband, Robert D. Manz, who has given me much useful criticism and invaluable moral support throughout this enterprise. Finally, and above all, I want to thank my mother, Dr. Anne P. Forbes, who has given countless hours of her time to make this work possible.

A note on usage and transcription

This work deals with a society which derived its names and terms from four languages: Arabic, Persian, Mongolian and Central Asian Turkic. I have used three different systems of transcription – one for Persian and Arabic, a second for Mongolian and a third for Turkic. For Arabic and Persian I have chosen a slightly simplified form of the *Encyclopaedia of Islam* transcription, making no distinction between the two languages. I have altered some consonants to conform with English usage (j instead of dj for instance) and have chosen to use q in place of ḳ. I have also omitted lines under compound consonants.

Mongolian and Turkic names present a number of problems. The Mongol ruling class changed its language from Mongolian to Turkic in the course of the thirteenth century. Names and terms from the early period I have therefore transcribed as Mongolian, using Professor Francis W. Cleaves' transcription, adapted to conform to English orthography: so for instance Chaghadai, Qubilai. Later names, from the western regions of the Mongol Empire after about 1300, are transcribed as Turkic. For this reason, while Chinggis Khan's son is referred to as Chaghadai, the polity named after him, formed after 1300, is called the Ulus Chaghatay. For terms, since most refer to the later period, I have used a Turkic version (e.g. *yasa*, *yarghu*, *khurïltay*) giving the Mongolian in parentheses where appropriate. Turkic transcription is much the most problematical, since we have no widely accepted transcription system for Chaghatay Turkic. On consonants I have used the same transliteration as for Persian and Arabic, but on vowels I have used modern Turkish usage, distinguishing between front and back rather than long and short, and have assumed vowel harmony.

For names and terms, I have used full diacriticals. To form the plural I have added an *s*, except in compounds and in cases where the collective noun is a standard term. Hence *amīrs* but *umarā' dīwān* and *ᶜulamā'*. Names of dynasties are spelled according to modern usage, without diacriticals. Place names are also written without diacriticals. The best known cities and provinces are given in modern usage (Khorasan, Herat) but for smaller places I have used the vowelling of classical usage.

For dates I have given both *hijra* and Christian years. For some parts of Temür's career an exact chronology has been preserved, while for others we have few dates, and on the early parts of his career the major sources disagree among themselves. Where I have known the month or season of the *hijra* date I have indicated the specific Christian year; elsewhere I have given both possible years.

CHAPTER 1

Introduction

Tamerlane moved like a whirlwind through Eurasia and left a name familiar throughout the world. The record of his campaigns is long and vivid. From 1382 to 1405 his great armies criss-crossed Eurasia from Delhi to Moscow, from the T'ien Shan Mountains of Central Asia to the Taurus Mountains in Anatolia, conquering and reconquering, razing some cities, sparing others. His activity was relentless and unending. Throughout his life he kept his armies on the move – sometimes together, sometimes divided and dispersed throughout the countryside, but almost never at rest or at home. His fame spread quickly to Europe, where he remained for centuries a figure of romance and horror, while for those more intimately involved in his career his memory still remains green – whether as the destroyer of Middle Eastern cities, or as the last great representative of nomad power.

Tamerlane is more correctly called by his Turkic name, Temür; the western version of his name comes from the Persian Tīmūr-i lang, Temür the lame. He was born in Transoxiana near Samarqand probably in the 1320s or 1330s.[1] Transoxiana had been part of the Chaghadayid khanate, the region of Chinggis Khan's second son Chaghadai, and the Barlas tribe to which Temür belonged was descended from the Mongol Barulas tribe of Chinggis Khan's confederation. The Barlas and the other tribes of Transoxiana had remained nomadic but lived in close contact with the settled population, and through the adoption of Islam had come to participate in its culture.

Temür's career belongs to the history both of the Middle East and of the steppe and marks an important watershed in each. On the one hand Temür represents the culmination of an old tradition – he is the last of the great nomad conquerors. He rose to power within a nomad confederation and the members of this confederation formed the backbone of his army throughout his career. However, Temür's conquests were in one crucial sense different from those of Chinggis Khan and most other earlier nomad conquerors; the world he conquered was not an alien one, but a known entity, almost all of which had been previously ruled by Mongols. Temür moreover aspired to rule not over the steppe, but over the sown. He made no effort to secure his gains in Zungaria or the territory of the Golden Horde, but in his Middle

Eastern territories – Iran, Khorezm, Afghanistan – he established governorships and permanent garrisons. Other great steppe conquerors had also arisen in the borderlands between steppe and sown, but most consolidated their hold first over the steppe. Temür on the other hand overran the steppe but never aspired to rule it.

Within the Middle East Temür's conquests in the eastern Islamic world coincided approximately with the Ottoman conquest of its western regions, and represent a similar phenomenon. These were Turkic conquests from within, by tribal groups who were able to manipulate both steppe and Islamic traditions and institutions. They could constitute themselves as a separate ruling stratum over the subject population but they had sufficient knowledge of local traditions to rule directly and to participate from the start in Islamic culture. It is from this time that the Turkic people and the traditions of the steppe became truly indigenous to the Middle East.

Despite the extent of Temür's conquests, the realm which he left to his successors was neither enormous nor secure. His death brought a bitter succession struggle among his sons and grandsons which emptied the royal treasury and reduced the extent of the Timurid realm. Yet the ambiguities of his legacy did not dim the glory of Temür's achievement. What the Timurid dynasty lacked in power it made up for in cultural prestige, and its rulers actively cultivated the charisma of their ancestor as an integral part of their own legitimacy. Temür's successors ruled within the Islamic tradition, but continued to glorify their Turco-Mongolian culture, using its titles, its political institutions and its emphasis on dynastic charisma for their own purposes. In this mixed culture of Islamic and Turco-Mongolian origins, the figure of Temür retained a central place, along with that of Chinggis Khan. Temür now became a legendary figure, equipped with an elaborate and partly supernatural genealogy.

Temür's myth proved highly useful to the Turkic dynasties which followed the Timurids in the Middle East and Central Asia, and it continued to flourish in the eastern Islamic world into the nineteenth century. Temür's conquest marked the completion of the period of nomad conquest in the Middle East. While the Seljukid and Mongol sultans had ruled as outsiders Temür's successors ruled as indigenous leaders, and under their rule the mixed Turco-Mongolian culture from which they sprang became entrenched in the Islamic world as part of a mature cultural complex. The great empires of the early modern era – the Ottomans, Safavids and Mughals – owed much of their success to this new synthesis.

The Turco-Mongolian heritage

Both the tribal confederation within which Temür rose to power and the world he conquered were the products of the Mongol Empire; Mongol history and traditions defined his goals, his methods and his ideology. By the middle of the fourteenth century the Mongol empire had fallen apart but much of Eurasia still bore its imprint. Despite the decline of the Chinggisid dynasty, the steppe nomads they had led retained much of their power and prestige. They held the balance of power not only in the steppe but also in many of the surrounding areas of the Middle East and the Russian lands. These nomads preserved the Mongolian heritage of their ancestors in a new guise suitable to the rule of settled people, with whom most were now intimately involved.

As the Mongol rulers had adapted to the needs of the individual regions they ruled, they had not abandoned their nomad heritage, but had created a new culture combining steppe principles with strong elements of the heritage of their subject populations – both the Turkic nomads of the western steppe, and the settled peoples of their agricultural regions. The spoken language of this new culture was Turkic, its religion Islam and its political legitimation Mongolian. The Turco-Mongolian tradition became predominant throughout all the western Mongol domains from Central Asia to Russia, with only Mongolia and China remaining apart. In most of the lands it affected the Turco-Mongolian heritage was not the only cultural system. It coexisted with Persian culture in the Middle East and with Russian culture in Russia and the Ukraine, but it affected all aspects of political and military life throughout the large area of its influence.

The Turco-Mongolian heritage owed much of its success to the strength and adaptiveness of steppe traditions developed over centuries of contact with settled cultures. This tradition had its origins in the pre-Mongol period, and achieved its classic formulation during the rule of Chinggis Khan (1206–27). Chinggis Khan's career brought profound and lasting changes to the steppes of Eurasia. What determined his importance in the history of the steppe and its surrounding regions was not so much his military prowess as his great administrative ability and his astute use of steppe traditions. Chinggis began the organization of his realm well before he won it, while he was still struggling to gain control over his own tribe, so that by the time he had attained power he had a governmental system already tested and refined. Although he was in contact with the Chin dynasty of Northern China early in his career, he chose to base his administration on nomad customs and this gave him and his successors independence from the institutions of the settled societies they conquered. Their empire therefore had a central organizational tradition which could withstand its conquest of settled lands and even its own political breakdown.[2]

The administration which Chinggis developed became the model for the government of nomad states down to the nineteenth century. Its original basis was his personal following: the band of people whom he had gathered around himself during his rise to power, and whose loyalty attached to him personally. From these people he chose his household officers – his cook, his falconer, his stablemaster – whose positions soon expanded to become part of an institutionalized tradition of court administration. Chinggis adopted the decimal military organization common in the steppe, using it to break up the tribal structure of his nomadic subjects, and placing his personal followers at the head of many of the larger units. For his chancellery he adopted the script used by the settled Uighur Turks of the Turfan basin.

With the rapid acquisition of new regions after 1209 Chinggis had to control an ever growing dominion of varied population from Turkic and Mongolian nomads to the settled populations of Iran and northern China. To do this he developed a system which moved individuals and populations thousands of miles from their place of origin, settling Persians in China and nomads deep in settled territories. In the cities of his conquered regions he stationed military governors, mostly of Inner Asian provenance, with Mongol militias. To further secure unity and control within his realm he garrisoned the settled regions with separate elite units (*tamma*) drawn usually from a number of different tribes and areas and representing the whole of his army. At the same time, Chinggis made use of the expertise of Chinese and Iranian bureaucrats in the administration of his realm; a few of these men rose to positions of great power over regions far from their native lands and wielded influence in the central administration. In this way he began the opening of horizons and the mixing of sedentary and nomad populations which wrought a profound change in the social structure of Eurasia during the Mongol period.

Chinggis divided his steppe empire into four great territories, later known as the four *uluses*, which he assigned to his sons along with sections of his army. The descendants of his eldest son Jochi received the western portion of the empire, "as far as Mongol hoofs had beaten the ground," his second son Chaghadai received the steppe portion of Transoxiana with the territories north of the Pamir and T'ien Shan mountains, and his third son, Ögödei, received the territory east of Lake Balkhash (Zungaria). In agreement with Mongol traditions the youngest son, Tolui, received the original center of Chinggis Khan's power in Mongolia, along with Chinggis's personal thousand and the greatest part of his army. These four *uluses* remained at the base of Mongol organization and politics throughout the centuries of Mongolian influence and rule.

Although Chinggis Khan was extraordinary for both his military and his administrative abilities, his career of conquest was not unique. What was exceptional was his ability to pass on his power undiminished to his successors, who raised the nomads of the Eurasian steppe to a position of unprecedented power. After Chinggis Khan's death in 1227 his appointed successor Ögödei became the Great Khan of the Mongol empire. Under him and the next two Khans, Güyüg and Möngke, the Mongol empire retained its basic unity and continued to expand to become the largest empire ever known, comprising the Eurasian steppe from Russia to Mongolia, Iran, Afghanistan, China, and Korea.

It is this period, from 1227 to 1260, which gave to the Chinggisid dynasty its unique charisma as the rulers of most of the known world. It also established the basis for a common political culture throughout the Eurasian steppe and neighbouring settled lands. Among Turco-Mongolian populations from the Crimea to Mongolia the Chinggisid tradition survived as long as nomads held power. Through the nineteenth century the supreme titles of rule in the steppe, "khan" and "khaqan," were reserved for those who claimed descent from Chinggis Khan, and the cult of Chinggis has lasted even into this century.

Despite the existence of separate *uluses* and constant quarrels within the dynasty the great khans were able to maintain considerable unity of administration. Reforms instituted by Ögödei and Möngke imposed a fairly standard and regular administration within the conquered territories – China, Russia, Turkestan and Iran – with similar systems of taxation, military support and local government.[3] The empire was further linked through its famous postal system, the *yam* (Mongolian, *jam*), and subject both to universal censuses and conscription, and to the ideology of the Mongol law, the *yasa* (Mongolian, *jasagh)*.[4] Even the steppe traditions which worked against strong central rule could be manipulated at this period to enhance the unity of the empire. The settled regions of the empire had remained the joint property of the members of the Chinggisid dynasty. In these areas – Iran, Transoxiana and China – the early khans developed what have been called "satellite administrations." These were governments containing agents representing the princes of the four main *uluses* as well as the Great Khan.[5] This system did much to create a common system and common experience in widely different parts of the empire.

The khans further strengthened joint interests in conquered territories through their choice of the troops sent to conquer and to garrison them, drawn from all the *uluses* of the empire and led by princes chosen from several dynastic lines.[6] The system of joint conquest and administration provided a common population and system for the whole of the empire. The same offices and institutions were found throughout the Mongol dominions and different territories also contained members of the same tribes and adherents of the same dynastic and political factions.

With the death of Möngke Khan in 1259 the unity of the Mongol empire collapsed. The primary cause of the breakdown was a protracted succession struggle between two of Möngke's brothers, Arigh Böke, based in the steppe, and Qubilai, who based his power on his possession of northern China. Qubilai won this contest largely because of his superior resources, but he was unable to win recognition from the heads of all the other Mongol *uluses*, and ruled only over part of Mongolia and over China, where he founded a new dynasty, the Yüan. He and his successors still claimed the title of Great Khan but only the Mongol Ilkhanid dynasty of Iran recognized their claim.

Qubilai's reign began a new era in the history of the Mongol empire, which had lost not only its unity but also its center of gravity. The peripheral areas, supported by income from their agricultural and urban populations, now emerged as the crucial centers of power. By 1309 the center of the Mongol empire had become the property of the Mongol khanates which ringed it. Most was controlled by the Yüan khans of China and part went to the Chaghadayid khanate which controlled eastern and western Turkestan. Iran was now an independent region under the descendants of Qubilai's brother Hülegü, who bore the title Ilkhan. The western part of the Mongol empire, the Golden Horde, had long been almost independent under the powerful descendants of Jochi. These Mongol dynasties were not only separate; they were most usually at war with one another.

The breakup of the Mongol empire did not bring an immediate decline. The Mongol khanates continued to increase their holdings and to improve the control and exploitation of the regions they held. Chinggis Khan's descendants still monopolized power throughout much of Eurasia and imposed their own political and military traditions over their dominions. Nor did the political dissolution of the empire destroy its cultural unity. Despite the enmity among the Mongol khanates the different regions of the empire continued to share much common experience. The *uluses* within the Mongol empire now began to adapt themselves to local conditions and to the populations they ruled. Many scholars have seen this process as the end of a common Mongol experience, but a closer look shows strong similarities in the process of adaptation in different areas; the changes during this period occurred at much the same time in different areas and often took very similar forms.

In adapting its rule to settled ways the Mongol ruling class retained its own traditions while adding the elements of foreign culture it could best assimilate. This process marks the creation of a new heritage, often called Turco-Mongolian, which combined the two great steppe cultures. One can date the beginning of the Turco-Mongolian age approximately from the early fourteenth century; this was the age when the Mongol rulers began to deal directly with their settled subjects while these subjects on their side began to accept some of the traditions of the Turco-Mongolian elite who ruled over them.

The first of the changes leading to the formation of the Turco-Mongolian tradition was the formal conversion of the shamanistic Mongols to the faiths of their new subjects. The first official Mongol conversion was to Buddhism; in 1253 Qubilai Khan became closely associated with the Tibetan 'Phags-pa Lama and when he took the title of Great Khan in 1260, he gave great power and honour to the Buddhist church. This was a formal and political conversion limited probably to the members of the dynasty, for whom it proved highly useful.[7] The official institution of Islam in the western Mongolian khanates began later, at the very end of the century, and had much more lasting consequences. In 1295 the Ilkhan Ghazan made a public confession of Islam and decreed the destruction of the churches, synagogues and Buddhist temples constructed by his infidel predecessors. His actions were imitated later by Özbek Khan of the Golden Horde (1312–41), then in the Chaghadayid khanate, within the western section under Tarmashirin Khan (1326–34) and within the eastern section a generation later, under the khan Tughluq Temür (1347–63).[8]

Another process occurring at the same time in the western part of the Mongol empire was the gradual replacement of Mongolian by Turkic as the spoken language of the ruling class. Unlike the official conversion to Islam, which was a public and political act, the Mongols' adoption of Turkic is hard to trace and date, and it is the subject of some controversy among scholars. The written evidence is particularly hard to evaluate because Mongolian retained its prestige for several centuries as the language of the Great Khans, and Mongolian scribes were maintained in chancelleries long after Mongolian had probably ceased to be a common spoken language.[9] In the Golden Horde, where much of the conquered population was Turkic, the adoption of Turkic apparently began very early. There is evidence that by the late thirteenth century its rulers knew and used Turkic and in the early fourteenth century Turkic titles had begun to replace Mongolian ones, although the formal language of administration may still have been Mongolian.[10] At this time the Mongol rulers of several other khanates also spoke primarily Turkic; this is the language in which their utterances are recorded by the travelers and scholars who visited them.[11]

By the fourteenth century then the ruling class throughout the Mongol empire had begun to assimilate itself to the population of its conquered territories, adopting the religions of its settled subjects[12] and the language of its nomadic ones. In the sphere of government on the other hand Mongolian prestige remained paramount and the Chinggisid order retained its overwhelming prestige. Both the written language developed under Chinggis and the offices which he established continued in use throughout the Mongol dominions. The same Turco-Mongolian titles – *beg*, *bahadur*, *noyan* – the same administrative and military terminology – *tümen*, *qoshun* – and the same offices of *darugha*, *yarghuchi* (Mongolian *jarghuchi*), were used throughout the empire. Mongol dynastic law, the *yasa*, likewise continued in force despite the adoption of settled religions with separate legal traditions.

The strength of the common Turco-Mongolian tradition is well illustrated in the reforms instituted by the rulers of different Mongol states during the late thirteenth and early fourteenth centuries. These reforms, introduced first in China by Qubilai (1260–94), then in Iran by Ghazan Khan (1295–1304), in the Golden Horde by the khans Toqta (1290–1312) and Özbek

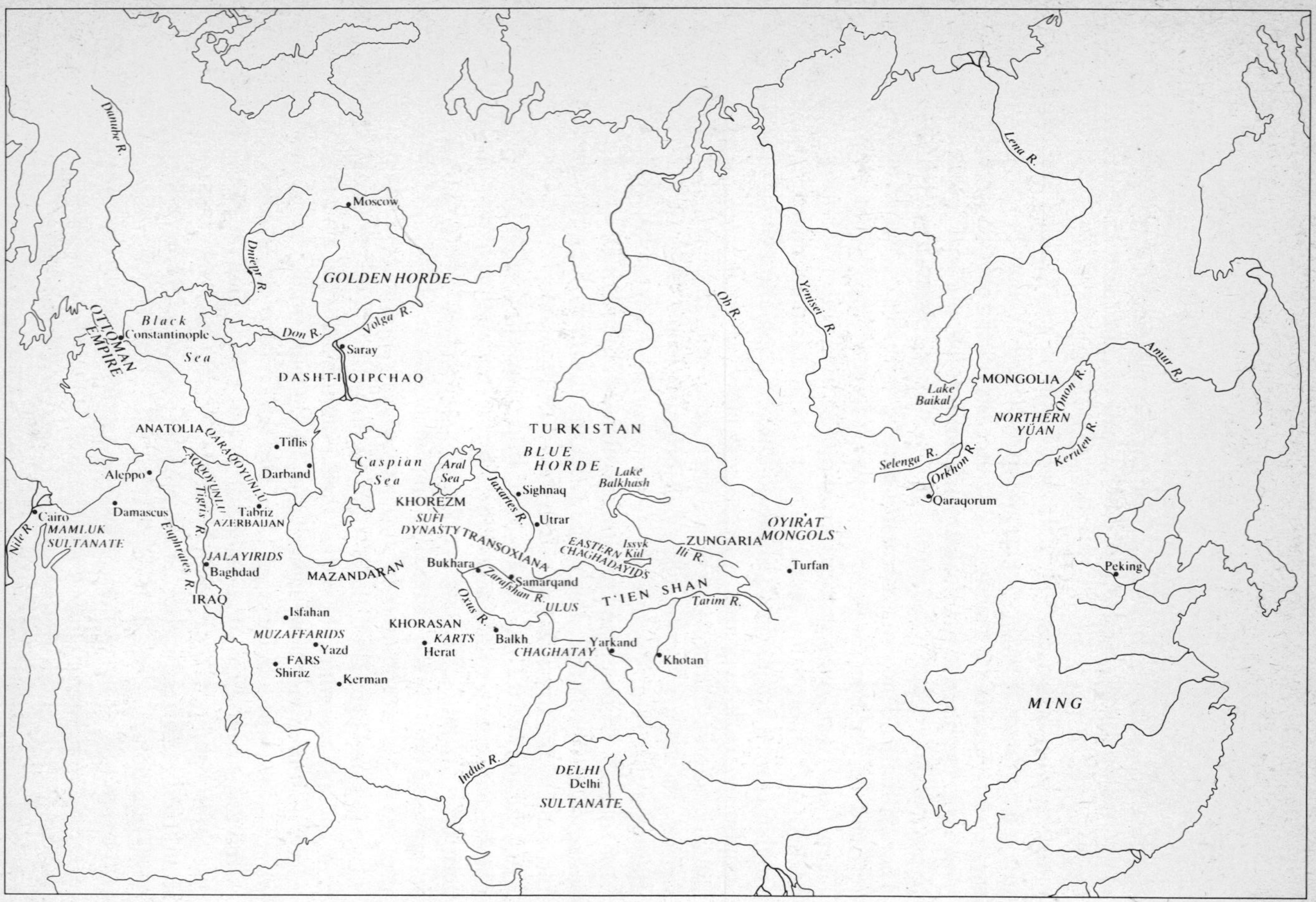

1. Eurasia in 1370.

(1312–41) and in the Chaghadayid khanate by Kebeg (1318–26) had much in common. The similarity and the timing of these reform programs suggest that the Mongol leaders looked as much to each other for models as to the traditions of the regions they ruled.

One of the crucial needs in each emerging Mongol state was a consistent currency accepted throughout the realm. In 1264 Qubilai introduced paper money into Yüan China and fixed the value of the most important products; about thirty years later in 1294 his great-nephew the Ilkhan Geikhatu attempted the same experiment in Iran, with the help of Qubilai's representative in Tabriz, Bolad Ch'eng-hsiang.[13] Shortly thereafter Geikhatu's successor Ghazan introduced a more successful currency reform together with a major revision and systematization of the tax structure. Similar currency reforms were introduced in Transoxiana first in the 1270s then more fully under Kebeg Khan, and later in the Golden Horde by Toqta Khan.[14]

Other reforms enacted in this period further illustrate the importance of Mongolian tradition. The systematization of regional administration undertaken by Kebeg and Özbek Khan was designed according to steppe models. Kebeg reorganized and systematized the *tümens* of the Chaghadayid realms; these were at once administrative and military entities based on the nomad decimal system. Özbek developed hereditary regional governorships throughout the Golden Horde with bureaucracies containing both Islamic and Turco-Mongolian offices.[15]

The military reforms which Ghazan instituted in Iran, giving hereditary land grants to the commanders in his army for the support of his troops, are usually compared to the earlier Middle Eastern tradition of the *iqṭāᶜ*, but they are even more similar to the system of military colonies which the Mongols had developed in China. They could well have been inspired by the Chinese system, as we know that Ghazan's minister, Rashīd al-Dīn, was closely associated with Qubilai's official Bolad, whose influence on currency reforms I have mentioned above.[16] It seems likely that the Chaghadayid khanate had a similar system, as I shall discuss later in this work.[17]

The khans of the Mongol successor states then, while they regularized their governments to improve the administration of their subject populations, used very similar models in their different areas. The Mongols had adapted to the cultures they ruled; they had converted to major religions and become adept at ruling over settled populations, they had intermarried with many of their nomadic subjects and had adopted their spoken language. In doing so they had not lost the Mongol heritage but replaced it with a similar Turco-Mongolian tradition, containing elements of the subject cultures they ruled over and fitted to the needs of a more evolved and sophisticated society in which nomad and settled lived closely together. This new culture held sway throughout the western regions of the former Mongol empire, from eastern Turkestan to Hungary.

The Turco-Mongolian world at Temür's time

By 1360 when Temür began his career, the Mongol khanates had become fragmented and large areas – Iran, Transoxiana and after 1368 also China – were no longer ruled by descendants of Chinggis Khan. The Mongol empire as such had ceased to exist. Only in the northern steppe territories did Chinggisid khans vie with each other for control over diminished realms.

Despite the collapse of the empire, the nomads retained power and prestige even in the lands now lost to the Chinggisid dynasty, and in many cases it was Turco-Mongolian tribes who assumed power in the place of Mongol khans. Instead of a royal dynasty and a small foreign ruling class, governing through intermediaries over a strange population, the western regions of the Mongol empire now had a relatively homogeneous population of Turkic nomads controlling a population whose languages and ways they had come to know.

A hundred and fifty years of Mongol and Turco-Mongolian rule had blurred the differences between nomad rulers and settled subjects, and had softened the boundary between the steppe and the settled regions which surrounded it. They remained separate in character and in consciousness, but they were now closely in contact, sharing common traditions and experience and acutely aware of each other's activities. The Mongol empire had left behind itself a fractured world, but a single one. It was this world which produced Temür, and which he set out to conquer. Despite the enormous extent of his campaigns Temür passed out of the territory of the Mongol empire only briefly, in his campaigns into Syria, Anatolia and India, and even these territories were ruled by Turkic dynasties, connected to an earlier steppe tradition.

Just as the whole of the Mongol empire was bound together by common traditions, the regions within it, though ruled by innumerable dynasties, remained connected through complex political ties and struggles. The easternmost regions of the former Mongol realm were the most separate and distinct. Here most of the Mongols had abandoned their settled territories. China was ruled by a dynasty of settled origins – the Ming – while the Mongols in the steppe regions raided, traded and bargained with the Chinese in much the same way they had always done. The Mongols of Mongolia and Zungaria, north of the T'ien Shan, had remained eastern in their outlook; most had remained unconverted and they retained the Mongolian language. This region was not totally separated from the Islamic and Turco-Mongolian sections of Eurasia. The Ming dynasty had a wide world view and an agressive interest in the western regions. It maintained diplomatic relations with the Chaghadayid realm, and kept its eye on the silk road through the Tarim River basin, a region officially under the rule of the Chaghadayids and of great interest also to the Oyirat Mongols in Zungaria, north of the T'ien Shan mountains.

The Chaghadayids were now divided into eastern and western branches. The khans of the Eastern Chaghadayid realm maintained an interest in the western region and were quick to interfere with its politics when their struggle with insubordinate tribal leaders allowed them the leisure and the military forces. The rulers of the western section, the Ulus Chaghatay centered in Transoxiana, likewise retained an interest in the regions surrounding them; they were particularly active in Khorasan, and also maintained close relations with Khorezm and with the Jochid khans on their northern frontier.

The Jochid realm had always been a decentralized one and was at this time in considerable disarray. Between 1350 and 1370 the Golden Horde was ruled by three different khans, each in his own capital. This disorder benefitted the Blue Horde to the east of the Volga, also of the Jochid house, which had become independent in the early fourteenth century. Now, under its powerful ruler Urus Khan (c. 1361–80), it began to interfere in the affairs of the Golden Horde. Khorezm, bordering Transoxiana on its western side, had in about 1361 also become independent from the Golden Horde, and was ruled by the so-called Sufi dynasty, of the Qungirat tribe.[18]

After 1335 the former Ilkhanid realms in Iran were controlled by innumerable small dynasties of different origins, Mongolian, Turkic, Iranian and Arab. One can discern within this confusion three major regions. The eastern Iranian region of Khorasan centered its politics around the Kartid kings of Herat, members of an Iranian dynasty formerly tributary to the Ilkhans. The strongest power in central Iran was also an Iranian one, the Muẓaffarid dynasty of Fars and Kerman; between its realm and Khorasan lay Mazandaran, ruled for some time by the last Mongol pretenders to the Ilkhanid throne. The western regions of Iran were disputed among several nomadic confederations of which the most powerful at this time was probably the Turco-Mongolian Jalayirid federation, based in Baghdad. Its position however was challenged by two Turkmen[19] dynasties which arose about 1380: the Aqqoyunlu, based in Diyar Bakr and eastern Anatolia, who competed with the Jalayirids on their western border, and the Qaraqoyunlu, who began as vassals of the Jalayirids and soon gained sufficient power to take Azerbaijan from them.

This list gives only a simplified picture of the political situation in Iran at Temür's time. Besides the dynasties I have listed there were innumerable smaller ones, and many pasture areas of the Middle East were inhabited by semi-independent tribes, active in political and military affairs; all of these actors engaged in frequent contests for control over neighboring territories. While few dynasties within the former Mongol Empire held power over a large area, almost all were closely involved with neighboring powers, through alliance and through conflict, and through their neighbors, also with a larger world. They also shared common traditions. Almost no power within the western part of the former Mongol domains was totally unconnected with Mongol rule; even the Middle Eastern dynasties of settled, Persian or Arab origin had for the most part won their position as vassals of the Mongol Ilkhans.

Just as the Mongol empire had continued to grow after its political dissolution, so its traditions and methods spread after its decline even beyond the frontiers of Mongol control. Not only nomad, but even settled rulers accepted the Mongol charisma and adapted it to their own use. The Mamluk sultanate, which had successfully resisted frequent Mongol attempts to incorporate it, had nonetheless copied in its own dynastic monuments the grandiose style of Ilkhanid architecture and had adopted the practice of judging some legal cases according to the Mongol *yasa*.[20] The Qaraqoyunlu dynasty which was of Turkmen origin and therefore outside the Turco-Mongolian tradition nonetheless manufactured a connection to the Chinggisid dynasty to bolster its own dynastic claims.[21] Both the Mamluks, imported individually from the steppe regions, and the Turkmen Aqqoyunlu came from a tradition related to the Mongol one, and thus compatible with it. The Russian princes originated outside this world, yet they too continued to honor and to use the Mongol heritage well after they had won their independence from Mongol rule. The defense of Chinggisid legitimacy sometimes served as a justification for military campaigns and in later years the terminology and iconography of Mongol sovereignty entered into that of the emerging Tsardom of Muscovy.[22]

The world of Temür's time then was one in which nomad power remained paramount while the Chinggisid dynasty was in decline, in which the Mongol traditions remained a powerful source of legitimacy while the settled population, formerly subject to the Mongol khans, slowly regained some of its former independence. Nomad and settled were much closer and much more equal than they had ever been before, and each accepted part of the other's tradition while maintaining strongly separate identities and spheres.

The rule of Temür

Into this world in 1370, Temür catapulted with overwhelming force. Aspiring first to lead his tribe, next to control the Ulus Chaghatay, then to maintain his precarious position of leadership and finally to conquer most of the known world, Temür pursued power with an awesome singleness of purpose. His career was in many ways strikingly similar to those of earlier nomad conquerors. He rose to power within a confederation of unruly tribes, whose loyalty he could keep only by means of a career of conquest, and whose mobility and military skill made these conquests possible. Like many other nomad leaders, Temür did not establish a highly structured administration, preferring a personal rule over his own followers, and a relatively loose overlordship over settled territories. He was interested in controlling and garrisoning the largest cities, in collecting and organizing taxes through the use of bureaucrats from his settled territory, and in using soldiers from these territories in further campaigns. Within these limits local rulers could continue to hold power. Many settled leaders rose up against Temür's rule in the course of his reign, but these uprisings did not seriously injure his prestige and could easily be put down. With a large army which he wished to keep occupied there was no disadvantage in conquering the same area twice, and collecting two ransoms instead of one.

This method of holding and wielding power required constant effort, both military and political. Temür and his army were thus never at rest, and neither age nor increasing infirmity could halt his growing ambitions. When he departed on his last and most fantastic campaign to conquer China he was too weak to walk, and had to be carried in a litter.[23] He nonetheless mustered an enormous army and proceeded north to winter in the city of Utrar, but there, on 17 or 18 February 1405, he died.

While Temür, in his unceasing military activity, resembled his nomad predecessors, many of his successes and his limitations stemmed from the age he lived in. Just as Chinggis Khan had made use of the earlier steppe heritage and its adaptation of settled, especially Chinese traditions, so Temür used the developed Turco-Mongolian tradition for his own ends. The unprecedented speed and extent of his conquests owed much to the remains of the Mongol Empire, which provided him both with administrative structures and with an imperial ideology. At the same time, the unique and continuing charisma of the Chinggisid dynasty made a new imperial dispensation difficult to effect.

The world into which Temür emerged was a relatively easy one for him to conquer and rule. As I have shown above, the Middle East and the western steppes were politically fractured, but still connected by recognition of Mongol traditions and a habit of nomad rule. A conqueror rising to power within this world could well aspire to rule the whole of it. Temür moreover came to power in a particularly favorable region. In the Eurasian politics of Temür's time the Ulus Chaghatay held not a powerful but a central position. Both settled and nomadic populations were strongly entrenched within it, and its borders touched on both steppe and settled powers. There was almost no important Eurasian region with which the Ulus Chaghatay did not have some contact; on its eastern border it adjoined the eastern Chaghadayids and the cities of the Silk Route, on the North it bordered the Jochid powers and to the south the Iranian principalities. A leader of the Ulus Chaghatay might start from a relatively weak position, but he had an almost unlimited field of vision.

The remains of an earlier structure and the mixing of nomad and sedentary populations allowed Temür to mobilize great resources within a very short time. In his early struggle, to gain power within the Ulus Chaghatay, he benefited both from the existence of dynastic and regional armies created by the Chaghadayid khans, and from the wealth of the settled population. He used these resources first to gain control over the tribes of the Ulus Chaghatay, and then to begin his conquest of the outside world. When Temür took over new territories in the Middle East, he had ready-made a system for their exploitation, and was able immediately to establish a fairly direct rule, to collect taxes, to restore trade and agriculture and to conscript new troops. These new resources then permitted him to proceed immediately to the subjugation of new areas. Just as Qubilai had defeated his rival Arigh Böke through the superior resources of China, so Temür used the resources of the Middle East to triumph over the Golden Horde.

Temür then was a nomad ruler but one who from the first based his strength on the exploitation of settled populations. Unlike Chinggis Khan, he had inherited a system of rule which could encompass both settled and nomad populations. He did not therefore have to create a new system or a new ideology. This allowed him to conquer and incorporate new regions with great speed, but it made it more difficult to establish himself as the founder of a new and lasting dynasty.

The legitimation of Temür's rule

It is in Temür's use of the Mongol imperial ideology that we can see most clearly the opportunities and limitations which the Turco-Mongolian tradition offered him. On the one hand he could invoke steppe traditions of universal rule, and familiar mythology connected with dynastic founders. On the other hand, the achievements of the Chinggisid dynasty had given it a unique charisma, and according to the traditions of the Mongol empire accepted throughout Temür's dominions, only Chinggis Khan's descendants could adopt the title of khan and aspire to sovereign power. Temür therefore was hampered in the formal legitimation of his rule by his lack of royal descent. Despite his enormous realm and the autocratic nature of his rule, he adhered to this restriction with scrupulous correctness, and used simply the modest title of *amīr* – "commander" – embellishing it sometimes with the adjectives *buzurg* or *kalān* – "great." He was quick to point out the moderation of his official claims even to people outside his jurisdiction and his tradition.[24]

To further bolster his position he adopted the pose of a supporter of the Chinggisid line, installing a puppet khan and ruling in his name. He further acquired the title of royal son-in-law, *güregen*, by virtue of his marriage to a princess of the Chinggisid line.

Such legitimation through association was sufficient to justify Temür's rule for the space of his lifetime, particularly among the nomads whose support was most important to him. Its drawback was that it intrinsically relegated him to second place, and did not develop for him or his family the prestige which would turn him from the restorer of the Chinggisid empire into the founder of a new dynasty, able to claim power on its own merits.

Temür needed something beyond his formal legitimation to express his position as sovereign over a new and large dominion. He achieved this by fostering a personal myth based largely on reality, which showed him in the traditional mold of nomad conquerors and dynastic founders – most particularly that of Chinggis Khan.[25] The tradition of the steppe favored the legitimation of personal power, glorifying the self-made man and seeing in a successful career of conquest and rule a proof of the favor of God. A successful conqueror was the possessor of a unique good fortune, and to resist such a man was to oppose the will of God.[26] Some aspects of this ideology coincided with Iranian and Islamic ideas. Both the Qur'anic notion that military and political success could prove God's favor and the Iranian idea of charismatic royal favor had been exploited by earlier rulers within the Middle East.[27] Temür therefore was able to adapt these ideas to his own situation and use them to counter the weakness of his official legitimation.

One trait common to most major nomadic dynastic founders was their difficult youth. Temür accordingly emphasized his own modest beginnings – if he did not invent them – and made no secret of his early career as a livestock-thief, while still claiming an aristocratic lineage. He also followed earlier nomad sovereigns in his claim to special heavenly favor and support. Here again he underlined his early obscurity, stating that he owed all his success to divine intervention. Temür's references to divine favor were not all modestly expressed. He claimed to have direct contact to the spiritual world through an angel which appeared to him and to have supernatural powers in the perception of other people's motives and plans.

In the method of his conquests and the disposition of his realm, Temür approximated the course of Chinggis Khan's career, and this was probably not fortuitous. Temür's conquests were extraordinary not only for their extent and their success, but also for their ferocity. This trait is the more striking because few of the regions Temür conquered were foreign to him. Nor was it the actions of Temür's nomad army which precipitated the massacres for which his campaigns were famous, as Temür held exceptionally firm control over his soldiers.[28] Temür's ruthlessness could have been due simply to his personality, but there may well also be a more deliberate reason for it – a desire to recall the conquests of Chinggis Khan and to assert a similar level of personal force. For a conqueror originating within the Middle East and sensitive to the value of trade and agriculture Temür's ferocity was unexpected, but as a means of establishing him as a leader and a dynastic founder comparable to Chinggis Khan it was an effective policy.

Temür also echoed the style of the Mongol Great Khans. The account by the Spanish ambassador Ruy Gonzalez de Clavijo of his sojourn at Temür's court clearly recalls earlier European reports of the court of Qaraqorum.[29]

Although Temür did not pretend to sovereignty beyond the borders of his conquests, in his reception of Clavijo he echoed the universalistic claims of the early Mongol khans, asking after the health of "my son, the king of Spain."[30]

Temür also ruled over a large settled population of Iranians and Arabs and here his sovereignty took a different expression; he was concerned less with the legitimacy of his rule than with its extent and completeness. In this case too there is a contrast between Temür's modest formal claims and his much more extravagant symbolic ones. He himself almost never used the title of *sulṭān*, and in fact during his conquests he overthrew few of the dynasties in his conquered territories, contenting himself usually with submission and the provision of taxes, and with the mention of Temür and the Chaghadayid khan in the *khuṭba*. At his court on the other hand, Temür displayed his dominion over his settled subjects without false modesty, indeed with elaborate ostentation. He named the new suburbs of Samarqand after the great cities of the lands he had conquered and imported craftsmen of all regions to turn Samarqand into a true imperial capital.

Temür's personality

While the histories of Temür's reign give ample detail on his military activities and sufficient material to analyze his political methods, on his personality and beliefs they offer little reliable information. Here we can construct at best a fragmentary picture.[31] What emerges most strikingly from the accounts of Temür's life is his extraordinary intelligence – an intelligence not only intuitive, but intellectual. He was first of all a master politician and military strategist, able to win and keep the loyalty of his nomad followers, to work within and to transform a highly fluid political structure, and to lead a huge army to conquests of unexampled scope. These are the skills that one expects of a nomad conqueror, and which are learned and sharpened during the long tribal power struggle which precedes most nomad conquests. Temür was likewise adept at ruling over the Arabo-Persian lands that he conquered. Although he punished recalcitrant cities and imposed ruinous ransoms on even submissive towns, he showed a clear understanding of the value of trade and agriculture and took measures to promote both, using his army to restore the areas and cities it had ravaged. He was skillful also in the manipulation of settled cultural symbols – the use of building for self-aggrandizement, and of religion for the justification of his conquests and his rule.

What is most impressive, because least expected, is the scope of Temür's intellectual interest and ability. Although he could neither read or write he had the use of those who could, and he was thus effectively literate in both Turkic and Persian. The histories of his reign extol his knowledge of medicine, astronomy and particularly of the history of the Arabs, Persians and Turks. His delight in debating with scholars was inexhaustible and in his opinion at least he often had the better of them.[32] The Timurid histories might be expected to present a favorable picture of Temür's intellectual abilities, but they are borne out by an independent source: the autobiography of Ibn Khaldūn, who met Temür after the siege of Damascus in 1400–1. The two men discussed a number of topics and Ibn Khaldūn remarked on Temür's impressive intelligence and his fondness for argumentation.[33]

The question of Temür's religious beliefs has been a matter of controversy ever since he began his great conquests.[34] His veneration of the house of the Prophet, the spurious genealogy on his tombstone taking his descent back to ᶜAlī, and the presence of Shiᶜites in his army led some observers and some later scholars to call him a Shiᶜite. It is unlikely that this was true since Temür came from a strongly Sunni area, and on occasion moreover used his protection of Sunnism as a pretext for campaigns aganist Shiᶜite rulers. His official religious counselor moreover was the Hanafite scholar ᶜAbd al-Jabbār Khwārazmī.[35] Temür's religious practices with their admixture of Turco-Mongolian shamanistic elements belonged to the Sufi tradition of the marches, and his primary religious loyalty belonged almost certainly to the Naqshbandi Sufi order whose power and influence was already well fixed in Transoxiana.[36]

In religion as in other aspects of his life Temür was above all an opportunist; his religion served frequently to further his aims, but almost never to circumscribe his actions. His attitude towards men of religion is well summarized in Jean Aubin's felicitous phrase, as a mixture of "intellectual curiosity and superstitious prudence."[37]

It was in the justification of his rule and his conquests that Temür found Islam most useful. Temür's campaigns against the kings of Georgia, the Shiᶜite *sayyids* of Amul in Mazandaran and the non-Muslim populations on his route to India were all ostensibly undertaken with the preservation of the *sharīᶜa* in mind.[38] He cultivated the Sufi *shaykhs* of Transoxiana and Khorasan to bolster his standing both among his Chaghatay followers and his settled subjects; not only did they attest to his superior spiritual powers, they also served to justify his invasion and conquest of Islamic lands. In 1382, for instance, timely visits to the powerful *shaykhs* of Andkhud and Turbat-i Shaykh-i Jam in Khorasan elicited their endorsements of his forthcoming attack on the Kartid dynasty of Herat.[39]

Temür's patronage of religion also served to enhance his charisma and that of his dynasty. He placed the mausolea he erected for the members of his family close to the shrines of important Sufis or graced them with the remains of a Sufi *shaykh*. One of the most splendid and beautiful building complexes done at Temür's orders was the shrine of Shaykh Aḥmad Yasawī.[40] Throughout his life Temür showed honor to Sufi *shaykhs*, who belonged to his inner circle.[41] Temür thus paved the way for the extensive patronage of religious figures, both *ᶜulamā'* and Sufi shaykhs, in the later Timurid period. During his rule however power remained securely with the sovereign himself and neither the *ᶜulamā'* nor the Sufi shaykhs he favored seem to have had independent political power within the court.

While Temür's religious feelings were securely under the control of his outstanding intelligence, one passion overcame even this – his overweening jealousy of power.[42] Temür led almost all important expeditions in person and took care to claim credit for the few independent campaigns he allowed to his chief commanders. Although he assigned his sons and grandsons to the provinces of his dominions and his followers to the command of large bodies of troops, he took care to limit their powers and to keep them securely under his eye. This was to some extent a necessary precaution to prevent the formation of rival powers within a loosely structured army and administration. Temür however carried this policy so far that he damaged the efficiency of his administration and more importantly, made it difficult for his descendants to maintain control over their own territories after his death.

It was in his treatment of his own family particularly that Temür's unwillingness to share power proved destructive. He clearly felt a strong affection towards the members of his family and he attempted, in articulating his legitimacy and charisma, to apply these to his descendants.[43] Despite this, Temür did not fully trust his offspring and did not allow any one of them the power and prestige necessary to assert full control over the territories they governed. At his death his chosen successor was unable to back his claim against the resistance of the other princes, and none of Temür's descendants was able to command the full loyalty even of his own troops. The resulting succession struggle was unusually long and destructive, and left behind it a dynasty both economically and politically weak.

The purpose of this study

This book is an analysis of Temür's career as the founder of a nomad conquest dynasty. Despite his involvement with the settled regions he ruled, Temür began and ended his life as a leader of nomads – it was the tribes of Transoxiana who formed his political style, and it was the heritage of the Mongol empire which molded his administrative system and determined the scope of his ambitions. The histories of Temür's reign describe in some detail the course of his rise to power and give us an opportunity to examine the society from which he came rare in the study of nomad conquest dynasties. It is possible to trace the history not just of groups but of individuals from before Temür's rise to power into the reign of his successors, and thus to examine in unusual detail the dynamics of tribal politics and of the formation of sovereign rule.

The organization of this study does not accord with that of the histories it uses, which chronicle Temür's campaigns but give little information on his goals, his motives or his methods of organization.[44] The administrative manuals which exist for many other periods are unavailable for the period of Temür's life, nor are any of the contemporary histories of his reign written by bureaucrats who served under him. Only two sources give direct information on the structure of his administration: the *Dastūr al-wuzarā'* of Khwāndamīr which briefly outlines the careers of a few Persian bureaucrats, and a genealogy of the Timurid house, the *Muᶜizz al-ansāb*, which lists the holders of different offices under Temür and his sons. Most of the conclusions I have drawn here therefore come from incidental information pooled from various parts of different sources. Taken together they are sufficient to form a relatively clear picture both of the society Temür ruled and of the way in which he ruled it.

In this book I use the history of the Ulus Chaghatay and of Temür's career to describe the logic underlying the politics of a tribal confederation and the practice of personal government. Both Temür himself and the tribal confederation from which he sprang show many similarities to earlier nomad societies and rulers. One of the most striking traits they share is the apparent confusion of their political systems – from the endemic warfare and constantly switching alliances within a tribal confederation, to the personal and unstructured rule of a nomad sovereign. This seems to be a government of overlapping structures and undefined institutions, in which personality and opportunity are the determining factors. One can regard this as a sign of primitivism, and emphasize the apparent failures of Temür and other nomad sovereigns – the unnecessary cruelty of his campaigns, the confusion of his administration, his tendency to conquer the same region not once but several times, and his inability to provide a smooth succession.

It is no small task to conquer western Asia or to rule even the section of it which Temür held. What has struck me in my study of Temür's career is not failure but success, not confusion but system. The tribal confederation which formed the Ulus Chaghatay was able to hold together for a full generation without strong central rulership or intolerable violence. Temür, once he came to power, was able to maintain his position and use it to begin a career of conquest. The extent of his campaigns was extraordinary and not fortuitous. What made them possible was Temür's ability to exert full control over a growing dominion and a huge heterogeneous army. He did this through a government which was highly personal but not, I believe, without system.

In this study I attempt to examine the organization which lay behind the active tribal politics of the Ulus Chaghatay, and the successes of Temür's career. To do this one must look beyond the structures of tribe and administration, to the dynamics of their interaction. When we look at the uses to which institutions were put, we can understand the advantages of political fluidity and of institutional confusion. It may be then that these traits continued not because no one could change them, but because they were part of a system which worked. It was a system not without drawbacks and not without failures, but it also had successes, and these could be spectacular.

Because of the importance of the Ulus Chaghatay in determining the character of Temür's rule, I have devoted considerable space to it in this study. The second and third chapters of the book deal with the Ulus Chaghatay as it was before and during Temür's rise; one chapter describes the society of the Ulus, the other examines its political dynamics and the way that Temür rose to power within it.

The middle section of the book deals with the consolidation of Temür's control over his settled and nomadic subjects. I examine his use of both settled and nomad manpower in his army and administration, showing the way in which he mobilized these populations while minimizing the dangers they could pose to his personal power. The last section chronicles the events of the first four years after Temür's death, in order to demonstrate the changes his rule had brought about in the political structures and dynamics of the regions he ruled. These changes were considerable, and fateful for the dynasty he left behind him.

It is the question of control which is central to this study, as it was, I believe, central to Temür himself. This is a study in the exercise of control over a tribe, a tribal confederation, then a large dominion, and the effects of that control on the population it encompassed. In particular it is a study of the contest between politics and control. The politics central to the functioning of the tribal confederation within which Temür rose to power worked in favor of his rise, but against the maintenance of his position; thus the suppression of political activity became a necessity in the maintenance of control over his nomad followers.

This book relates the history of an exceptional ruler, able to amass enormous personal power and to transform the society he ruled into a tool for his personal ambitions. In analyzing his methods of rule and their effect on the society of the Ulus Chaghatay I hope both to contribute to the understanding of Tamerlane himself, and to use his career as an example of larger and more general questions.

CHAPTER 2

The Ulus Chaghatay in the mid fourteenth century

For the study of Temür's life the Ulus Chaghatay is of central importance; this was the world within which Temür rose to power and which remained at the center of his realm throughout his life. Its structure and politics shaped his career from before his assumption of tribal leadership to his final campaign against China. Although he conquered an enormous territory and spent most of his later years outside the lands of the Ulus, he carried the Ulus with him throughout his life; its nomads made up the core of his army and administration and its traditions determined his goals. Indeed it was the control of the Turco-Mongolian nomads of the Ulus which was his most central concern even while he conquered and ruled his new domains.

The history of the Ulus Chaghatay presents a valuable opportunity to study the composition and structure of a tribal confederation. Its early history is known at least in its outlines and the Timurid sources give a fairly full description of Temür's rise to power; this allows us an unusually detailed picture of a medieval nomad society. We can analyze the component parts of this confederation, see something of the varying structures within it and of the dynamics of its political system, and even to some extent trace the evolution of a self-conscious identity within it.

The Ulus Chaghatay came into being with the break-up of the Chaghadayid khanate after 1334. It was a confederation of Turco-Mongolian tribes, ruled at first by a khan of the Chaghadayid house and later by a succession of non-royal tribal commanders (emirs), most of whom maintained puppet khans to legitimate their rule. In the middle of the fourteenth century the Ulus comprised a large area, including Transoxiana and much of the northern and eastern parts of what is now Afghanistan. The people of the area were highly diverse; there were large urban and agricultural populations, numerous nomadic Turco-Mongolian tribes, and the mountain peoples of Badakhshan and the Hindu Kush. While at this time the nomads held decisive political power, the settled peoples were an important factor in the economic life of the Ulus.

The geography of the Ulus Chaghatay encouraged a dual economy, pastoral and agricultural. This area was the steppe frontier of the Islamic world, bordered to the north by the great Qipchaq steppe, and to the east by the Pamir and T'ien Shan mountains, the domain of the Turco-Mongolian nomads. Although it was a borderland it was not an area of marginal culture, either for the settled or for the nomad societies it nourished. Both Transoxiana and northern Khorasan were ancient centers of trade and agriculture; at the same time this had long been a region of crucial interest to the steppe nomads, who often controlled it. The Oxus region contains both excellent farmland and steppe, and these moreover are often interspersed. Even within rich and irrigated agricultural areas – the Ferghana and Zarafshan river valleys and the plains of northern Khorasan – there is much land which is suitable only for nomadic exploitation. The many rivers of the region create large areas of brackish marshland, useful for nomads wintering in the lowland steppes. Almost no part of this region moreover is distant from the mountains whose foothills provide summer pastures.[1] The mountain massif of central and eastern Afghanistan likewise contains large valleys suitable for agriculture, along with mountain pastures for the nomads who winter in the plains below them.[2] The nomads of the Ulus lived in close contact with its settled population, whom they controlled and exploited directly. They knew the value and the requirements of the agricultural and urban economies, and were able to deal easily with the leaders of the settled communities under their control.

The sources available to us on the Ulus Chaghatay permit us to analyze its Turco-Mongolian population in some detail, but provide very little information on the other people of the area. In the context of this study, the Chaghatay nomads holding the balance of political power are in any case the most important actors, and most of this chapter therefore will be devoted to the analysis of their structure and organization. Just as the geography of the Ulus Chaghatay had determined the diversity of its inhabitants, its history under the Chaghadayid khans had formed the structure and tradition of its nomad population. The Mongols had brought a large new population of nomads into Central Asia – some organized as armies under a single tribal commander, serving a Mongol prince, others as garrison troops, conscripted from different tribes and different sections of the Mongol army – and as time went on, new groups were added. These groups varied considerably both in their organization and in the extent of their power. Since they defined and controlled the politics of the Ulus Chaghatay, it is important to understand both what they were and how they differed from each other. This chapter therefore is devoted to their analysis and description.

The formation of the Ulus Chaghatay

At the time of Temür's rise to power, the Ulus Chaghatay was a loose confederation of mixed population without central leadership, but possessing nonetheless a definite identity. The nomad ruling class maintained a strong identification with the Ulus Chaghatay, which lasted even through Temür's career and beyond. They were referred to as "Chaghatays" both by Timurid histories and by foreign observers. This was an identity at once linguistic, political and cultural, and was built on common traditions and common historical experience. Much of the social and political structure of the Ulus Chaghatay was inherited from the Chaghadayid khanate. The Ulus evolved gradually, partly through the actions of the khans, partly through tribal activities, partly by chance. Chaghadayid rule had provided little strong central leadership, but perhaps partly for that reason it had produced an entity which could survive without this.

The Chaghadayid khanate originated as the territory of Chinggis Khan's second son, Chaghadai, whose lands centered on the Issyk Kul and the Ili river, and included the Muslim territory of Central Asia in Transoxiana.[3] Along with this land Chinggis granted to Chaghadai a portion of his army, including four regiments of a thousand each led by an important tribal commander. This khanate was one of the most conservative and least centralized of the early Mongol *uluses*. It was affected by its location close to the heartland of the Mongol realm; this enabled its rulers to maintain their steppe traditions and it also embroiled them in the power struggles centering within this region. The early history of the khanate was troubled and not conducive to the creation of orderly or centralized government.[4]

The connection between Transoxiana and the eastern section of the Chaghadayid khanate was often tenuous. The first Chaghadayid khans and their followers remained in the region of the Ili and Talas rivers and had little to do with governing the settled areas within their dominions. These areas were administered largely by powerful Middle-Eastern bureaucrats, working within a satellite administration, jointly responsible to the Great Khan and the rulers of the four main Mongol realms.[5]

In the middle of the thirteenth century, the Chaghadayid khans began to show a more direct interest in the settled regions of Central Asia. Chaghadai's grandson Alughu, who held power from 1261 to 1266, occupied Transoxiana and expelled the governors answerable to the khan of the Golden Horde.[6] Alughu's successor, Mubārakshāh, was a Muslim and was raised to the throne near the Angren river, close to Transoxiana.[7]

Mubārakshāh's successor Baraq also based himself in Transoxiana; eastern Turkestan and the Ili region had now come under the control of one of Ögödei's descendants, Qaidu, whom Baraq was forced to recognize as his sovereign.[8] It was not until about 1306, after the death of Qaidu, that the Chaghadayid khans regained the Ili and Talas regions.[9]

By the end of the thirteenth century then, the Chaghadayid khans had begun to make their seat in or near Transoxiana. Nonetheless they still had little involvement with the settled population and its culture. The khans and their followings continued to live in the mountainous and steppe areas of Transoxiana while the cities and agricultural regions were administered by

Middle-Eastern bureaucrats, and many cities in Transoxiana remained under the leadership of local dynasties.[10]

In the early fourteenth century the Chaghadayid khanate began to develop a more organized government and to resemble the other better developed Mongol realms. Kebeg Khan (1318–26) built his residence, later known as Qarshi, near Samarqand and began to take a greater interest in the settled population. He introduced a uniform currency of unusual purity, and began minting coins in his own name as khan. He also reorganized the *tümen* system, as I have mentioned above.[11]

Kebeg's successor Tarmashirin Khan (1326–34) converted to Islam and followed a policy of greater assimilation with Islamic culture, abandoning many of the Mongolian traditions honored by his predecessors, including apparently the yearly journey to the eastern and less settled region of his realm. This behavior alienated some of his more conservative followers, who rebelled and deposed him. In the disturbances which followed Tarmashirin's downfall the Chaghadayid khanate split into two parts: the western section, Transoxiana, became known as the Ulus Chaghatay, and the eastern section, containing the more conservative nomadic population, as Moghulistan.[12] From its inception then the Ulus Chaghatay was a voluntary confederation, based on the common interest and common culture of those who made it up – Turco-Mongolian tribes who, while maintaining their loyalty to the Mongol tradition, were willing to coexist with a Muslim settled population.

The decade after Tarmashirin's downfall was a confused period within the Ulus Chaghatay, and one we know very little about – we cannot even be certain who ruled it for much of this time. We can state definitely only that by the mid 1340s its ruler was the Chaghadayid khan Qazan b. Yasa'ur. In 1346–7 he was defeated and killed by one of his emirs, and the Ulus Chaghatay came under the control of tribal leaders.[13] The eastern part of the Chaghadayid khanate was now separated from the Ulus Chaghatay, but the Ulus contained large new territories south of the Oxus which had not originally been part of the khanate. These areas – northeastern Khorasan, Qunduz, Baghlan, Kabul and Qandahar – had become incorporated into the Chaghadayid khanate in the course of the late thirteenth and early fourteenth century. This occurred through a gradual process of infiltration and attraction.

The Chaghadayid khans were from the beginning interested in the lands south of them, but their raids on the area rarely resulted in the direct annexation of new territory.[14] The Ilkhans succeeded in repulsing most Chaghadayid campaigns in Khorasan from the 1260s through the 1320s, though it is possible that the Chaghadayids acquired the region of Balkh in the course of these raids, since we are told that it was an area favored by Kebeg Khan.[15] The numerous political struggles within the Chaghadayid khanate led to the emigration of dissident princes into Khorasan. This became especially frequent in the early fourteenth century, which was a period of confusion and strife within the khanate.[16] The Ilkhans welcomed these dissidents and gave them territories and people over which to rule, a policy which did much to increase Chaghadayid influence in Khorasan and the regions south of it. One of the most important of these grants was the territory which the Ilkhan Öljeytü gave to the dissident Chaghadayid prince Yasa'ur in 1313–14. This stretched apparently from Balkh to Kabul, and included the mountains of Badakhshan and those of Qandahar.[17] Yasa'ur brought with him some of his own followers and shortly after he had been installed at Badghis he undertook a campaign to Transoxiana, captured a great number of people, and resettled them in Khorasan.[18]

Another large area to the south of the Oxus, stretching from Baghlan and Qunduz down to Ghazna, came into the Chaghadayid khanate as a result of the allegiance of the Qara'unas, a large body of Turco-Mongolian troops which had originated as the garrison (*tamma*) troops sent to Qunduz and Baghlan early in the thirteenth century. (See Appendix A, Qara'unas.) Since the Qara'unas and their territory constituted an important element of the Ulus Chaghatay, I shall examine here the process through which they became part of it. There is some disagreement about when this occurred, and the problem is complicated by uncertainty among historians, both medieval and modern, about the exact identity of the Qara'unas and the extent to which they can be considered to be a single entity or to be the same entity over a long period of time.[19] What follows therefore is only a tentative sketch.

In 1271–2 the Ilkhans welcomed the deposed Chaghadayid khan Mubārakshāh b. Qara Hülegü, and installed him as governor of the Negüderī troops, a section of the Qara'unas centered in the region of Qandahar. After this the Negüderī remained largely under the leadership of Chaghadayid princes, who as time went on began to obey not their new masters, the Ilkhans, but their relatives, the Chaghadayid khans. From the end of the thirteenth century, scholars agree that the Negüderī were under Chaghadayid control.[20]

According to Ḥāfiẓ-i Abrū, Öljeytü, when settling Yasa'ur in northern Khorasan, had ordered that the emirs of that area obey him.[21] Among these was Baktut b. Uladu b. Sali Noyan, who had inherited the command of several Qara'unas *tümens*. He was a close and trusted companion to Yasa'ur and sided with him when he rebelled against the Ilkhanids.[22] It may be that the northern Qara'unas became part of the Ulus at this time. In any case we know that the Qara'unas – or most of them – were considered part of the Ulus Chaghatay soon after this, since the Arab traveler Ibn Baṭṭūṭa reports that during the rule of Tarmashirin (1326–34) their central areas – Qunduz, Baghlan, and Ghazna – were governed by Boroldady, one of Tarmashirin's most trusted emirs.[23]

By the time of Tarmashirin Khan therefore large regions south of Trans-

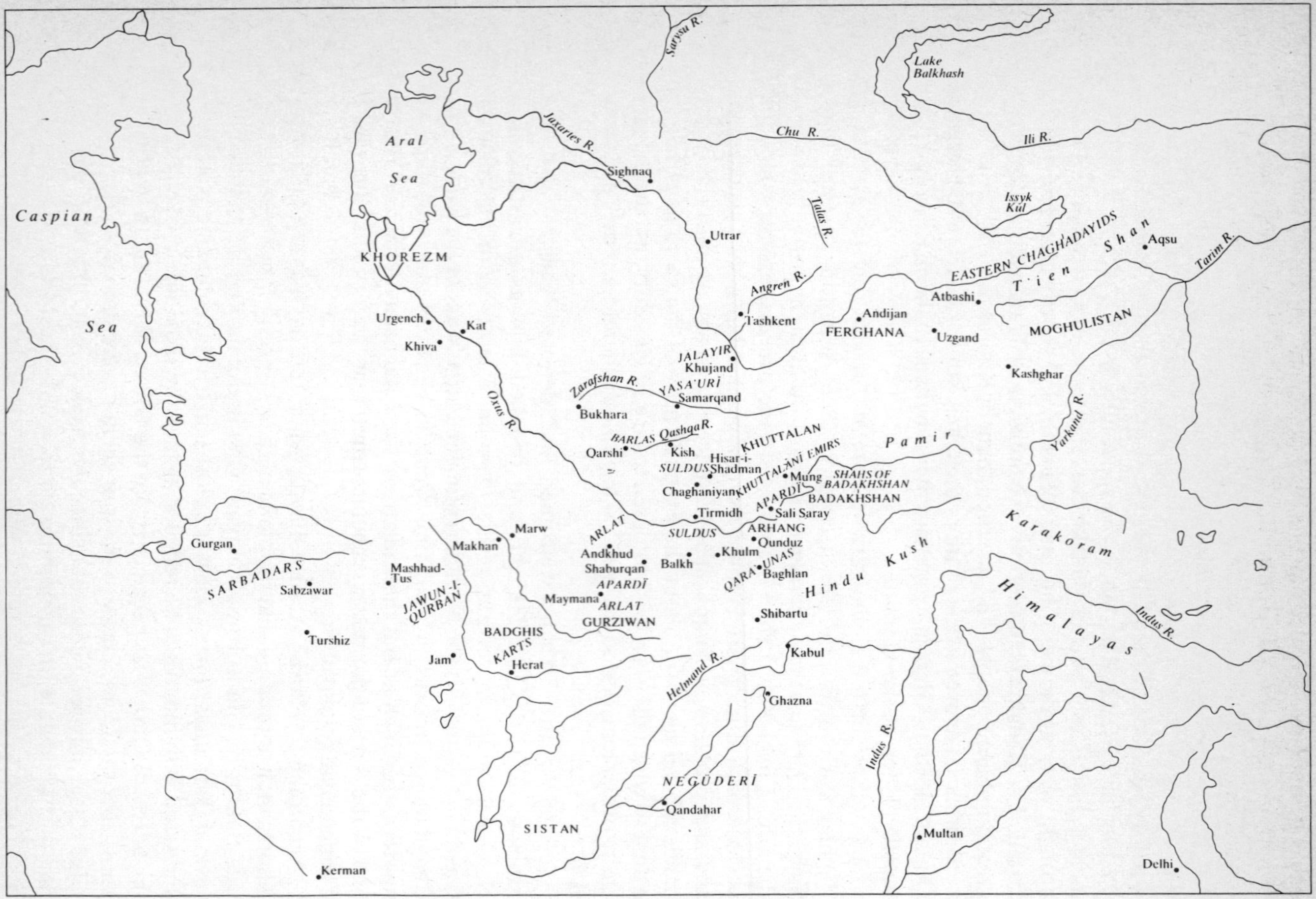

2. The Ulus Chaghatay in 1360.

oxiana including those of Balkh, Qunduz, Baghlan and Qandahar had become part of the Chaghadayid khanate. After the division of the khanate, these areas remained as part of the Ulus Chaghatay. They were in no way an appendage, but an important and integral part of the Ulus. The last of the Chaghadayid khans to hold power over the Ulus Chaghatay, Qazan, was connected with Khorasan; he was the son of the prince Yasa'ur, who had earlier held the region of Balkh under the Ilkhans.

Once the Ulus Chaghatay had assumed its new shape, it retained it without change from the time of Tarmashirin to that of Temür. Despite frequent changes in the central leadership and the weak rule of many of those who held the throne, the Ulus lost neither territory nor membership, and kept a sense of common and separate identity. It had formed gradually, through an evolving sense of common interest, and required no compulsion to keep it together.

The powers within the Ulus Chaghatay

I have outlined the territory of the Ulus Chaghatay; we now have to discuss the people within it. All the main sources on early Timurid history contain the same list of the groups which made up the Ulus Chaghatay during the brief rule of Buyan Suldus who held power around 760–1/1358–60, on the eve of Temür's rise to power. The information in these passages agrees fully with other evidence concerning the membership of the Ulus, and I will therefore give a summary of it here.

By this time, the various groups within the Ulus had made themselves independent under their own chiefs. Even within the Suldus tribe Buyan did not hold full power; he controlled the region of Chaghaniyan north of the Oxus but the region of Balkh was held by another Suldus emir, Öljey Bugha. Two tribes occupied the center of Transoxiana; Ḥājjī Beg headed the Barlas in the region of Kish and Qarshi, while the Yasa'urī under Khiḍr Yasa'urī held the region of Samarqand. The northernmost part of the Ulus was the region of the Jalayir, under Bāyazīd; their seat was in Khujand. The southern part of the Ulus, below the Oxus, contained a number of powers. The Apardï tribe was based in Shaburqan, led by Zinda Ḥasham from the Nayman tribe, and in Khuttalan there were more Apardï led by Öljeytü b. Apardï who ruled the area in conjunction with Kaykhusraw Khuttalānī, emir of the *tümen* of Khuttalan. In the mountains of Badakhshan, the kings of Badakhshan held sway. Finally there was Amīr Ḥusayn, at the head of the Qara'unas, whose region centered in Qunduz and Baghlan.[24]

The only tribe which is not included in this description but can definitely be said to belong to the Ulus is the Arlat of Andkhud and Gurziwan. They are mentioned by Temür's biographer Ibn ᶜArabshāh as one of the four tribes of the Ulus, and passages in the contemporary histories also indicate that they were part of it.[25] Their omission here is probably due to the fact that they were not a large or important tribe at this time.

The brief description which I have reproduced above gives little indication of the complexity and variety of the groups which made up the Ulus Chaghatay. A detailed account of all of them would require too much space to include in this chapter. (For a fuller discussion see Appendix A.) I will limit myself here to short descriptions. Several of these groups – the Barlas, Arlat, Jalayir and Suldus – bore the names of Turco-Mongolian tribes known from the time of Chinggis Khan and were presumably offshoots of those tribes. We know definitely that the leading clan of the Barlas tribe traced its origin to Qarachar Barlas, head of one of Chaghadai's regiments. As there were Jalayir and probably Suldus emirs at the head of other regiments given to Chaghadai, their presence in the Ulus can be explained in the same way.[26] The Arlat tribe had been settled in northern Khorasan from the period of the Mongol conquest, and had become part of the Ulus Chaghatay presumably when the Qara'unas and their allied tribes joined it.[27]

The other powers mentioned in this passage were of different kinds. The shahs of Badakhshan were indigenous rulers who had retained their hold on the region since the time of the Mongol conquest, and were included in the Ulus by geographical happenstance.[28] The other four groups, the Yasa'urī, the Apardï, the Khuttalānī emirs and the Qara'unas, were of fairly recent origin and had come into being as armies attached to either a place or a person.[29] The Yasa'urī, and I believe also the Apardï, had begun as the troops of an individual leader, while the Khuttalānī emirs led what had probably begun as a regional army, perhaps one of the *tümens* of the Chaghadayid khanate; all of these groups apparently functioned in much the same way as the older Turco-Mongolian tribes. The Qara'unas were quite different from these. As I have written above, they originated as garrison troops serving the Ilkhanids first, and then the Chaghadayids. At this period the Qara'unas represented a large and powerful force within the Ulus Chaghatay – they numbered apparently three *tümens*. The internal structure of the Qara'unas however is difficult to discern, and it is not even entirely clear which groups should be included within them. (See Appendix A: Qara'unas.)

These then were the most prominent members of the Ulus Chaghatay: the old Turco-Mongolian tribes – Barlas, Arlat, Suldus and Jalayir – the troop contingents under their own leadership – Yasa'urī and Apardï – the Khuttalānī emirs in control of a regional army, the indigenous Shahs of Badakhshan, and, at the head of the Qara'unas, Amīr Ḥusayn.

The structure of the tribes

I have used the word tribe up to now without explanation or definition, and these must now be provided. This is not an easy task. Anthropologists have provided us with some definitions and typologies of tribes but even to a scholar living within one and able to elicit information at will, the tribe remains an elusive entity. The historian attempting to determine what it is he is dealing with must construct as complete a picture as he can, then make his way through the controversies of the anthropologists, and finally decide on the strength of usually very meager evidence which definition best fits and explains his case. Here I shall try to do just that.

In analyzing the structure of these tribes, we can draw only limited help from the terminology used in the sources. The authors of most of these works came from outside the nomad tradition and wrote in Persian or Arabic, and they do not tell us what the Chaghatays themselves called the various groups within the Ulus. The word most frequently applied to the major powers of the Ulus is the Arabic word *qawm*, most usually translated as "tribe." Within the sources this has many uses; it is most frequently used for a tribe, but it can designate the following of any given person (here apparently a translation of the Turkish *il*, frequently used with that meaning), and it can also be applied to a nation, like the Moghuls, or even a sedentary political entity.[30]

The other term applied to the tribes of the Ulus was that of *qabīla*, also translated often as "tribe." This word occurs less frequently than *qawm*, and seems usually to designate a smaller unit; it is used once or twice for a section within a tribe, and elsewhere almost always for small tribes.[31] The vocabulary of the Persian sources therefore does suggest a certain segmentation within tribes, and a ranking of tribes by size and importance. It does not however provide an understanding of the structure of the Ulus powers or of the differences among them.

One can then turn to scholarship and consider the meaning given to the word tribe in secondary sources. Some anthropologists and historians have depicted the tribe as a relatively fixed and stable entity, bound together by kinship, whether real or fictive. This might be the relatively egalitarian segmented tribe described by Evans-Pritchard, or the stratified tribe of conical class which Paul Kirchhoff has delineated.[32] Most recent scholarship has stressed the flexibility of tribes, both in structure and in membership. According to this formulation tribalism should be seen not as a fixed state, but as a repetitive, dynamic and even reversible process.[33] Some scholars have suggested that the tribe served a primarily political and temporary purpose; its members were all those who followed its chief, and at his death or defeat, the tribe collapsed.[34]

This more dynamic definition of a tribe probably comes closer to historical reality, especially in defining a successful tribe at a time when nomads still held military and political power. A strong leader in a nomad society could attract many people, and might well make little distinction between newer and older followers. Fredrik Barth's description of the Basseri tribe of Iran gives a vivid picture of the disparate elements making up the tribe, and the free movement of tribal sections among the various tribes of the area.[35] The evidence we possess about the Turkish and Mongolian tribes of the medieval steppe suggests a similarly complicated and fluid tribal structure.[36] If then one is to define a tribe at any given moment, one might best describe it as all followers of a tribal chief. For a detailed analysis however, and especially for an analysis of changes over time, we need also a more complex and exact definition, which will allow distinctions among groups of different sizes and structures.

One of the first tasks of this book is an examination of the dynamics of tribal politics: the relationships within tribes, among tribes, and between tribes and a supra-tribal leader. I shall be describing the history of the tribes over a considerable period, from before Temür's rise to the succession struggle after his death, attempting to determine how they were changed with the transformation of the Ulus Chaghatay into the Timurid realm. For this purpose, it is important to determine what units made up a tribe, and which of these were most securely attached to it.

It is clear that not all members of a tribe are equally committed to it; most tribes have both central and peripheral members. Paul Kirchhoff has suggested that the tribe had within it gradations of membership, depending on nearness to the chief of the leading clan, and through him to its common ancestor.[37] Another way to define how closely bound a group is to its tribe is to determine whether it possesses a separate or alternative identity outside the tribe. This becomes very important in the active and fluid political system of a tribal confederation like the Ulus Chaghatay. A section of the leading clan of a tribe might rebel, but it could less well defect to another tribe or power than could for instance the remnant of a different tribe more recently absorbed by its powerful neighbor, still retaining a separate name and a corporate identity.

In discussing the tribes of the Ulus Chaghatay, I shall try to identify a number of the parts which I believe made them up. The first was the leading lineage or clan, the tribal aristocracy, from which the leadership of the tribe was traditionally drawn. Under the control of this group, there seems to have been a body of tribesmen closely attached to it. These two elements could be considered the core of the tribe. Tribal leaders could also attract to themselves a shifting body of tribesmen belonging either to distant sections of one or another tribe, or to small and relatively powerless tribes within the Ulus. Besides these tribes, there was a sizable population I have defined as non-tribal which provided additional manpower for the tribal leaders; these will be discussed in the next section.

We must now look closely at the individual groups within the Ulus Chaghatay. At the head of most powers within the Ulus were a few people bearing the tribal name; we usually know of ten to twenty such people, spread over several generations. From among them came the chief of the tribe, or *beg*. The four Turco-Mongolian tribes of the Ulus, the Arlat,

Barlas, Jalayir and Suldus, were all ruled by such aristocratic clans. In the case of the Barlas, we have a genealogy of the leading clan, tracing its descent back to Chaghadai's emir, Qarachar Noyan. Of the Barlas emirs mentioned in the histories, almost all are to be found within this family tree. (See Appendix A: Barlas.)

Almost all the other powers of the Ulus had originated as troop formations. Some were led by their own leaders and acted as independent powers. Each of these, the Yasa'urī, the Apardï, the Khuttalānī, and the Negüderī, was led by an extended family or clan, which passed on power within itself, although not always from father to son. In many cases the leading clan contained two different lineages, competing for power. This clan had hereditary rights over a body of troops and a territory for their upkeep. These were, therefore, simply younger tribes, originating in much the same way as had the older ones.

The leading clans within the Ulus tribes are fairly easily identified, because their members appear in the histories. The body of the tribe, providing the tribal troops, also appears but is much harder to classify. References to tribal troops are not very frequent and are often oblique, particularly in the accounts of the period before Temür's takeover. The Timurid historians refer to them in a number of different ways: sometimes as the following of the tribal leader, at other times by the tribal name or by the name of the region which their leader controlled. There is mention of a Jalayir *hazāra* (thousand) in Temür's army before he came to power and of Jalayir troops on two early expeditions of Temür's army after he came to power.[38] Since later in Temür's life the Jalayir *beg* is mentioned as heading his own *tümen*, it is likely that his tribal troops continued to exist as a unit.[39] As for the other tribes, there are several mentions of Suldus and Apardï troops, and one of Yasa'urī soldiers, as well as some mentions of the troops of smaller tribes. In no case is there information about the composition of these armies.[40]

It is interesting that Barlas troops are never mentioned as such. Within the Barlas there is mention of the "*ulugh ming*," "the great thousand," controlled by the chief of the tribe. In his early years Temür was granted the "hereditary *tümen*," or the "*tümen* of Amīr Qarachar."[41] As I have stated above, the Barlas, Suldus and Jalayir may well have originated from three of the thousands granted to Chaghadai. It seems likely that the basic troops of the Barlas, and perhaps also of the Suldus and Jalayir, were descendants of the thousands of their ancestors; these then would be the "hereditary *tümen*."[42]

In addition to tribal sections closely attached to the leading clans, there was apparently a sizable population belonging to smaller tribes or tribal sections, from which chiefs could attract and attach followers. It seems for instance that the Arlat, at least those at Andkhud, were under the control of the Apardï emirs at Shaburqan, while the Qipchaq troops may have been part of the Jalayir army (see Appendix A). There were also a number of emirs active within the Ulus Chaghatay who bore names of tribes which the histories never mention as a whole, and to which they ascribe no territory. As examples one can cite emirs of the Nayman, Taychi'ut and Nüküz.[43] Their presence can be explained if one assumes that these were small tribes or remnants of tribes, absorbed into the larger ones while still retaining some separate identity. In this way the tribes of the Ulus resembled the Basseri of Iran, whom I have mentioned above.

It is probable that the tribes of the Ulus were not all identical in structure, although evidence on this subject is very limited. There are indications for example that the Jalayir and Suldus were more segmented than the Barlas. The Barlas had within it five main lineages, carefully recorded in the tribal genealogy, and we hear of one possible subtribe, but these did not apparently function as political units.[44] For both the Jalayir and Suldus however, there is evidence of more independent units within the tribe. There are several mentions of subgroups within the Jalayir, often acting independently from one another. In one case we know the name of a section of the tribe, in another the name of a section's leader.[45] In the case of the Suldus, one emir is identified as leader of a *qabīla*, probably a subsection of the tribe, since he was not the tribal chief.[46] The Suldus also were divided territorially, between Chaghaniyan and Balkh.

Non-tribal troops

The groups which I have described above were all relatively similar; they were led by a chief originating within the tribe, they had a definite corporate identity, and occupied a specific tribal area. Not all of the Turco-Mongolian population however belonged to such tribes – the Ulus Chaghatay contained numerous other nomad groupings, varying considerably in structure and importance, some with a definite corporate identity and some without. In attempting to define and describe the variety of groups making up the Ulus and to analyze their activities and importance within it, I have made a distinction between two types, one classified as tribal and the other as non-tribal. I have identified as tribes those groups which originated from older Turco-Mongolian tribes, and also newer groups which possessed a corporate name and identity and had an internal political system able to supply the leadership of the tribe from within. In the context of this study, which deals primarily with political dynamics, the second of these criteria is crucial. Groups which originated outside of the tribal structure and which did not have independent internal leadership I have defined as non-tribal.

This distinction is in some ways an arbitrary one, but it is useful in analyzing the Ulus Chaghatay because the tribal and non-tribal populations had quite different political roles, and posed different problems and opportunities to leaders within the Ulus. While the tribes of the Ulus provided much of its political leadership, the non-tribal troops provided an additional pool of manpower which could be used by both the tribal and the supra-tribal leaders of the Ulus.

Nomads traditionally organized in tribes or sections might switch their allegiance to a different tribe, but their tradition dictated that they belong to one tribe or another. People of a non-tribal background, whether settled leaders or nomads who had been part of a garrison or standing army, might serve under tribal leaders but could probably more easily defect from the tribal enterprise to go back to their former life and identity. They could also be more easily won away by the central leadership which had originally created them, and this is what happened when Temür rose to power. In this way the non-tribal troops formed a swing population whose control either by the various tribal leaders or by a central leader could strongly influence the balance of power within the Ulus.

In this section I shall attempt to analyze the non-tribal component of the Ulus Chaghatay – groups which apparently did not provide their own leadership from within, and had originated outside the tribal system. I am not dealing here with the mass of the settled population, but with the nomad and Turco-Mongolian military manpower available either to tribal leaders, or to supra-tribal ones.

Most of the non-tribal leaders of the Ulus Chaghatay were remnants of armies created by the Chaghadayid dynasty. One major source of non-tribal power was the regional armies of Transoxiana, probably the remnants of the *tümens* organized by the Chaghadayid khans. There was besides this a military class or group bearing the title *qa'uchin*, appearing in the armies of the Ulus Chaghatay both before and after Temür's rise to power. This set of people has never been satisfactorily identified, and must be examined. Another source of manpower specifically identified in the sources was the troop formations remaining from earlier times, both personal followings and garrison troops. There were as I have stated quite a number of these and they should be discussed in some detail here, because they were an important source of manpower in the Ulus. There were four such regiments: the Qara'unas, within which were found the smaller Borolday, the *tümen* of Kebeg Khan, and the Dulan Jawun.

The Qara'unas were much the most important of these; they were both more and less than a tribe. Traditionally they were attached to a single emir whose position seems to have been sometimes hereditary and sometimes appointive. While the Qara'unas did not always choose their leadership from within they did retain some corporate identity, and at this time their soldiers apparently did not fight under outside leaders, unless at the express command of their own emir. The Qara'unas could be an important source of manpower to the khan or central leader, and could also be a major power in their own right; their emirs at this time claimed leadership over the Ulus Chaghatay. Qazaghan, who had taken control over the ulus in 747/1346–7, had been succeeded by his son ᶜAbd Allāh. After ᶜAbd Allāh was killed by Buyan Suldus, Qazaghan's grandson Amīr Ḥusayn had retained power over the Qara'unas, though not over the Ulus. Within the Qara'unas there was a separate formation, known as the Borolday *hazāra* or *tümen*, which seems to have provided significant numbers of troops. This had originated as the troops of the Qara'unas commander Borolday and was controlled personally first by Qazaghan and then by Amīr Ḥusayn.[47]

In the region of Balkh there was a separate formation, known as the *tümen* of Kebeg Khan; according to the medieval historians Kebeg before he became khan was allowed to collect around himself the rich people from every *ulus*, and their descendants still called themselves "the *injü* of Kebeg."[48] The presence of this *tümen* at Balkh may be explained by Kebeg's interest in the area. He is said to have rebuilt the city, which had been ruined by Chinggis Khan.[49] There was another troop contingent in Khorasan which was apparently attached to Temür himself. This was the Dulan Jawun, described as the "*hazāra* of Khulm."[50] The name of this contingent comes from the Mongolian "*dolughan jaghun*," meaning seven hundred, and it probably began as a local garrison army.[51] It is not clear whether the Dulan Jawun were attached to the Barlas as a whole or only to Temür's family, but the tie is said to be an ancient one. Temür used them twice before he took over the Ulus Chaghatay; it is worth noting that he had to come to Khorasan to conscript these troops.[52]

Such troop contingents were an important part of the military manpower available to the Ulus Chaghatay, but they were available only to the fortunate few who inherited rights over them, or could seize such rights. Another and even more important question is whether there were other non-tribal troops which were available to all of the tribal leaders in the Ulus Chaghatay. The sources give indications that this was so.

It is clear that not all of the soldiers available in any region were considered members of the tribe that held the area. As I have written above, the histories often identify armies according to the region they came from. This is particularly true of the army of Kish, controlled by the Barlas, which is invariably identified by its area rather than by tribal name. When Temür gained control over the Barlas he was also granted governance of the region of Kish and Qarshi, and he is frequently mentioned recruiting troops there.[53] Of the emirs connected with this region many were Barlas, but a number were not. We hear for instance of Temüge Qa'uchin joining Temür near Kish in 765/1364, and a few years later a Qara'unas army camped near Qarshi succeeded in winning over many local emirs; of those mentioned several had armies, and only one was mentioned with a tribal affiliation.[54] In other tribal regions there were also emirs not clearly belonging to the tribe. About the Suldus region of Chaghaniyan it is specifically stated that not all its troops were Suldus. At one point in Temür's early career he sent one of his followers out to collect the army of the region, "Suldus and others."[55]

In one region, Khuttalan, it seems likely that the tribal and regional armies had remained quite separate, and that the regional army had by Temür's time begun to function as a tribe. The histories state that Khuttalan and Arhang were controlled jointly by two men: Kaykhusraw Khuttalānī and Öljeytü Apardï. The army and the *tümen* of Khuttalan are mentioned a number of times and were clearly attached first to Kaykhusraw Khuttalānī, and then to his relatives.[56] Öljeytü's personal base was at Arhang and his troops presumably were largely tribal, although no specific information is given about them in the sources. Some support he must have had, since he held a high position within the Ulus, and his power was clearly separate from that of Kaykhusraw.

It is clear then that various regions of the Ulus Chaghatay had troops attached to them which might be partly tribal, but were not entirely so. It seems likely that there was considerable variation within the Ulus. When discussing tribal armies I began with the Jalayir, who were most often referred to by the name of their tribe. It is interesting and perhaps significant that the army of Khujand, which was their seat, is never mentioned as such. It is possible that theirs was an almost purely tribal army. The southern and less mountainous areas, controlled by the Barlas in Kish, the Suldus in Chaghaniyan and Balkh, and the Apardï/Nayman in Shaburqan, had tribal armies and also regional ones including, in the case of Balkh, troops of former leaders.

One should probably connect these regional armies with the *tümens* which the Arab historian Ibn ᶜArabshāh mentioned in his description of the Ulus Chaghatay. According to Ibn ᶜArabshāh there were seven *tümens* in the Samarqand region and nine in Ferghana; he defines a *tümen* as a population which produces ten thousand soldiers.[57] Unfortunately we know little about the *tümens* of Transoxiana. It is clear that a census was taken in Transoxiana, as elsewhere, and that population and land were divided into decimal units. There is some disagreement as to whether these divisions represented troops or tax units. Some "thousands" apparently represented civilians providing income for the Mongol princes to whom they were assigned.[58]

It remains likely however that decimal units also provided direct support for Mongol troops.[59] The other major Mongol successor states – the Ilkhanids, the Golden Horde and Yüan China – all had decimally organized and largely non-tribal armies, whose commanders at a certain point were given land from whose revenues they could support themselves.[60] If the Chaghadayid *tümens* represented a similar military system it might explain the presence of non-tribal troops on the land. The similarity of the reforms instituted within different areas of the Mongol empire at this time make this a definite possibility.

The creation of *tümens* probably also entailed the conscription of some of the indigenous population into the army, and might have led to the sedentarization of some of the nomad armies.[61] Unfortunately it is impossible to tell from the sources whether the regional armies were made up wholly or largely of Turco-Mongolian nomads. We must therefore leave this question unresolved.

One more group of people remains to be considered: the *qa'uchin*. This was a special class or group of military men important both before and after Temür's rise to power, making up part of his personal following in his early career and later part of his army. Their origin and their place in the Ulus Chaghatay have remained unclear and the available evidence unfortunately does not allow us to determine who and what they were. Here I shall suggest some possible interpretations. A full discussion of the *qa'uchin* is found in Appendix A.

The *qa'uchin* were a recognized and hereditary class or group of people, whose members are identified as such in the sources, but they do not seem to have been attached to any one region of Transoxiana or to have had any clear internal leadership. *Qa'uchin* emirs appear in the sources both before and after Temür's rise to power and seem to have played a significant though not outstanding role at both periods. Whether they originated as a personal army loyal to the Chaghadayid khan or as the standing army of the Chaghadayid khanate, it seems likely that they did have independent access to land, because they were able to survive as a class after the downfall of the Chaghadayid khans. They should therefore be included among the non-tribal troops of the Ulus, available to both tribal and supra-tribal leaders.

These then were the troops of the Ulus Chaghatay: the tribesmen, the remains of personal followings and garrison troops, regional armies of various regions – indigenous, Turco-Mongolian or both – and finally the *qa'uchin*, who may perhaps be identical with the local troops or be part of them. It seems clear that after the power of the Chaghadayid khans had dwindled, some part at least of their administrative and military structure remained and the districts of the Ulus Chaghatay, when taken over by tribal leaders, still held non-tribal soldiers placed or organized there by the Khan. One can say with some certainty that a significant number of the troops of the Ulus Chaghatay were non-tribal in their origin and organization.

Nomad and settled populations

The evidence we have about Transoxiana during Temür's time does not permit us to reconstruct its society and economy in detail, but does allow us an overview. It shows two distinct societies, nomad and settled, both highly developed and living in close propinquity to each other. It is clear that much of the Turco-Mongolian population of the Ulus Chaghatay was still nomadic. While the members of the leading clans probably owned agricultural land, and lived in close contact with the settled population, most tribesmen continued to rely for their daily sustenance on their herds and to migrate regularly between summer and winter pastures.

Both the Spanish ambassador Clavijo and Ibn ᶜArabshāh state that Temür and his ancestors were shepherds, or nomads, and Clavijo described the "Chaghatays" as nomads, travelling with their flocks and herds and accompanied on their campaigns by their women and children.[62] The descriptions of the Ulus Chaghatay at this time suggest a society depending on livestock and practicing regular migration. When Amir Qazaghan of the Qara'unas gained control of the Ulus Chaghatay in 747/1346–7, he established his winter pasture (*qïshlaq*) on the Oxus at Sali Saray, and his summer capital at Shahr-i Mung in the mountainous region to the north.[63] The account of Amīr Ḥusayn Qara'unas' formal takeover in 765/1364 states that as he put his realm in order the nomads were settled in their original *yurts* (territories) and that they divided up their pasture and wells.[64]

The disposition of tribal territory also suggests a nomadic life. It is notable that the areas held by the local powers of the Ulus almost all contained both the river valleys and marshes suitable for winter pasture and the mountains necessary for summer grazing. The Barlas held the area from Qarshi on the Kashka river, where Temür sometimes wintered, to Kish and the mountainous region surrounding it.[65] A number of groups held two distinct areas which from their geographical location would seem to have been originally summer and winter pastures.[66]

Although the members of the Ulus Chaghatay continued to practice nomadism, they did not depend on it for the whole of their wealth and power and much of the territory their leaders controlled was urban or agricultural. The great cities of Samarqand and Bukhara, with smaller ones such as Qarshi, Kish, Khujand, and Shaburqan were under nomadic overlordship and the tribes sometimes stationed governors (*shaḥna*) in these cities.[67] Several of these districts were well known for fertility and prosperous agriculture.[68] The goods and income produced by the settled population were almost certainly a significant factor in the strength of the tribes. The histories give very little insight into administrative affairs, but on one or two occasions they do mention the collection of taxes or levies (*māl-i dīwān*, *kharāj*). We are informed of one occasion during the period we are discussing when Temür sent people to collect taxes; Ḥājjī Maḥmūdshāh Yasa'urī went at his orders to get the taxes from Bukhara which was his region and two of Temür's servitors were assigned to collect from the region of Kish.[69] The population of Samarqand, attacked from outside and abandoned by their Chaghatay overlords, complained that they paid taxes, but received no protection in return.[70] Individuals within the leading families of the tribes also had direct ties to the land and its settled population. Some were apparently attached to specific regions and sometimes owned land; a *waqfnāma* of 1326 mentions a number of farms in the possession of Turco-

Mongolian emirs.[71] When Bahrām Jalayir took over control of his own tribe with Temür's help, he pillaged the lands of his defeated rival.[72]

The nomads moreover seem to have made free use of cities during their campaigns. There are several mentions of sieges in which one Chaghatay army fought from within a city and another besieged it from without; the fortified towns of Transoxiana therefore could serve as refuges for the nomads who controlled them. It is clear also that some of the settled population served in the various Chaghatay armies. The sources mention Tajiks and footmen in the Yasa'urī army defending Bukhara, and both are mentioned in some of the armies led by other Chaghatay commanders within the Ulus.[73]

The enjoyment of the benefits of settled territories for income, refuge and additional manpower and the ties of individual emirs to specific areas help to explain the strong attachment of the tribes to the lands they held. It is noticeable that the tribal holdings were constant throughout a long period with only intermittent central control. Moreover, while the chiefs of tribes or their rivals often fled their territory and even the Ulus Chaghatay, the greater part of the tribe stayed where it was. For instance when Ḥājjī Beg, the chief of the Barlas, fled before the invading Moghuls in 761/1360, he seems to have taken with himself only a small group of people, leaving most of the tribe behind.[74] After the second invasion by the Moghul khan Temür, then chief of his tribe, fled with a few followers while the other emirs of the Barlas remained in Transoxiana.[75]

The tribes and other groupings of the Ulus Chaghatay must be seen as nomads, but nomads particularly well acquainted with the settled world and closely bound to it. They resembled in this way the nomads of the Middle East – the "enclosed nomads" – making use of marginal lands and mountain pastures within an agricultural society. The crucial difference was that the Chaghatay nomads held the balance of political and military power within the districts they inhabited, and that part of their power and wealth came from the control of settled societies. As the ruling group moreover, they preserved intact the cultural traditions of their nomad forbears.

The settled population, though it undoubtedly played a role in the politics and economy of the Ulus Chaghatay, appears in the sources almost exclusively in relation to the activities of the Turco-Mongolian tribes. The histories of the period, written by historians from other regions at the order of the victorious nomads, rely on Chaghatay traditions and give little information about the settled peoples.[76] Several individuals and groups from the settled population do appear in the accounts of Temür's rise to power and his early rule, discussed in the next chapter, but the sources tell us essentially nothing about their background and importance. The brief account of their actions therefore gives us no insights into the structure or the relative power of the settled society of the Ulus Chaghatay.

At the time of Temür's rise to power the inhabitants of the Ulus Chaghatay included two main groups of people: Turco-Mongolian nomads, known as Chaghatays, and settled peoples, including urban, agricultural and mountain populations. Although one can assume that most urban and agricultural affairs were in the hands of local leaders, the settled population lived under the overlordship of the Chaghatay nomads.

The tribes of the Ulus Chaghatay formed a confederation united less by common leadership than by shared interest and traditions. The Ulus had come into being neither by conquest nor by fiat, but by a process of gradual separation and amalgamation. Its members shared a common loyalty to the house of Chaghatay and used structures remaining from the khanate's military and administrative system. Even in the absence of central leadership the Ulus remained a constant entity with a corporate identity. From the time that it had separated from the Chaghadayid khanate to the time of Temür's rise to power it had retained the same shape and the same membership.

In discussing the Chaghatay nomads, I have distinguished between tribal and the non-tribal populations. The tribes, as I have defined them, were groups which had not only a corporate name and identity, but also internal leadership: one or two families whose members had a hereditary right to rule the tribe. These tribes had originated in different ways. Some, like the Barlas, Jalayir and Suldus, were descended from the Turco-Mongolian tribes of Chinggis Khan's army. Others, such as the Yasa'urī or the Khuttalānī, had been troop contingents, either personal or regional, and had more recently become tribes.

In the middle of the fourteenth century the tribal chiefs controlled the political life of the Ulus Chaghatay, and had at their disposal most of the wealth and the military manpower of the region. They did not owe all their strength to the tribesmen whose loyalty they commanded directly but could attract followers also from a large swing-population consisting of small tribes or sections of tribes. Moreover, with the overthrow of the Chaghadayid khans and the decline of central leadership, the tribal leaders had taken control over much that had previously been the province of the central government or of members of the royal dynasty. The regional armies originally organized by the khans now campaigned under the tribal leaders who held their territory and the *qa'uchin* troops were available to at least some of the tribal leaders. The tribal chiefs might also attach to themselves the troop contingents – originally garrison troops or personal followings – which had been created by the Chaghadayid dynasty. Individually each of these troop contingents, most especially of course the Qara'unas, lent considerable power to the person who controlled it. Together they provided a significant part of the military manpower available to the tribal and supratribal leaders of the Ulus Chaghatay.

The Chaghatays, while remaining nomadic, lived in close propinquity to the settled population of the Ulus Chaghatay which provided them with a significant proportion of their wealth and power. Tribal leaders stationed governors in the cities under their control and collected taxes from them. They made use of fortified cities for defense in war and even apparently conscripted settled soldiers into their armies. Individual tribal emirs moreover owned land and controlled their own territories. For this reason, the tribes of the Ulus remained strongly attached to their regions, and while tribal leaders might flee the Ulus, they could not take the whole of their tribe with them. To retain control over their tribes and to benefit from them, they had to remain within the Ulus. This was a confederation of many heterogeneous groups who lived, for the moment, in balance. Settled and nomad, tribal and non-tribal, shared common interests and could work to each other's advantage. This structure was maintained by a highly active and fluid political system which will be described in the next chapter.

CHAPTER 3

Temür's rise to power: the politics of the Ulus Chaghatay

A description of the territory, tribes and other population of the Ulus Chaghatay cannot by itself give a full picture of the Ulus or an understanding of its identity and its internal life. One must not only examine the structure of the Ulus and the powers that made it up, but also discover what these structures meant to the people within the Ulus: how the tribes molded the loyalties and actions of their members, what kept the tribes together, and what, in the eyes of its own population, constituted the Ulus Chaghatay. To find this out we must examine the political life of the Ulus, for it is here that we find the fullest expression of its traditions and loyalties.

I have characterized the Ulus as a tribal confederation, not because all of its population was tribally organized – as I have shown above it was not – but because its political life centered around the tribes. It was the tribal leaders who controlled the resources of the Ulus, and it was the contests within and among the tribes which motivated much of the political activity in the Ulus. One could define the membership of the Ulus Chaghatay as those groups within it which owed allegiance to the house of Chaghadai, or much less reliably as those who were willing to follow whoever was supreme leader of the Ulus. It would be most accurate to define it as those who were involved in deciding who would rule the Ulus, and who would lead the tribes within it.

It was political conflict at all levels which constituted the central concern of the members of the Ulus and formed the bond which kept them together as a single and stable entity. The political activity most basic to the Ulus was the struggle for leadership within the tribes. The causes of this internal political struggle were inherent in the tribal structure. The leadership of a tribe was open to all those within its ruling clan, and could be won and kept only through the support of the tribesmen. This was a politics of consent. Chieftainship could be inherited not just by the sons of the former leader, but also by his brothers, nephews or cousins, or in some cases by the members of a rival lineage. For this reason contests for succession were common. Moreover, once someone had become chief of a tribe, he had still to remain so. Tribesmen were quick to desert an unpopular or unsuccessful leader, and the large number of eligible successors ensured them an alternative candidate whom they could support. For the members of the leading clans the tribe was less an object of loyalty than a prize to fight over.

Another focus for conflict was the leadership of the Ulus itself. The Ulus had inherited from the Chaghadayid khanate a tradition of central leadership. As a concept this leadership remained crucial to its Turco-Mongolian population. The ideal of khanship was part of their Mongol heritage, and the house of Chaghadai an important focus for their loyalty. In reality however central leadership was often contested and rarely fully effective. The Ulus had developed without the help of a strong ruler and was able to continue without one. Its tribes, controlling settled territory from which they extracted wealth and non-tribal populations which provided them with military manpower, had little economic or social need to band together with other tribes under a supra-tribal leader. They did however have need of outside alliances for a different reason – because these alliances were necessary for the political struggles within the tribes themselves.

Since candidates for leadership of the tribe could not count on fellow tribesmen for support, they had instead to look for help outside the tribe. Both tribal chiefs and their rivals depended on alliances with the members of other Ulus tribes. What was most useful of all was an alliance either with the leader of the Ulus or with a powerful candidate for that position. It was of course difficult to know who would be successful in attaining leadership over the Ulus. In the struggles over power within the confederation therefore, one sometimes finds members of the same tribe on different sides of the conflict. Each of the rivals for power within the tribe hoped that his candidate for the leadership of the Ulus would win, and install him as chief of his tribe.

Politics within the tribes therefore was closely connected with the politics of the Ulus. The leadership of both individual tribes and of the confederation was often contested, among the same set of people – the members of the aristocratic clans. Once the Chaghadayid khans had been deposed any person from the tribal aristocracy was potentially eligible to lead either his tribe or the Ulus, and all used the same tools and the same stratagems in pursuit of either position.

This system was both fluid and tightly interdependent. It was also, for just these reasons, a system which bound together those who participated in it almost as firmly as would a strong central leadership. The constant political activity and change within the Ulus kept its members occupied within its sphere, and firmly enmeshed in a net of alliances and rivalries with other members of the confederation. Since alliances changed frequently, there were few permanent splits within the Ulus.

The political conflict within the Ulus Chaghatay was expressed largely in military action, and one might therefore expect its history to be a violent one, but this was not the case. Although the men of the Ulus spent a considerable amount of time armed and on horseback they spent much less time in actual combat. A commander who knew himself outnumbered usually retreated before a battle; a large part of a commander's skill therefore lay in the accurate assessment of his opponent's strength. Here leaders were aided by the fluidity of Ulus politics and the frequent changes of alliance among its members – most of their opponents had at some point been their allies, and were thus familiar to them. In general commanders joined battle only when they were relatively evenly matched, and their battles rarely lasted more than one or two days. After this time either the commander or the troops of the weaker side were ready to retreat.[1] For this reason it was possible for the Ulus Chaghatay to sustain its internal conflicts over several decades, without serious harm to its population, or attrition within its leading class.

To illustrate the way in which the Ulus Chaghatay functioned, I shall give here an account of its history during the second half of the fourteenth century, and of the way in which Temür rose to power within it. Temür began his career in a relatively low position, and the story of his rise serves to show the system he worked in and the tools he had at his command. It also gives us an indication of the political acumen which characterized Temür throughout his career.

Events in the Ulus Chaghatay before Temür's rise to power

The Ulus Chaghatay, formed after Tarmashirin's death in 1334, remained only a short time under Chaghadayid leadership. In 747/1346–7, the emir of the Qara'unas, Qazaghan, killed the Chaghadayid khan Qazan and himself assumed control of the Ulus Chaghatay.[2] Qazaghan did not attempt to assert full sovereignty over the Ulus. He contented himself with the title of *beg* or *amir*, and maintained a Chinggisid puppet khan to establish the legitimacy of his rule. At this time the Ulus Chaghatay was apparently divided into two groups of tribes. The southern one was dominated by the emir of the Qara'unas and included beside the Qara'unas the Arlat, the Apardï, and the Khuttalānī emirs.[3] This was a fairly cohesive group, and a strong one. The northern section consisted of the Yasa'urī and the old Ulus tribes: the Barlas and the Jalayir. The Suldus tribe seems to have wavered between the two groups. With the takeover of the Ulus by Amīr Qazaghan, the southern part of the Ulus gained the upper hand and it maintained its advantage until Temür's assumption of power in 771/1370.

Although Amīr Qazaghan held power for twelve years – up to 759/1357–8 – it is not clear to what extent he commanded the loyalty of the northern tribes. What little information we have about his reign suggests that both his support and his concerns centered in the southern part of the Ulus, the region where the Qara'unas had traditionally been active. While he stationed his son in Samarqand, he ruled from the Qara'unas territories in the southeast, Sali Saray and Shahr-i Mung. Most of the emirs mentioned campaigning with him were southern – the Arlat, Apardï and Khuttalānī emirs, and the Shahs of Badakhshan.

Like the Chaghadayid rulers before him Qazaghan maintained an interest in India. He raided it once, and he provided a force of auxiliaries to the Delhi sultan Muḥammad Tughluq in 751/1350–1.[4] He also mounted a campaign against Herat at the request of the Arlat and Apardï emirs and the *shaykhs* of Jam.[5] The histories describe this expedition in some detail, and give the names of the emirs who accompanied Qazaghan. The only member of the expedition who was not part of the southern coalition was Buyan Suldus, whose holdings lay between the two sections of the Ulus.[6]

In 759/1358, Amīr Qazaghan was murdered by the son of Borolday, the former emir of the Qara'unas, angry that the command of his father's troops (the Borolday *tümen*) had been denied him.[7] Qazaghan's son ᶜAbd Allāh succeeded him, and seems to have had more ambitious ideals than his father, wishing apparently to extend his power over the northern part of the Ulus. The histories reflect clearly the negative reaction of the tribal leaders to ᶜAbd Allāh's northern interests. During Qazaghan's lifetime, while ᶜAbd Allāh had been stationed in Samarqand, he had undertaken a campaign to Khorezm. This expedition is reported with disapproval, and Qazaghan supposedly was angered by it.[8] After his father's death ᶜAbd Allāh decided to move his capital to Samarqand, despite warnings from his advisors against abandoning his native place. Before he had been long in office moreover he killed his father's puppet khan Buyan Qulï Khan and replaced him with a different one. These actions along with his youth and inexperience, cost him his position. In 760/1358–9, Ḥājjī Beg Barlas and Buyan Suldus chased him out, killed his brothers and his khan, and installed Buyan Suldus as emir of the Ulus. ᶜAbd Allāh fled to the Qara'unas territories where he soon died, but his nephew, Amīr Ḥusayn b. Musalā b. Qazaghan, survived and led a precarious life on the southeastern fringes of the Ulus Chaghatay.[9]

In giving reasons for ᶜAbd Allāh's overthrow, the histories emphasize his unlawful execution of the khan his father had appointed. The killing of a puppet khan seems to have been taken lightly enough however on other occasions; both Qazaghan and Temür did this without bad consequences. It is probable that it was ᶜAbd Allāh's decision to move his capital to Samarqand which was the decisive element in his downfall. The two emirs who killed him, Buyan Suldus and Ḥājjī Beg Barlas, both held territories close to Samarqand. Ḥājjī Beg was at Kish, Buyan at Shadman. The prospect of a central leader with a sizeable regiment of Qara'unas troops so close to their regions would not be appealing. Nor was the statement of absolute sovereignty implied in the occupation of what had been the khan's region and an area controlled by tribes who were not close associates of the Qara'unas. The northern tribes had little to gain and much to lose from this arrangement.

Buyan Suldus apparently never attempted to assume full control over the

Ulus; the sources report favorably on his personality but state that he gave himself up to drink and pleasure. Taking advantage of the confusion within the Ulus the eastern Chaghadayid khan Tughluq Temür invaded Transoxiana in Rabīᶜ II 761/February to March 1360. This invasion provoked no resistance from the tribal leaders, who either took advantage of the invasion to better their positions or fled the Ulus. Bāyazīd Jalayir and his tribe, whose lands were on the Moghul frontier, joined the Moghuls and went with them against Samarqand and Kish. Ḥājjī Maḥmūdshāh Yasa'urī, whose territory was close to that of the Barlas, decided to take this opportunity to pillage their region at the head of a Moghul contingent. The chief of the Barlas, Ḥājjī Beg, first gathered his army to resist but then, deciding that the enemy was stronger than he, chose instead to flee into Khorasan.[10]

Temür's rise to power

It was at the time of the Moghul invasion that Temür made his first bid for the leadership of the Barlas tribe. This was not at all a coincidence; it was the Moghul khan who installed Temür as chief of his tribe. The history of Temür's assumption of leadership over the Barlas and of his struggles to keep this position illustrates the importance of outside support for a tribal emir. Temür at first accompanied Ḥājjī Beg on his flight before the Moghuls but when they reached the Oxus, he asked permission to return to Kish to keep hold of the Barlas region. Ḥājjī Beg granted his request, and Temür made his way back. The reason the histories give for Temür's return is his fear that the Barlas *ulus* would fall into confusion if left without leadership, but subsequent events make it clear that Temür recognized this as an opportunity to seize leadership of the tribe.[11]

One should consider here what position Temür held within his tribe, and why he felt ready to make a bid for leadership. He was a member of one of the five main lineages of the Barlas clan, but not apparently one of the most prominent, and he was not closely related to the tribe's chief. There is little information available about either his father or any other recent ancestor, which may suggest that his family did not hold a very high position. Both the Spanish ambassador Clavijo and Ibn ᶜArabshāh explain that Temür started out his career as a petty brigand, stealing sheep, and gradually attracting to himself a band of followers which increased as his depredations became more extensive. It is of course possible that this story was a fabrication or an exaggeration to show Temür in the mold of a dynastic founder. It is clear from other evidence that by the time Temür made his first bid for power within his tribe, he possessed a personal, non-tribal, following.[12]

In the accounts of Temür's early campaigns the identity of many of his personal followers becomes clear, though it is not possible to identify them all. Only a few of them were members of the Barlas tribe, and there were also few members of the other important tribes of the Ulus Chaghatay. For some people the sources mention no tribal affiliation, others, such as Sayf al-Dīn Nüküz, ᶜAbbās Qipchaq, and Dā'ūd Dughlat, belonged to tribes without a strong presence in Transoxiana. The size of this following is not clear. Ibn ᶜArabshāh gives its number at forty, while Clavijo states that Temür eventually had three hundred horsemen under his command. These estimates may not in fact be contradictory; it is possible that Ibn ᶜArabshāh was counting only the emirs in Temür's following, while Clavijo counted also the soldiers each brought with him.[13]

Temür was not cutting himself off from his tribe in forming his band, rather he was building up an instrument of power within it. A group of followers who, unlike tribesmen, could be counted on in adversity and even exile was a great strength for politics inside the tribe as well as outside it. Other members of the tribal aristocracy at this time apparently had similar bands. The Jalayir emir Bahrām, for instance, left for Moghulistan with his "companions and personal army."[14] It is possible also that the troops of Öljey Bugha Suldus near Balkh, mentioned in the last chapter, could have had their origin in such a following.

By the time of Tughluq Temür's invasion, Temür had sufficient standing inside and outside his tribe so that he could hope to lead it. Nonetheless he was presumably not the only Barlas emir who could hope to rule, nor was he the only one to remain in Transoxiana when Ḥājjī Beg left. We need some further explanation for the immediate success of his bid for power. The answer probably lies in the personal connections he had with the tribes and possibly the khans of Moghulistan.

As I have mentioned above, one of Temür's early followers was Amīr Dā'ūd of the Dughlat, a tribe which held enormous power and territory in Moghulistan, intermarrying with the royal line and often making and unmaking khans. Amīr Dā'ūd was married to Temür's sister, Qutluq Türken Agha, who had earlier been married to another member of the tribe, Sulṭān Dughlat.[15] There are other indications also of personal connections with Moghulistan. Temür had allies within the Merkit tribe, whose lands lay on the border with Moghulistan, and the father of an important Moghul emir, Amīr Ḥamīd Kerai't, had been a friend of Temür's father.[16] There is an indication also that Temür held some personal possessions near Tashkent, then part of the eastern Chaghadayid territories.[17] Whether for these or other reasons, Tughluq Temür Khan received Temür cordially and granted him the region of Kish and the Barlas *tümen*.[18]

Temür now proceeded to gather an army of nomads "from the Oxus to Samarqand" and to forge a set of alliances with the leaders of other tribes, choosing as his allies people unfriendly to Ḥājjī Beg Barlas. First of all he attached himself to Amir Khiḍr Yasa'urī, who was head of the Yasa'urī tribe and related by marriage to Temür's cousin Ḥājjī Maḥmūdshāh Yasa'urī, last mentioned preparing to pillage the Barlas lands. At this time the Moghuls fell out among themselves and left the region. Taking advantage of this,

Qazaghan's grandson, the Qara'unas leader Amīr Ḥusayn, returned from Kabul and asked Khiḍr, Temür and Bāyazīd Jalayir to go with him against Buyan Suldus, seeking revenge for the murder of his uncle and other members of his family. This Khiḍr and Temür agreed to do, while Bāyazīd expressed interest but avoided the campaign.[19] One should recall here that Ḥājjī Beg had been the partner of Buyan Suldus in the murder of Amīr Ḥusayn's uncle ᶜAbd Allāh for which revenge was now being sought. Both Khiḍr and Amīr Ḥusayn could be expected to continue supporting Temür when Ḥājjī Beg returned.

Now that he had gained the support of Amir Khiḍr and Temür, Amīr Ḥusayn was a major force within the Ulus. The three emirs went towards Shadman to attack Buyan Suldus, but when Buyan heard of their approach he fled to Badakhshan; when they pursued him to that region its ruler, Shāh Bahā' al-Dīn, also fled without battle. Amīr Ḥusayn then claimed control of the region and leadership of the Ulus Chaghatay. Thus with the help of Temür and the Yasa'urī, the rule of the Ulus had once again returned to the southern coalition and Temür, preparing to face Ḥājjī Beg, had gained a powerful new ally. Amīr Ḥusayn's claims however did not go uncontested. Shortly after the return of Khiḍr and Temür to their lands, they received word from Amīr Ḥusayn that Tughluq Suldus, the chief of one section of the Suldus, had become inimical. Khiḍr and Temür answered his appeal, gathered their armies and met with Amīr Ḥusayn, but Tughluq had already fled.[20]

At this time Ḥājjī Beg Barlas returned and set out to regain power over his tribe. He did not go directly against Temür but went instead to an outside ally, Bāyazīd Jalayir, with whom he attacked Temür's prestigious associate, Amīr Khiḍr Yasa'urī. Hearing of this attack, Temür joined his army to that of Khiḍr. The sources disagree on the outcome of the first battle between the armies, but agree about its result; the Barlas emirs decided to return their allegiance to Ḥājjī Beg Barlas and most of the army of Kish deserted Temür, with the sole exception of his personal follower Chekü Barlas. Temür and Chekü therefore decided to return their allegiance to Ḥājjī Beg. This is not a surprising decision; within an insecure and changeable system, emirs switched allegiance as they found it expedient and their leaders, if they wanted to retain their followers, had to accept this behavior. When Temür had to cede his position he was accepted back into his tribe, and then quickly turned against his recent ally, Khiḍr Yasa'urī. Together with Bāyazīd, Ḥājjī Beg and Temür now went against Khiḍr, whom they fought and defeated. This victory enlarged Amīr Bāyazīd's territories, and served to confirm Ḥājjī Beg as leader of the Barlas.[21] Temür's first bid for power had failed.

In Jumādā I, 762/March to April 1361, Tughluq Temür Khan again invaded, and Temür's fortunes once more improved. As the Moghul forces reached Khujand, Bāyazīd Jalayir submitted and when they had reached Samarqand, Buyan Suldus followed suit. Ḥājjī Beg Barlas planned to do the same until he heard that the Khan had executed Bāyazīd Jalayir; then he decided to flee to Khorasan. He passed through Kish to collect some troops, and chased by the Moghul army, crossed the Oxus into Khorasan where he was surprised and killed. Temür remained behind and went as before to the khan. His family's ally Amīr Ḥamīd Kerai't, spoke for him and he was once again given the area of Kish, at the same time becoming commander of a *tümen*.[22]

Temür however did not remain long in this position. The Moghul Khan had apparently decided to subjugate the Ulus Chaghatay more completely than he had done before, and soon began to attack all the powerful leaders within it. His first move was a campaign against Amīr Ḥusayn. Amīr Ḥusayn prepared to resist him but when the two armies met he was deserted by Kaykhusraw Khuttalānī, whose brother he had executed when assuming leadership of the Ulus a year or two before. Amīr Ḥusayn fled without a battle. When Tughluq Temür returned from this expedition he executed Buyan Suldus and a number of other emirs whom he considered troublesome.[23] Having disposed of the most powerful chiefs of the region, Bāyazīd, Buyan Suldus, Ḥājjī Beg and Amīr Ḥusayn, Tughluq Temür appointed his son Ilyās Khwāja to rule Transoxiana.

According to the sources, the Moghuls opened the door of tyranny, and oppressed the local emirs. Finding this pressure unbearable, Temür left with a few followers and went to join Amīr Ḥusayn near Khiva. This was the first of many periods of exile for Temür. The presence of refuge areas near the Ulus Chaghatay made it possible for him and Amīr Ḥusayn to continue their political and military activity in neighboring lands when they were unable to do so within the Ulus. For the next three years both men spent much of their time outside the Ulus – largely in Khorasan – with only a small number of followers. These were not easy years for Amīr Ḥusayn and Temür and they suffered several humiliating defeats by local powers. However Temür at least also gained some valuable allies during this time. Most notable among these were Malik Muᶜizz al-Dīn Kart of Herat and Mubārakshāh Sanjarī, a Turkmen chief holding an area near Makhan, who was later a close ally of Temür's.[24]

In Khorasan Temür and Amīr Ḥusayn were able gradually to regroup around themselves some of the emirs of the Ulus Chaghatay. Temür returned inconspicuously to Transoxiana to recruit support for an expedition to Sistan; this trip was apparently successful since in 765/1364 he and Amīr Ḥusayn campaigned for one of the kings of Sistan, at the head of a thousand men. It was on this campaign that Temür received the wound to which he attributed his lameness.[25] Soon after this the two emirs began to gather an army with which to attack the Moghuls.

Although Tughluq Temür Khan had met almost no resistance on either of the two occasions that he invaded the Ulus Chaghatay, most of its emirs were now eager to join Amīr Husayn against the Moghul forces. Their alienation from the eastern Chaghadayids was due probably to the Khan's attempt to assert full sovereignty over them. The sources complain of the tyranny exercised by the Moghuls after their second invasion. One should remember their similar reaction to the pretensions of ᶜAbd Allāh b. Qazaghan. Another cause for complaint was the Moghuls' treatment of the important emirs of the Ulus Chaghatay, most of whom they either executed or forced into flight. At this time executions were apparently rare in the Ulus Chaghatay and it was particularly unwise to execute tribal emirs since the Ulus operated on a system of collective tribal vengeance.[26] Both the goals of the Moghuls and the methods they used to attain them were unacceptable to the tribal leaders of the Ulus, used to weak central leadership and a low level of political violence.

Amīr Ḥusayn therefore was able to attract a large number of followers for his campaign, including many of the tribal aristocracy. He and Temür were joined by some Barlas emirs who had decided to desert the Moghuls, and by several other powerful leaders – Mūsā Taychi'ut, Bahrām Jalayir, and Ūlmās b. Tümen, perhaps the son of Tümen Negüderī.[27] They also had with them Shīr Bahrām Khuttalānī, a relative of Kaykhusraw's who had apparently gained control of Khuttalan when Kaykhusraw deserted.[28]

The two emirs however did not rely only on the tribal aristocracy in their attempt to take back the Ulus Chaghatay. An important part of their army consisted of non-tribal troops, and it was at this time that they began to gain control over the additional troop contingents which became an important part of their strength. Within their army there were a number of personal followers, and many people without tribal affiliation, some of whom commanded infantrymen. They also conscripted several local armies: the Dulan Jawun of Khulm who were attached to Temür, the Borolday, attached to Amīr Ḥusayn, and the army of Badakhshan under its shahs.[29]

Amīr Ḥusayn was not able to enlist or to keep behind himself the whole of the tribal aristocracy of the Ulus. His relations with the Khuttalan emirs were always difficult, perhaps because they were such close neighbors, and now when Amīr Ḥusayn and Temür reached Khuttalan on their tour of conscription Amīr Ḥusayn quarreled with Shīr Bahrām Khuttalānī who then deserted them.[30] As they approached Balkh, from which they wished to invade Transoxiana, they met a more active challenge from Mengli Bugha Suldus who had inherited the *tümen* of Öljey Bugha Suldus. Mengli Bugha was joined by two local emirs,[31] and with them opposed Amīr Ḥusayn and Temür, but was defeated. Balkh and its armies – the *tümens* of Öljey Bugha Suldus and of Kebeg Khan – now fell to Amīr Ḥusayn and Temür.[32] These two armies remained thereafter under their control and contributed significantly to their strength.

With this army, made up of personal followers, tribal emirs, and non-tribal contingents, the two emirs attacked the Moghuls. The Moghuls themselves however were not entirely without support from Chaghatay emirs; in this case, as in many others, the tribes of the Ulus were split. The Suldus and Khuttalānī tribes had emirs on both sides of the dispute. The Moghuls had behind them Kaykhusraw Khuttalānī and Tughluq Suldus, both of whom had earlier fought Amīr Ḥusayn, and had taken refuge in Moghulistan. Amīr Ḥusayn and Temür fought an indecisive battle with the Moghul forces, then put them to flight through a ruse. Shortly thereafter the Moghuls left Transoxiana on hearing that Tughluq Temür Khan had died. Shaykh Muḥammad Suldus, chief of the Suldus tribe, now joined up with Temür, as did Shīr Bahrām Khuttalānī.[33]

The position of the Khuttalānī emirs in this contest is quite clear; Shīr Bahrām, despite initial reluctance, was active on Amīr Ḥusayn's side, while his relative Kaykhusraw fought on the side of the Moghuls, who had provided him refuge and continued to do so until 769/1368. For the Suldus it is less clear, since we know nothing of either Tughluq Suldus or Mengli Bugha after this, and nothing of Shaykh Muḥammad Suldus before he joined Temür following the Moghul defeat. What is evident is that the three emirs were acting independently – one in Balkh, against Amīr Ḥusayn and Temür, one in Transoxiana, eventually at least with Amīr Ḥusayn and Temür, and one with the Moghuls against the two emirs. Like the earlier invasion, this contest for leadership over the Ulus provided an opportunity for ambitious men within the tribes to make bids for personal power.

After the victory over the Moghuls Amīr Ḥusayn held a great convocation or *khurīltay* and installed himself once more at the head of the Ulus, appointing a puppet khan to legitimate his rule, as his grandfather had done. This happened at the end of 765/1364.[34] Once Amīr Ḥusayn had taken power, he and Temür began to disagree with increasing frequency. It is hard to evaluate Temür's position within the Ulus Chaghatay at this point. He was certainly at the head of his tribe, and his close alliance with Amīr Ḥusayn probably lent him additional prestige. It is doubtful however that he held the leading position which the sources ascribe to him; one must assume that this was won gradually over the next several years. Temür's estrangement from Amīr Ḥusayn therefore is probably symptomatic of the actions of other emirs within the Ulus Chaghatay, once again reacting against the assertion of central control.

Amīr Ḥusayn spent the winter in his own seat, Temür in his, and in the spring, hearing that the Moghuls were planning another invasion the Chaghatay emirs went out to confront them. They fought the Moghuls in Ramaḍān, 766/May, 1365 and were badly defeated. The Timurid histories blame the defeat on Amīr Ḥusayn, and it brought about the first serious rift between him and Temür. Each collected his own following and retreated across the Oxus; Amīr Ḥusayn to Shibartu which had earlier served as his refuge area, and Temür to Balkh, where he collected around himself his own men and the *tümens* of Kebeg Khan and Öljey Bugha.[35]

With the loss of power, relations between Amīr Ḥusayn and Temür again improved. In the fall they heard that Samarqand had been successfully defended by its own inhabitants, under the leadership of a small group which the sources call Sarbadars, and that the Moghuls had left Transoxiana because of a horse-plague. Temür immediately left for Qarshi and in the spring of 767/1366 Amīr Ḥusayn arrived with a large army containing the troops of Balkh, Badakhshan, Qunduz, Khuttalan, Hisar-i Shadman, Andkhud and Shaburqan – the whole southern part of the Ulus Chaghatay, including the areas of the Suldus, Arlat and Apardï. The two emirs reassured the Sarbadars with promises of friendship, then seized and killed many of them.[36]

When they had regained their positions within the Ulus, Temür and Amīr Ḥusayn again fell out. Amīr Ḥusayn levied a large tax on a number of Temür's closest associates, most of them part of Temür's personal following. The insult presumably was aimed at Temür, and indeed it was he who paid the money.[37] The events of the next years are described as a duel between the two erstwhile allies, but they probably represent a more general and recurring pattern – the erosion of tribal support for a leader asserting sovereignty, and the related struggle for power within the tribes. The next disagreement between the two men is ascribed to the machinations of other tribal emirs. This began with a plot against Temür by several men: ᶜAlī Darwīsh b. Bāyazīd Jalayir, Amīr Mūsā Taychi'ut who was married to ᶜAli Darwīsh's sister, and Farhād, probably Farhād Apardï. The histories relate that these emirs wrote a letter to Amīr Ḥusayn accusing Temür of plotting against him. It seems likely that the prime mover behind the affair was ᶜAlī Darwīsh. He was in an ambivalent position at this time. As the son of the former Jalayir leader, Amīr Bāyazīd, who had been inimical to Temür and Amīr Ḥusayn, he seems to have been out of favor – for the few years preceding this event, the Jalayir emir mentioned most frequently is Bahrām, who had taken part in a number of campaigns with Temür and Amīr Ḥusayn, and seems to have been allied particularly with Temür.[38] ᶜAlī Darwīsh however had a special connection with Amīr Ḥusayn, since his mother, daughter of Tarmashirin Khan, had been taken by Amīr Ḥusayn after Bāyazīd's death. He may well have hoped that by discrediting Temür and his allies he could shake Bahrām's position, and get control of the Jalayir tribe.

Mūsā Taychi'ut was an interesting figure, and should be described here. Although the Taychi'ut are not mentioned as a tribe within the Ulus, Mūsā clearly had great power and influence. He had a troop contingent attached to him – the *hazāra-i ghancha* – and had marriage alliances with the Jalayir tribe and the Chaghadayid dynasty.[39] Yazdī's *Ẓafarnāma* states that ᶜAlī Darwīsh was the brother of Mūsā's wife – if these were full siblings then Mūsā, like ᶜAlī Darwīsh, was now related by marriage to Amīr Ḥusayn.[40] This would explain both his involvement in this affair and his close alliance with Amīr Ḥusayn.

Temür now began preparing to oppose Amīr Ḥusayn, in alliance with Bahrām Jalayir and Shīr Bahrām Khuttalānī. The stake that Bahrām Jalayir had in this is fairly clear; the case of Shīr Bahrām is less so, but it should be remembered that he had once already quarrelled with Amīr Ḥusayn, and that relations between Amīr Ḥusayn and the Khuttalānī emirs were often strained. The three emirs agreed to ally against Amīr Ḥusayn, and each was to gather an army in his own region. Shīr Bahrām went off to Khuttalan, began to gather troops, and entrenched himself in a fort in the mountains.

It is possible of course that these actions had preceded those of Temür's adversaries ᶜAlī Darwīsh and Amīr Mūsā, and that the letter they had sent to Amīr Ḥusayn contained truth rather than fabrications. This is something that we shall never know, as the histories all agree in their version of the story. Temür in any case had acted too soon, and quickly found himself deserted by his allies, who had little faith in their prospects of success. The speed with which Temür's backing dispersed at this time shows clearly how little either tribesmen or allies could be relied on under adverse circumstances. Amīr Ḥusayn soon won Shīr Bahrām back to his own side, and Bahrām Jalayir also deserted Temür. He had gone with two of Temür's personal followers to Khujand to take over the Jalayir. Together they put ᶜAlī Darwīsh and Amīr Mūsā Taychi'ut to flight, then Amīr Bahrām gathered the Jalayirs and became ruler of the region. However, Bahrām almost immediately began to doubt his and Temür's chances of success, so after pillaging ᶜAlī Darwīsh's lands and killing off his dependents, he fled with his own following to Moghulistan.[41]

Pessimism about Temür's prospects now spread to his closer associates, and members of his own tribe began to desert him. He did however succeed in winning over to his side the Yasa'urī, including Khiḍr's brother ᶜAlī, and ᶜAlī's brother-in-law (Temür's cousin) Ḥājjī Maḥmūdshāh. The Yasa'urīs were frequently Temür's allies – connected to him by marriage and as his closest neighbors. They were however unreliable, as the Khuttalānī emirs were to the Qara'unas leaders, perhaps also because of the tensions of close propinquity. On this occasion they deserted him shortly after he set out against Amīr Ḥusayn. According to the histories, Amīr Ḥusayn falsely proposed peace, then killed Shīr Bahrām Khuttalānī who was with him, and attacked Temür. Temür did not have the strength to resist him and retreated to the region of Marw in Khorasan, where he could count on the help of his old ally Mubārakshāh Sanjarī.[42] The army of Amīr Ḥusayn, led by Mūsā Taychi'ut, now took over the Barlas lands at Qarshi.

Much of the next two years, 768–9/1366–8, Temür spent outside the Ulus Chaghatay, seeking support against Amīr Ḥusayn, and mounting periodic expeditions into the territory of the Ulus. The willingness of neighboring powers to lend him help made it possible for him to retain some of his power and prestige throughout this long exile. Temür remained in the Marw region for several months, sending out messages to both Malik Muᶜizz al-Dīn Kart of Herat and the leader of the Turco-Mongolian Jawun-i Qurban tribe at Tus. He then returned to Transoxiana with a small army made up largely of his following. He took Qarshi in a surprise night attack and succeeded in holding it despite a siege by Amīr Mūsā with some Qara'unas forces. He then spent the winter of 768/1367 in Qarshi and started to reassert his control over the area, sending Ḥājjī Maḥmūdshāh Yasa'urī to govern Bukhara and collect its taxes. The Yasa'urī however once again turned out to be unreliable; ᶜAlī Yasa'urī now left Temür, joined his brother-in-law Ḥājjī Maḥmūdshāh in Bukhara and refused to return to Temür or to deliver the taxes.[43]

Amīr Mūsā meanwhile rejoined Amīr Ḥusayn, who gathered an army of southern emirs, and with a large army of Qara'unas, set out to attack Temür. Temür thought it prudent to retreat to Bukhara, where he was received by ᶜAlī and Ḥājjī Maḥmūdshāh Yasa'urī, but he soon retreated again to Makhan. The Yasa'urī emirs decided to remain and with the help of the Bukharan population, tried to hold the city against Amīr Ḥusayn and Mūsā, but after one battle they were forced to flee and rejoined Temür at Makhan, where he received them well. Amīr Ḥusayn meanwhile set up a governor in Bukhara, and returned to Sali Saray.[44]

Temür now turned to the king of Herat. His emissary was received with honor but the sources claim that Temür, suspicious of the Herat kings, refused to meet Malik Muᶜizz al-Dīn and kept his distance. Nonetheless the king continued to support Temür.[45] In the summer of 768/1367 Temür headed back to Transoxiana and made a surprise attack on Qarshi, which in the absence of Amīr Mūsā Taychi'ut, he succeeded in taking. It turned out however that a Qara'unas army was camped nearby, and was attracting to itself a number of local emirs with their armies, including Amīr Sulaymān Yasa'urī. Temür set off to attack them accompanied by a very reluctant ᶜAlī Yasa'urī, put on his horse almost by force; he also had in his army an emir apparently from the settled population, Mawlānā Badr al-Dīn, who fled along with ᶜAlī Yasa'urī. One incident in this battle provides a good illustration of the relative lack of violence in this warfare. Among Temür's opponents in the battle were two of his old friends, whom Temür's soldiers failed to recognize and killed. This upset Temür considerably and he arranged to have the two men buried at Kish and to have prayers read over their bodies.[46]

Temür won this battle and headed for Samarqand on the advice of his emirs; here he was resisted by one of Amīr Mūsā's commanders. He defeated these forces, but soon heard that the armies of Öljeytü Apardï and Amīr Ḥusayn had taken Kish. He clearly could not hold out against them, so having given the army of Kish permission to return home, he retreated north to Tashkent, accompanied by the six hundred men he had brought with him from Khorasan.[47]

Temür now sought help from two other estranged emirs of the Ulus

Chaghatay, Bahrām Jalayir and Kaykhusraw Khuttalānī. Kaykhusraw had presumably been in Moghulistan from the time that he had deserted Amīr Ḥusayn shortly after Tughluq Temür's second invasion of Transoxiana in 762/1361, and Bahrām since his desertion of Temür in 767/1366. The khan had assigned seven thousand Moghul troops to these emirs and they had settled in the region of Tashkent the governorship of which had been granted to Bahrām Jalayir. Temür now came to them asking help against Amīr Ḥusayn. Bahrām refused, finding perhaps that his position in Moghulistan was comfortable enough. Kaykhusraw on the other hand had less to keep him in Moghulistan and a stronger feeling against Amīr Ḥusayn, who had killed his brother. He therefore invited Temür to him and treated him well. Kaykhusraw was a valuable ally for Temür. He was someone whose power base lay right in the region of Amīr Ḥusayn's heartland, yet his feelings for Amīr Ḥusayn made him unlikely to switch sides. After several years in Moghulistan he had ties to that region including a marriage alliance with the Chaghadayid dynasty; he had married Tümen Qutluq, a cousin of Tughluq Temür's. The daughter of this union was now betrothed to Temür's son Jahāngīr.[48]

Temür and Kaykhusraw, with the backing which they could elicit from the Moghuls, clearly presented a considerable threat to Amīr Ḥusayn, and one he could not afford to ignore. He therefore now gathered a large army and went against Temür along with Mūsā Taychi'ut, Shaykh Muḥammad b. Buyan Suldus, and Öljeytü Apardï. Temür and Kaykhusraw marched against them with a body of Moghul troops. After a number of skirmishes Temür and Kaykhusraw retreated, and Temür wintered in Tashkent, sending emissaries off to the Moghuls to request troops.[49]

In the spring Temür's emissaries returned to him, saying that a Moghul army was following. When Amīr Ḥusayn learned of this, he sent a delegation of religious figures to plead with Temür to reconsider, pointing out the harm that a Moghul invasion would bring on the settled population. Temür apparently realized that he would lose sympathy if he arrived with the Moghul army, and so agreed to call it off. After some delay and a few minor skirmishes, Temür and Amīr Ḥusayn made peace, and Temür returned to Kish.[50] The two emirs, now reconciled, spent the summer of 769–70/1368 putting down disturbances on the southern edge of the Ulus. The shahs of Badakhshan showed signs of insubordination, and were brought to order by Amīr Ḥusayn. At the same time Malik Muᶜizz al-Dīn Kart raided the regions of Balkh and Shaburqan. Temür went against him, and he retreated.[51]

Having made peace with Temür who was probably by this time his most powerful rival, Amīr Ḥusayn began to think of asserting his sovereignty over the Ulus Chaghatay. This action soon cost him his position. On the return from Kabul he informed Temür that he wanted to make Balkh his residence and rebuild its fortifications. Temür advised against this, citing the misfortune which had come to Amīr Ḥusayn's uncle ᶜAbd Allāh when he deserted his homeland to make his residence among strangers at Samarqand. Despite Temür's advice, Amīr Ḥusayn went ahead with his plan.

This incident has been cited by scholars to show that Temür respected the nomads' dislike for large cities and especially for fortifications, and they have suggested that in disregarding this Amīr Ḥusayn lost popularity among his tribal supporters.[52] Within the Ulus Chaghatay however this seems an unlikely explanation as the Chaghatay nomads frequently took refuge within fortified cities. One should note moreover that when Temür gained control over the Ulus a year or two after this, he immediately built fortifications at Samarqand; had Amīr Ḥusayn owed his downfall to such an action, it is doubtful that Temür would have imitated it. The main argument that the histories give against the plan moreover, both for ᶜAbd Allāh and for Amīr Ḥusayn, is that they were abandoning their home territory and that of their closest supporters: "To leave one's own territory and make a home among strangers is far from the path of wisdom, since if something happens strangers will not come forth and give help."[53] ᶜAbd Allāh indeed had been leaving the area of his father's supporters, making his capital near where the khans had had their palace and in the territory of tribes much less securely allied to him. In settling in Balkh Amīr Ḥusayn was not moving as far from his own territory, but he was moving into the territory of the Suldus, whose loyalty to him was questionable at best.[54]

It is probable that both Amīr Ḥusayn and ᶜAbd Allāh were making political statements with their moves, asserting their supremacy over defeated opponents – in ᶜAbd Allāh's case the former Chaghadayid khans, and in Amīr Ḥusayn's the Suldus emirs, since Buyan Suldus had held the emirate of Transoxiana before him. The claim to sovereignty over the whole of the Ulus suggested by these moves was apparently unacceptable to the tribal leaders. In moving to Balkh, moreover, Amīr Ḥusayn was coming closer to Temür's territory, putting himself in a better position to block Temür off from his refuge area at Marw and from his Khorasanian allies. This may explain Temür's personal opposition to the move.

Since Amīr Ḥusayn would not give up his plan however, the two emirs went together to Balkh, and at the end of 769/1368 began to build the fortifications. The reaction was not long in coming. The Timurid histories are eager to justify Temür's role in the opposition to Amīr Ḥusayn and their account, though consistent, should probably be treated with reserve. They ascribe the first actions against Amīr Ḥusayn to two other emirs, Shaykh Muḥammad Suldus and Kaykhusraw Khuttalānī, who they report allied against Amīr Ḥusayn and wrote a letter to Temür asking for his support. This was intercepted by Amīr Ḥusayn, who did not mention it to Temür, but made secret plans against him. When Temür returned from Kish, he heard that Amīr Ḥusayn and Amīr Mūsā had plotted to seize him. Nonetheless he went to see Amīr Ḥusayn and agreed to go against the dissidents with Zinda

Ḥasham Apardï. Hearing of their approach these emirs fled and Amīr Ḥusayn took up residence in Balkh.[55]

Temür was now Amīr Ḥusayn's major rival and relations between them worsened steadily. The sources list several grievances which caused Temür to break with Amīr Ḥusayn. It seems likely that Amīr Ḥusayn was trying to assert his authority over Temür and force him to accept a clearly subordinate position. He sent emissaries to transport some of Temür's people to Balkh, and also sent someone to fetch Shīrīn Beg Agha, Temür's sister and the wife of Mu'ayyad Arlat who had just, in a fit of drunkenness, murdered one of Amīr Ḥusayn's followers. Temür took this provocation as occasion to oppose Amīr Ḥusayn, finding that a large number of emirs had become dissatisfied with him. He consulted with Amīr Mūsā Taychi'ut and other emirs, and all agreed to resist Amīr Ḥusayn. One person opposed this plan, namely the ever reluctant ᶜAlī Yasa'urī, and he was summarily executed despite his projected marriage to Temür's daughter. Temür now sent an emissary to summon Shaykh Muḥammad Suldus back from Moghulistan, and then headed against Amīr Ḥusayn. Despite the prompt desertion of Mūsā Taychi'ut from Temür's army, Amīr Ḥusayn's forces fled without a battle.[56]

It is clear that by this time Temür had most of the tribal chiefs on his side. He was further encouraged by Sayyid Baraka, a religious leader near Andkhud, who came forward and presented him with a drum and standard.[57] Temür now began seriously to gather armies. He camped in Chaghaniyan and sent out Chekü first to gather the army of that region, both Suldus and others, and then to Khuttalan to gather an army there. When Temür went to Khulm he was joined by the Dulan Jawun, also by Öljeytü Apardï whom Amīr Ḥusayn had left in Qunduz, and by Shāh Shaykh Muḥammad of Badakhshan. Next came Kaykhusraw Khuttalānī and Amīr Chekü with the army of Khuttalan. Thus, as the sources report, Temür had on his side almost all of the emirs of the Ulus Chaghatay.[58]

With this army behind him Temür raised his own candidate to the dignity of khan, and organized his army for an assault on Balkh. He was joined here by Zinda Ḥasham Apardï with the Apardï army of Shaburqan. Thus even Amīr Ḥusayn's most faithful supporters – the Apardï emirs of Arhang and Shaburqan – had gone over to Temür's side. Amīr Ḥusayn's forces were unable to hold out, and after two days' battle he surrendered. Despite promises of safety he chose to flee, but was found and brought before Temür.[59]

According to the Timurid histories, Temür wished to spare Amīr Ḥusayn's life, although Kaykhusraw Khuttalānī pleaded to be allowed to take vengeance on him for his brother's death. It is likely that Temür used Kaykhusraw's vengeance as a way to legitimate the killing of Amīr Ḥusayn; since this was retribution for past killing, it did not bring further vengeance on Temür himself. This was common practice in the Ulus Chaghatay, as will be seen below. The unwillingness of the Timurid historians to ascribe responsibility for Amīr Ḥusayn's death to Temür reflects the sanctions against executions within the Ulus. As the historians report, when Temür did not give in to Kaykhusraw, Öljeytü Apardï arranged for Mu'ayyad Arlat and Kaykhusraw to take Amīr Ḥusayn off secretly and kill him. Temür's responsibility in this remains unclear, but the treatment meted out to Amīr Ḥusayn's sons, two of whom fled and two of whom were killed along with Amīr Ḥusayn's Chinggisid khan, suggests some hostility also on his part.[60]

Temür now had the pleasant task of handing out Amīr Ḥusayn's wives. He used their distribution to enhance his own prestige and to win over tribal emirs. He kept four wives for himself; these included Saray Malik Khanïm, who as the daughter of Qazan Khan provided him with a connection to the Chaghadayid dynasty, and two non-royal women, Ulus Agha, daughter of Buyan Suldus, and Islām Agha, daughter of Khiḍr Yasa'urī, both of whom gave him useful tribal alliances. The others he gave away. Sevinch Qutluq Agha, daughter of Tarmashirin Khan, he gave to Bahrām Jalayir, Dilshād Agha to Zinda Ḥasham, and ᶜĀdil Malik, the daughter of Kayqubād Khuttalānī, to his follower Amīr Chekü. The first two of these gifts seem to be attempts to win over questionable allies, since Bahrām had not been very firmly behind Temür and was still apparently in Moghulistan, while Zinda Ḥasham had joined Temür's forces only at the last minute. The gift of Sevinch Qutluq Agha to Bahrām Jalayir is particularly interesting, since she was almost certainly the widow of Bāyazīd Jalayir and the mother of ᶜAlī Darwīsh Jalayir. Temür therefore was delivering over to Bahrām the mother of his chief rival.[61]

Temür at the head of the Ulus Chaghatay

Yazdī's *Ẓafarnāma* lists the emirs whom Temür had led against Amīr Ḥusayn and who now recognized his position. They were Shaykh Muḥammad Suldus, Amīr Kaykhusraw Khuttalānī, Öljeytü Apardï, Dā'ūd Dughlat, Sarïbugha Jalayir, Chekü Barlas, Zinda Ḥasham Apardï, Mu'ayyad Arlat, Shāh Shaykh Muḥammad of Badakhshan and Ḥusayn Bahadur, as well as a number of religious figures including Sayyid Baraka and the Khāndzāda shaykhs who had ruled Tirmidh.[62] Thus the people who gathered behind Temür included the leaders of the major tribes and some of the religious leadership, as well as the members of his personal following. He now headed for Samarqand, leaving one of his own tribe, Murād Barlas, as governor of Balkh.

Temür almost immediately began to formalize his position. Like Qazaghan and Amīr Ḥusayn, he contented himself with the title *amīr*, but he increased his prestige by associating himself in various ways with the family of Chinggis Khan and the charisma attached to it. He had already appointed a puppet khan of the Chinggisid line, and now began to use the title *güregen*. He started to make Samarqand, close to the old seat of the

Chaghadayid khans, into a royal capital and built up fortifications around it. On 12 Ramaḍān 771/9 April 1370, he had his government formally reaffirmed by the members of the Ulus Chaghatay.[63] He also created the beginnings of an administration, handing out offices both in the army and in administration.[64]

This was not the end of Temür's labors. It was much easier to gain power over the Ulus Chaghatay than to keep it. Like the other emirs who tried to exercise leadership over the Ulus, Temür soon found the tribal leaders turning against him, and for the first twelve years of his rule he remained constantly insecure in his position. Indeed the tribal leaders had little to gain by continuing to support Temür after he had taken power. As long as the leadership of the Ulus was contested, political initiative lay with the tribal aristocracy, but a strong central leader would inevitably try to limit the power of the tribal chiefs. Furthermore, the threat of a Moghul invasion, which had helped Amīr Ḥusayn to rise to power, had now disappeared with the overthrow of the eastern Chaghadayid khan, Ilyās Khwāja, and the beginning of dissensions among the Moghul tribes.

Despite this Temür was able to remain in power, and eventually to become sovereign over the Ulus Chaghatay. There are a number of reasons for his unusual success. Even at the beginning of his rule Temür had certain great advantages which made it difficult for any one other emir to challenge him. In the course of their long struggle for power, he and Amīr Ḥusayn had taken control over almost all the non-tribal troop contingents of the Ulus Chaghatay. On Amīr Ḥusayn's death these fell to Temür. He had behind him therefore not only the Barlas tribe, but also the Qara'unas armies and several smaller contingents. Temür did not repeat the mistake of the Suldus and Barlas emirs, who having killed the Qara'unas leader ᶜAbd Allāh with some of his family had left the Qara'unas intact and leaderless, thus permitting Amīr Ḥusayn to return and regain control. Instead Temür incorporated the Qara'unas troops into his own army, putting them under the command of his closest and most trusted follower, Chekü Barlas.[65] Since the leadership of the Qara'unas had often been appointive this move provoked no overt opposition. The Qara'unas were probably the largest body of troops in the Ulus and they had provided both Qazaghan and Amīr Ḥusayn the strength to rule. Now that Temür had them securely under his own control, he commanded the largest army within the Ulus Chaghatay. In killing Amīr Ḥusayn, he had destroyed the last rival around whom the tribal leaders could rally successfully.

The tribal chiefs moreover were vulnerable to Temür. Many of the resources in land and manpower which they enjoyed had originally been organized by a central government, and could be won back by a supra-tribal leader; indeed Temür had already taken over many of the armies formerly available to the tribes. The settled population, which provided much of the tribal income, had a natural interest in having a central leadership which might impose the peaceful conditions conducive to settled prosperity. The tribal leaders moreover were unsure of the loyalty of their tribal followers. Since the internal politics of the tribe depended heavily on alliances outside it, particularly with candidates for supra-tribal leadership, Temür was able to interfere in tribal affairs without violence to the tribe and without violating the traditions of the Ulus Chaghatay.

Thus Temür was able to deal successfully with the conspiracies and desertions of the tribal leaders, and to do so without using more violence than was acceptable. While the use of force and the number of executions gradually increased as Temür became more assured, very few tribal emirs were executed or deprived of command until they had rebelled several times. When Temür did order the execution of an emir he followed the practice of earlier leaders, and handed the culprit over to someone whom that man had wronged. If Temür was gentle towards the tribal leaders he was even more so towards the tribes as a whole. Of the many tribes that resisted his rule none were permanently broken up and only one was put under the leadership of an emir totally unconnected with it.

The first emirs to desert Temür were his rival's former allies. Foremost among these was Amīr Mūsā Taychi'ut, who had in fact deserted even before Temür's final battle with Amīr Ḥusayn. Someone was sent to fetch him, and he fled first to the north, then when he discovered that he was not safe there, to Zinda Ḥasham Apardï at Shaburqan. When Temür summoned the Ulus emirs to a *khurïltay* that summer, Zinda Ḥasham and Mūsā did not come. Not content with this they held up and killed two Arlat emirs who had been unfriendly to Amīr Ḥusayn and were on their way to congratulate Temür on his victory. Temür appealed to Zinda Ḥasham's relative Öljeytü Apardï to go bring him to order. Öljeytü asked to be excused, saying that Zinda Ḥasham could not be persuaded, and that he himself therefore would be shamed. Temür accepted this excuse, and sent Öljeytü's son Khwāja Yūsuf instead. Zinda Ḥasham promptly imprisoned him.[66]

It seems likely that Öljeytü was the senior emir of the Apardï, and as the Khuttalan and Shaburqan Apardï were connected, he was probably considered the head of the tribe.[67] To try and fail to control Zinda Ḥasham would have been a blow to his prestige and position; his son could better afford the humiliation. Temür's acceptance of Öljeytü's excuses suggests that he did not wish to upset the internal affairs of the tribe. Temür himself however would not accept such an insult, and so raised an army and went against Shaburqan. Zinda Ḥasham capitulated fairly rapidly, getting Öljeytü Apardï to intercede for him. He surrendered Amīr Mūsā and gave his younger brother to Temür as hostage. It is clear that Temür could not yet afford to deal harshly with two such powerful emirs as Mūsā and Zinda Ḥasham; he therefore forgave them both and reconfirmed their positions, taking Mūsā however back with him to Samarqand.[68]

It did not take Zinda Ḥasham long to find another ally against Temür.

This time he joined up with the ruler of Tirmidh, Khāndzāda Abū'l-Maᶜālī, who had recently sworn allegiance to Temür. Now, having seen the Prophet in a dream, Abū'l-Maᶜālī announced the approaching end of the world and proclaimed himself an appointed leader in the confirmation of the faith. Together he and Zinda Ḥasham plundered the lands around Tirmidh and Balkh. Temür put them to flight, installed a governor (*darugha*) in Tirmidh, and then sent Chekü with the armies of Khuttalan, Qunduz and Baghlan to besiege Zinda Ḥasham at Shaburqan. Chekü wintered there, and in the spring Zinda Ḥasham again surrendered and was brought to Temür, with whom various emirs interceded for him. Temür spared him and gave him a number of presents, but this time he did not allow him to return to Shaburqan. This occurred in 772–3/1371–2.[69]

At this time Temür began to turn the energies of the Ulus outwards, undertaking a number of campaigns against the Qungirat Sufi dynasty, which controlled Khorezm, and into the Ferghana, Ili and Talas regions against Qamar al-Dīn Dughlat and the other Moghul emirs who had taken power in Moghulistan after the murder of Ilyās Khwāja Khan. For the next nine or ten years, until 782/1380–1, Temür alternated invasions of Moghulistan and Khorezm. This was a common way to retain the loyalty of nomad followers and indeed the one emir who had succeeded in holding power over the Ulus Chaghatay, Qazaghan, may have owed much of his success to his frequent campaigns in to the south. Nonetheless, despite Temür's successful campaigns which provided occupation and booty for the emirs of the Ulus, the tribal leaders continued to resist him.

It was not long before the leaders of the northern tribes, neighbors and traditional allies of the Barlas, joined the southern leaders in their resistance. In 773–4/1372–3, as Temür returned from an expedition against Moghul territories, he faced a revolt from a number of the emirs both from the southern and the northern sections of the Ulus. These were once again Zinda Ḥasham Apardï, Amīr Mūsā, and Khāndzāda Abū'l-Maᶜālī of Tirmidh, now joined by Khiḍr Yasa'urī's son Abū Isḥāq, and Shaykh Abū'l-Layth Samarqandī.[70] These men had apparently conspired to seize and kill Temür, but were discovered. Temür did not treat them harshly. He exiled Abū'l-Maᶜālī and Abū'l-Layth, and once again forgave Amīr Mūsā, this time ostensibly because Temür's daughter was betrothed to Mūsā's great-nephew. He also forgave Abū Isḥāq Yasa'urī, whose brother-in-law, Temür's personal follower Sayf al-Dīn, interceded for him. Zinda Ḥasham however Temür imprisoned and took back to Samarqand where he died. His lands were handed over to Buyan Temür b. Aqbugha Nayman. The Apardï thus remained under Nayman leadership, but since Aqbugha was Temür's personal follower, his son's loyalty could be counted on.[71]

Temür now turned his attention to the Sufi dynasty of Khorezm and set out against it in the spring of 773 or 774/1372 or 1373.[72] In the course of the Khorezm campaign Kaykhusraw Khuttalānī deserted Temür and tried to ally with the Khorezmians. When Temür returned, he handed Kaykhusraw over to the people of Amīr Ḥusayn to be executed in vengeance for his killing of Amīr Ḥusayn. He then returned the *tümen* of Khuttalan to the other side of the Khuttalānī family, giving it to Muḥammad Mīrkā, the son of Shīr Bahrām.[73] It was rare for Temür to punish disloyalty so quickly and so severely. Kaykhusraw had been a close ally of his from 769/1367 when Temür had taken refuge in Moghulistan from Amīr Ḥusayn. It was due to his alliance to Temür that Kaykhusraw had been able to return to the Ulus, and regain control over his tribe. This may have made his desertion particularly unacceptable to Temür.

Kaykhusraw's execution was not without its effect; his son Sulṭān Maḥmūd now fled to Yūsuf Ṣūfi in Khorezm with two Yasa'urī emirs, Abū Isḥāq b. Khiḍr and Ḥājjī Maḥmūdshāh. With their encouragement Yūsuf Ṣūfī raided the regions of Kat. In response to this Temür undertook another campaign to Khorezm in 774–5/1373–4, which quickly elicited an apology from Yūsuf.[74] In 776–7/1375–6, Temür faced yet another conspiracy from his tribal emirs. On his way back from a campaign against Moghul territories he stopped in Khujand, where he was received by Bahrām Jalayir's son ᶜĀdilshāh, now chief of the Jalayir. Here Temür discovered a plot against him by ᶜĀdilshāh, Shaykh Muḥammad Suldus, and Türken Arlat, the ruler of Gurziwan in Khorasan. On this occasion, Temür chose simply to leave. When ᶜĀdilshāh later came to him, he readily forgave him.[75]

Although Temür was clearly not ready at this time to challenge the leader of the Jalayir tribe, he did feel secure enough to assert his authority over the Suldus. Before leaving for another expedition to Khorezm the next spring, he had Shaykh Muḥammad Suldus up before the tribunal and, judging him guilty, handed him over for execution to a kinsman whose brother he had killed. He then gave command of this part of the Suldus tribe to his personal follower, Aqtemür; this was the one Ulus tribe which Temür put under outside leadership. At the same time, he executed Bāyazīd Jalayir's two sons, ᶜAlī Darwīsh and Muḥammad Darwīsh. The histories mention no uprisings by these last two emirs. Since as sons of a former chief they were ᶜĀdilshāh's potential rivals, their execution was probably a bid to buy ᶜĀdilshāh's loyalty, or perhaps part of a deal with him.[76]

Temür's attempt to bring the tribal leaders to order through a mixture of severity and conciliation proved to be a failure. The tribal emirs continued unreliable, particularly the Jalayir leaders, to whom Temür had shown consistent favor. At this time Temür sent an army against Moghulistan under ᶜĀdilshāh and Sarïbugha Jalayir and himself undertook another expedition to Khorezm. Both these campaigns were hampered by recalcitrant emirs. The first desertion was that of Türken Arlat who, on the border of Khorezm, left to flee back to Gurziwan. When Temür sent someone after him, he fought his pursuers and he was killed in the ensuing battle. Soon after this Temür learned of a much more serious uprising: that of ᶜĀdilshāh and

Sarïbugha Jalayir. After Temür's departure they had joined with the *darugha* of Andijan and gone with their followings, both Jalayir and Qipchaq, to besiege Samarqand. Temür hurried back and put them to flight. They took refuge first in the Dasht-i Qipchaq with Urus Khan of the Blue (eastern) Horde, then with the Dughlat emir Qamar al-Dīn in Moghulistan. Most of the Jalayir army had remained behind, and this Temür divided among his emirs. He also installed his son ᶜUmar Shaykh in Andijan.[77]

The Jalayir emirs however had not lost interest in the Ulus Chaghatay. In 778–9/1376–8 Qamar al-Dīn, helped by ᶜĀdilshāh and Sarïbugha, went against Andijan and attacked ᶜUmar Shaykh, who was deserted by part of his army and had to be rescued by Temür. Soon thereafter news reached Temür that ᶜĀdilshāh Jalayir was in the mountains to the north of the Ulus. He sent two emirs after him; they eventually came up to him and killed him. Later, after two years away, Sarïbugha returned to Temür and was given control of the Jalayir tribe.[78] From this time on he and his followers remained loyal.

The Jalayir had been Temür's strongest and most determined opponents. After their submission Temür had only sporadic trouble with the tribal leaders of the Ulus Chaghatay. He had put down resistance from almost all of the tribes within the Ulus: the Apardï of Shaburqan, the Arlat, the Khuttalānī emirs, the Suldus, the Yasa'urī and the Jalayir. He had dealt with all of these successfully, and in many cases had replaced the leadership of the tribe. The most powerful tribes of the Ulus – the Jalayir, the Suldus and the Apardï of Shaburqan – were now led by members of Temür's personal following. After twelve years of rule, Temür had gained control over the Ulus Chaghatay.

Between Temür's first bid for power within his tribe and his takeover of the Ulus Chaghatay there were ten years of incessant political activity, and almost incessant campaigning. The story of Temür's fortunes during these years is illustrative of the politics of the Ulus Chaghatay. Although his first objective was control of his own tribe, to achieve this Temür had to use alliances outside it. His personal following was non-tribal, built up partly by his predatory activities, partly by marriage; two of his closest supporters, Mu'ayyad Arlat and Dā'ūd Dughlat, were his brothers-in-law. The most decisive factor in his takeover was probably his connections with the Moghuls, who were easily persuaded to give him the leadership of the Barlas. As long as the former chief of the tribe, Ḥājjī Beg, was still alive, Temür remained insecure. He thus chose to strengthen his position by finding outside allies, choosing people unfriendly to Ḥājjī Beg, most notably Amīr Ḥusayn of the Qara'unas, whose uncle Ḥājjī Beg had helped to depose. When, in 762/1361, Temür achieved permanent leadership over his tribe, he had a ready made set of tribal alliances, acquired in the course of his rise.

The way in which Temür gained power within his tribe was probably not atypical. In other tribes also leadership could be contested, and power could be gained through outside support, particularly through alliance with a candidate for the leadership of the Ulus. The history of the tribes during the years of alternating alliances and rivalries between Temür and Amīr Ḥusayn show splits within the tribes, as rivals pinned their faith on different contestants for power.

I have given several examples of such actions in this chapter. In 765/1364, when Temür and Amīr Ḥusayn attacked the Moghul army in Transoxiana, both the Khuttalānī and the Suldus tribes were divided, with one candidate for tribal leadership on the side of the Moghuls, and another on that of Amīr Ḥusayn and Temür. When Amīr Ḥusayn and Temür were fighting each other in 767–8/1366–7 the Yasa'urī emirs chose different sides – one going over to Amīr Ḥusayn while two others backed Temür. It was possible also for a power struggle over the leadership of a tribe to encourage a contest over the Ulus; this can be seen in the quarrel between Amīr Ḥusayn and Temür in 767/1366. In this case it was ᶜAlī Darwīsh Jalayir hoping to gain control over his tribe who provoked Amīr Ḥusayn against Temür, while his competitor, Bahrām Jalayir, encouraged Temür to resist.

Tribal leaders and their rivals required support outside the tribe partly because the tribe itself could not be relied on. The Barlas tribe went over to Temür both times that Ḥājjī Beg left the Ulus, and later, in 767/1366, some of them deserted Temür in his fight against Amīr Ḥusayn. The tribe served its chief in much the same way the Ulus served its leadership; these were both entities to be won and kept, but not to be counted on.

In their search for outside allies, tribal leaders and contestants for power over the Ulus did not limit themselves to the powers within the Ulus. The polities surrounding the Ulus Chaghatay – in Khorezm, Khorasan and Moghulistan – were very willing to give help and refuge to dissidents from the Ulus Chaghatay, and their assistance was often critical in determining the outcome of struggles within it. Thus Amīr Ḥusayn and Temür were able to survive in Khorasan while the Moghuls controlled Transoxiana, and to use that area as a base from which to organize a successful counterattack. In the same way Temür, when at odds with Amīr Ḥusayn, used the refuge and help available to him in Khorasan and Moghulistan to continue his resistance until he was able to return to the Ulus on terms that were satisfactory to him. After Temür's assumption of power, dissident emirs fled to Khorezm and Moghulistan and encouraged the rulers of these territories to attack the Ulus.

Such a situation made it very hard to resolve disputes within the Ulus or to maintain power over it. This served to enhance the power of the tribal leaders, who profited from the insecurity of the central leadership to retain wealth, manpower and political initiative in their own hands. The chiefs had considerable interests in the contests for power over the Ulus Chaghatay, since these were closely connected with the power struggles within the tribes. Once an emir had been installed as leader of the confederation however, tribal leaders had little desire to promote his power. Thus they almost immediately turned against any supra-tribal leader who tried to claim sovereignty over them, and few such leaders succeeded in retaining power over the Ulus. The rule of Amīr Qazaghan and of Buyan Suldus, neither of whom attempted to claim full control over the Ulus, provoked no major resistance. The leaders who tried to assert their position however – ᶜAbd Allāh b. Qazaghan, Tughluq Temür Khan, Amīr Ḥusayn and finally Temür – soon found themselves opposed by most of the tribal emirs of the Ulus Chaghatay.

What made this situation tenable was the relative lack of violence within the Ulus. Battles were short, and often avoided altogether. Leaders had considerable tolerance for desertions and changing alliances, and very few tribal emirs were executed for resistance to the central leader. What shows of force there were moreover provoked opposition; the Moghuls executed several of the most important tribal chiefs in 762–3/1361–2, and found almost the entire Ulus united against them in 765/1364, at the first opportunity for resistance. Likewise, Amīr Ḥusayn executed Kayqubād, brother of Kaykhusraw Khuttalānī, in 761–2/1360–1, and as a result was deserted by Kaykhusraw when he fought the Moghuls in 763/1362.

The way in which Temür dealt with the desertions and conspiracies of the tribal leaders at the beginning of his rule shows the caution with which he had to proceed. His mastery of the Ulus tribes was an exercise more of patience than of force. Zinda Ḥasham had rebelled three times and killed two of Temür's supporters before he was imprisoned, while Mūsā Taychi'ut was never punished at all for the trouble he caused. Temür was particularly cautious in using force against the more powerful tribes, and he piled favors on both Bahrām and ᶜĀdilshāh Jalayir despite their inconstancy to him.

When Temür did order the execution of an emir, he kept his hands clean by handing over the culprit to someone that man had wronged, a practice common among the leaders of the Ulus. His most inspired use of this technique was with Kaykhusraw Khuttalānī and Amīr Ḥusayn; having allowed Kaykhusraw to kill off Amīr Ḥusayn in vengeance for his brother, he then handed Kaykhusraw in his turn over to the remaining relatives of Amīr Ḥusayn for vengeance. In this way Temür avoided taking full responsibility for the execution, and did not call forth the vengeance of the victim's tribe.[79] If Temür was gentle towards the tribal leaders, he was even more gentle towards the tribes themselves. Only one tribe, the Suldus, were put under leadership unconnected with the tribe. The Jalayir, though temporarily broken up, were soon reunited under Sarïbugha Jalayir.

It is fairly clear why Temür feared the use of force against members of the Ulus Chaghatay. It is rather less obvious how he could succeed in keeping control without it. There are several reasons why this was possible. The tribes, dependent for part of their strength on outside resources, could lose much of their power when these were taken from them, as they might be by a strong central leader. After his victory over Amīr Ḥusayn, Temür had acquired valuable new non-tribal troop contingents, now attached personally to him and these, with the forces he had already controlled, made him much the largest power in the Ulus, irrespective of tribal support.

The chief cause of Temür's success however was the fact that he had no serious rival. The tribes were too strongly attached to the Ulus to defect, though their leadership might and sometimes did. Without an alternative candidate around whom to unite, the tribes could not offer effective resistance, and had little incentive to do so. Without a rival the central leader therefore was much less vulnerable to the whims of the tribal emirs. They on the other hand continued just as vulnerable to him. If a tribal leader rebelled, the leader of the Ulus could still easily find another candidate within the tribe to take his place, without violence to the tribe as a whole, or even a rupture of tradition. Thus despite constant and continuing opposition from the leaders of the Ulus tribes, Temür was able to assert his control, and to maintain his position. The strength of the tribal leaders depended on the insecurity of central leadership, and when faced with a strong supra-tribal leader, they were unable to retain their advantage.

Nonetheless, the political system of the Ulus Chaghatay could not continue unchanged without posing a threat to Temür's sovereignty. The Ulus derived much of its identity and cohesion from the active practice of intertribal politics, which depended not on a central leader, but on the tribes themselves. It had a political culture and a set of accepted practices which allowed this active conflict to continue without unacceptable violence. Under this system the idea of central leadership was necessary, but its reality was inconvenient. As long as the Ulus Chaghatay remained unchanged, a strong sovereign would be unwelcome.

CHAPTER 4

Temür's army of conquest: the Ulus Chaghatay

In the foregoing chapter I have discussed the first two periods of Temür's career which he spent maneuvering in a political system dominated by the tribes of the Ulus Chaghatay – succeeding first in gaining power and then, more surprisingly, in holding it. In this chapter I shall discuss the transition to the next stage of Temür's career, that of his great campaigns, and shall examine the ways in which Temür became sovereign over the Ulus Chaghatay and the conqueror of vast territories. These two processes were closely connected, and it is doubtful that either could have succeeded without the other. Although Temür did have sufficient strength to put down the tribal uprisings against him, the real threat to his position came not from individuals but from the political system as a whole. He remained insecure in his position as long as this system remained in place. Because the tribal aristocracy who controlled the Ulus found instability more advantageous than strong central leadership, the rewards Temür offered them could not secure their loyalty. Nor, within the political culture of the Ulus Chaghatay, could Temür use violence to subdue the tribal leaders.

What Temür had to do to maintain and secure his position was to subvert the political system – to change the Ulus Chaghatay from an active tribal confederation into a loyal and subservient army, dependent on his favor. The first step in this process was the creation of a reliable group of subordinate commanders. Like many other sovereigns, most notably Chinggis Khan, Temür promoted a new elite made up of his personal followers and the members of his family. With these men he gradually displaced the tribal aristocracy from the center of power. Temür's new ruling group did not depend for its strength on outside support; its members had risen to power through Temür's activities, and were dependent on Temür's personal favor.

In order to create this elite and to promote its power over that of the older ruling group, Temür needed to acquire additional wealth, manpower and political rewards to bestow on its members. To transform the Ulus Chaghatay, Temür had to make it grow. Thus almost as soon as he came to power he began a series of campaigns against the neighbors of the Ulus. These expeditions served both to keep the tribal leaders of the Ulus occupied and to provide Temür's new elite with additional sources of wealth and promotion. By 781/1379 when Temür brought the last of the Ulus tribes under his control, the transfer of power was relatively complete. The tribes had now lost much of their former strength, and had done so less through their defeats at Temür's hands than through the changes Temür had wrought in the politics of the Ulus. The new Ulus Chaghatay was a larger and richer polity than the old, and the tribes controlled a much smaller share of its wealth and manpower.

Temür however was still not fully secure in his position. He had to make sure, first that the tribal leaders could not regain the position they had lost, and second that the new elite would not take over the political activity he had suppressed among the tribal chiefs. In a society as unstructured and as politically active as the Ulus Chaghatay, this was not an easy task. To secure his new order Temür employed the same method he had used to create it – he went to war. After 786/1384–5 Temür and his army undertook a series of distant and far-ranging campaigns from which they returned only rarely and usually briefly to Transoxiana. For the business of politics he now substituted that of conquest.

Even when he was not campaigning, Temür kept much of his army outside the territory of the Ulus Chaghatay. In the regions over which he imposed control he installed his sons or grandsons as governors and appointed with them large Chaghatay armies, made up of the different groups within the Ulus. At the same time, he moved a new and foreign army into Transoxiana, thus providing himself with a politically inactive population in the center of his realm and ending the constant maneuvering within the Ulus. The history of Temür's career therefore shows two parallel and closely related lines of activity – the one military, the other political. While Temür successfully put down tribal uprisings and engaged in military campaigns of ever increasing range and duration, he was also effecting a major political transformation within the Ulus Chaghatay. This transformation, changing an unruly tribal confederation into a huge army subordinate to one man, enabled Temür to embark on his unrivalled career of conquest and the conquests in their turn secured the change he had wrought, and enabled Temür to remain what he had first set out to be: sovereign over the Ulus Chaghatay.

The great campaigns

Temür did not secure his new order through the installation of a new structure, but through a career of constant maneuver and movement similar to his activities within the Ulus Chaghatay. It was crucial that this movement be solely under his control. This he managed through conquest, and the history of his career as full sovereign of the Ulus Chaghatay is one of almost ceaseless military activity in foreign lands. Temür's campaigns had many political advantages for him. First of all, the conquest of foreign lands offered an

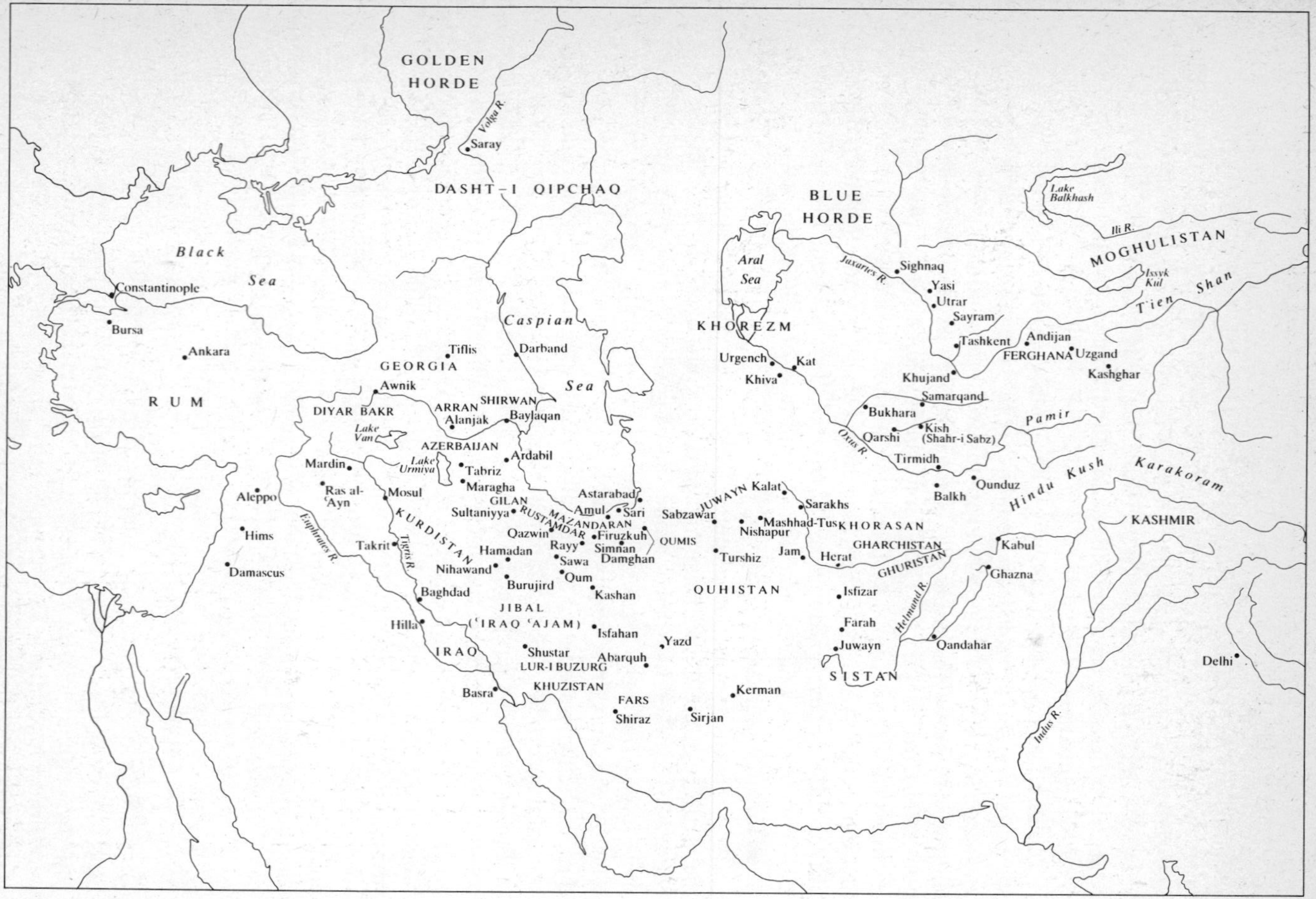

3. The area of Temür's conquests.

occupation other than the practice of politics, and numerous rewards to take the place of the political advantages which had motivated much of the military activity within the Ulus up to this time. Not only was there rich booty to distribute; there were also new troops to put under the command of his own followers and increasing numbers of offices within a growing army and expanding administration which could be used to reward those who served Temür.

Above all Temür's campaigns served to interrupt the political processes of the Ulus by taking the Chaghatay emirs out of the territory around which their political interests had centered. In this regard the great campaigns after 782/1380–1 differ markedly from the military expeditions of Temür's first years in power. Temür's early campaigns against Khorezm and Moghulistan were frequent but relatively short. Thus although the army was frequently outside the Ulus Chaghatay, it was still based in its original territory, and its political life, still led by the tribal leaders, remained active. Once he began his conquest of the Middle East however, Temür led his army far from the territory of the Ulus, and kept it away for long periods of time.

Temür began his rule over the Ulus Chaghatay with forays against his neighbors to the north, closely connected to the Ulus through political and cultural ties. These powers had long served as refuge areas for dissidents, and often disputed the borders of the Ulus. His campaigns against them were not designed for conquest but as an assertion of superior power and an indication to neighboring states that Temür would tolerate no threats to his power, whether through the protection of dissidents or the assertion of rival claims. The first region to attract his attention was the eastern Chaghadayid realm, Moghulistan, where the Dughlat emir Qamar al-Dīn had usurped power but had failed to keep the loyalty of all the tribal emirs. In the years 772 or 773/1370–2[1] Temür and his army undertook two brief but successful campaigns into Moghul territory, where they collected plentiful booty and installed local allies. Qamar al-Dīn himself however remained elusive.

Temür next turned against the Qungirat dynasty of Khorezm, whose leader, Ḥusayn Ṣūfī, held Kat and Khiva – both formerly part of the Chaghadayid khanate. Temür demanded these territories and when his request was refused invaded Khorezm in 773–4/1372–3. Ḥusayn Ṣūfī died and his son Yūsuf made peace with Temür, but soon thereafter raided Chaghatay territories. The next year Temür invaded again; this expedition produced a quick apology. Temür then turned again against Moghulistan, where he campaigned several times but once more failed to inflict a definitive defeat on Qamar al-Dīn. He did however annex the rich Ferghana valley, where he stationed his son ᶜUmar Shaykh as governor with an army of Chaghatay troops.

In 777 or 778/1375–7 a new opportunity offered itself. Tokhtamïsh, one of the contestants for leadership over the Blue Horde north of the Jaxartes, sought refuge with Temür. Temür received him enthusiastically and set him up as khan on his northern borders in the region of Utrar and Sighnaq, the capital of the Blue Horde. Tokhtamïsh however proved unable to hold his own against the attacks of the Blue Horde's khan Urus who demanded Tokhtamïsh's extradition. Temür refused, and set out for the first of his many expeditions into the Dasht-i Qipchaq. After considerable effort, Temür and Tokhtamïsh succeeded in defeating the sons of Urus Khan who himself died in the course of this campaign, and Tokhtamïsh became khan of the Blue Horde.[2]

Soon after this, Temür turned his attention to the settled regions on his southern border. In 782/1380–1 he appointed his son Amīrānshāh as governor of Khorasan, and began to plan the subjugation of this area.[3] His first campaigns here were relatively small and brief, like his northern expeditions. Temür called the leaders of Khorasan to attend a *khurïltay* but the king of Herat, Malik Ghiyāth al-Dīn Kart, failed to attend. The next spring therefore Temür attacked his territories, besieged Herat and took the city without difficulty in Muḥarram 783/April 1381. The other major powers in Khorasan – the Sarbadar leaders of Sabzawar and the Turco-Mongolian Jawun-i Qurban tribe of Mashhad-Tus – showed appropriate submission, and were not disturbed.[4]

Since the powers of Khorasan did not cease their political and military activity, Temür returned twice in the next years to strengthen his control. He first attacked the head of the Jawun-i Qurban tribe, who with the ruler of Mazandaran, Amīr Walī, had attacked Sabzawar.[5] After a long siege the Jawun-i Qurban were forced to surrender. During this time, at the end of 784/early 1383, there was a major rebellion in Herat; Temür now removed the Kartid kings and put the city directly under Chaghatay control. He also mounted a campaign against Sistan in 785/1383–4, replaced its ruler with a more compliant relative, took the city of Qandahar and razed its fortification. The method that Temür used in conquering Khorasan – beginning with a brief campaign to extract submission from local rulers and following this with one or several punitive campaigns against insubordinate powers – was one that he continued throughout his life. This was a system which worked well for him. The activity of campaigning was favorable to his prestige and each campaign produced both booty for his army and ransom money from the cities for his treasury. He had little interest therefore in establishing firm control on his first expedition to a new area.

Temür's campaigns against western Iran began in 786/1384–5 with an expedition against the troublesome ruler of Mazandaran, Amīr Walī. Amīr Walī fled and Temür took Astarabad, one of the chief cities of Mazandaran, then proceeded west to Rayy and Sultaniyya. Sultaniyya had been in the power of the Turco-Mongolian Jalayir dynasty, whose leader, Sulṭān Aḥmad, retreated before Temür. On this expedition Temür contented himself with installing a compliant ruler in Sultaniyya and Tabriz, and returned home in 787/1385–6.

By this time Temür's former protégé Tokhtamïsh had begun his own career of conquest and had succeeded in taking over the Golden Horde. He now became a major competitor to Temür, and as a descendant of Chinggis Khan and ruler of the powerful Ulus Jochi, he could claim a higher station in the Turco-Mongolian world. Two men of such ambition could not comfortably coexist. During the winter of 787/1385–6, Tokhtamïsh attacked and pillaged Tabriz, now counted among Temür's dependencies. To reassert his own power, in 788/1386 Temür began the first of his major campaigns, the three-year campaign to Iran and the Caucasus. He took with him a large part of his army, which could be divided up to produce a bewildering display of military activity. His campaign had no single goal but was aimed against large and ever expanding areas. Temür headed first to the region of Luristan in southern central Iran, which had been a center of banditry, and then against Azerbaijan, where Sulṭān Aḥmad Jalayir had reestablished his influence in the wake of Tokhtamïsh's attack. After defeating Sulṭān Aḥmad, Temür campaigned in Georgia, took Tiflis, and captured its king whom however he soon reinstated. Other rulers of this area from the Caucasus to Gilan now hastened to tender their submission.

At the beginning of 789/1387, Tokhtamïsh again prepared to attack the Caucasus; Temür now sent an army against his troops, and defeated them. He next campaigned against the Turkmen Qaraqoyunlu to the west, in the region of Lake Van. He then turned east again, campaigned briefly in Kurdistan, which he left in the hands of its former ruler, then headed towards Fars, held by the Muzaffarid dynasty. Temür took Isfahan, which first submitted but then rebelled and suffered a major massacre. As his army approached Shiraz Zayn al-ᶜĀbidīn Muẓaffarī fled without joining battle, and other members of the dynasty came to offer their submission.

At the end of 789/1387, Temür learned that Tokhtamïsh had attacked Transoxiana and pillaged it right up to the Oxus. Leaving Fars under the governance of the more submissive members of the Muzaffarid dynasty, he returned to Transoxiana where he spent the next four years fighting against his northern neighbors. These were punitive campaigns from which Temür gained little new territory. His first campaign was against the Sufi dynasty in Khorezm, which had joined Tokhtamïsh in his invasion.[6] This time Temür was not content merely to exact submission from the Sufi dynasty, but ruined its capital city and deported large numbers of its people. The winter of 790–1/1388–9 Temür spent successfully repulsing Tokhtamïsh's attacks on his northern borders, and in the next years undertook two campaigns against the Moghuls, now again nominally under the leadership of a Chaghadayid khan, Khiḍr Khwāja – like the Sufi dynasty, they had cooperated with Tokhtamïsh during his invasion. In the late fall of 792–3/1390 Temür began preparing for a major expedition against Tokhtamïsh. He wintered in Tashkent, and in June fought and defeated Tokhtamïsh whom his troops chased up to the Volga. After collecting massive booty and celebrating his victory in the capital of the Golden Horde he returned to Samarqand.

In the fall of 794/1392, Temür set out for another campaign to Iran, known as his five-year campaign. He went against a rebellious leader in Mazandaran, then sent his sons to pacify Kurdistan and Luristan while he headed against southern central Iran, where Shāh Manṣūr, a member of the Muzaffarid dynasty, had succeeded in unseating most of his relatives and in amassing an unacceptable amount of power. Temür defeated him in the spring of 795/April 1393, and destroyed the Muzaffarids, placing their lands under the governorship of his son ᶜUmar Shaykh. At about the same time he installed his third son, Amīrānshāh, as governor of the western regions of Iran and set out to wrest these areas from the primarily nomad dynasties who controlled them. In the summer of 795/1393 he took Baghdad from Sulṭān Aḥmad Jalayir, sent emissaries to the two Turkmen dynasties of western Iran and Anatolia, the Aqqoyunlu and the Qaraqoyunlu, suggesting that they show their submission, then attacked and conquered many of their territories in the northern Tigris-Euphrates region.

Towards the end of 796/1394, hearing that Tokhtamïsh had again raided in the Caucasus, Temür went against him. Tokhtamïsh was unable to withstand his army and Temür advanced as far as Moscow, plundering along the way, then looted Hajji Tarkhan and Saray before returning through Darband in the spring of 798/1396. This was a blow from which the Golden Horde never fully recovered. After this, Temür returned slowly to Samarqand, chastising insubordinate rulers along the way. As a result of this campaign, Tokhtamïsh lost his throne and the Golden Horde ceased to be a threat. Temür was content with its chastisement and made no attempt to establish permanent control over it.

Temür now turned his attention to the glory of his capital city, and spent several months in the construction of palaces and gardens, the reception of foreign ambassadors, the investigation of officials, and gifts to the poor. In the spring of 800/1398 he set off in a new direction, heading south to northern India. In Rabīᶜ II 801/December 1398, he reached Delhi which his army sacked and burned. This was apparently one of the few occasions on which Temür lost control of his troops and they inflicted damage which he did not intend. After this Temür and his army campaigned briefly along the Ganges before returning to Samarqand in the spring of 801/1399.

After only a short stay in Samarqand, Temür learned that Amīrānshāh, governor of western Iran, had begun to behave unacceptably. The Timurid histories ascribe his actions to insanity following a fall from a horse, but it is more likely that he was trying to assert his independence.[7] In the beginning of 802/Fall 1399, Temür headed west again for his longest expedition, the so-called seven-year campaign. He sent an emir ahead to investigate Amīrānshāh, who hastened to meet his father; he was ordered to accompany Temür's army and after some time removed from his governorship, but suffered no other punishment.

In the course of this campaign Temür reasserted his control over the Georgians and retook Baghdad from Sulṭān Aḥmad Jalayir, who had regained it in his absence; he also campaigned again through Kurdistan and fought the Qaraqoyunlu Turkmens. Temür now extended his campaigns further to the west, campaigning in Syria against the Mamluks and in Anatolia against the Ottomans. Both of these dynasties had given refuge to Temür's Qaraqoyunlu and Jalayir opponents, and had refused Temür's requests for their extradition. They also represented strong independent traditions outside of Mongol jurisdiction. Temür's campaigns against them were not aimed at annexation, but like earlier campaigns in the steppe were demonstrations of superior power and prestige. Temür attacked Syria in the winter of 803/1400–1. Here he contented himself with a relatively brief campaign, in which he captured several major cities, notably Aleppo, Hims and Damascus; Aleppo submitted without a struggle and was spared, but Temür subjected Damascus to looting and massacre.

One probable reason for these western campaigns was simply the desire to continue military activity. It is notable in this context that Temür pressed on with his campaign even when his commanders tired of it. In 803/1400, for instance, his emirs tried to dissuade him from attacking Syria, saying that they had undertaken many difficult expeditions, and that he should allow the army to disband and rest.[8] On the same campaign, Temür's commanders expressed doubt about undertaking an expedition to Anatolia against the Ottoman sultan Bāyazīd.[9] In both cases Temür decided to continue his campaigns despite the objections from his army.

He set out against the Ottomans in the spring of 804/1402, and in Dhu'l Ḥijja/July met and defeated the Ottoman army near Ankara, taking Sulṭān Bāyazīd himself captive. Temür's armies then campaigned through the Ottoman territories, collecting ransom money from their major cities. Sulṭān Bāyazīd, though well treated, died within a few months of his capture. Temür, satisfied with this blow to Ottoman hegemony, now returned east without leaving any permanent administration in Anatolia. In the spring of 806/1404 he headed back towards Samarqand, stopping on his way to put down a major rebellion in Mazandaran – that of his former subject, Iskandar Shaykhī.

In Samarqand Temür staged a great *khurïltay* at which he received numerous ambassadors including some from China and the Spanish embassy of Ruy Gonzalez de Clavijo. After only a few months in the capital he began preparing for the greatest exploit of his life – a campaign against China. He gathered together a large army and a mass of supplies, and in the late fall of 807/1404, he set off for Utrar where he planned to spend the winter. Here however Temür became ill, and on 17/18 of Shaᶜbān 807/17–18 February 1405, he died, leaving China still unconquered.

The formation of a new elite

Temür's great conquests were the work not only of a superior military genius, but also of an exceptionally loyal and disciplined army. The troops that achieved this were no random collection of tribes in search of booty but a centralized force, led by commanders personally loyal to Temür. This army was the result of a major political and social transformation in the Ulus Chaghatay begun soon after Temür came to power. During his first twelve years in power, Temür changed the Ulus Chaghatay from a tribal confederation into an army of conquest, in which tribes played only a subordinate part. Temür had two groups available to him whose loyalty and dependence he could confidently count on – the members of his family, and his personal following. These men owed their position to Temür and were bound to him by ties of personal loyalty; thus unlike the tribal leaders they had an interest in preserving his rule. They also differed from the tribal chiefs in having no outside source of power which had to be maintained through political activity. At the beginning of Temür's reign this ruling class commanded only a small proportion of his army. As time went on however the forces previously held by tribal leaders came increasingly under their control. The new troops acquired in the course of Temür's campaigns also went to this new elite, further reducing the relative power of the tribal chiefs.

Temür's personal following, serving him from his youthful days of brigandage, formed the larger part of the new ruling class. As I have written above, estimates of its numbers range from forty to several hundred men, the smaller estimate probably representing the number of important emirs in it, and the larger one the total number of soldiers. The evidence in the sources allows us to identify eighteen men as followers of Temür. These were presumably the most prominent members of the following and those closest to Temür. I have used several criteria to decide who was a member of Temür's following. The first is inclusion in Ibn ᶜArabshāh's list of Temür's followers in the account of Temür's early career.[10] Other indications of membership are participation in certain campaigns during Temür's early years on which he took only an army of a few hundred or less, or mention in a list of men close to Temür of which most others can be identified as followers.[11] Finally I have assumed that Temür's followers remained consistently loyal to him through the political upheavals of the Ulus Chaghatay, and had no independent involvement in tribal politics. Not all the men whom I have identified as Temür's followers meet all of these criteria, but all do at least meet several.

Temür drew his following from a variety of tribal and non-tribal groups. Two of his followers were his brothers-in-law – Dā'ūd Dughlat and Mu'ayyad Arlat. Two were Barlas, Chekü and Ḥusayn.[12] There were two Qipchaq emirs, ᶜAbbās and Khitay, and two *qa'uchin*, Tābān and Qumarī Īnaq. Aqbugha Nayman and Sayf al-Dīn Nüküz both came from tribes not strongly represented in the Ulus Chaghatay. Several followers are without tribal names – these include Elchi, Shaykh ᶜAlī, Aqtemür, and Eyegü Temür. Sarïbugha Jalayir was unusual among Temür's followers in that he led a small contingent of tribal troops; nonetheless the circumstances of his career suggest that he was a member of the following. These fifteen men can definitely be identified as personal followers of Temür; three more were probably followers, but the evidence is not clear enough to make this absolutely definite. These are Üch Qara, Ghiyāth al-Dīn Tarkhan, and Temür's second cousin Taghay Bugha Barlas, all of them important men during Temür's reign. Some of this following may have been of slave origin; this was apparently Üch Qara's provenance, and has been suggested also for Ḥājjī Sayf al-Dīn Nüküz.[13]

Temür began the promotion of his followers as soon as he took power over the Ulus Chaghatay in 771/1370; he gave them nearly all the important military and civilian posts which he distributed at that time. A few other *qa'uchin* emirs and some men whose origin and careers are not known also received military command, but no tribal leaders were thus honored.[14] It is not clear what troops Temür was now putting under the command of his followers or what forces they already led. Each of the emirs within Temür's following probably commanded a small troop contingent and Sarïbugha Jalayir at least had behind him a section of his tribe, but their forces were certainly small. The accounts of his early campaigns and the estimates of outside observers suggest numbers ranging from three hundred to six hundred.[15] Temür also had at his disposal several contingents of non-tribal troops which he and Amīr Ḥusayn had attached to themselves and some of these undoubtedly formed the armies he distributed to his followers.

During the next years the army commanded by Temür's followers grew as Temür gradually removed troops from the control of the tribal leaders and placed them under the command of the new elite. This process is difficult to follow; much of it must be reconstructed through indirect evidence, and the troop numbers given in the histories are often vague. Nonetheless it is possible to trace the transfer in its broad outlines and to account for the armies of many, though not all, of Temür's followers.

In Temür's early campaigns against Khorezm and Moghulistan, the participation and importance of his personal followers was about equal to that of the tribal chiefs, among whom Bahrām Jalayir and his son ᶜĀdilshāh, Shaykh Muḥammad Suldus, Khwāja Yūsuf b. Öljeytü Apardï, and Kaykhusraw Khuttalānī all continued active and powerful.[16] The balance however soon began to change. In 773/1372 Temür assigned the region of Kabul, Qunduz and Baghlan with its troops to Chekü Barlas; this was the Qara'unas army numbering three *tümens*, one of the largest within Temür's army. As the tribal leaders continued to resist Temür he began to put their troops under the control of followers. In 772–3/1371–2, after Zinda Ḥasham's third uprising, Temür gave the region of Shaburqan and the

Apardï army to Buyan Temür, the son of Aqbugha Nayman. The Suldus troops went to another follower, Aqtemür, in 777–8/1376–7. In 781–2/1379–80 Temür gave command of the Jalayir tribe to his follower Sarïbugha Jalayir, and at some time before 793/1391 the Qipchaq troops came under the control of ᶜUthmān b. ᶜAbbās Qipchaq, the son of one of Temür's followers; these troops, or some of them at least, had earlier apparently campaigned under the Jalayir emirs.[17]

There were also numerous special regiments which Temür placed under the control of his followers. For instance, Shaykh Nūr al-Dīn, who was the son of Sarïbugha Jalayir and particularly close to Temür, headed a *tümen* of special troops attached to the court (*khānabachagān-i khāṣṣ*).[18] Rustam b. Taghay Bugha Barlas, son of Temür's cousin and follower, commanded the "*tümen-i san-siz*,' ("the numberless *tümen*") defined as "the personal servitors and intimates of the court" (bandagān-i khāṣṣ wa muqarrabān-i dargāh).[19] One special regiment consisted of *qa'uchin*, and this was led by Allāhdād, the brother of Temür's powerful follower Ḥājjī Sayf al-Dīn Nüküz.[20]

We cannot unfortunately discover from the sources what all these troops were or where they came from. The terminology suggests that some were slave troops either purchased or acquired as prisoners of war from Temür's numerous campaigns.[21] It seems likely that many others were soldiers who had previously campaigned under the leadership of the tribal chiefs who had led not only their tribal contingents, but also numerous smaller tribes and sections of tribes, along with the regional armies of the lands they controlled. It is likely that as Temür and his new ruling group succeeded in maintaining and strengthening their position at the expense of the tribal leaders, an increasing proportion of the local troops came under their command. In some cases Temür acquired these through direct action – this was the case for instance with the regions where he installed Barlas governors who took command over the local troops, as will be discussed below.

The transfer of troops to Temür and his followers however may also have been a natural process. The continued control of troops depended on the power of the tribal chiefs; to keep the command of the regional armies they required a firm hold over the tribal lands, and to attract additional tribal population they had to be powerful enough to promise advantages to those who joined them. As the tribal leaders failed to unseat Temür or hold their position against him, the smaller tribes and sections of tribes may well have chosen to switch their allegiance to more successful leaders. As the tribes lost their hold on tribal lands the regional armies and the *qa'uchin* likewise came under Temür's command. This is a supposition which cannot be proved with the evidence that is available. It does however seem a likely explanation for the striking change in the relative power of the tribal emirs and of Temür's new elite.

By 782/1380–1 the transfer of power within Temür's army was far advanced, and after 793/1390–1 it seems to have been complete. By this time most of Temür's followers led large bodies of troops. Of the fifteen known members of Temür's following, eleven had *tümens*.[22] By the time of Temür's first campaign to western Iran in 786/1384–5 therefore the larger part of the manpower of the Ulus Chaghatay had moved from the tribal leaders to members of Temür's following.

Within Temür's army the command of troops was usually hereditary, and Temür's followers passed their troops on to their descendants. Many of them had several sons and grandsons; thus Temür had at his disposal an increasing number of people personally loyal to him, and under them he placed an ever larger number of troops.[23] At the same time, the number of Temür's own sons and grandsons increased markedly, and these also acquired armies. Temür had four sons who survived to maturity. The two eldest were Jahāngīr and ᶜUmar Shaykh, born in the mid to late 750s.[24] Temür's sons were married young and began to participate in political and military activities in their early teens. In 776–7/1374–5, Jahāngīr began to campaign at the head of an army, and in 779–80/1377–9 ᶜUmar Shaykh likewise began to appear on campaign. Jahāngīr died in 777–8/1376–7 leaving behind two sons, Muḥammad Sulṭān and Pīr Muḥammad, both of whom were old enough to hold important positions by the early 790s/1388–96. ᶜUmar Shaykh also died during Temür's lifetime, in 796/1394, leaving several sons three of whom, Pīr Muḥammad, Rustam and Iskandar, were active and important figures during the second part of Temür's reign.

Temür's third son Amīrānshāh was born about 768/1366–7 and in 782/1380–1 at the age of fourteen received the governorship of Khorasan. Several of his sons – Abā Bakr, ᶜUmar, and Khalīl Sulṭān – were active as commanders and governors during Temür's lifetime. Temür's youngest son, Shāhrukh, was born in 779/1377 and was participating in campaigns by 793/1390–1. His sons were not old enough to be active political or military figures before Temür's death, although two of them did receive governorships. Thus by the end of Temür's life he had a large number of children and grandchildren active on campaigns, many of them governors of large provinces.

Like his followers, Temür's sons were provided with armies, and some led more than one *tümen*. In the latter part of Temür's career there were at least nine *tümens* led by his offspring, as well as the thirteen *tümens* and several smaller regiments led by his followers.[25] It is notable that these *tümens*, under Temür's followers and family, constitute the majority of all the *tümens* mentioned in the histories.[26] One must consider here what these troop figures suggest. It is I believe unlikely that these *tümens* actually contained the ten thousand soldiers that their name implies, or even the potential to raise that many.[27] Nor is it certain that the *tümens* mentioned in the accounts of Temür's campaigns were all the *tümens* or all the troops that existed – they almost certainly were not.[28] Nonetheless it is clear that a *tümen* represented a sizable force, and that the men who commanded them held very considerable power.

Almost all the most conspicuous commanders in Temür's army were his family, his followers or their sons and relatives. This was the ruling group of the Ulus Chaghatay. It soon became a closed and self-perpetuating class, strengthened by numerous marriages between Temür's followers and his family. Some of Temür's followers were related to him by marriage; the descendants of these men now continued to marry into Temür's family, and others of his followers also married his descendants. When Temür's grandchildren arrived at marriageable age, they began to marry among themselves. There was a strong tendency under Temür to continue to intermarry with the same families, a custom common among Turco-Mongolian tribes.[29] We can take as an example the family of Dā'ūd Dughlat, one of Temür's closest and most prominent followers, who was married to Temür's sister. His son Sulaymānshāh in turn married Temür's daughter Sulṭān Bakht Begim. Later, Sulaymānshāh's son Yūsuf married the daughter of Temür's grandson Muḥammad Sulṭān.[30] Several other members of Temür's following who were not originally connected to him married their descendants into the royal family. Two examples are Temür's powerful followers, Ḥājjī Sayf al-Dīn and ᶜAbbās Bahadur Qipchaq.[31] Such followers then added to their personal favor and military power a direct relationship to the dynasty, and many came close to the royal princes in prestige and power.

These marriage alliances further encouraged the formation of a relatively closed class which increased less by the admission of new members than by natural reproduction. This new ruling group was radically different from the tribal aristocracy who had held power earlier. It was a smaller group of people and one without the outside loyalties and political affiliations which had made the tribal leaders such unsatisfactory subjects. This new elite was loyal personally and exclusively to Temür, and dependent on him for their position. Most importantly this new class based its power on a stable political order, controlled by Temür, rather than the fluid and changeable system which had been favorable to the power of the tribal leaders, and which they had sought to perpetuate.

The powers of the Ulus Chaghatay and their decline

As Temür strengthened the position of his new elite, the power of the tribes and other independent groups within the Ulus Chaghatay steadily declined. At the beginning of Temür's rule the tribal leaders held very considerable power within his army but as each tribe in turn rebelled and was subdued their forces decreased. The last major tribal uprising within the Ulus Chaghatay occurred in 790/1388–9 when the Borolday *tümen* and the Khuttalānī emirs rebelled.[32] Temür's sons quickly put them down and after this tribal commanders played a relatively minor role in Temür's campaigns, commanding apparently small numbers of troops.

Because of the insecurity of tribal leadership, Temür could suppress tribal power without having to destroy the tribal aristocracy or break up the tribes themselves. Throughout Temür's career the tribes remained intact and largely unchanged in structure. What Temür did was gradually to remove from the tribes their greatest sources of power, the control of the troops and the land of the Ulus Chaghatay. What they retained was the basic, hereditary troops of the tribe, which now represented a much smaller percentage of the manpower of Temür's expanding army. In the last section I described the way in which Temür transferred troops from the tribes to the members of his following. It is more difficult to follow the removal of land from the tribes. We know relatively little about Transoxiana and the territory of the Ulus Chaghatay during Temür's reign, since he spent much of his time outside it, and the histories follow him on his campaigns. What we do know suggests that the tribes lost much of the control they had had over their regions, and in some cases moved quite out of their original territories.

This process appears clearly in the case of two tribes whose territory was at the center of the Ulus Chaghatay: the Suldus and the Yasa'urī. At the beginning of Temür's career the Suldus held the regions of Balkh and Chaghaniyan with the fortress Hisar-i Shadman. During Temür's rule however, Balkh was governed by Barlas emirs, and one of them, Yādgār, is mentioned leading its armies in 790/1388.[33] While Mengli Bugha Suldus, who held control in that area before Temür's takeover, commanded a *tümen*, his son, Pīr ᶜAlī Tāz, inherited apparently only a *hazāra* from his father.[34] The areas of Hisar-i Shadman and Chaghaniyan continued to be the seat of some of the Suldus tribe, but were not fully under their control. In 790/1388 these areas were occupied by Barlas and Suldus, both of whom were still active there after Temür's death.[35]

The Yasa'urī lost control of their lands more completely than did the Suldus. This was probably inevitable, since they had been based in the regions of Samarqand and Bukhara, at the center of Temür's realm. Samarqand was now of course directly under Temür's control, administered by a succession of trusted emirs, and Bukhara was governed first by Temür's cousin Taghay Bugha Barlas, and then by his sons.[36] There is no indication of Yasa'urī power or even presence in these regions. We know less about other tribal holdings, but what evidence we do have points in the same direction. Khujand, which had been the central region of the Jalayir, is not mentioned during the succession struggle after Temür's death under their control; they seem more closely connected with the region of Utrar.[37] Information about the holdings of the Arlat and Apardï tribes during Temür's lifetime is unfortunately very scant. We know nothing at all about the Arlat holdings; the Apardï apparently lost control of Shaburqan, but retained their holdings in Khuttalan.[38] The evidence presented above is fragmentary, but it does all point in the same direction; by the middle of Temür's career, the tribes of the Ulus Chaghatay no longer held full control over their lands. With these territories they had lost their independent access to much of the wealth and manpower of the Ulus Chaghatay, which had been a major component of their power. These resources now belonged to Temür and his new elite.

One method Temür used to remove the control of land from the tribal leaders was the appointment of Barlas emirs to govern regions previously held by the tribes, most notably the regions of Balkh and Bukhara, formerly under the Suldus and Yasa'urī. He then further weakened the hold of the tribes over their territories by importing and settling large numbers of foreign troops in Transoxiana. To garrison the forts on the borders of Turkistan, he brought in soldiers from almost all the regions he had conquered – importing Indians, Khorasanians, ᶜIraqis, Syrians and several nomad populations.[39] Within the area of Transoxiana, Temür installed a new nomadic population, brought primarily from Rum, Azerbaijan and ᶜIraq; this included the Qaratatars from Anatolia and some of the Jalayirid confederation of ᶜIraq.[40] Thus in the course of his reign Temür had radically altered the military population within the original territory of the Ulus Chaghatay; in the place of local troops campaigning under tribal leaders, the armies of Transoxiana now held mostly foreign soldiers who owed obedience to Temür himself and to the commanders appointed by him.

One of the most striking aspects of Temür's treatment of the tribes is his avoidance of violence, against both tribal chiefs and the tribesmen they led. It was not only people whom Temür spared, but also structures; he chose not to break up the tribes, but rather to push them aside. Despite their loss of power and independence the tribes and other groups of the Ulus Chaghatay continued to exist for the rest of Temür's career and changed remarkably little in structure. By 782/1380–1, when Temür had consolidated his power, many of these groups were under new leadership and some were no longer called by their old names, but almost all are still discernible throughout Temür's career.

Temür's treatment of his own tribe, the Barlas, provides a good illustration of the way in which he preserved formal tribal structures while denying the tribes the independent political power and activity which had threatened him. As the tribe of the new ruler the Barlas could not be robbed of all its power. Temür granted it an honorable place in his realm, but it was not as powerful as one might expect, or as some scholars have suggested.[41] The Barlas did not become a focus of strength; they did not share Temür's power with him but rather served him as a resource, a source of people whom he trusted more confidently than the members of other tribes though not apparently as much as his personal followers. Temür gave important governorships to several members of the tribe, but few Barlas held high command in the army and those who did were connected with Temür rather by ties of loyalty than of blood.

Temür's reign caused remarkably little change in the internal structure of the Barlas. When he took leadership of the tribe in 762/1361 he did not elevate his own lineage over others within the tribe; aside from his sons only one member of his lineage held a prominent place during his reign.[42] The Barlas emirs whom Temür most favored were the relatives and children of his follower Chekü Barlas, of a family different both from Temür's and from Ḥājjī Beg's. This lineage now held command of the Qara'unas troops and Chekü's nephew Edigü received the governorship of Kerman.[43] The other lineages of the Barlas continued, as they had before Temür's takeover, to provide some emirs and to wield a moderate amount of power.[44] It is notable moreover that the hereditary troops of the Barlas, the *ulugh ming*, were held not by Temür but by the nephew and grandson of the former chief, Ḥājjī Beg.[45] It appears that once Temür was secure in his position he allowed these troops to return to the family of their former commander. The amount of military power they provided was probably not in any case very great.[46] After taking over the Ulus Chaghatay then, Temür did not emphasize his position as head of the Barlas tribe, and may not even have kept it. By retaining the old order of the Barlas, under emirs who were no longer powerful, he made the Barlas a formal structure outside the new centers of power.

We know less about the other powers of the Ulus Chaghatay, but we can trace their existence throughout Temür's lifetime. The groups which had been robbed of their own chiefs and put under members of Temür's following now constituted an element in the power of their new leaders. Foremost among these were the Qara'unas who had provided Amīr Qazaghan and Amīr Ḥusayn with the strength to rule. After Temür's assumption of power he gave them to his follower Chekü Barlas, and thereafter they appear in the histories only as the troops of Qunduz and Baghlan.[47] During most of Temür's life they served Chekü's son Jahānshāh, probably the most powerful emir in Temür's army.[48] Clavijo, describing Jahānshāh's power, wrote that he had an immense following of clansmen and possessed extensive lands and much wealth.[49] Since nothing in the histories suggests that Chekü or Jahānshāh possessed a large following within the Barlas, this refers almost certainly to the Qara'unas. It seems indeed that the forces of Qunduz and Baghlan remained intact throughout the Timurid period, and that while their name and their leadership had changed, their numbers and the power that they lent to their leaders remained constant up to the time of the Uzbek invasion.[50]

After the Qara'unas emirs, the Jalayir had been perhaps the strongest force within the Ulus Chaghatay. Like the Qara'unas they are rarely mentioned by their tribal name after 782/1380–1, and while their emirs remained prominent throughout Temür's life, they owed much of their power to personal favor. Sarïbugha, whom Temür installed as chief of the Jalayir, owed his appointment as head of the tribe to his membership in Temür's following, and it is notable that all of the Jalayir emirs mentioned in the accounts of Temür's later reign were his relatives.[51] The descendants of the former Jalayir chiefs, Bāyazīd and Bahrām, do not appear in the histories after 777/1375–6.

The Suldus and the Apardï tribes also remained intact under the leadership of members of Temür's following. The Apardï formed part of the army of Temür's follower Buyan Temür b. Aqbugha, who campaigned with the army of Khorasan.[52] In 777–8/1376–7 Temür handed over the Suldus *tümen* to his personal follower Aqtemür. At Aqtemür's death in 788/1386 the Suldus troops passed to his son Shaykh Temür, and later probably formed the *tümen* of the powerful emir Dawlat Temür, who may well have been Shaykh Temür's son.

The Suldus tribe had been split at the beginning of Temür's career, with part of the tribe at Chaghaniyan and the other section under Öljey Bugha Suldus at Balkh. This division continued to exist throughout Temür's life. The other section of the Suldus, based in Balkh, apparently continued under the leadership of Öljey Bugha's grandson, Pīr ᶜAlī, mentioned a number of times in the histories of Temür's reign. Pīr ᶜAlī rebelled after Temür's death, basing his power apparently on Suldus troops.[53]

The tribes which remained under their own leadership – the Barlas, the Khuttalānī emirs, the Apardï of Khuttalan and the Yasa'urī – also continued intact, but they held only a low place in Temür's army. A good example of this is the branch of the Apardï based in Khuttalan, which had previously been at least as powerful as the Apardï of Shaburqan, and was in fact the senior branch of the tribe. This section of the Apardï still continued to exist but was not powerful or prominent after Temür's takeover. Its emirs are rarely mentioned after 790/1388, and then only on occasions when a large proportion of the army was mustered for a single campaign.[54] It is notable that while in 773–4/1371–3 the Apardï emir Khwāja Yūsuf stood at the head of a *tümen*, neither he nor his children are again mentioned with such a large number of troops, although he and his son took part in Temür's later campaigns.[55]

The Yasa'urī of Samarqand and Bukhara, less important than the Apardï to begin with, lost even more of their strength. The Yasa'urī emir Ḥājjī Maḥmūdshāh, who was Temür's cousin, continued until 795/1393 to exercise power and influence despite a temporary desertion to Yūsuf Ṣūfī of Khorezm,[56] but after this there are very few mentions of Yasa'urī emirs, and there is no mention of Yasa'urī troops.[57] The Khuttalānī emirs retained their power somewhat longer, but they too suffered a marked decline under Temür. They continued to reside in Khuttalan, and the army of Khuttalan is mentioned among Temür's troops during his great campaigns, but the

Khuttalānī emirs themselves do not appear in the accounts of Temür's later career.[58] Thus the army of Khuttalan was incorporated into Temür's army but did not provide its original emirs with significant power.

Like the tribes of the Ulus Chaghatay, non-tribal troops continued to exist, many of them under new leadership. The army of Balkh participated in campaigns in 790/1388 and 807/1404; in 790 it was commanded by the *darugha* of Balkh, Yādgār Barlas.[59] The *tümen* of Kebeg Khan, also based in the region of Balkh, likewise functioned as a unit and it is mentioned in 796/1393 and in 800/1398, both times under the same man, Shaykh Arslan.[60]

Most of the groups which had made up the Ulus Chaghatay thus retained much of their original structure; Temür could allow this because they no longer provided their leaders with a strong independent power base. The possession of a tribal following did enhance the strength of some of Temür's followers, but it was not itself sufficient to ensure a high position. The emirs who led tribes and who played a prominent part in Temür's army were those who belonged to Temür's personal following. Jahānshāh b. Chekü, Buyan Temür b. Aqbugha and his sons, Shaykh Temür b. Aqtemür, and the sons of Sarïbugha Jalayir were indeed powerful men, but they owed much of their strength to personal favor. Most of these men moreover were not significantly more powerful than other members of Temür's following who had not been given tribal troops; Sulaymānshāh b. Dā'ūd, Shāhmalik and Sayf al-Dīn Nüküz for instance were all equally prominent.

Without the advantage of membership in Temür's following the control of a tribe brought with it little power or importance. The tribal leaders who had retained control over their own tribes did not hold a high position: Khwāja Yūsuf b. Öljeytü Apardï and Ḥājjī Beg's nephew Muḥammad Darwīsh Barlas for instance were both successors to men of considerable power, but neither played an important part in Temür's campaigns. By this time therefore, the troops which came with the control of a tribe were not by themselves large enough to place their holders among the main commanders of Temür's army. This army still contained tribes, but after 782/1380–1 it was not structured as a tribal army.

The Ulus Chaghatay as an army of conquest

What Temür now ruled can best be called an army of conquest. Temür's new elite was above all a military class, whose power and position depended largely on the number of troops its members commanded, and the allocation of these troops was in Temür's hands. In its new form Temür's army was similar in many ways to the most famous of the Turco-Mongolian conquest armies – that of Chinggis Khan. Both of these conquerors owed much of their early success to their personal followings whose members they used to staff the top command in the army and administration.[61] Neither Chinggis Khan nor Temür separated their personal followings from the rest of the army. In this they differed from many rulers who retained their tribal troops intact and added to them an elite force formed from their personal followings.[62] Instead, both Temür and Chinggis used their followings to provide the highest level of command over the whole of the army, and removed troops from the tribal chiefs to put them under the leadership of this new elite.[63] In this way both leaders transformed a decentralized and tribally organized society into a unified army subservient to one man. The commander of such an army held much greater power and a much more secure position than could the leader of a tribal confederation.

Nonetheless, despite the changes Temür had instituted, his position remained insecure. Although he had dismantled the political system which threatened his power at the beginning of his career, he had not destroyed it. He had not broken up the tribes, nor had he obliterated the tribal aristocracy which had led them. The new elite which he had placed at the center of his army and administration was personally loyal to him, but it consisted of people who had come to maturity within the Ulus Chaghatay and had been trained within its fluid and active political system.

It was not enough for Temür to install a new system – he had also to maintain it. He had to prevent the tribal leaders from regaining the power which had been taken from them, and also to keep the new elite from taking over the political activity denied to the tribal chiefs and turning the troops now under them into tribes of their own. This was the more necessary because troops within Temür's army were usually conscripted and equipped by the emirs who led them. The commanders in charge of conscription – *tovachïs* – were charged with determining the number of soldiers in the army and making sure that the emirs of the Ulus and the governors of regions provided the appropriate number of troops, properly equipped.[64] Thus it was quite possible that the primary loyalty of these troops would focus on their immediate commander and that they could become a source of independent power.

The armies of the princes

As I have mentioned above, Temür prevented independent political activity among his following partly by keeping them constantly on campaign. He then further settled much of his army in the territories he had conquered. After 795/1392–3 much of the military segment of the Chaghatay population no longer inhabited Transoxiana but was scattered over a wide area of newly conquered lands, separated both from their territory and from their kinsmen. As Temür's sons and grandsons came of age he made them governors of his new provinces, and assigned emirs to serve them. These emirs were chosen to be representative of the whole of the ruling class; each army included members of several different tribes or groups, and also the relatives of Temür's personal followers. In this way Temür created a new regional base for armies which had previously depended on Transoxiana. Since each princely army mirrored the composition of the whole Chaghatay army, people from various tribes and even from the families of Temür's followers were assigned to different armies.

The first princely army which Temür created was that of his son ᶜUmar Shaykh, whom he appointed in 778–9/1376–8 to rule the regions of Andijan and Kashghar.[65] Among his emirs were two of Temür's followers, Khitay and Elchi, along with the son of a third, Anūshīrwān b. Aqbugha. He had with him also the son of a Qipchaq emir, and one Moghul emir.[66] His army included parts of several tribes; he was sent to Uzgand with an Apardï *tümen*, a Qarluq *hazāra* and others.[67] In 795/1393 Temür moved ᶜUmar Shaykh from Andijan and gave him the province of Fars. He now added several important new emirs to ᶜUmar Shaykh's army, all sons or relatives of personal followers.[68]

Amīrānshāh's appointment as governor of Khorasan in 782/1380–1 is described in more detail, and provides a much fuller list of his army. Temür appointed with him two Barlas emirs, two *qa'uchin* emirs, Qumarī Ïnaq and Tābān Bahadur, both members of Temür's following, and several other followers or their relatives, including Sayf al-Dīn Nüküz, Aqbugha, ᶜUthmān b. ᶜAbbās, Urus Bugha, brother of Sarïbugha Jalayir, and Muẓaffar b. Üch Qara. In addition to these men Amīrānshāh had with him Ḥamza, probably the son of Mūsā Taychi'ut.[69] Thus his army had in it representatives of three tribes, Jalayir, Taychi'ut and Barlas, as well as six members of Temür's following, several of them very prominent.

We are also given extensive lists of the emirs appointed to Kabul with Pīr Muḥammad b. Jahāngīr in 794/1391–2 and to Khorasan with Shāhrukh in 799/1396–7, and these strongly resemble the lists of emirs given in the descriptions of earlier appointments. They contain a few Barlas emirs and numerous sons or relatives of Temür's followers, some of them powerful and important men.[70] The representative character of the princely armies was not coincidental; in describing the appointments of Pīr Muḥammad and Shāhrukh, Yazdī's *Ẓafarnāma* specifically states that all the important emirs sent a brother or son, and that one person was sent from each *tümen*.[71]

The creation of provincial armies therefore served to scatter the members of families and groups which, if they had stayed together, might have formed independent centers of power. The Barlas and *qa'uchin* emirs were dispersed and so, significantly, were the families of Temür's personal followers. Thus for instance of the sons of Ḥājjī Sayf al-Dīn, one was appointed to Khorasan with Shāhrukh, and another to ᶜIraq with Abā Bakr b. Amīrānshāh.[72] The sons of Shaykh ᶜAlī Bahadur were also separated; one was assigned to Transoxiana with Muḥammad Sulṭān, one to Khorasan with Shāhrukh, and one to Kabul with Pīr Muḥammad b. Jahāngīr.[73]

Armies of this kind existed also under other nomad dynasties. Similar ones were created by the Aqqoyunlu confederation; their princes held appanages, each with an army drawn from all of the confederate clans.[74] The practice is reminiscent also of the *tamma* system used by the Mongols, in which princes or emirs from various tribes and from each *ulus* combined to make up a garrison army.[75] In the case of the Timurids however the members of a new army were chosen less from the tribes under Temür's command than from the families of his personal followers. It was these, with a few Barlas emirs, some *qa'uchin*, and occasionally the son of a particularly prominent emir of the Ulus Chaghatay, who were chosen for the provincial armies. This is a striking illustration of the new power structure within Temür's army, and the extent to which strength and numbers had passed from the tribes to Temür's own following.

The Timurid princes were now potentially the strongest centers of power in the realm, but Temür was careful not to allow them to build separate power bases. One should not consider the provincial armies as a real division of the army of the Ulus Chaghatay, or believe that the princes became truly independent actors. Temür used a number of methods to limit their power. One of the most effective of these was the appointment of senior members of his following to the provincial armies. Many of these men were Temür's contemporaries, and a number had marriage alliances to the Timurid dynasty. They had been closely involved in administrative affairs since Temür's assumption of power and had close personal ties to him. In power, prestige and closeness to Temür they fell little behind the princes. Since many princes were appointed to governorships very young, such emirs acted not as servitors but as guardians or watchdogs, monitoring the activities of the princes they served. Even while making up part of the army of a prince they continued to give their primary loyalty to Temür and their presence could override the authority of their masters. Although most emirs were appointed permanently to one princely army these senior appointments were often temporary. Later the same emirs might be appointed to serve another prince or return to Temür.

Amīrānshāh was fourteen when he was appointed to Khorasan in 782/1380–1, and four senior emirs were sent with him including two of the most powerful members of Temür's following, Aqbugha Nayman and Ḥājjī Sayf al-Dīn. All of these emirs remained involved with Amīrānshāh and the affairs of Khorasan until about 790/1388, after which only Aqbugha remained in his service.[76] There are several other examples of such appointments. Sevinchek, who inherited the place of Temür's follower Khitay, was assigned to ᶜUmar Shaykh in Fars in 795/1392–3. When later he quarreled with ᶜUmar Shaykh's son and successor Pīr Muḥammad, he caused a major split among Pīr Muḥammad's followers. He was then sent to India as punishment, and later assigned to ᶜIraq with Abā Bakr b. Amīrānshāh.[77] Jahānshāh b. Chekü, probably Temür's most powerful emir, was assigned to western Iran in 806/1404 with ᶜUmar b. Amīrānshāh, then about twenty-one years old. Jahānshāh apparently soon came to feel that ᶜUmar showed too little respect for Temür's ordinances, disagreed with him during Temür's life and rebelled against him soon after Temür's death.[78]

Temür further limited the power of his descendants by continuing to treat their armies as part of his own. The provincial armies did not serve only under the prince to whom they were attached. Shāhrukh's army for instance accompanied Temür on the Indian campaign in 800–1/1398–9, while Shāhrukh himself remained in Khorasan.[79] Part at least of Amīrānshāh's *tümen* fought in Temür's siege of Takrit in ᶜIraq in 796/1393 while Amīrānshāh himself raided Hilla and Basra.[80] Individual emirs also sometimes served in Temür's armies quite independently of the princes to whose army they belonged, and of the other emirs who served in it with them.[81] Thus the power bestowed on the princes in the assignment of armies and provinces remained conditional and subject to Temür's control.[82] Although Temür's army was nominally divided, the emirs in the princely armies continued to make up part of Temür's forces, and many remained loyal primarily to Temür himself.

Yet another method of control was Temür's frequent reassignment of provincial governorships. This served to divide and reapportion the princely armies, and to prevent strong local loyalty. For much of his reign Temür continued to reorganize his dominions, moving princes from the governorship of one province to another, often at the other end of his realm.[83] Of Temür's sons and grandsons both ᶜUmar Shaykh and Amīrānshāh, appointed as governors during the first years of Temür's reign, were removed to new territories during the five-year campaign and replaced in their original posts by younger princes.

The death in 805/1403 of Temür's heir apparent, Muḥammad Sulṭān, occasioned the final reorganization of the provinces, which culminated in the division of his realm into four sections, each held by the family of one of his sons. The dominions of Hülegü Khan were now apportioned among Amīrānshāh's sons; Khalīl Sulṭān governed the regions of Baylaqan, Arran, Armenia and Georgia, Abā Bakr ruled ᶜIraq and Baghdad along with Kurdistan, Mardin, Diyar Bakr and the Oyirat tribe, while Azerbaijan went to ᶜUmar.[84] The regions of central Iran became the province of the sons of ᶜUmar Shaykh, who had died in 796/1394. Pīr Muḥammad governed Fars, Iskandar was now granted the regions of Hamadan, Nihawand, Burujird and Lur-i Kuchik, while Rustam held Isfahan.[85] Shāhrukh had governed Khorasan since 799/1396–7, and Temür now installed his sons in the provinces to the north of it. He granted the borders of Moghulistan, including Andijan and Kashghar, previously under the rule of Iskandar b. ᶜUmar Shaykh, to Shāhrukh's son Ibrāhīm Sulṭān in 807/1404, and he installed Shāhrukh's other son, Ulugh Beg, on the Turkistan frontier, to guard the regions of Tashkent, Sayram and Ashbara.[86]

Thus at the end of Temür's life he had organized all of his dominions into provinces governed by his sons and grandsons, and had further divided his realm into four main regions, ruled by the families of his sons; the northwestern area was under Amīrānshāh and his children, the southwestern under the sons of ᶜUmar Shaykh, the southeastern under the rule of Jahāngīr's son Pīr Muḥammad, who had been appointed governor of the area in 794/1391–2, and the northeastern under Shāhrukh and his sons. Like Chinggis Khan, Temür appointed one person as his successor, and instructed the others to defer to him.[87]

The army of conquest serving under Temür during his great campaigns was a very different entity from the Ulus Chaghatay over which he had taken power. The people who made it up were the same and most of the groups which had held power before Temür's rise continued to exist within his army, many under new leadership, but almost none much altered in structure. The dynamics of power however were radically changed. Whereas earlier the tribal leaders had held the upper hand, controlling both land and large numbers of soldiers, now they had given way to a new elite consisting of Temür's own family and his personal followers. The tribes had lost most of the control they had held over their territories, and much of their earlier manpower had now gone to provide Temür's followers with armies. Tribes put directly under the members of Temür's following remained intact and contributed to the strength of the new elite, while tribal leaders who were not members of Temür's following now held only a low position. Power depended not on tribal strength, but on closeness to Temür.

Temür achieved this change in the power structure of the Ulus Chaghatay gradually during his first twelve years in power. At the beginning of his rule much of Temür's army still consisted of tribesmen under their own leaders, and while this was so his position was challenged by a long succession of conspiracies and desertions. In the course of putting these down Temür succeeded in transferring much of the tribal manpower to his followers and other people loyal to him. Some of the methods he used were direct. He put members of his following at the head of several recalcitrant tribes; this happened to the Jalayir, the Suldus, and the Apardï of Shaburqan. He also sent tribal troops away, dispatching a *tümen* of the Apardï to form the garrison army of Uzgand and Kashghar under ᶜUmar Shaykh.

These measures served to weaken the tribes, and Temür prevented the tribal aristocracy from regaining power by reorganizing the Ulus Chaghatay. First he appointed Barlas governors to several regions previously controlled by tribes – most notably the areas of the Suldus and the Yasa'urī. Secondly he imported numerous foreign soldiers, both of settled and of nomad origin, and established them as the army of Transoxiana. In this way he removed two crucial sources of tribal strength – the regional armies of Transoxiana and the wealth of its settled inhabitants. The tribal leaders were also deprived of the constant political and military activity within the Ulus which had helped them to attract and keep followers, and their efforts to continue this and to defy Temür's rule ended in repeated failure. As the smaller tribes and military groups of the Ulus began to perceive Temür and his new elite as the most successful powers in the Ulus, they probably found it advantageous to switch their allegiance. Thus as Temür's rule continued, the tribal leaders had ever fewer troops at their command.

By 782/1380–1, the transfer of power was essentially complete, and from this time on there was very little change in the structure of power. Temür's descendants and his more prominent followers now held almost all important positions of command within the army. His personal followers were closely connected to his family, both by intermarriage and by their appointment to the armies of the princes. Together these two groups came to form a closed elite, controlling most of the high military command.

Even after he had established his new elite however, Temür could not consider himself secure – he had still to make sure both that the new order remained intact and that his new elite did not develop centers of power and political interests which could threaten his position. He did this by undertaking a war of conquest which kept him and his followers out of the Ulus Chaghatay almost constantly for the rest of his life. Temür's conquests form a constant background to his transformation of the Ulus Chaghatay. They provided the additional wealth and manpower which raised his new elite above the tribal aristocracy. They also allowed him to remove the members of the Ulus Chaghatay around which their political life had centered, and thus to interrupt the political processes whose continuance had threatened Temür's rule. At the same time conquest provided a substitute for political activity, and this new movement was fully under Temür's control.

Temür further strengthened his new order by settling the Chaghatay armies in the provinces of his new realm. By providing each prince with an army representative of the whole of the Ulus Chaghatay Temür created an intermediate level of command, and by assigning members of each tribe and powerful family to different armies, he prevented the creation of independent centers of power. The princes themselves were kept from gaining undue strength by the appointment of powerful emirs to supervise them, by changes in the governorships granted to them, and by Temür's use of their armies and their emirs in their absence.

Temür then could control the Ulus Chaghatay only by going beyond it. The history of his career is one of noise, destruction and violence throughout the world, serving at once to facilitate and to obscure a quiet change at its center. It is this transformation within the Ulus Chaghatay, from an active tribal confederation to an army of conquest whose movement depended on Temür, which lies at the heart of Temür's success. Without it, he could not have remained at the head of the Ulus Chaghatay, and certainly could not have undertaken his extraordinary career of conquest.

CHAPTER 5

Temür's army of conquest: outsiders and conquered peoples

Those who saw Temür's army described it as a huge conglomeration of different peoples – nomad and settled, Muslims and Christians, Turks, Tajiks, Arabs, Georgians, and Indians. Temür conquered a huge territory of varied population and resources and he was not slow to put these to use in his new enterprise. Here I shall examine the position of the conquered peoples within Temür's army and his realm: how they were conscripted, how they were controlled, and to what extent they truly became part of Temür's army.

Temür conquered and subdued new territories with a systematic ferocity quite at variance with his gentle treatment of powers within the Ulus Chaghatay. His methods of control however were not much different. Temür overthrew only a few of the most powerful dynasties in the lands he conquered and left almost all the smaller ones in power under compliant rulers. The regions he conquered were ruled by small dynasties vying for power within and among themselves, and it was not difficult to find allies among them who were interested in a new enterprise.

Temür did not treat all conquered regions and people alike and the variations in his policies illustrate the challenges and opportunities which different regions offered him. In many of the territories he conquered, such as northern India, Syria, Anatolia, Moghulistan and the Qipchaq steppe, Temür contented himself with the collection of ransom money and the destruction or chastisement of unfriendly leaders, leaving no permanent administration behind him. The areas over which he did assert control were those which were similar to the Ulus Chaghatay in population and structure: lands of mixed populations which had previously been ruled by Chinggisid dynasties. These areas – Ferghana, Khorasan, Sistan, Khorezm, western Iran and ᶜIraq – Temür and his Chaghatay emirs could adapt to easily and rule directly.

It is significant that all of these areas contained a largely settled population and were strongly Persian in culture. Temür's neighbors to the north – the Jochids of the Dasht-i Qipchaq and the Turco-Mongolian tribes who made up the eastern Chaghadayid realm – were also close to the Ulus

Chaghatay in history, culture and geography, and like the regions south of the Ulus, had been involved with its politics. Nonetheless, Temür did not incorporate these territories into his realm, with the exception of the predominantly agricultural region of the Ferghana valley.

The incorporation of new land, soldiers and elites offered both an advantage and a threat to Temür. On the one hand the influx of wealth and of manpower from his new territories added enormously to the size and power of his army. On the other hand, his realm now included a large population with no traditional ties of loyalty to him. Temür's profit from these new people depended therefore on how fully he could control them and how much service he could extract from them. This in turn depended on their relation to him and his army – both how well equipped they were to withstand Chaghatay control, and how much advantage they could gain from joining Temür's enterprise. In these respects, the populations Temür conquered differed considerably among themselves. Those who proved most tractable and most useful were not the nomads, similar to the Chaghatays in tradition and lifestyle, but the settled and largely Persian dynasties of the Middle East. It was these people who joined Temür's enterprise, whether by force or by attraction, while nomads remained largely outside.

The subjugation of settled populations

The bloodshed which accompanied Temür's campaigns in the Middle East masks a policy of preserving local rule even in areas where his army encountered resistance.[1] The regions he conquered had been controlled by innumerable small dynasties; now that Temür was predominant in the region, their land and soldiers were largely at his disposal. Two dynasties, the Karts of Herat and the Muzaffarids of Fars, controlled very considerable territory and wielded influence far beyond their actual holdings. These could be a threat to Temür and he eliminated them, murdering most members of both dynasties. The areas they had held – Herat, Badghis and Ghuristan in Khorasan and in western Iran the cities of Isfahan, Yazd, Shiraz and Kerman, with their large regions – came directly under the rule of Timurid governors, and became important centers of Timurid power. Most smaller dynasties remained in place. Many rulers submitted voluntarily to Temür, and were promptly reconfirmed in the control of their territories.[2] Their submission was due partly to fear, but partly also to the recognition of the benefits of alliance with a successful enterprise.[3]

Temür was able to control the local dynasties of his conquered lands without destroying them or taking over their territories directly. He ensured their compliance by replacing their leadership if they resisted him, sometimes several times, and by restricting their power within the territories they ruled. In many cases, where Temür encountered resistance, he merely replaced an uncooperative ruler with a more compliant member of the same family, or with another dynasty which had claims to the same area. The endemic struggles for local power made this a relatively easy task.[4] The rulers whom Temür removed he usually put into captivity, often deporting them with their families to Transoxiana or to the borders of Turkistan. This made it possible for him to reinstall them if the men put in their places proved unreliable. Thus for instance when in 794/1392 the *sayyids* controlling Amul and Sari in Mazandaran began to show rebellious tendencies Temür went against them and granted their region to two other local leaders, one of them Iskandar Shaykhī, whose father they had displaced.[5] When Iskandar Shaykhī rebelled in 806/1403–4, Temür brought back Sayyid Ghiyāth al-Dīn, the son of the former ruler who had been exiled in Khorezm and returned the region of Amul to him.[6]

Temür often kept local dynasties under control by repeatedly replacing their leaders with other members of the same family. The most striking case is that of Lur-i Buzurg. Its *atabeg*, Aḥmad, had been dispossessed by the Muzaffarids. After his conquest of southern Iran Temür returned Lur-i Buzurg to Aḥmad, taking his two brothers Afrāsiyāb and Masᶜūdshāh to Samarqand. Later Temür returned Afrāsiyāb to his homeland, dividing the region between him and Aḥmad. The two brothers soon began to fight, as indeed they had done before. Temür's grandson Pīr Muḥammad who was then governor of the region preferred Afrāsiyāb, and so arrested Aḥmad and sent him to Temür, but Temür returned him. After Temür's death Pīr Muḥammad again arrested Aḥmad, but he was soon freed by a later Timurid prince governing the region.[7] Such constant change and interference made it difficult for local rulers to retain an independent power base.

Although Temür left most small dynasties intact, he did sometimes constrict the territories they ruled. Thus in 788/1386 he removed the cities of Qazwin and Tarum from the control of the Gilani ruler, Sayyid ᶜAlī Kiyā, without making any attempt actually to depose him.[8] Similarly when Temür reinstalled Sayyid Ghiyāth al-Dīn of Sari and Amul in 806/1404 after the rebellion and defeat of Iskandar Shaykhī, he gave him only the city of Amul, while one of Temür's own emirs remained stationed in Sari.[9]

These methods of control, not particularly original ones,[10] were in many ways similar to Temür's treatment of the tribes of the Ulus Chaghatay. Temür imposed more frequent changes in leadership on the settled regions, and often accompanied these changes with considerable bloodshed, but the method was not significantly different from the one he had used within the Ulus Chaghatay. Like the tribes, the conquered territories continued to offer sporadic resistance. No dynasty however was strong enough to rebel successfully, or to hinder Temür in his continuing conquests. It seems likely that uprisings by settled dynasties posed little threat to Temür, since his army was almost constantly on campaign and could easily put them down, collecting additional booty and ransom as it did so. The rebellions of settled peoples were probably not particularly harmful to his prestige, as long as they were suppressed quickly and effectively. These were merely conquered subjects, whose loyalty and obedience were not necessary to the maintenance of Temür's charisma. The control of settled populations did not pose a major problem for Temür.

Temür was quick to make use of the local rulers under his control, but much slower to trust them. His reaction to these men depended both on their previous relationship to the Ulus Chaghatay and on their readiness to submit, and some enjoyed considerable favor. Almost none however became full members of Temür's elite. Newly subjugated leaders and their armies were partially incorporated into Temür's forces but they did not become an integral part of his army. Besides the ransom money (*māl-i amān*) and subsequent taxes that they paid into the Timurid coffers, they were obligated to provide a certain number of troops, and either to accompany Temür on some of his campaigns, or to send a member of the family to do so.

In general, local leaders accompanied Temür's armies only on expeditions relatively close to their own regions. Thus for instance Sayyid Ghiyāth al-Dīn, son of the ruler of Sari, went with Temür on his two Iranian campaigns, but not apparently on his campaigns to the Qipchaq steppe.[11] Malik ᶜIzz al-Dīn Kurd of Armenia likewise campaigned in Temür's army against the Qaraqoyunlu Turkmens, while the ruler of Shirwan, Shaykh Ibrāhīm, was in Temür's army for several of his western and northern campaigns against Georgia, the Qipchaq steppe, Anatolia and Gilan.[12] Neither of these men however is mentioned on Temür's eastern or southern expeditions. It is unclear what percentage of their troops local rulers had to put at Temür's disposal; this probably depended both on their own enthusiasm and on Temür's needs. Sayyid Ghiyāth al-Dīn of Sari and Amul, never a whole-hearted subject, went to join Temür with "some men of the army."[13] Shaykh Ibrāhīm of Shirwan, a close ally of Temür's, is mentioned "with the army of Shirwan," and as emir of a *tümen*.[14]

Local rulers and their troops sometimes became part of the provincial armies commanded by Temür's sons. One example of this is the army led from Khorasan against Sultaniyya by one of Amīrānshāh's most powerful emirs. Muḥammad Sulṭānshāh, himself of Khorasanian descent. This included several local leaders – Pīrak Pādishāh of Mazandaran, Nīkrūz Jawun-i Qurban, Mulūk Sabzawārī of the Sarbadars, and Dawlat Khwāja Abīwardī.[15] The armies of ᶜUmar b. Amīrānshāh, appointed to Azerbaijan in 806/1403, are listed in the *Muᶜizz al-ansāb*, and contain numerous emirs of that region.[16]

For leaders who had been out of power in the regions Temür conquered, the arrival of Temür's army presented less a threat than an opportunity. Just as the neighbors of the Ulus Chaghatay had earlier provided refuge to its dissidents, now Temür's army, passing through new territories, attracted men who were eager for an alternative career or an outside ally who might help them regain their holdings. One of the most prominent of such people was Iskandar Shaykhī, mentioned above, who joined Temür on his Khorasanian campaign. His father had been deposed by the father of Sayyid Kamāl al-Dīn, who ruled Amul. On the loss of his region, Iskandar Shaykhī joined the service of the Kartid kings, bringing with him one thousand horsemen, and at the fall of the Kartids he joined Temür's army.[17] On Temür's second Iranian campaign in 795/1393 Iskandar Shaykhī accompanied him and encouraged him to attack the Sayyids. Temür did so and granted the region of Amul to Iskandar.[18]

A number of other emirs of less prominence left the employ of regional rulers to seek fortune in Temür's forces. Two examples are Muḥammad Sulṭānshāh, who came to Temür from the kings of Herat, and Mubashshir Kartī, who had apparently left Khorasan for Transoxiana even before Temür's rise to power.[19] These men seem to have had no local attachments or regional power, and perhaps for this reason they were more fully accepted into Temür's army than most rulers from his conquered territories.[20] A number of emirs from ᶜIraq and Syria likewise joined Temür, although they did not attain as prominent a position as the Khorasanian emirs. Many of them, instead of campaigning with Temür's army, were sent to garrison the Turkistan frontier.[21]

The new members of Temür's army were less loyal than his Chaghatay emirs, and constituted a less privileged class. They were not accorded the rights and privileges held by the Chaghatays, and led a highly precarious existence. Temür was quick to feel displeasure with the local leaders who had joined his train, and quick also to act on his feelings. On his first Iranian expedition he assigned Sārū ᶜĀdil, a powerful emir who had served both the Jalayirids and the Muzaffarids, to Tabriz. Sārū joined Temür's army with over seventeen *qoshuns*.[22] He had served Temür for only two years after his appointment when Temür suspected him either of treachery or of mental imbalance (presumably a leaning towards ambition) and killed him, along with many of his relatives.[23] The *atabeg* of Lur-i Kuchik, Malik ᶜIzz al-Dīn, fared only slightly better; he was defeated in 790/1388 and taken captive with his son to Samarqand, then after three years returned and reinstalled as ruler of his region. In 806/1403–4 however he was executed because his son was dilatory in the collection of taxes.[24]

Even rulers not specifically suspected of bad intentions were sometimes required to send their children or relatives to Temür as hostages. I have cited the example of Atabeg Aḥmad of Lur-i Buzurg whose brothers Temür held in Samarqand. In 806/1403–4 Temür applied this requirement to all the commanders of ᶜIraq (here probably ᶜIraq-i ᶜAjam), ordering them to send sons or brothers to accompany him.[25]

It is clear from the evidence presented above that most local leaders, while they did campaign in Temür's armies at the head of their own troops, did not become members of the Timurid elite. They were only temporary members of Temür's army, holding a subordinate and highly precarious position within it. The exceptions to this rule were the leaders from areas with which the Ulus Chaghatay had been familiar before the beginning of Temür's conquests – those of Khorasan, Sistan, and to a lesser extent Mazandaran and Khorezm. These were the first areas Temür conquered, and they had long standing political connections with the Ulus Chaghatay.

This was particularly true of Khorasan, as several scholars have noted.[26] The Sarbadarids of Sabzawar are a good example. Their leader Khwāja ᶜAlī Mu'ayyad was quick to submit to Temür on his first expedition to Khorasan and accompanied him on his western campaigns thereafter.[27] At Khwāja ᶜAlī's death in 788/1386 Temür divided his holdings among several of his relatives. One of these, Khwāja Masᶜūd Sabzawārī, seems to have held a high place under Temür. He campaigned at the head of the Sarbadar troops and was made governor, first of Shushtar, and then of Baghdad, both important cities.[28] Temür's favor to the Sarbadar dynasty was strong enough even to survive treacherous behavior on their part. Mulūk Sabzawārī, a relative of Khwāja ᶜAlī's who ruled Juwayn, joined the uprising of Ḥājjī Beg Jawun-i Qurban in 790–1/1388–9, and somewhat later fled to the Muzaffarid ruler Shāh Manṣūr, whom he aided against Temür. Despite this, Temür continued to favor the other members of the family, and allowed even Mulūk himself to return to service; in 796/1393–4 he left him in Basra to organize it after its conquest, a position of some responsibility and trust.[29] Thus Temür treated the Sarbadars with almost as much leniency as he did the Chaghatay emirs under him, in sharp contrast to his treatment of most of the foreign rulers under his control.

Several other Khorasanian emirs also played an important part in Temür's campaigns. The careers of Mubashshir and Muḥammad Sulṭānshāh have been mentioned above, and we know of Khorasanian emirs on the Indian campaign and at the siege of Damascus.[30] In addition to commanding troops many Khorasanian emirs became governors over conquered cities. I have mentioned the governorships of Khwāja Masᶜūd Sabzawārī above. Malik Muḥammad Ūbahī, a relative of the Kartid kings, received first the governorship of the fortress Qalᶜa-i Safid in Fars after its conquest in 795/1393, and then that of Alanjak in Azerbaijan in 803/1400.[31] Temür gave control of Damghan and Sari to Jamshīd Qārin of Quhistan in 790/1388. In 805/1402–3 after Jamshīd's death, the governorship of Sari went to Shams al-Dīn Ghurī of the Herat region.[32]

After Khorasan, the nearby provinces of Sistan and Mazandaran provided the greatest number of outside commanders for Temür's army. Shāhshāhān-i Sīstānī, given the rule of Sistan by Temür in 785/1383, accompanied Temür even on distant campaigns; he is mentioned at the head of the army of Sistan in Kerman, Syria and Rum.[33] Iskandar Shaykhī of Mazandaran, to whom Temür returned the rule of his native city Amul, has been mentioned several times.[34]

Thus throughout his lifetime Temür retained within his army a consciousness of the borders of the Ulus Chaghatay and its relations with its neighbors. The highest positions in his army were reserved for the members of the Ulus Chaghatay, but the rulers and emirs of areas close to it were also incorporated into his forces and given positions of some prestige. The more distant areas of Temür's conquests such as western Iran and ʿIraq had had little contact with the Ulus Chaghatay before Temür's conquests. The rulers and emirs of these regions remained outsiders within his army, kept under control less by the promise of wealth and advancement than by the constant threat of punishment.

The conscription and utilization of foreign troops

The discussion above has centered on the upper levels of command – the rulers or emirs of the conquered regions and their role in the army Temür led. To understand fully the utilization and control of conquered peoples, we must look also at the lower levels. This section of the chapter will discuss the use of the common soldiers recruited from Temür's new realm. The large number of foreign troops which observers noted in Temür's army was not due entirely to the forces led by the rulers who had submitted to him. There were in addition some soldiers from the conquered regions who were recruited and commanded more directly by Temür's emirs. Some of these were used only on local campaigns but others became a fairly permanent part of the army and campaigned even on distant expeditions.

It is hard to tell who made up the new troops that Temür's army recruited, or to discern the details of their conscription and command within the Chaghatay army. We do not really know what for instance the histories mean by the army of Shiraz or the infantrymen of Qum. Were these peasants forcibly conscripted, armies settled on the land by an earlier regime, or tribesmen? These are important questions in determining the quality of such troops and the role they played in the Timurid army. The answers however are elusive; neither the sources on Temür's reign nor the military history of the Middle East provide much evidence about such forces. All I can do here is to review the available information and suggest one or two possible ways to interpret it.

Before analyzing the meager evidence of the Timurid sources we should examine the tradition and history of the lands Temür conquered, and consider what sort of armies one would expect to find there. Scholars writing on the military history of Islamic lands agree that the Middle East under the later caliphate was peculiar in being a highly militaristic society without an indigenous army. The armies both of foreign and of native dynasties consisted primarily of slave soldiers attached personally to the ruler, and secondarily of mercenary troops – often Kurds, Daylamites or nomadic Arabs – hired to supplement them.[35] This system remained in force even after the influx of new nomad manpower which accompanied the Seljukid invasion.[36]

Towards the end of the caliphal period, under the Buyids and Seljukids, it became customary to finance the army by granting assignments of land or its revenue (*iqṭāᶜ*). This connected the army closely to the land, but it did not create a military class attached to a specific area. Even when grants of land revenue did become hereditary, frequent invasions and changes of government prevented the formation of a permanent military class. The men who held *iqṭāᶜ* grants were the members of a standing army, most of them Turkish military slaves personally attached to the ruler they served.[37]

In addition to their slave troops, rulers might recruit local forces of various kinds, most of them probably serving as mercenaries. The Kurds, Arabs and Daylamites served in this capacity throughout the Middle East, and the Khalaj Turks, the Ghurids and peoples of Gharjistan served in Khorasan. Some rulers swelled their forces with sectarian religious groups, vigilantes, and for campaigns against non-Muslims, *ghāzīs*, or volunteers.[38] Other than this we know little about locally recruited armies. The military system of the later caliphate thus fostered the development not of regional but of dynastic armies, attached to the person of their leader, made up primarily of slave troops, tribesmen and soldiers of fortune. This does not seem to fit what indications we have about the troops in the provinces of Temür's realm, which are usually identified by region, and which were often found in the settled and urban areas.

To explain these armies one must turn to the Mongol period, which brought in large numbers of nomad troops and caused a major shift in the supply and the use of military manpower. This change was formalized by Ghazan Khan (1295–1304) who in order to pay his troops handed out to them large tracts of land from whose income they could support themselves. He distributed land to commanders of thousands to divide among commanders of hundreds and tens. These grants were a form of *iqṭāᶜ* but differed from earlier *iqṭāᶜ* grants in several respects. The land grants to individuals were smaller, and the holders were now interposed directly between the peasants and the central government, rather than between the landlord and the government as in earlier times. This gave beneficiaries much more direct control of the land. Grants in the Mongol period moreover were universally hereditary.

Like other Mongol states, the Ilkhanids divided their territories into *tümens* and organized the local population for military service.[39] One of the levies due from the population was that of *cherik*, the provision of troops. Conscription was calculated apparently at one soldier for every nine households for the settled population, while among the nomads all adult males were expected to serve.[40] The non-Mongol forces thus recruited were decimally ordered, and were often used to guard border areas.[41]

The slave troops so prevalent earlier were now largely replaced by an army settled on the land and subject to general conscription. In many ways the military order completed by Ghazan Khan resembles less the earlier Islamic practice whose terminology it borrowed than the systems of universal conscription introduced by other Mongol states. This institution is most clearly documented in China. There a general census allowed systematic conscription from the Chinese population, and the creation of hereditary military households, both Mongol and Chinese, provided for the support and continuance of a standing army.[42] As I have mentioned above, the Ilkhans and their bureaucrats were well informed about Yüan government, and sometimes influenced by it.

In attempting to analyze the regional armies under the Timurids we must consider the possibility that something still remained of the universal army created by the Ilkhans. We know this was operative at least until the 1330s, fifty years before Temür's conquest.[43] In addition we must take into account the types of manpower used in Middle Eastern armies before the Mongol conquest – the slave troops had probably declined, but the same tribes of nomads and mountain peoples were available and the same population of adventurers to be coerced or attracted into the army. A conqueror as active as Temür, needing manpower at once to take new territories and to guard past conquests, might be expected to use most of the manpower available to him and this indeed is what Temür did.

In some cases it seems possible that Temür simply conscripted peasants along his path to use temporarily either for fighting or for other work. The sources several times mention the conscription of local armies, sometimes specifically of foot-soldiers, for local campaigns. One example is the recruitment of infantry from the regions of Rayy, Qum, Kashan, Isfahan and Qumis to put down a rebellion in 806/1403–4.[44] Since Mazandaran was heavily wooded and difficult of access for horsemen, these infantrymen could have been wanted as much for making paths through the woods as for fighting. In 795/1392, having dealt with the *sayyids* of Sari, Temür stopped to collect an army in Shasman before continuing on his way.[45] Either of these might have been simple conscription of local populations.

On the other hand it is clear that not all of Temür's infantry consisted of peasants recruited for short-term use. The infantrymen of Khorasan were used on Temür's Indian campaign at a considerable distance from their place of origin, and many of the troops left to garrison cities included infantry.[46] Foot-soldiers moreover did not always remain unmounted; when in 802/1399–1400 Amīrānshāh's emirs were called before the tribunal to be judged for cowardice in battle, they were fined from fifty to three hundred horses each, and these horses were given to the foot-soldiers of the army.[47] Such treatment does not seem consistent with an infantry of conscripted peasants, and it is likely that many of Temür's foot-soldiers came from peoples with a military tradition. Some may well have been soldiers from the marches of Khorasan and Afghanistan, and also perhaps the mountain peoples –

Merkits and Badakhshanis – who made up part of the army of the Ulus Chaghatay.

We must consider also whether some of these soldiers represented the remains of the Ilkhanid armies; there are some indications that this could have been the case. As I have stated above, one of the levies owed to the Ilkhans by the population under them was the military levy, or *cherik*. This term was also used to denote troops conscripted from the subject population and local militias,[48] and it is with this meaning that we find it used in Yazdī's *Ẓafarnāma*. At Temür's period the *cherik* troops were commanded by the local Chaghatay governors – *darughas* – appointed to the cities and towns of the conquered regions. These men commanded both small Chaghatay forces and locally recruited ones. During the rebellion in Yazd in 797–8/1395–6 Pīr Muḥammad, governor of Fars, sent messengers to the regions of Fars, Kerman, Khorasan and ᶜIraq calling for the gathering of armies. He was joined by the *darughas* of several regions including Isfahan, Kerman, and Quhistan with their own troops and also with the *cherik* of their regions.[49] The local governors' command of regional armies is confirmed by the account of disturbances in Mazandaran, in which Jamshīd Qārin, governor of Sari, went to the aid of another local ruler with his own *nökers* and what troops he had, men of Mazandaran and of Khorasan.[50]

The Ilkhanid use of the term *cherik* for both military levies and local militias suggests that these forces were conscripted from local populations. It seems quite possible that the *cherik* led by Temür's *darughas* could be the remnants of these armies. There is some indication also that regular conscription continued in the later Timurid period, and that the men being recruited were not peasants, but men from a military class. The sources mention a "*qoshun* tax," an occasional levy which was paid by the common people at times of conscription, since the army being recruited consisted only of nobles (*aᶜyān*).[51]

Another thing which could indicate the existence of troops attached to an area is the custom of identifying armies by region or city. Such a usage might sometimes refer to the Chaghatay troops of a region, or to those attached to local rulers, but in one or two cases this does not seem a likely interpretation. At ᶜUmar Shaykh's appointment to Fars, for instance, the army of Shiraz (or according to some sources of Fars) was put under him.[52] In Kerman the Chaghatay and local armies are mentioned separately; Edigü Barlas, governor of Kerman, went to besiege Sirjan with the Moghul[53] army and the army of Kerman.[54] The evidence presented above suggests the Ilkhanid armies may still have existed, and may have made up a part of the local manpower which Temür conscripted. These forces, along with various auxiliary troops of nomads and mountaineers, and perhaps some conscripted peasants, now served to swell the ranks of Temür's army.

In considering the conscription and the use of local troops one further question presents itself: that of their leadership. This question, like so many others in the history of Temür's reign, is difficult to answer. There is no doubt that many regional troops were led by their own leaders; I have discussed above the rule of local rulers and their armies. On the other hand it is clear that Chaghatay emirs held command over a number of local troops. The soldiers of Khorasan, for instance, although sometimes under their own leaders, were also conscripted and led by Chaghatay emirs.[55] On the Indian campaign, the Chaghatay emir ᶜAlī Sulṭān Tovachï was in charge of the footmen of Khorasan.[56] Similarly, on the campaign in Syria there is mention of an emir called ᶜAbd al-Raḥmān, *tovachï* of the foot army.[57] There may also have been a special section of the army consisting of soldiers from the settled regions; Jalāl Islām, an emir who for a time headed Temür's *dīwān*, was at his removal from this post appointed as head of the Tajik forces.[58]

The conscription of foreign troops directly into Temür's army served not only to increase the number of troops at his command, but also to increase his control over local rulers who might formerly have conscripted the same forces. Rulers within the conquered provinces, though left in charge of their territories and part of their former troops, now had a much smaller reserve of manpower on which to draw. Many of the tribal peoples who had formerly been available to them were part of Temür's army. The regional armies of conquered areas might serve either in the *cherik* troops attached to Chaghatay *darughas* or in special forces directly attached to Temür's army. While local rulers within Temür's dominions could maintain their positions, their ability to expand their forces was severely limited.

The nomads of the conquered regions

So far in discussing the rulers of the lands Temür conquered I have examined the settled leaders and their followers. Temür also conquered large areas inhabited primarily by nomads such as the Qipchaq Steppe and Moghulistan, and the Middle East at this time also contained sizeable enclaves of tribal, nomadic or semi-nomadic peoples. These regions presented a more difficult challenge to Temür's rule; they were harder both to control and to exploit. Temür had no consistent policy towards nomads and tribes. Many he raided, some he transplanted, and some he seems to have left untouched.

Temür did not court the nomads he came across on his conquests; indeed he was often harsher to them than he was to settled dynasties. In dealing with the large nomadic confederations of the Jalayir, Aqqoyunlu and Qaraqoyunlu he made no attempt to win over individual tribes from them to add to his own armies. Instead he dealt directly with the leaders of these confederations, taking over those of their territories he wanted to incorporate, and plundering others. A few emirs from these groups came into Temür's service, but most remained with their former masters.

In discussing the tribes and nomads of the areas Temür conquered, we should recognize first that we are dealing with groups of different types – from the Turco-Mongolian tribes of Moghulistan to the probably semi-nomadic tribes of Luristan – and second that we know very little about many of them. Since a detailed investigation of all these peoples would be too long a project, I shall not here go beyond a brief discussion of those central to the history of Temür's reign. Many of the tribes or tribal peoples of the regions that Temür incorporated seem to have had at that time relatively little power; they are mentioned only as a unit, and their influence apparently did not extend beyond local politics. One can take as examples the Khalaj Turks of Jibal, the Baluch in Khorasan, and perhaps also the Saki and Feili tribes of Khuzistan.[59]

In western and southern Iran Temür had to deal with tribes of Lurs and Kurds, most of them under the control of their hereditary dynasties: the atabegs of Luristan – Pīr Aḥmad of Lur-i Buzurg, and ᶜIzz al-Dīn of Lur-i Kuchik – and Malik ᶜIzz al-Dīn Shīr Kurd, all of whom I have mentioned above. In addition to these there were three large nomad confederations which had arisen on the decline of Mongol power in Iran: the Jalayirids under Sulṭān Aḥmad b. Uways, based in Baghdad, and the two Turkmen confederations of the Qaraqoyunlu and Aqqoyunlu, vying for power in northwestern Iran. Finally there were the great Turco-Mongolian nomad powers of the Dasht-i Qipchaq and Moghulistan whom Temür fought repeatedly but never removed from power.

Certain tribal peoples, especially the smaller ones, Temür could simply leave unmolested and conscript into his armies when he needed them, as rulers of the same areas had often done before him. This he did for instance with the Ghurs and the mountain population of Gharjistan in Khorasan, who now became part of Temür's Khorasanian army.[60] In the region of Sawa, Qum and Kashan Temür conscripted the tribes of Arabs and Khalaj in order to put down a rebellion in Mazandaran in 806/1403–4.[61]

Most tribes and nomads mentioned in accounts of Temür's campaigns however were being plundered by the Timurid army. In Khuzistan Temür's troops raided the Saki or Sulaki and Feili tribes and the nomads of the Shushtar region; in Syria they went against the Turkmen confederation of Dhū'l-Qadr, and they undertook raids also against the Oyirats in ᶜIraq and the nomads near Baghdad, Mardin, and Ras al-ᶜAyn.[62] During the campaigns in Rum and the Qipchaq steppe, Temür took the opportunity to plunder numerous tribes.[63] These raids were probably undertaken to replenish the livestock of Temür's army, and the sources often explicitly mention the seizure of animals.[64] Temür's campaigns were arduous and sometimes fought under conditions highly destructive to livestock. Large numbers of animals died, especially during the expeditions Temür undertook against his northern neighbors.[65] Temür's was a nomad army, accompanied by the wives and children of its soldiers and requiring large quantities of food. To provision it he had to renew his stock by taking animals from the nomads he encountered along the way.

Temür moved large numbers of Chaghatay nomads into the territories he conquered, and stationed them there as garrison forces. They were thus competing with local nomads for available pasture. This may be one reason why Temür transported large numbers of nomads from the lands he conquered, to resettle in Transoxiana and on its northern borders. He achieved this often quite brutally, and it could cost many lives. The best known example is the transplantation of the Qaratatars from Rum to Transoxiana; according to the histories Temür forced thirty or forty thousand households to move. They rebelled on the way and were slaughtered in large numbers.[66] Temür also transported some of the nomads he had conquered on his campaign in the Qipchaq steppe, and many from Azerbaijan and ᶜIraq.[67]

Small groups of nomads Temür could either conscript or raid but larger nomad powers proved more resistant. His campaigns against his northern neighbors, especially those against the Golden Horde, were indeed successful; he defeated his opponents when they were willing to engage in battle and returned with massive amounts of booty. But he annexed very few territories in these regions and seems also to have attracted few new followers, despite the stunning successes of his armies.

This is particularly surprising in the case of the eastern Chaghadayids and Khorezmians, who were closely related to the Chaghatays in tradition, and had been actively involved in the affairs of the Ulus Chaghatay before Temür's rise to power. In spite of these links Temür's army apparently contained few Moghul or Khorezmian emirs, even though some of those who did join Temür rose to high positions. The actual number of Moghul and Khorezmian emirs is difficult to judge because they are much harder to identify than those of settled regions.[68] The sources mention an emir called Yayïq Ṣūfī, almost certainly one of the Sufi dynasty of Khorezm, who had been given the *tümen* of his region, and according to the histories was one of the greatest emirs in the right wing of Temür's army. He rebelled in 796/1393–4, and was imprisoned.[69] Two easily identifiable Moghul commanders are found in Temür's armies, equal apparently to most Chaghatay emirs. One of them was Buyan Temür b. Bekichek Chete. He was prominent in ᶜUmar Shaykh's army and was made *atabeg* or guardian of ᶜUmar Shaykh's son Iskandar.[70] Another Moghul was Amir Quṭb al-Dīn, brother of Qamar al-Dīn Chete, who was in Amīrānshāh's *tümen* at the siege of Takrit in 796/1393.[71] There may have been more Moghuls than this, but the histories do not identify them directly. Temür's army certainly did contain contingents of soldiers from Khorezm and Moghulistan, but most of these may have been prisoners of war, rather than troops campaigning under their own leaders.[72]

From the Golden Horde also Temür apparently attracted few new recruits, although some prominent emirs did join his forces temporarily.[73] The most notable of these was Tokhtamïsh. Three others were Künche Oghlan, Temür Qutluq and Edigü, all of whom deserted Tokhtamïsh to join Temür in or before 790/1388, but in the course of Temür's campaign against the Ulus Jochi in 793/1391 they deserted Temür and returned to the Golden Horde.[74] Thus even the few emirs that Temür did attract from the nomad khanates often proved temporary and unreliable subjects.

Temür's dealings with the nomad confederations within the Middle East – the Jalayirids, Qaraqoyunlu and Aqqoyunlu – were not very successful. Despite numerous raids and campaigns against them he could do no more than displace them temporarily; after his death they quickly regained their strength. He drove the Jalayirid leader, Sulṭān Aḥmad b. Uways, out of Sultaniyya and Tabriz in 786–7/1384–5, and in 795/1393 out of Baghdad, where Temür then installed his own governor. Nevertheless Sulṭān Aḥmad found refuge first in Egypt and then with the Ottomans, and he was able to retake Baghdad for a short time during Temür's life and soon again after his death.[75]

The Qaraqoyunlu, based in eastern Anatolia and parts of Azerbaijan, remained consistently hostile to Temür as he was towards them. Although he undertook several campaigns against them, he only pushed them back temporarily. Both Qara Muḥammad and his successor Qara Yūsuf resisted Temür stubbornly and both succeeded in retaking Tabriz during Temür's absence – Qara Yūsuf indeed several times.[76] Qara Yūsuf also succeeded in capturing and imprisoning one of Temür's emirs, and one of his foremost local allies.[77] Later on Temür's invasion of Anatolia he took refuge first with the Ottoman sultan Bāyazīd, then in ᶜIraq with Sulṭān Aḥmad Jalayir, and finally in Damascus. Soon after Temür's death he retook his old territories in eastern Anatolia and Azerbaijan.[78]

With the Turkmen Aqqoyunlu confederation, much less powerful at this time, Temür had relatively friendly relations. Qara ᶜUthmān, who was the greatest power within the confederation, chose to submit to Temür about 1399–1400, largely out of fear of the Ottomans whom he encouraged Temür to attack. He served Temür at the head of his own army in Syria and in return Temür granted the city of Amid to Qara ᶜUthmān's son Ibrāhīm.[79] The Aqqoyunlu however did not become an integral part of Temür's army; like the settled rulers who submitted to Temür they joined him only on campaigns close to their own region. Their attraction to the Timurids stemmed primarily from the weakness of their position between the Ottomans, the Mamluks and the Qaraqoyunlu. It was the Aqqoyunlu leadership which chose to ally with Temür; Qara ᶜUthmān used this alliance to enhance his position within the confederation, and the power of the confederation in relation to its rivals. Temür therefore left the three tribal confederations of western Iran no less powerful at the end of his reign than they had been before; the Aqqoyunlu profited from its alliance with Temür, and the Jalayirids and Qaraqoyunlu suffered temporary setbacks but were not destroyed.

Temür's failure to subjugate the nomad confederations of western Iran was not due to insufficient military power. He defeated both the Jalayirids and the Qaraqoyunlu several times, and he succeeded in capturing some of the nomads of the Jalayirid confederation, whom he transported to Transoxiana.[80] Nor does his inability to subdue the nomads along his path suggest a loss of nomadism among his own following. Clavijo gives clear evidence, cited in Chapter 2, that the Chaghatays were still nomadic at the end of Temür's life. What made it difficult for Temür to weaken other nomad powers was a lack not of nomadism but of tribalism. To destroy the nomad confederations he fought, military defeat was not sufficient; it was also necessary to remove their support by attracting away from them some of the tribes that made them up, and this Temür could not do. Membership in Temür's army offered few attractions to nomads from outside the Ulus Chaghatay.

Dynasties with tribally organized armies, like the Safavids and the Aqqoyunlu, could swell their numbers by winning over tribes from their rivals and expand their power through the incorporation of new tribes as well as new territories.[81] The Timurid army however could not attract tribes because the army that Temür led, although it contained tribes, was no longer tribally organized. Temür had not won over the tribes of the Ulus Chaghatay but suppressed them. He had been able to do this partly because these tribes had lost much of their mobility. Temür's rule was too strong to permit tribes to function as autonomous units; new tribes or groups could not enter his army as confederates but only as subordinates. This prospect was unlikely to appeal to the members of a tribal confederation which allowed considerable autonomy to the tribal leaders within it. Temür did not incorporate other nomadic tribes fully into his army. While some groups without significant power, like the Arabs and Khalaj of Qum and Kashan, and the Aqqoyunlu, did serve for a time in Temür's armies, they did so only as temporary troops.

Since Temür could not lure away tribes from the large nomad confederations, he could not permanently subjugate them, or even weaken them significantly. It is probably for this reason also that the large nomad powers he fought – the Moghuls and the Golden Horde – contributed so few emirs to Temür's army, despite the relatively high position he granted to those who did join him. Most of those who did join him moreover found little satisfaction and did not remain loyal.

In his great conquests Temür ravaged innumerable cities and regions, but destroyed very few dynasties or tribes. It was only the most powerful polities in the lands he conquered that he could not accommodate: among the settled dynasties the Karts and the Muzaffarids, whom he eliminated, and among the nomadic ones the Jalayirids and the Qaraqoyunlu, whom he pushed back but could not destroy.

The local rulers whom Temür subjugated owed him military service, but few became real members of his army or achieved power within it. Those whom he did favor were those close to the Ulus Chaghatay in geography rather than in culture – the emirs of Khorasan, Sistan, and Mazandaran who had dealt with the Ulus Chaghatay before the beginning of Temür's great conquests and were thus familiar to Temür and his followers. The rulers of more distant territories remained outsiders within Temür's armies even when campaigning beside his emirs, and led a highly precarious existence.

Temür incorporated many troops from the conquered regions directly into his army. His emirs conscripted and led local troops with which they sometimes campaigned quite far afield, and the *darughas* of cities commanded, along with their Chaghatay troops, some locally conscripted militias. The smaller tribes and mountain peoples who had served in the armies of earlier dynasties now served Temür. The recruitment and use of regional troops did more than swell the ranks of Temür's army; it also removed from the grasp of local rulers much of the manpower on which they might have drawn. While they were left in command of their armies, their opportunities to expand them were much restricted.

Temür's treatment of subjugated rulers thus resembled in many ways his handling of the tribes within the Ulus Chaghatay, differing primarily in his greater harshness to the newly conquered peoples. Like the tribes, local dynasties were left in place but robbed of much of their political, regional and military power. Their leaders were repeatedly replaced, their lands constricted, and their military manpower limited. In structure Temür had changed relatively little and had merely added a new level of command at the top. This however was sufficient to keep the conquered areas under his control for the duration of his reign, and to keep their rulers in a clearly subservient position.

Temür's new settled subjects were vulnerable because their resources were stationary and could be taken over by conquest. They were furthermore easy to locate and to punish in case of misbehavior. For them moreover Temür's rule had certain advantages. He offered a valuable opportunity for younger brothers or deposed rulers to gain power, and the unification of the Middle East clearly could benefit urban and commercial classes. In any case, submission was advisable, since Temür could not be resisted.

Foreign nomad populations had much less to offer Temür, and on their side at once less to fear and less to gain. Instead of providing grain, they competed for pasture. Since they could retreat they could not be subjugated by force, and while they could be punished, this was a costly process. Most nomads served Temür simply as a useful source of free livestock gained on plundering expeditions or of moveable manpower. Temür also had few advantages to offer nomad tribes outside the Ulus Chaghatay, since he was unwilling to incorporate them fully into his army. Moreover he made no effort to attract the nomads of the regions he conquered.

Temür then was not able to deal successfully with the large nomad confederations of western Iran. To weaken these he would have had to attract away some of their membership, and this he could not do. His army was not tribally organized, and his rule was detrimental to tribal power. New tribes therefore could be accommodated only in a clearly subordinate position, and were more likely to join the army through coercion than through attraction. His victories over his nomad opponents remained temporary and could not last beyond his death. The large areas of nomad population in Moghulistan and the Dasht-i Qipchaq he conquered but never incorporated. Though he might push the Turkmen confederations of the Middle East out of their eastern territories, he could not co-opt their manpower as he had done that of the settled leaders. Settled populations Temür could subdue and make use of with relatively little change, but nomadic tribal populations had to be robbed of tribal power before Temür could safely use them. This he could do to the nomads of the Ulus Chaghatay, but not to those in his new territories.

CHAPTER 6

Structure and function in Temür's administration

Temür spent almost all of his long career on campaign, and did not attempt to construct a comprehensive new governmental structure. Like other premodern leaders, he ruled through people rather than institutions and used men according to their personality and relation to himself. His government was that of an individual, who interfered at will in the affairs of his subordinates and demanded direct and complete loyalty from his subjects – loyalty not to his office, nor to his government, but to his person. For the period of his life this administration served its purpose well. He was able to govern his territories, to reward his men with rank and power as well as booty, and to control both his army and the subject population under him.

In its outlines Temür's administration was similar to those of the other nomad polities which preceded and followed his. He had inherited two well developed systems of government – one Turco-Mongolian and one Arabo-Persian. These two he combined and adapted to his own needs. He made use of the scribes and the bureaucracy of his settled territories to administer the lands which he had conquered, while imposing above this bureaucracy another administration organized in the Turco-Mongolian tradition and staffed by members of the Chaghatay ruling elite. The ranks and offices found within Temür's government are similar to those found in other nomadic polities of the period – the Ilkhanids, the Golden Horde, the Aqqoyunlu and the Qaraqoyunlu. The nomenclature of Timurid administration is therefore familiar and well attested. An examination of the functions of the offices discussed in the sources shows moreover considerable agreement with information on the same offices in other polities.

Identifying the offices of Temür's administration will not explain how it worked. Despite its developed nomenclature this administration remained loose and unarticulated. The Timurid histories do not illuminate the workings of even the main institutions within Temür's government, while the perquisites and functions of offices are often unclear. It is difficult to determine the range of responsibilities attached to a given office, and it is even more difficult to discover how positions shaped the careers of the men who held them. This is due partly to lack of information, but also to the fact that the formal structure of this administration did not determine how it functioned.

In trying to analyze Temür's methods of control one must examine not one system, but two. The first is the formal one, mentioned explicitly though usually briefly in the historical sources. This consists of a number of offices designed to perform a specific set of tasks and to define the spheres and activities of groups within Temür's government. Behind this system lies another one, based on the same offices, but used for a different purpose. Temür had not only to govern his extensive realm, he also had to reward and to control his ruling class. His elite had to be repaid for their support, and the granting of offices in his administration was an important element of this reward. An office presented to its holder not only a set of duties and an opportunity for income, but also a certain amount and type of power. This was an important consideration in an army and administration as loosely structured as Temür's. If the ruling class was not to threaten Temür's position it had to be controlled, and this too was done partly through the judicious allocation of ranks and offices.

It is the dynamics of Temür's government which form the central concern of this chapter. The structure of his administration – its ranks and offices and its formal organization – are described at the end of the book in Appendix C. Here I shall examine the way the administration worked, particularly in relation to the ruling class itself. The first question to pose is the relevance of the administration's structure to its functioning. It is important to determine whether the actual working of the administration adhered to the divisions drawn up among different spheres and offices. A second aspect of the question is how the formal structure served to define the actions of the ruling class – to what extent the office a man held determined his activities and the shape of his career.

The second question I have posed is how Temür used his administration to enhance his own position and to manipulate his ruling class. Here one should regard an office within Temür's administration as an opportunity for wealth, power or access to the sovereign, given as a reward for service. In this aspect of his administration Temür showed a definite regard for system, and it is possible to discern regular patterns of allocation, indicating a clear and consistent set of concerns.

The relevance of structure

The fundamental division within Temür's government was between the settled and Turco-Mongolian spheres. In the sources on Temür's administration this distinction is clearly drawn; there was one set of offices for the Persian bureaucrats who served him and another for his Turco-Mongolian followers.[1] As in other nomad states, military matters, honorary court offices and the administration of Chaghatay affairs belonged to the Turkic sphere, while the settled bureaucrats continued to administer financial affairs, tax collection, and much of local government. Temür's administration contained two central *dīwāns*: the *dīwān-i aᶜlā*, within which the Persian bureaucrats worked, and the Chaghatay *dīwān*, known as the *dīwān-i buzurg*. These two *dīwāns* were not parallel institutions. The *dīwān-i aᶜlā* was an administrative *dīwān* with wide responsibilities, while the *dīwān-i buzurg* seems to have functioned principally as a tribunal for Chaghatay emirs.

In Temür's government, as in those of most nomad dynasties, it is impossible to find a clear distinction between civil and military affairs, or to identify the Persian bureaucracy solely with civil, and the Turco-Mongolian solely with military government. It is in fact difficult to define the sphere of either side of the administration and we find Persians and Chaghatays sharing many tasks. (In discussing the settled bureaucracy and the people who worked within it I use the word Persian in a cultural rather than ethnological sense. In almost all the territories which Temür incorporated into his realm, Persian was the primary language of administration and literary culture. Thus the language of the settled *dīwān* was Persian, and its scribes had to be thoroughly adept in Persian culture, whatever their ethnic origin.) Temür's Chaghatay emirs were often involved in civil and provincial administration and even in financial affairs, traditionally the province of the Persian bureaucracy.

The lack of differentiation between the settled and Chaghatay arms of the government was due in part to the Chaghatays' familiarity with settled culture. The involvement of Chaghatay emirs with settled and particularly Persian culture even before the beginning of Temür's conquests shows clearly in the Timurid histories. The tribes of the Ulus Chaghatay had depended for part of their wealth on the taxes they collected from their settled subjects, and the Turco-Mongolian emirs of the Ulus Chaghatay had maintained close contact with the settled *ᶜulamā'*, whom they used as envoys and mediators in both internal and external disputes.[2] Some of Temür's emirs moreover were themselves adept in Persian culture. One of his earliest and most powerful followers, Ḥājjī Sayf al-Dīn, wrote poetry both in Persian and in Turkish, and Temür's grandson, Khalīl Sulṭān, studied poetry with the Persian poet ᶜIsmat Allāh Bukhārī.[3] Temür and his followers therefore were fully capable of understanding the needs and uses of their settled subjects. The administration of settled territory was not new to them and they were capable of supervising most aspects of civil and even of financial administration. They needed Persian scribes primarily for the technical side of their administration, which required specific skills in writing or accounting.

The close connection of Persian and Chaghatay personnel is seen in the *dīwān-i aᶜlā*, which was the Persian *dīwān*, but in whose affairs Chaghatay emirs were intimately involved. There are several references in the sources to the *amīrs* of the *dīwān-i aᶜlā* which apply almost certainly to Chaghatay commanders, including some of Temür's most important followers.[4]

The collection of taxes, a central concern of the *dīwān-i aᶜlā*, provides a good illustration of the way in which tasks were shared between Chaghatay and Persian personnel. The first tax to be collected from a conquered city was the ransom money, or *māl-i amān*. Usually high-ranking Chaghatay emirs took charge of this and sometimes no Persian agents are mentioned.[5] In other cases the emirs worked together with two or three of the highest bureaucrats of the *dīwān*. At Damascus in 803/1400–1 for instance, the collection of money was organized by three emirs – Shaykh Nūr al-Dīn, Shāhmalik, and Allāhdād – with two scribes, Masᶜūd Simnānī and Jalāl Islām. These five men sat together by the one open gate of the city, registering the money brought them by the *muḥaṣṣils* who worked inside the walls.[6] A second source of wealth from newly conquered cities was the city treasuries. It was apparently the especial task of the Persian scribes in the *dīwān-i aᶜlā* to appropriate and register this wealth. The collection of regular taxes from the provinces of Temür's realm was also done by both Chaghatays and members of the settled bureaucracy, although in this case most usually they did so separately. Of the men sent to oversee the collection of taxes in a province, we know of three who were Chaghatays and four who were Persians.[7]

After the collection of taxes the most important function of the settled bureaucracy was the inspection of local *dīwāns* in Temür's provinces, and this too the Persian bureaucrats shared with Temür's Chaghatay emirs. It is not clear whether there were regular tours of inspection to provincial *dīwāns*, but we do know that Kerman at least received periodic visits. These were sent from the central *dīwān*, and each delegation consisted of one Chaghatay emir and one Persian official.[8] Delegations investigating specific problems often contained both emirs and scribes. Thus for instance in 802/1399 when Temür heard of Amīrānshāh's misbehavior he sent an emir and a scribe to settle the financial and other problems involved.[9] Likewise when Pīr Muḥammad b. ᶜUmar Ṣhaykh, then governor of Fars, failed to go on campaigns as ordered, both Temür's follower Allāhdād and the prominent Persian bureaucrat Muẓaffar al-Dīn Naṭanzī went to look into the affair.[10]

In other cases, sometimes important ones, Persian scribes undertook such missions alone. When Edigü Barlas, governor of Kerman, was discovered embezzling local funds agents of the *dīwān-i aᶜlā* were sent to right matters, without apparently any emir as escort. In the end however, the matter was settled privately; Edigü's wife, who was Temür's cousin, repaid the money herself.[11] Thus in the investigation of abuses the Persian scribes seem to have been somewhat more active than the Chaghatays, perhaps because most of the abuses being investigated were financial.

In the allocation of offices, as in the distribution of tasks, the two sides of Temür's government were not entirely separate. Some offices could be held either by scribes or by emirs and some, though they usually belonged to one sphere of government, might occasionally be filled by someone from the other. On occasion Chaghatay emirs held the position of vizier or had power directly over the *dīwān*. We are told for instance that Dawlat Khwāja Ïnaq, probably a *qa'uchin*, and certainly an emir, was vizier and *nāyib*[12] for Amīrānshāh at the time he asserted himself.[13] In Khorasan Temür's emirs apparently oversaw the functioning of the local *dīwān*. Muḥammad Sulṭānshāh is described as administering the *māl-i dīwān* and controlling the appointment and dismissal of its agents. One of those under him was the Persian *ṣāḥib dīwān*.[14] On the other side, the office of *darugha*, entailing military leadership, was normally part of the Chaghatay sphere but on occasion Temür appointed scribal or religious figures to this post. When he was in India for instance, he appointed as *darugha* of Ajodhan a religious scholar, Mawlānā Nāṣir al-Din ᶜUmar, and the son of one of his scribes, Khwāja Maḥmūd Shihāb.[15]

Some of Temür's scribes were also active as military commanders. Mawlānā Nāṣir al-Dīn ᶜUmar, for instance, is mentioned campaigning as well as supervising the *khuṭba* after the conquest of Delhi.[16] The head of Temür's *dīwān*, Khwāja Masᶜūd Simnānī, also apparently took part in the army's campaigns; he was killed by an arrow at the siege of Baghdad in 803/1401.[17] His successor, Jalāl Islām, was just as active in the army as in the chancery. He campaigned with Temür's army in India, and on his dismissal from the *dīwān* was put in charge of the Tajik forces. He was active later on Temür's campaign in Rum, during which he was killed in battle.[18]

The involvement of scribes from the settled bureaucracy in military campaigns was not unique to Temür's army. This seems to have been common practice also under other nomad dynasties. Seljukid viziers accompanied the sultan on military expeditions, and sometimes indeed led such expeditions themselves.[19] Minorsky has noted that the civil dignitaries of the Aqqoyunlu had armed followings, and under the early Safavids Persian viziers sometimes led very important military expeditions.[20]

One can suggest several reasons for the close connection between the Persian and Chaghatay spheres. In the course of a reign spent entirely on campaign, it was natural that all members of government should participate to some extent at least in the military undertaking. Likewise, since Temür's army was much the largest institution under him, it is not surprising that those in it should have been involved also in civil administration. Above all, the Chaghatay emirs whom Temür led were familiar with Persian culture and were able to communicate with the Persians who worked for them. The Persian bureaucrats on their side had had long experience with Turco-Mongolian rulers. There was therefore no obstacle to close cooperation between Chaghatay emirs and Persian bureaucrats.

Just as the division of Temür's administration into two spheres did not in fact entail a strict division of tasks or a separation of Chaghatay and Persian personnel, so the existence of specific offices neither limited nor defined the careers of those who held them. Few positions granted a clear mandate to their holders or gave them a definite and pre-determined place in Temür's administration. The tasks supposedly attached to a specific office might well be undertaken by men who did not hold that position. Emirs assigned to govern cities and districts within Temür's realm continued to campaign in his army, while those assigned to military posts were sometimes involved in the collection of taxes or the restoration of cities.

One would have expected for instance that the *muhrdār*, since he was the keeper of the seal and the official who controlled access to the sovereign, would remain close to Temür but the men who held this office campaigned sometimes at a considerable distance from him.[21] The *darugha*, though appointed to an office which was ostensibly local and fairly stationary, might well continue to be part of the army in its far ranging campaigns. The *darughas* of cities and regions within Temür's realm sometimes left their areas quite soon after their appointments and rejoined Temür in his campaigns. Temüge Qa'uchin for instance became *darugha* of Yazd in 795/1393 and in 796–7/1395–6 left to join Temür's campaign in the Dasht-i Qipchaq.[22] Lālim Bahadur Qa'uchin was appointed *darugha* of Abarquh in Fars in the spring of 795/1393, and participated in the siege of Takrit in ᶜIraq in the fall of that year.[23]

Temür distributed the work at hand to the men who were available and capable, regardless of the positions they held. Thus for instance, although the *darugha* was usually the first official appointed to a newly conquered city, in some cases Temür simply left behind one of his emirs who remained for a few months to organize the city. He charged Mulūk Sabzawārī with the organization of Basra after its conquest, and entrusted Isfahan to Ḥājjī Beg Jawun-i Qurban.[24] The reconstruction of cities, usually part of the *darugha*'s duties, might be assigned to other people. Temür on his way to India for instance left several emirs behind to restore the city of Iryab.[25]

One final example of the freedom with which Temür distributed tasks among his subordinates is the conscription of troops. This was one of the duties of the *tovachï*, and indeed some of the men mentioned conscripting troops did hold that office.[26] At other times however Temür sent out different emirs to gather armies. When Iskandar Shaykhī rebelled in 806/1403 for instance, Temür sent off two of his grandsons with Pīr ᶜAlī Suldus to collect the army of Rayy, and sent Sulaymānshāh to conscript footmen in the area of Qum and Kashan.[27] A little later he dispatched Sulaymānshāh and Miḍrāb b. Chekü Barlas to mobilize the army of Khorasan.[28]

The vagueness of government ranks under Temür, the confusion in the duties attached to offices and the freedom with which Temür assigned tasks to his subordinates need not surprise us. Engaged for the whole of his long career in unending conquests, Temür could hardly be expected to construct a regular and established administrative machinery. The Turco-Mongolian administrative tradition moreover encouraged vague and overlapping spheres of responsibility.[29] Nor would a more formally organized system have enhanced Temür's personal power, as I have attempted to show elsewhere.[30] Temür's administration allowed him to delegate necessary tasks, while retaining control over his subordinates and the functioning of all aspects of his government. No office or task was sufficiently routine to escape the sovereign's attentions, and he was free to use the people under him according to their individual abilities. The formal structure of Temür's administration did not determine the working of his government. Instead it was an instrument to be manipulated or ignored by the sovereign in person and at will.

The control of the Persian bureaucracy

The lack of articulation noticeable in Temür's administration does not mean that he governed without a system. We must remember that for Temür's lifetime his government achieved its goals; he kept firm control both over the territories he governed and over the people beneath him. This was a major accomplishment which could not be achieved without definite and well-conceived policies.

Temür had two sets of people to control within his government, Persians and Chaghatays, and he used different methods to limit the powers of each. The Persian bureaucrats serving Temür were largely without military resources, most of which belonged either to the Chaghatay army or to local rulers, but they were not without potential sources of strength. This class wielded considerable power under the rule of many nomad dynasties. They had the advantage of specialized training, of a separate independent network of influence and patronage, and sometimes of direct ties to the people they governed.

In this book I am concerned largely with the ruling elite, and thus will assess primarily the power and influence that the Persian bureaucrats wielded within the central government. Here the central *dīwān* was the crucial institution, and its scribes the major actors. The position of local *dīwāns* in the provinces of Temür's dominions and the extent of their control over the local population is a question of equal importance, but one which is much more difficult to answer with the evidence that is available to us. I shall deal here with the power they derived from local sources primarily as this affected their relation with Temür and his followers.

It is clear that Temür's Persian administration held an inferior position. We cannot even discover who headed the Persian *dīwān* for much of Temür's reign. Temür did not feel dependent on his Persian bureaucrats, and he used his Chaghatay emirs, conversant with Persian tradition and settled ways, to constrict their power and limit their independence. In his book on the viziers of Middle Eastern dynasties, the *Dastūr al-wuzarā'*,

Khwāndamīr wrote that viziers under the Timurids held exceptionally little power. He stated that the Timurid sultans were quick to appoint and dismiss viziers, and often appointed men of inferior abilities. This seems to have been particularly true in the time of Temür himself. The biographies Khwāndamīr gives for Temür's viziers are notably short and incomplete compared with those of later Timurid rulers.[31]

There are several reasons for the relatively low position of Temür's viziers. The attitude of Temür and his followers towards the Persians, combining familiarity with contempt, led them to constrict the role of Persian bureaucrats. The epithet "*Tājīk-mizāj*," "Persian-natured," is found in the histories as an expression of contempt.[32] When princes of the royal house misbehaved, as occasionally happened, the responsibility was quickly assigned to the Persians in their entourage; the influence of these corrupt people was seen as the cause for Amīrānshāh's excesses when he "went insane," for the failure of Pīr Muḥammad b. ᶜUmar Shaykh to go on campaign as ordered in 802/1399–1400, and for the defection of Temür's grandson Sulṭān Ḥusayn to the enemy at Damascus in 803/1400–1. In the cases of Amīrānshāh and Pīr Muḥammad, several Persian courtiers were executed.[33] Temür also did not hesitate to change decisions made by the *dīwān-i aᶜlā*, as is shown by his decision to lower the tribute that the *dīwān* had set for the ruler of Kashmir.[34]

The officials of the central *dīwān*, which moved with Temür and was therefore constantly under his eye, seem to have held particularly little power. There is no indication that the viziers or the *ṣāḥib dīwān* had any influence over Temür's policy towards the settled peoples. The heads of the *dīwān* whom we know about are mentioned almost exclusively in connection with the collection of ransom money or the registration of wealth taken from the treasuries of conquered cities.

The heads of the provincial *dīwāns*, where they were not supervised by powerful emirs, probably had greater possibilities for independence. They had some important sources of strength. The political fragmentation of Iran before Temür's conquest had led to regional administrations, and probably made it difficult to centralize the settled bureaucracy. It is clear from even the scanty evidence available that local bureaucrats could have considerable local influence. Two provincial bureaucrats are mentioned in terms which suggest that they held a high position; Khwāja Muẓaffar Naṭanzī is referred to as *ṣāḥib-i ikhtiyār*, "preeminent," in Persian ᶜIraq, and Khwāja Jalāl al-Dīn, the *ṣāḥib dīwān* in Samarqand, had his orders obeyed throughout all regions.[35]

This potential for independence seems to have been of concern to Temür and he placed a number of checks on the power of these bureaucrats. They had above them the provincial governor with a large following of Chaghatay emirs, many of whom might be involved in civil government. Each major city in addition had a *darugha*, almost always Chaghatay, closely involved with civil as well as military government, and often connected with the local *dīwāns*.[36] Furthermore the heads of the provincial *dīwāns*, though in charge of financial administration, did not themselves control the collection of taxes. Tax officials were sent out directly from the *dīwān-i aʿlā*, and probably served to exert some central control over local *dīwāns*. The people who actually collected taxes were the *muḥaṣṣils*, most of whom apparently were Chaghatays. It is not clear to whom the *muḥaṣṣils* were answerable. In the case of Khorasan they seem to have been appointed by Temür's emirs, Ḥājjī Sayf al-Dīn and Muḥammad Sulṭānshāh, as overseers of the *dīwān*, but the administration of Khorasan may have been exceptional. Judging from the descriptions given of the *muḥaṣṣils*' actions elsewhere it seems probable that little control was exerted over them from any quarter (see Appendix C).

In this way the heads of provincial *dīwāns* were limited by the tax collectors sent out from the central *dīwān* to supervise them and both sets of scribes were placed between two Chaghatay layers of administration, the *darughas* and the *muḥaṣṣils*, neither subject to their control. Temür checked tendencies towards power and independence in the provinces of his realm also through a policy of inspection and punishment, directed particularly against the provincial *dīwāns*. Whereas the most severe punishment meted out to the heads of the central *dīwān* seems to have been dismissal or imprisonment,[37] members of local *dīwāns* were not infrequently executed.[38] Temür showed considerable interest in discovering local abuses, especially at the end of his reign. In 806/1403–4, he requested tales of oppression in the provinces from the *ʿulamā'* in his *majlis* and sent representatives of the religious classes along with the *dīwān* scribes to all the regions of his realm to investigate and punish abuses.[39]

This action was not without consequences. In the same year, Temür ordered that Quṭb al-Dīn Quramī, apparently head of the *dīwān* of Shiraz, be imprisoned and tortured for extortion from the population.[40] The next year, when Temür headed back towards Transoxiana, he sent Khwāja Fakhr al-Dīn Aḥmad ahead to Herat to investigate and punish members of the *dīwān*, with drastic results.[41] On his arrival in Samarqand he executed three members of his *dīwān*, two for administrative abuses and one for miscalculation in the building of a mosque.[42] It is significant, considering the involvement of Chaghatay officials at various levels of provincial administration, that it was almost always the Persian bureaucrats singled out for punishment. We know of no Chaghatay *muḥaṣṣils* who were punished for misbehavior, and of only one *darugha*.[42]

Although Temür may have permitted in his Chaghatay officials what he punished in his Persian bureaucrats, he probably did not have to fabricate the charges he levelled against local *dīwāns*. The members of Temür's settled bureaucracy were placed in positions which facilitated extortion; they were assigned the task of exploiting the subject peoples, rather than protecting or benefiting them. The imposition of taxes, confiscation and registration of the contents of local treasuries, and the investigation and punishment of local abuses were none of them activities designed to endear Temür's bureaucrats to the local population. It is clear that Temür and his followers not only allowed but sometimes encouraged Persian bureaucrats to overburden the people under their charge. In describing the conquest of Syria, Ibn ᶜArabshāh gives a list of local people whom Temür recruited to squeeze wealth from the population.[44] Temür also continued the Mongol custom of expecting officials to present lavish gifts to the sovereign, a practice which naturally encouraged corruption.[45] It was in fact in connection with the extortion of wealth for a gift that Temür punished the head of the Shiraz *dīwān*, Quṭb al-Dīn Quramī.[46]

This arrangement was not unique under Temür, and there is no evidence that it was a conscious policy. Nonetheless it probably did serve to prevent the settled bureaucrats from gaining power or prestige through the backing of the local populations. In this respect Temür's administration resembled that of the Ilkhans under whom also the Persian *dīwān* served its own interests and those of the sovereign at the expense of the people.[47]

It was Temür who took the role of champion of his subjects, punishing the Persian *dīwāns* for their excesses, something which he did publicly and with *éclat*. The task of repairing the ravages of Temür's campaigns went to Temür's emirs and his army. Temür was actively interested in both agriculture and trade. His army undertook the rebuilding of cities, the construction of new buildings, and large-scale agricultural works, while his *darughas* and governors were often assigned as one of their duties the restoration of the regions under them. Temür and his princes had large irrigation canals dug at Qarabagh, in Khorasan, and near Kabul, had forts with surrounding irrigation works built on the Turkistan border at Shahrukhiyya, Ashbara and Bash Khamra, and undertook numerous other smaller construction projects such as mosques, city palaces, and city walls. The work on these projects was usually divided among several Chaghatay emirs, sometimes *tovachïs*, supervising the work of the soldiers under them.[48]

The Persian bureaucracy on the other hand seems rarely to have sponsored construction of any kind during Temür's reign. Only twice are Persian scribes mentioned in connection with building projects undertaken at Temür's orders. Jalāl Islām, a scribe who was also active as a military commander, was assigned with Shāhmalik to repair the mosque at Iryab, on the way to India.[49] The *ṣāḥib dīwān* of Samarqand was involved in the building of a mosque while Temür was on his seven-year campaign; he made a mistake in the building and was executed as a result.[50] The histories of Yazd, in which the construction of buildings is very fully documented, show a striking lack of activity during Temür's reign, contrasted to active periods of building right before and after, when notables and civil dignitaries often ordered the construction of buildings.[51] The one major edifice built by an individual in Yazd during Temür's lifetime, the Dār al-Fatḥ which Ghiyāth al-Dīn Sālār

Simnānī constructed, is mentioned not only in the histories of Yazd but in most of the general histories of the period, something which suggests that this was no ordinary action.[52] The histories mention no other building projects by Persian dignitaries. Thus the Persians under Temür did not help to restore the cities and countryside ravaged by Temür's army. Nor apparently did they play a role in protecting the population from the depredations of an alien ruling group.[53] Quite the contrary, they were assigned the task of exploiting the subject population. When they carried this out with too much zeal, Temür investigated and punished them, with fitting pomp and publicity.

A comparison of Temür's bureaucrats with those who served other similar dynasties – the Seljukids, Mongols and Safavids – serves both to emphasize the weakness of Temür's Persian viziers and to clarify the reasons for their position. Under the other dynasties I have mentioned, the vizier or *ṣāḥib dīwān* usually held a prominent and powerful position. Nor was this true only after the dynasty had become established; many of the viziers of dynastic founders, the Seljukid Toghrïl Beg, the Ilkhan Hülegü and the Safavid Shāh Ismāᶜīl, were powerful men.[54]

These dynasties allowed power to their Persian officials for various reasons. The Seljukids and the Mongols, neither very familiar with the culture and politics of the Middle East, recruited the bureaucrats of Khorasan and relied on them both to administer the settled population and to negotiate with local powers. The Seljukids, already Muslims, were considerably less alien to their new dominions than were the Ilkhans. Nonetheless their sultans' desire to adopt the Perso-Islamic monarchical and governmental tradition and to base their legitimacy on Middle Eastern traditions ensured their viziers a crucial and powerful position.[55] The early Ilkhans had little desire to adapt themselves to the Middle East and based their dynastic claims on Mongol traditions. They were however much in need of knowledgeable administrators for their new territory and relied heavily on their Persian officials, appointing them not only to financial positions but also to governorships of large provinces.[56]

The Safavids promoted the power of their Persian bureaucrats for other reasons. Like the Timurids, they rose to power within the Middle East and were fully conversant with its culture and politics. They did not therefore need to rely heavily on the settled bureaucracy to administer their territories and this is reflected in the relatively low position held by a number of viziers under Shāh Ismāᶜīl.[57] They did however need their Persian officials for another purpose: to counter the power of the tribal chiefs who led most of the troops in their army. It was for this reason that in 1508 Shāh Ismāᶜīl began to fill the office of *wakīl* – vice-regent for civil, religious and sometimes military affairs – with Persian officials rather than Turkmen emirs. The policy of promoting the power of Persian bureaucrats over the less controllable Turkmen tribal chiefs continued under Shāh Ismāᶜīl's successors.[58]

There were then several different ways in which nomads might use settled officials, all of which promoted the power of the Persian bureaucrats. Scribes might be used to administer settled territories whose needs and possibilities the nomads understood little about. They might likewise be used to construct or negotiate a position and legitimation for the ruling dynasty within the traditions of its new dominions. Finally they, and the bureaucratic system they staffed, could be used to counteract the power of tribal chiefs.

Temür however needed the settled officials for none of these purposes. He and his followers were familiar enough with the territories they conquered to oversee their administration themselves. He based his dynastic legitimacy less on Middle Eastern traditions than on those of the Mongol empire within which he had come to power and whose attitudes towards settled people he and his followers had inherited. Nor did Temür need to use his Persian bureaucracy to decrease the power of his nomadic followers, since he had already devised other and effective means to control them. What remained for Temür's Persian officials therefore was a relatively minor and constricted role: the technical administration of financial and local affairs. Such a position gave them little opportunity for significant power or prestige within the central government.

The Chaghatay sphere

To control the Persian bureaucrats who served him Temür used his Chaghatay followers, but he was not content to maintain the supremacy of nomad over settled. He wanted also to preserve his personal supremacy, and here his Chaghatay elite was as much a threat as an asset. Temür's Chaghatay followers, though more closely under his supervision than many of his Persian bureaucrats, also had greater opportunities to amass personal power. The tribal political system had been pushed to one side and it had not been replaced with a fully functional alternative system. The lack of articulation in Temür's government – the lack of separation between different offices and tasks, and the resulting overlap in spheres of responsibility – served to enhance Temür's personal power. It could do so however, only if he used it with care and forethought.

Temür's army in particular could pose a threat to his supremacy, since there was no institutional check on the power of military commanders. Chaghatay soldiers were mustered and equipped not by the central government, but by the emirs who led them. Under these circumstances it was unsafe to entrust great power to any one individual, even among those most faithful to Temür. Even less was it desirable to build up a class of people possessing independent strength. In the organization of his administration, as in the distribution of his forces, Temür constantly guarded against the development of independent positions.

Temür enhanced his power through the systematic control of an ill-defined set of ranks and offices. The offices in his administration provided both an opportunity and a danger to the sovereign and their allocation was in many ways as important as their function. It is here that the logic of Temür's administration becomes clear. Temür used the offices and ranks in his gift as instruments of reward and control, to secure his new political order while preventing its members from developing the independent power their predecessors had enjoyed.

We find a good illustration of his policies in his distribution of the rank of *amīr*. This title was one of considerable prestige and was held only by major figures, but its duties and perquisites remain unclear (see Appendix C). It was one that Temür used systematically to delineate the new Chaghatay elite and to establish grades within it; at the same time it was an instrument of exclusion. In the course of Temür's career we see significant change in the identity of the men holding this rank. At the beginning of his reign Temür granted the title of *amīr* to a number of tribal leaders; this was probably an attempt to win their loyalty and give them a stake in his success. Several of the tribal emirs who were prominent in the early part of Temür's career are listed as *amīrs* in the *Muᶜizz al-ansāb*; these were Ḥājjī Maḥmūdshāh Yasa'urī, ᶜĀdilshāh Jalayir, and Shaykh Muḥammad b. Buyan Suldus. All of these men however died fairly soon after Temür's takeover, and none passed on his position to a descendant.[59] Temür's attempt to win the loyalty of tribal chiefs had not succeeded and after this we find few members of the major Ulus tribes among the many people listed as Temür's *amīrs*. Several tribes are left totally unrepresented. The Apardï of Arhang and Khuttalan, the Arlat, and the Khuttalānī emirs for instance all remained active for some time after Temür's rise to power, yet none of them appear here.

What is more striking is that while many of Temür's followers were *amīrs*, few of the men he had placed at the head of tribes are included in the list. While ᶜĀdilshāh Jalayir appears here, Sarïbugha who was given control of the Jalayir a few years after ᶜĀdilshāh's death is not listed, nor for that matter does he appear in the lists of other office holders.[60] Temür's follower Aqtemür, who was given control of the Suldus, is not listed as an *amīr*, nor is his son Shaykh Temür who inherited his troops.[61]

In this way Temür separated the chieftaincy of a tribe from the attainment of rank and honor within the Ulus Chaghatay. When his attempt to win over the tribal aristocracy had failed he chose to exclude tribal chiefs systematically from his elite, and to deny the rank of *amīr* even to members of his personal following if they held the leadership of a tribe. Temür's *amīrs* were people who won their position through personal service, rather than through outside strength. In this regard Temür differed from many nomad polities, such as the Safavids, who bestowed this title primarily on tribal chiefs, and used it to tame and institutionalize the existing tribal structure.

Temür made an exception to his policy for his own tribe, the Barlas, which he did admit to the ruling group in a position somewhat lower than that of his family and personal followers. The representation from the Barlas tribe among Temür's *amīrs* was strikingly regular; there was one *amīr* from each of the five main Barlas lineages, and these *amīrs* passed on their positions to their sons or brothers. These are almost the only Barlas emirs listed.[62] The appointment of Barlas among Temür's *amīrs* shows Temür's strategy of according honor and position to his own tribe and preserving, at least formally, its original structure. Temür used the position of *amīr*, of considerable honorary value but uncertain duties, to distribute prestige evenly among the members of his tribe and to give it an honorable position within his realm without surrendering significant power to it.

Below the rank of *amīr* was that of *bahadur*, of yet more uncertain meaning. Temür seems to have used this rank as a way of bestowing recognition on the second level of men among his elite, those whom neither birth nor service entitled to the rank of *amīr*. Among the *bahadurs* one finds several of Temür's followers, a number of *qa'uchin* emirs, and some people of unknown origins, but no members of important Ulus tribes. Fewer of the men listed as *bahadurs* in the *Mu*ᶜ*izz al-ansāb* figure prominently in the histories of Temür's reign, though several of Temür's important followers do appear on this list – most notably Shaykh ᶜAlī Bahadur, Aqtemür, and Khitay Bahadur. These were apparently among Temür's less well-born followers; Shaykh ᶜAlī and Aqtemür have no known clan affiliation, while Khitay came from the Qipchaq tribe, subject first to the Jalayir and then to Temür.

The bestowal of rank under Temür was thus as much an exercise of exclusion as of inclusion. Members of the new elite received titles, while members of the old did not. Temür's own tribe and his following figured prominently among the new elite, while even the new leadership of the other Ulus tribes was excluded from its first rank. The titles of *amīr* and *bahadur* were used to formalize and perpetuate the new political order.

Temür was systematic also in the allocation of offices bringing with them more definite responsibilities. What apparently determined the apportionment of positions was the consideration of the amount and kind of power they granted to their holders. Power of any given kind went where it would create the smallest challenge to the sovereign. Above all Temür clearly distinguished the military and provincial spheres of activity from each other; he tended to separate the control of large numbers of troops from the secure possession of a region.

In Chapter 4 I discussed the distribution of power within Temür's army. The largest numbers of troops within it were controlled either by Temür's descendants or by the members of his following and their relatives. At first glance Temür's distribution of military offices seems to favor the members of his personal following, who received the most prestigious and powerful positions within the army. The office of commander-in-chief, *amīr al-umarā'*, for instance, belonged to the family of Temür's closest personal follower, Chekü Barlas, who also controlled the important Qara'unas troops.[63] The position of *tovachi* also went frequently to the members of Temür's following. It was held by Chekü, passing to his son Jahānshāh and grandson Burunduq. ᶜAbbās Bahadur and his son Shams al-Dīn were also *tovachis*.[64]

Granting high military office to men who already controlled large numbers of troops might seem to encourage the concentration of power in the hands of individuals. However the offices of *amīr al-umarā'* and of *tovachi*, prestigious though they were, did not provide an independent power base to their holders. The men who held these offices worked closely with Temür, and under his supervision – their positions provided them neither troops nor land nor, as far as we know, definite control over any one part of the army. The choice of followers and *qa'uchin* emirs for these two posts was highly logical. Both groups were skilled in military affairs, and the members of Temür's following had long-standing personal ties to Temür, useful in offices which involved close contact with the sovereign. Another post rather similar to these in its requirements and perquisites was that of *muhrdār*, keeper of the seal, and this also went to members of Temür's following, largely to the family of Eyegü Temür.[65] This position, like those discussed above, seems to have lent considerable standing to its holder but it entailed no separate sphere of interest and did not provide a base for independent power.

The office which provided the best opportunity to build up a personal power base was that of *darugha*, which involved the control of territory and could keep its incumbent at a distance from the sovereign. It is notable that this post was granted most usually to members of the Barlas tribe, to *qa'uchin* emirs, or to Khorasanians, and in the case of the latter two groups the governorship was usually distant from their native territories. The members of these groups had relatively little power in the army and controlled substantially fewer troops than did Temür's personal followers.

In contrast, the members of Temür's personal following rarely received territory except the tribal areas which had been transferred to some of them along with tribal troops. Only a few of Temür's personal followers were made *darugha*, and these appointments were usually of short duration. Although Temür appointed Dā'ūd Dughlat *darugha* of Samarqand in 771/1370, after 773/1371–2 he left Samarqand in charge of other people, usually a different one each time he went on campaign.[66] Shaykh ᶜAlī Bahadur became *darugha* of Khorezm in 781–2/1379–80, but this was either a very short appointment of one which bestowed only partial power, since we have evidence from the same year suggesting that Khorezm was held by Temür's protégé Tokhtamïsh.[67] Two other members of Temür's following served briefly as *darughas*.[68] What is striking here is not only the small number of appointments, but also the comparison with the numerous military and administrative posts granted to Temür's personal followers. The short period of tenure is also notable; the few followers who did serve as *darughas* were given no time to establish themselves as powers within the regions under their jurisdiction. Temür's policy in this regard differs from that in other Turco-Mongolian states, in which *darughas* were frequently members of the highest elite.[69] It is possible that Temür abandoned this policy at the end of his life, since in 806–77/1403–4 he did appoint several of his personal followers or their descendants to regional posts. Sulaymānshāh b. Dā'ūd was appointed to govern the region of Rayy and Firuzkuh after the defeat of Iskandar Shaykhī in 806/1404. In 807/1405, when Temür arrived in Utrar, he was received by Birdi Beg b. Sarībugha, who was apparently based there; it is not clear whether he had been officially appointed to govern this area but he is mentioned in Moghulistan with Muḥammad Sulṭān in 903/1401. Yūsuf Jalīl b. Ḥasan Jāndār is mentioned as *darugha* of Tabas soon after Temür's death. The results of these appointments serve to show the wisdom of Temür's earlier policy; both Sulaymānshāh and Yūsuf Jalīl rebelled soon after Temür's death, and while nothing is known of Birdi Beg after 807, his brother Shaykh Nūr al-Dīn opposed Temür's grandson Khalīl Sulṭān, and based himself in Utrar.[70]

The group most frequently appointed as *darughas* were the *qa'uchin*. Yazd, Tabriz, Rayy, Abarquh, Khorezm, Herat, Isfizar, and Awnik were all governed at one time or another by *qa'uchin* emirs.[71] Many of these were large and strategic cities, and they represent important posts for a group which otherwise seems to have been in the second rank within Temür's government. It is not clear how long the *qa'uchin* governors held their appointments. In general their tenure was quite short, though probably longer than that of Temür's followers.[72] Although the *qa'uchin* emirs probably originated as a military class, most of them did not lead great numbers of troops. Two *qa'uchin* emirs were among Temür's followers, but unlike most of Temür's following neither of them were powerful commanders, nor did they leave troops to their descendants and none of the *qa'uchin* emirs are known to have led *tümens*.[73]

The Khorasanian emirs appointed as governors usually held cities fairly distant from their place of origin, and most did not command very large numbers of soldiers. The largest following we know of was that of Khwāja Mas^cūd Sabzawārī, governor first of Shushtar and then of Baghdad, whose army numbered probably between one and three thousand.[74] The other Khorasanian emirs given governorships were less prominent men; since they have already been discussed I shall not enumerate them here.[75] Among the Barlas governors there were a few powerful commanders but these were a minority. Two Barlas governors were commanders of *tümens*: Yādgār Barlas, governor of Balkh, whose *tümen* may well have been made up of local troops, and Temür's cousin, Taghay Bugha, governor of Bukhara, commander of the "*tümen-i san sïz*" (the numberless *tümen*) made up of court troops.[76] The remaining Barlas governors are little mentioned outside the areas they governed, and never as leaders of large numbers of personal troops.[77]

Beyond Temür's immediate family, then, there were only one or two individuals who controlled both land and large troop contingents. Unlike the men appointed to military posts, the emirs whom Temür appointed to govern cities and territories came from groups without large military followings. Thus Temür made certain that there was no one class of people able at once to control land and large numbers of troops. Considered as a method to control and to reward the members of the ruling class, while distributing power in the way which would least threaten the authority of the sovereign, Temür's organization of offices reveals itself as a most efficient one. For those close to him and particularly for the members of his following and his tribe some share in Temür's newly won power was required. Those whom he rewarded most spectacularly after his immediate family were his personal followers. The largest number of troops, the positions of greatest personal prestige (*amīr al-umarā'*, *muhrdār*, *tovachi̇*) and the closest connection with the royal family were all bestowed on this group. While rewarding his followers, Temür took care to limit their opportunities for independence by excluding them from positions which involved the control of territories within his realm.

Another group which could expect to profit significantly from Temür's rise was the Barlas tribe. Within the steppe tradition of government the realm was to some extent the joint property of the ruling clan. Chinggis Khan and his descendants had responded to this tradition by establishing the practice of joint administration throughout much of their empire. Temür chose to share rather less of his new-found power. He included representatives of the Barlas lineages among his *amīrs*, thus counting them among the new aristocracy of the realm. Barlas emirs also received some share in the actual governance of the realm: they were appointed as *darughas* to positions of regional power within the original area of the Ulus Chaghatay. To balance this Temür gave the Barlas little power within his army. In the command of troops and the possession of military offices they lagged far behind the members of his personal following. The *qa'uchin* emirs, less close to Temür than his followers and less prestigious than the members of his tribe, but consistently loyal to him, were rewarded only a little less generously. Although few apparently ranked as *amīrs*, quite a number were *bahadurs*. Several moreover were *tovachi̇s*. None commanded very large numbers of troops, but many were appointed as *darughas*.

One more aspect of Temür's administration remains to be considered – the transfer of offices. In a system which was newly instituted and not always orderly, it is striking to what extent power and positions of all kinds were hereditary. The control of troops, the ranks of *amīr* and *bahadur*, the office of *muhrdār*, *amīr al-umarā'*, and often that of *tovachi̇*, all passed on within the same families. Hereditary succession to troops and offices was common among Turco-Mongolian governments – it can be found for instance under the great Mongol khans, and in China under the Mongols.[78] What we must determine is why Temür chose to continue this practice.

The inheritance of offices can be regarded as a limitation on the power of the sovereign, since it prevents him from choosing his office holders and lessens the number of positions in his gift. For Temür however, this system probably had many advantages. Having managed with considerable effort to remove power from the tribal chiefs and to bestow it on his own followers and tribe, Temür had little interest in maintaining open access to positions of power and prestige. The inheritance of offices and of troops served to strengthen the groups that he had favored, and to continue the exclusion of those from whom he had taken power. It also helped to perpetuate the division he had installed between holders of military and of regional power.

Moreover the inheritance of offices did not entirely remove them from Temür's control. In the absence of primogeniture there were usually several possible candidates for an office or command, the more so since positions could pass on to nephews or cousins as well as to sons. In some cases at least it was Temür who chose the successor to an office. When Chekü Barlas died in 785–6/1383–4, for instance, Temür gave his place to his son Jahānshāh. At the death of Eyegü Temür in 793/1391, Temür showed honor to several of his relatives, but particularly favored Shāhmalik, to whom he granted Eyegü Temür's position of *muhrdār*.[79]

It is significant that the position of *darugha* was less consistently hereditary than most offices. There were for instance several different *darughas* of Yazd: first Temüge Qa'uchin, then later Yūsuf Jalīl, and then ᶜAbd al-Raḥmān Qorchï, none of them as far as I know related to each other.[80] Buyan Qa'uchin, *darugha* of Rayy for some time, was transferred to Tabriz towards the end of Temür's reign.[81] In this regard Temür's practice differed from that of other Turco-Mongolian states in which the position of *darugha* was often inherited.[82] The only *darughas* who passed on their positions to their relatives were the Barlas emirs, and this may have resulted from the traditions of joint rule which I have discussed above. The cities of Balkh and Bukhara, held by Barlas emirs, remained throughout Temür's career in the same families.[83]

In the case of land therefore, inheritance was limited to Temür's own tribe, holding areas near the center of power. Governorships in the provinces, filled by men less closely attached to Temür, and presenting greater opportunities for independence, were not passed on within one family. Where the inheritance of position might have endangered Temür's power, it was not allowed. In other areas, the establishment of a fixed order worked to Temür's advantage, and offices were usually hereditary.

The administration of Temür's realm was no easy task, and the maintenance of sovereign authority over it was an even harder one. Both the Ulus Chaghatay and Temür's Iranian territories had existed before him without central leadership, under political systems which favored loose, localized rule – by the tribes within the Ulus, and by local dynasties in Iran. These had to be replaced by a centralized government, favoring the rule of an autocratic sovereign. In designing his administration, Temür used both the traditions available to him – the Turco-Mongolian heritage articulated in the Mongol world empire, and the Islamic bureaucratic system of the lands he conquered. From these elements Temür fashioned a government to fit his needs. For an active and diffuse political system Temür substituted a still and dependent one, designed as far as possible to suppress independent sources of power and the political activity which revolved around them.

Temür's administration was neither systematic nor highly articulated. The two spheres of government, separate in theory, were ill-distinguished in practice and overlapped substantially in their jurisdictions. The offices of Temür's administration did not determine clearly the careers of the men who held them. Tasks which came within the province of a particular office were often performed by people quite unconnected to it. The reconstruction and organization of cities for instance was not always left to the *darugha*, nor were troops always conscripted by *tovachïs*.

Nonetheless, this was not a haphazard government. To understand the logic of Temür's administration one must look beyond its structure to examine the use Temür put it to. He took advantage of the fluidity of his administration to enhance his own personal power; this was a system designed to be manipulated by the sovereign in order to control his subordinates and to keep all significant power to himself. Looked at this way, for its use of and effect on the ruling class itself, Temür's administration shows logic and consistency.

The overlap between Chaghatay and Persian spheres here shows as an advantage; Temür successfully used his Chaghatay followers to limit the power of his Persian bureaucracy. Temür's scribes had no independent sphere of their own. Their main tasks – the collection of taxes and the investigation of local abuses – were shared by the Chaghatay emirs who staffed the Turco-Mongolian arm of the government. Nor did the Persians under Temür have the privilege of protecting the settled population from its nomad rulers. The business which was assigned to them was that rather of exploiting the conquered peoples. The task of repairing the ravages of Temür's campaigns or of promoting agriculture was undertaken not by the Persians but by the Chaghatays themselves. The Persian bureaucrats could neither achieve strong influence within the ruling class, nor count on the support of the local population against its foreign rulers.

To control the Persian bureaucracy, Temür could make use of his Chaghatay followers, but these men also could pose a threat to his position. To use their skills without allowing them undue power Temür manipulated the administrative system he had inherited, using it to control his ruling class. It is in the allocation of ranks and offices that the logic of Temür's administration reveals itself. The difference between military and provincial offices in particular takes on much greater importance. Temür, having given to his followers large numbers of troops and a preponderant position in the army, took care not to bestow on them definite control over any region within his dominions. Instead they were placed in posts, usually military ones, which bestowed prestige on their holders but no independent position. The men to whom Temür did give regional commands – the Barlas, *qa'uchin* and Khorasanian emirs – were all people with relatively little standing in the army, and few soldiers under their command. Thus while Temür often assigned to one individual both civil and military tasks, he very rarely assigned power in both these spheres to the same person.

Temür could be threatened not only by the creation of separate centers of power, but also by the continuation of the political activity which had existed before his rise. Here also he was able to use his administrative structure to his own advantage. His use of rank and office to suppress political activity shows particularly clearly in his manipulation of the title of *amīr*. By refusing this rank to men who held tribal power, even to those who were his personal followers, he denied the tribes a position within his new order and further weakened them as a focus for independent political activity. When the chieftainship of a tribe conferred neither significant military power nor definite prestige, it ceased to be an object worth competing for. Since the contest over rulership of tribes had been a key factor in the political life of the Ulus Chaghatay, their removal from the center of power did much to create the still political system which Temür desired for the preservation of his own power. Likewise Temür chose to continue the traditional inheritance of rank and office, partly because it helped to perpetuate the new order he had set up. Since he was able to influence the choice among several candidates, inherited offices did not serve as a secure base for power, or as a focus for continuing political activity.

We find then that there is system within Temür's government; it is a system based less on the clear delineation of necessary tasks than on the careful division and limitation of power. Where the traditions he had inherited served his purpose, Temür preserved them, but where they might threaten his position he felt free to discard them. Thus although the Persian bureaucrats under Temür performed their traditional tasks, they had an unusually circumscribed role. While he followed Turco-Mongolian practice in making most offices hereditary and in placing his personal followers in most of the highest posts of his administration, he departed from this practice in two important ways – in his near exclusion of followers from the position of *darugha*, and his frequent change of personnel in that position.

For the space of his lifetime, Temür's administration worked extremely well. The lack of formal structure denied definite spheres of power to his subordinates and allowed him to interfere at will in their affairs. At the same time, his systematic policy in the allocation of offices suppressed both individual centers of power and the independent political activity which had revolved around such centers.

CHAPTER 7

The struggle for succession

After a reign of thirty-six years Temür died in Utrar, in February 1405. On his deathbed he designated as successor his grandson Pīr Muḥammad b. Jahāngīr but this prince, governor of the distant province of Kabul, had little chance of imposing himself. Within a few days of Temür's death his sons and grandsons, together with his closest followers, had begun drawing up their armies to begin a struggle for power which occupied the next fifteen years.

The events of the years after Temür's death tell us much about the structure of his realm and the changes his rule had brought about. The reign of a strong sovereign tends to suppress independent political activity, and the conventions of Persian historiography, concentrating on the exploits of a dynastic founder, make the study of subsidiary political actors almost impossible. After Temür's death, internal political activity again revived and became a fit subject for historians; thus from the history of these years we can discover the positions of the groups under Temür and the relationships among them.

In some ways the political situation after Temür's death resembled the one in which he had risen to power. The military activity of the Ulus Chaghatay, which Temür had diverted to outside lands, now turned back into the interior of his realm. Members of his dynasty vied among themselves, and political power was again difficult to maintain, as emirs switched their allegiance readily from one leader to another. In the struggle which followed Temür's death we find almost all the political actors who had played a part in his rise to power and his early rule. The members of Temür's family and of his personal following, the Turco-Mongolian tribes of the Ulus Chaghatay, local settled dynasties and the nomads of the Middle East all took some part in the civil war. But there were important differences. Although most of the earlier groups still existed, their relative power and influence had changed radically.

It is a tribute to Temür's success that almost all the prominent political actors in the contest following his death were people whom he had personally favored. The first to mobilize their forces and those who played the greatest part in the war of succession were the members of Temür's family; the princes quickly decided to ignore Temür's testament and set about asserting their own regional power while attempting to extend their control to the regions of their brothers and cousins. After his own family the people whom Temür had most trusted were the members of his personal following and their descendants. These men were also active participants in the power struggle; in the first five years after Temür's death most members of this class either deserted or rebelled against their new masters. The third politically active group was the local rulers whom Temür had favored – in Khorasan, Sistan, Mazandaran and to a lesser extent Azerbaijan. These men now began to assert independent control over their regions and to encroach on those of their neighbors.

The powers which had caused Temür trouble on the other hand were now much less active. The rulers or dynasties who had opposed him and whom he had chastised were very little in evidence in these years; their power had been effectively reduced. The tribes of the Ulus Chaghatay had remained intact and did participate in the political struggle, particularly in Transoxiana, but they were not nearly as active or as powerful as either Temür's family or his followers. The one set of people opposed to Temür whom he had not succeeded in neutralizing were the nomad confederations of western Iran, in particular the Jalayirids and the Qaraqoyunlu. As I have written above, these confederations had succeeded in maintaining their strength and cohesion throughout Temür's reign, suffering only a temporary loss of territory. They now repaired this loss and quickly regained their old regions.

What had changed most of all was the nature of political activity. Temür had come to power within a well functioning political system – one which while fluid and insecure was based on recognized political relationships and required relatively little violence. He had changed this to an almost equally unstructured system based exclusively on personal loyalty to the sovereign and fueled by constant conquests.

The death of a strong ruler, particularly a nomad one, often brought about a political breakdown and an armed succession struggle. The struggle after Temür's death was particularly long, bitter and destructive, partly because of his personal jealousy of power, and partly because of the exceptional success of his career. Temür's sons and grandsons, competing among themselves for power, found themselves engaged in a struggle without set rules and relationships. It was not clear in this world who owed loyalty to whom. The princes found not only that they could trust none of their brothers and cousins, but also that they could not trust their subjects – not the emirs in their armies, not the settled rulers of their regions, not the common soldiers of their armies. Their plight was the more acute because they had so few rewards to offer. With the end of the great conquests came the end of outside booty and constant growth. Princes fighting for power within the realm could offer no certain advancement, and only what money they could find in

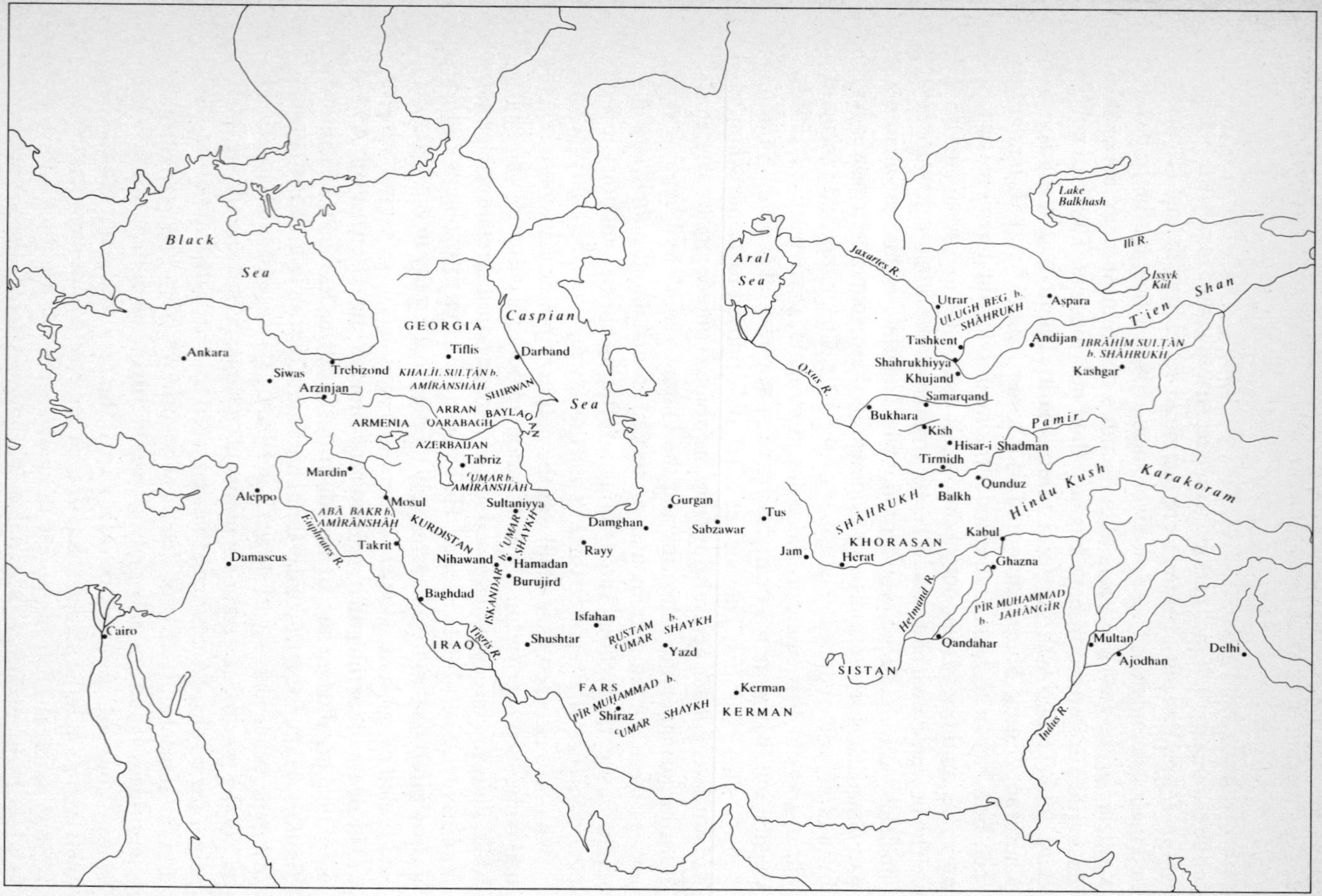

4. The disposition of Temür's realm.

their treasuries or from the exploitation of their realm. This struggle was fought at all levels and with all weapons, and it presents a vivid witness to the subversion which lay behind Temür's act of creation.

In this chapter I shall have to chronicle not one but several succession struggles. At Temür's death his realm broke down into four different regions, each one the scene of a separate fight for power. In Transoxiana, Amīrānshāh's son Khalīl Sulṭān early seized the throne and struggled against threats from Temür's designated successor Pīr Muḥammad, governor of Northern India, from Shāhrukh and from rebellious members of Temür's following. Shāhrukh had ruled Khorasan, Sistan and Mazandaran since 799/1396–7; no other member of the dynasty could dispute this territory with him but he had to contend with numerous insubordinate local dynasties and a series of rebellions by powerful members of Temür's personal following. In Fars three of the sons of ᶜUmar Shaykh b. Temür, each based in a different city, vied among themselves for control. Azerbaijan was held by Temür's son Amīrānshāh and his children, ᶜUmar and Abā Bakr, fighting for power among themselves and, unsuccessfully, against the Qaraqoyunlu confederation. The history of these areas illustrates different aspects of the situation in Temür's realm after his death. I shall therefore discuss each region in turn, omitting however the regions of Fars and Kerman, about which we have less information.

Transoxiana

Transoxiana, as the center of Temür's realm, was the theater of its central succession struggle. Temür's designated successor Pīr Muḥammad b. Jahāngīr was at much too great a distance from the capital to participate in the first part of the scramble for power; early success went not to those with the greatest strength, but to those close to the center of power. The major figure in this region was Khalīl Sulṭān who had spent the winter in Tashkent with a large part of the army gathered for Temür's Chinese campaign. At the news of Temür's death he laid claim to the throne of Samarqand with the support of several of the emirs who had wintered with him.[1] Khalīl Sulṭān was able also to persuade Temür's servitor Arghūnshāh who was in charge of Samarqand to deny access to anyone but himself. He entered the city in Ramaḍān 807/March 1405, and took power.[2] Arghūnshāh meanwhile had refused entrance to two of Temür's most favored emirs, Shaykh Nūr al-Dīn and Shāhmalik, who had been with Temür at his death and wished to install Pīr Muḥammad as successor according to Temür's testament. These men therefore went to Bukhara, along with the women and children of Temür's family, and later joined Shāhrukh.[3]

Khalīl Sulṭān had the advantage of propinquity and speed, and also the mixed advantage of an army made up of people from outside the Ulus Chaghatay without personal stake in the succession struggle. As I have explained in Chapters 4 and 5, the population of Transoxiana had not remained stable during Temür's reign. Many of the emirs and troops of the Ulus Chaghatay had been appointed to the new provinces of Temür's realm and foreign populations were moved into Transoxiana to take their place. All the histories of this period mention the foreign composition of Khalīl Sulṭān's army, which included soldiers from Hindustan, Khorasan, and ᶜIraq, with nomads from ᶜIraq and Rum.[4]

Indeed these troops along with some members of Temür's following made up almost the whole of Khalīl Sulṭān's army, while the tribal population of Transoxiana, including the Barlas, gave little support to him and in many cases seems to have kept away from political activity altogether. Khalīl Sulṭān therefore had an army which would not seek political power on its own, but which had few ties of loyalty either to him or to the dynasty. He had to buy their continued service through lavish disbursements from the rich treasury of Samarqand, which he had almost entirely depleted by the end of his four-year reign.

Khalīl Sulṭān's assumption of power in Samarqand was not acceptable to the Timurid princes near him. Temür's grandson Sulṭān Ḥusayn, the son of his daughter Agha Begi, made an attempt at power even before Khalīl Sulṭān arrived in Samarqand, and at the end of 807/1405 he tried to take over the army that Khalīl Sulṭān had sent with him on campaign, hoping to seize power for himself. His attempts failed and he fled to Shāhrukh, who executed him.[5] Shāhrukh also was displeased with Khalīl Sulṭān and seems to have planned an early expedition against him, but after a short skirmish he agreed to recognize Khalīl Sulṭān in return for the delivery of his personal possessions and those of his emirs from Samarqand.[6] One reason Shāhrukh abandoned this project was undoubtedly the beginning of local uprisings in Khorasan, starting at the end of 807/1405 and continuing for the next several years. Although Shāhrukh kept a guard on the Oxus and supported Pīr Muḥammad against Khalīl Sulṭān, it was not until 811/1409 that he invaded Transoxiana.

It was Temür's designated successor, Pīr Muḥammad b. Jahāngīr, who proved Khalīl Sulṭān's most determined opponent. At the end of 807/1405 he arrived at Balkh from Kabul to assert his claim to the throne. He requested help from Shāhrukh who appointed his son Ulugh Beg and one of his major emirs, Shāhmalik, with an army to the regions of Andkhud and Shaburqan, near Balkh. Pīr Muḥammad, with considerable effort, persuaded Shāhmalik to undertake a joint campaign against Khalīl Sulṭān; the armies met near Qarshi in Ramaḍān 808/February 1406, and Khalīl Sulṭān was victorious.[7] Pīr Muḥammad, along with his most powerful emir, Pīr ᶜAlī Tāz Suldus, soon regathered his forces and occupied the fortress Hisar-i Shadman, above the Oxus. In Ramaḍān 809/February 1407, Pīr ᶜAlī Tāz gathered a number of emirs around himself and murdered Pīr Muḥammad.[8]

The uprising of Pīr ᶜAlī Tāz deserves attention both because of its importance and because it was one of the few uprisings of this period which could be interpreted as being tribally organized. The activity of the Ulus tribes in this period can provide an indication of Temür's success in reorganizing the political and social structure of the Ulus. Pīr ᶜAlī was a Suldus emir and the area which he took over, Hisar-i Shadman, had been Suldus territory. It is possible then that this uprising represents an assertion of tribal power, although the histories do not present it as such. They do not mention his tribal name, nor do any of them mention him leading tribal troops.[9] Pīr ᶜAlī was the son of Mengli Bugha Suldus who before Temür's rise to power had inherited the *tümen* of Öljey Bugha Suldus, centered at Balkh. This was separate from the main part of the Suldus tribe which was based on the other side of the Oxus in Chaghaniyan. In 765/1364, Amīr Ḥusayn and Temür defeated and executed Mengli Bugha and took over the *tümen* of Öljey Bugha. Temür however took an interest in Pīr ᶜAlī and when he was twelve years old allowed him to inherit his father's property and his *hazāra.*[10] From 790/1388 on Pīr ᶜAlī participated in most of Temür's campaigns; he is mentioned in the army of Balkh in Khorasan in 790, and later on the five-year campaign to Iran, the Indian campaign and the seven-year campaign to the west.[11]

Pīr ᶜAlī was among those sent to Tashkent with Khalīl Sulṭān in 807/1404, but after Temür's death he left Khalīl and returned to Balkh.[12] He soon became Pīr Muḥammad's most important emir: according to Ḥāfiẓ-i Abrū he managed most of Pīr Muḥammad's affairs while the prince devoted himself to pleasure.[13] It was he who first occupied Hisar-i Shadman, encouraging Pīr Muḥammad to join him there and to resist Khalīl Sulṭān.[14] His choice of this location could well be significant since it had been the seat of the main branch of the Suldus at the time of Temür's takeover and was still occupied by Suldus emirs together with some Barlas ones.[15]

Pīr ᶜAlī's action could therefore represent an attempt to reunite the Suldus tribe. It is notable that the Suldus troops mentioned campaigning under Pīr Muḥammad in his battle against Khalīl in Ramaḍān 808/February 1406 were led not by Pīr ᶜAlī, but by emirs identified with the region of Hisar-i Shadman.[16] These troops had deserted in battle, causing Pīr Muḥammad's defeat, so it is also possible that this expedition was undertaken simply to gain full control of a region containing a valuable but unreliable army. Fairly soon after this successful move, Pīr ᶜAlī Tāz killed Pīr Muḥammad.[17] After Pīr Muḥammad's death Pīr ᶜAlī attempted to gain sovereignty in the area and although he did not succeed in taking it over, he did cause considerable trouble there for some time until he was defeated in 810/1407–8, and was murdered by his own followers.[18]

It does seem likely that Pīr ᶜAlī's tribal affiliation was an important element in the motivation and support for his rebellion. His attachment to the region of Balkh, the area of his section of the tribe, is shown by his eagerness to return to it after Temür's death, even though he had had no previous connection with Pīr Muḥammad who now controlled the area. His quick rise to preeminence among Pīr Muḥammad's emirs is an indication of the strength of his support within the area. The Suldus *tümen* of Balkh then was probably still an active political entity, one that lent support to its leaders and which was worth fighting for. It is notable however that Pīr ᶜAlī, who was the most powerful Suldus emir at this period, came from the section of the tribe that had earlier been weaker, and indeed had been taken over directly by Temür and Amīr Ḥusayn. Pīr ᶜAlī moreover owed both his position and his possession of troops to Temür's personal favor.

The one other major act of resistance which might be considered a tribal one was that of Shaykh Nūr al-Dīn, the son of Sarïbugha Jalayir, whom Temür had installed as chief of the Jalayir tribe. Shaykh Nūr al-Dīn left the service of Khalīl Sulṭān at the end of 807 or the beginning of 808/1405, settled in Utrar, and allied with Temür's follower Khudāydād. His actions should be considered together with those of Khudāydād, who was the first to resist Khalīl Sulṭān and the more constant in his opposition.

Khudāydād b. Ḥusayn Barlas was the son of one of Temür's personal followers and had inherited troops which were based apparently on the borders of Turkistan.[19] Unlike most of Temür's personal followers Khudāydād had a strong regional attachment, which he retained throughout Temür's career. He had been appointed with Temür's grandson Muḥammad Sulṭān in 800/1397 to secure the frontiers of Turkistan and remained there when Temür granted this area to Khalīl Sulṭān in 804–5/1402. Khudāydād and Khalīl soon became enemies, but Khalīl Sulṭān nonetheless reappointed Khudāydād as governor of the area beyond the Jaxartes, since he was not strong enough to refuse him the position. By the end of 807/spring 1405 Khudāydād had begun raiding Khalīl Sulṭān's territories.[20]

By this time Shaykh Nūr al-Dīn Jalayir had left Samarqand and settled in Utrar, which became his base.[21] This region had not been the area of the Jalayir tribe, nor did Shaykh Nūr al-Dīn have any personal connection with it. It was however the residence of his brother Birdi Beg, who had been appointed to the region in 800/1397 with Muḥammad Sulṭān b. Jahāngīr.[22] It seems likely that the tribal troops of the Jalayir had passed from Sarïbugha to Birdi Beg.[23] It is possible therefore that in going to Utrar, Shaykh Nūr al-Dīn was gathering around himself the Jalayir tribal troops taken there by Birdi Beg. The histories however mention neither Shaykh Nūr al-Dīn's troops nor his tribe.

Soon after he went to Utrar, Shaykh Nūr al-Dīn allied with Khudāydād against Khalīl Sulṭān. In the course of their raids, these emirs succeeded in gaining control of the whole of the border region, including Sayram, Tashkent, Andijan, Khujand, Shahrukhiyya, Utrar and Sighnaq. The westernmost of these, including Utrar and Sighnaq, were the territory of Shaykh Nūr al-Dīn, and those in the east, including Andijan, that of

Khudāydād. Although Khalīl undertook several expeditions against these rebels, he was never successful; they were able to keep their territory, and to raid as far as Samarqand.[24]

At the end of the winter of 811/1409 Khudāydād, probably with the collusion of Shaykh Nūr al-Dīn, wrote to Shāhrukh suggesting that he invade from the south while they attacked from the north. As Shāhrukh approached from Khorasan, Khudāydād succeeded in capturing Khalīl Sulṭān and took over Samarqand. According to Ibn ᶜArabshāh, Khudāydād was helped by information from Khalīl's closest emirs but Ḥāfiẓ-i Abrū denies this. The fact that Ḥāfiẓ-i Abrū finds it necessary to deny collusion however suggests that this might well have happened. As Shāhrukh approached Samarqand, Khudāydād retreated with Khalīl Sulṭān. A little later Khudāydād was killed by the Moghul emirs from whom he had requested help and Khalīl Sulṭān came to Shāhrukh; Shaykh Nūr al-Dīn also came to pay his respects. At the end of 811/Spring 1409, Shāhrukh took over Transoxiana, appointed Ulugh Beg as governor of the region and returned to Herat.[25]

The rebellion of Khudāydād and Shaykh Nūr al-Dīn does not seem to represent an assertion of tribal autonomy. Although it is possible that the Jalayir tribe formed part of Shaykh Nūr al-Dīn's armies, Shaykh Nūr al-Dīn owed his power not to his place within his tribe, but to his position as one of Temür's two or three most trusted emirs. The uprising therefore should be interpreted as the rebellion of two of Temür's most favored and most powerful followers, unwilling to be ruled by a prince of power and abilities much inferior to those of their original master. It was this group of people – the senior members of Temür's following – who presented the greatest challenge to the power of the Timurid princes within their territories. There were several similar uprisings by members of Temür's following in other provinces during these years. These men, owing their loyalty directly to Temür, did not consider themselves the subjects of his descendants but sought instead to take over the activities of the tribal aristocracy whose place they had inherited. They were returning to the system of the Ulus Chaghatay, in which loyalty was voluntary and alliances could be switched at will. Temür's emirs, particularly his personal followers, considered themselves allies of the princes, free to choose their course of action. The princes on the other hand saw their relative positions differently; they regarded the emirs as subjects, owing them obedience, and were quick to punish behavior which they considered unsuitable.

Besides the uprisings discussed above there were only minor disturbances by members of the tribes of the Ulus Chaghatay. I have mentioned above the desertion of Suldus troops during Pīr Muḥammad's battle with Khalīl Sulṭān in 808/February 1406. These troops were accompanied in their flight by two emirs of other tribes, Bāyazīd Borolday and Shīr ᶜAlī Barlas. Tāj al-Salmānī mentions that Khalīl Sulṭān undertook several unsuccessful expeditions against rebellious Barlas and Suldus emirs at Hisar-i Shadman.[26] Another rebellious Suldus emir deserted Khalīl Sulṭān in 809/1406–7 together with the Jawun-i Qurban and ᶜIraqi emirs whose flight will be discussed below.

On the whole the tribes of the Ulus were quiescent. It is notable that both Khuttalan and Arhang were still at this time governed by the sons or grandsons of their earlier tribal chiefs – Khwāja ᶜAlī b. Khwāja Yūsuf Apardï at Sali Saray in Arhang and Sulṭān Maḥmūd b. Kaykhusraw Khuttalānī in Khuttalan. The progenitors of these men had been very active and prominent figures during Temür's rise to power and his early rule, but Khwāja ᶜAlī and Sulṭān Maḥmūd are mentioned only once in the histories describing these years: in 810/1407 when they sent messengers and presents to Shāhrukh at Balkh.[27]

While Khalīl Sulṭān met with resistance from a few of the tribal emirs of Transoxiana, he received almost no support from any of them. Most of his army was made up of the new population of Transoxiana – the foreign emirs and nomads whom Temür had settled there. These forces served Khalīl fairly well for one or two years but then began to desert and return to their homes in large numbers, discouraged by his decreasing generosity and his lack of success. In Shawwāl 808/March 1406, the Qaratatars whom Temür had transported from Rum deserted, along with a number of ᶜIraqis, some of them probably from the nomadic Jalayirid confederation.[28] In the next year more ᶜIraqis deserted along with Kurds, Chaghatays, some Turkistani emirs and some of the Jawun-i Qurban tribe which Temür had transported from Mashhad.[29]

To keep the loyalty of such an army even to the extent that Khalīl Sulṭān succeeded in doing so required large amounts of money. Khalīl Sulṭān is noted in the histories for his extraordinary generosity. Before important campaigns he handed out lavish gifts to all members of the army, regardless of their ranks or their legitimate claims.[30] After a year or two of such activity he had used up not only the contents of the treasury but also the private wealth of members of the dynasty.[31] At this point it seems that his generosity began to decline particularly towards his foreign troops, and this was a major reason for their desertion.[32]

The history of Transoxiana during Khalīl Sulṭān's rule shows the extent to which Temür had transformed the central territory of the Ulus Chaghatay. During Temür's rise to power in the same region, the main political forces, the possessors of power and of armies, had been the Turco-Mongolian tribes of the Ulus. After his death most of these tribes still existed and two of them, the Suldus and the Barlas, continued to assert themselves but they were not the main actors in politics. The active contenders were the members of Temür's new elite, men who had been personally close to Temür, and personally promoted by him – Khudāydād, Shaykh Nūr al-Dīn and Pīr ᶜAlī Tāz. The succession struggle was fought among the new elite – Temür's family and personal followers – and was based primarily on their holdings outside the Ulus Chaghatay. The most successful and longest lasting of the uprisings against Khalīl Sulṭān was based in the outlying regions near or beyond the Jaxartes River. When Khalīl lost his throne, he lost it to Shāhrukh, basing his power on the possession of Khorasan. Khalīl Sulṭān neither held the throne of Transoxiana through the support of its original population, nor lost it through their opposition.

Khorasan

The situation in Khorasan was very different. Shāhrukh had been governor of the province since 799/1396–7, and had much too strong a hold on it to be successfully challenged by any other member of the dynasty. Nevertheless he found on Temür's death that he could not trust either the local Khorasanian powers or the commanders with his own army. The rulers of Khorasan, Mazandaran and Sistan had been particularly favoured by Temür and they had thus retained sufficient strength to resist his successors. Despite the length of time that Shāhrukh's emirs had been attached to him, they did not remain loyal, and he had to put down several uprisings by his most powerful commanders.

The first person to rebel against Shāhrukh was Sulṭān ᶜAlī Sabzawārī, the nephew of Khwāja Masᶜūd Sarbadār who with the rest of his family had been especially close to Temür, and had been allowed considerable autonomy within his dominions (see Chapter 5). Towards the end of 807/1405, Sulṭān ᶜAlī attacked Shāhrukh's governor in Mashhad–Tus. He was joined in his rebellion by the ruler of Astarabad in Mazandaran, Pīr Pādishāh, the son of Lughmān b. Taghaytemür, whom Temür had installed in the region when he took it over. Shāhrukh's emirs soon put the rebels to flight and conquered Sabzawar, and Shāhrukh had Sulṭān ᶜAlī executed in Ṣafar 808/July 1405,[33] but Pīr Pādishāh continued to resist for several more years.

At the beginning of 809/Summer 1406 Pīr Pādishāh aided the rebellion of several of Shāhrukh's emirs. This time Shāhrukh went against the rebels in person and chased them out of Mazandaran.[34] Pīr Pādishāh fled to Khorezm, where in 810/1407 he gathered about himself a number of soldiers who had fled from Khalīl Sulṭān in Transoxiana, including part of the Jawun-i Qurban tribe and a number of ᶜIraqis, many of whom Temür had forcibly settled in Transoxiana. This army besieged Astarabad, but fled at Shāhrukh's approach. Pīr Pādishāh retreated to Rustamdar in western Mazandaran, where he died later the same year.[35]

The other leaders who caused trouble for Shāhrukh were those of Ghur and Sistan. Temür had left the shahs of Sistan in charge of their own region, and they had been prominent in his army throughout his career. In Jumādā I 808/November 1405, Shāhrukh heard that the shahs at Farah were rebelling. He sent a force to Sistan to seize them and to repress also another rebellious leader, Mawdūd Ghurī.[36] The next year however the area was again in revolt; its rulers had killed several of Shāhrukh's officials and were plundering Ghur. Shāhrukh therefore sent another expedition into the area and dispersed the rebels.[37]

At the beginning of 811/1408 Amīrānshāh's son Abā Bakr, chased out of Azerbaijan by the Qaraqoyunlu, took refuge in Sistan. Shāh Quṭb al-Dīn received him with honor, seeing in this a way to show contempt for Shāhrukh. When Shāhrukh learned of this, he set off for Sistan and took the city of Farah, along with several other fortresses. When Shāh Quṭb al-Dīn failed to present himself as requested, Shāhrukh wrecked the dams on the Helmand river and systematically pillaged the region. Then, after installing new governors over much of this territory, he returned to Herat, appointing a number of his emirs to guard the borders of Sistan.[38] It was several more years however before he succeeded in asserting full control over this province.[39]

During the first years after Temür's death then, Shāhrukh was almost constantly engaged in putting down rebellions by local rulers all of whom, during Temür's life, had been exceptionally faithful and much favored. They had thus retained much of their power and made use of the dissension within the Timurid dynasty to advance their own aims.

At the same time Shāhrukh faced a number of desertions and conspiracies among his own emirs, particularly from the members of Temür's personal following and their sons. It was the most prominent emirs, closest to Temür, who caused the most trouble. These emirs demanded privileged treatment and if they failed to get it they made their discontent known. The first to resist Shāhrukh, in the beginning of 808/1405, was Sulaymānshāh b. Dā'ūd, related to the dynasty by marriage and recently installed as governor of Rayy and Firuzkuh. His resistance was motivated apparently by his unwillingness to submit to Shāhrukh's orders or to put up with actions of Shāhrukh's which went against his own wishes. Sulaymānshāh could well consider himself equal, in prestige or power, to the prince he served. He had been assigned to Khorasan with Shāhrukh in 799/1396–7 to act as guardian and advisor to the prince, then only twenty years old.[40] As I have explained in Chapter 4 such appointments were designed to curb the power of the Timurid princes and did not create a strong bond between the prince and the emir attached to him.

The immediate cause of Sulaymānshāh's revolt was Shāhrukh's execution of Temür's grandson Sulṭān Ḥusayn whom Sulaymānshāh had harbored for some time when he fled from Transoxiana after rebelling against Khalīl Sulṭān. When Shāhrukh ignored Sulaymānshāh's request that he punish the emirs who had executed Sulṭān Ḥusayn, Sulaymānshāh appropriated the funds which he had been given to arrange a feast and set off for the fortress of Kalat, turning a deaf ear to Shāhrukh's exhortation to do his duty by upholding the will of the dead sovereign. He was however soon defeated by Shāhrukh, and took refuge with Khalīl Sulṭān in Transoxiana.[41]

In the same year Shāhmalik, formerly keeper of the seal and one of Temür's closest followers, left Shāhrukh and went to Pīr Muḥammad b. Jahāngīr, but this was only a temporary misunderstanding and Shāhmalik soon returned to Shāhrukh's service.[42] At the end of 808/1406 several of Shāhrukh's most important emirs united against him. This uprising was led by the son of a member of Temür's personal following, Saᶜīd Khwāja b. Shaykh ᶜAlī Bahadur, and included several sons of two other members, Ḥājjī Sayf al-Dīn and Üch Qara Bahadur. Saᶜīd Khwāja had become very powerful; Shāhrukh had granted him the region of Mashhad–Tus earlier in the year, and he had distinguished himself in putting down the rebellion of Sulṭān ᶜAlī Sabzawārī. He may well also have enriched himself during this campaign, since he plundered many areas held by the rebels.[43]

Now Saᶜīd Khwāja began to gather emirs around himself and left Herat heading for his own territory of western Khorasan. Neither his motivation nor his plans are consistently presented in the histories but he does appear to have received encouragement from princes outside Khorasan, either from Khalīl Sulṭān or from Iskandar b. ᶜUmar Shaykh in Fars. As it happened, Saᶜīd Khwāja received material help from neither prince but he was joined by the Persian ruler of Turshiz, near Mashhad, and by Pīr Pādishāh b. Lughmān. Shāhrukh mounted a large expedition against these armies and succeeded in dispersing them. Saᶜīd Khwāja fled to Shiraz but Pīr Muḥammad b. ᶜUmar Shaykh delivered him up to Shāhrukh who had him executed. Some of the emirs who had joined him returned to Shāhrukh; others remained in Fars.[44]

At the end of 810/1408 another group of Shāhrukh's most prominent emirs conspired against him. The leader of the conspiracy was Jahānmalik b. Mulkat, who was a relative of two members of Temür's following, Aqtemür and Qumarī Īnaq.[45] Jahānmalik had been assigned to Shāhrukh's service while the prince was still an infant, and had enjoyed great favor.[46] The cause of the conspiracy he led was the threat of high taxation by Shāhrukh's vizier who wrote a detailed list of all the possessions and land holdings of Shāhrukh's notables, much exaggerating their worth. As a result a large group of emirs decided to leave Shāhrukh.[47] Almost all of the emirs involved in this conspiracy were sons or grandsons of Temür's most prominent followers.[48] These men left Herat, hoping to get control of the armies prepared for an expedition to Sistan, but Shāhrukh chased them and scattered them. He captured many of them, executed Jahānmalik and Saᶜādat b. Temürtash and forgave most of the others. Several of them escaped to Fars where they were well received by Rustam b. ᶜUmar Shaykh.[49]

Like the other princes of this time, Shāhrukh needed material rewards to keep the loyalty of his army. The histories of the period mention few disbursements from Shāhrukh's treasury to his troops. This may be chance, but it could indicate an unwillingness to squander the contents of his treasury, which had been gathered during his own rule in Khorasan. Unlike Khalīl Sulṭān, he had a strong and long-standing attachment to the region he governed and a direct stake in its well-being. It is perhaps significant that in 807/1405 when Shāhrukh was contemplating a campaign into Transoxiana to unseat Khalīl Sulṭān, he sent some emirs to gather an army and money from his own province, while at the same time he sent Shāhmalik to Bukhara to bring the contents of its treasury.[50]

What Shāhrukh did use to reward his commanders was grants of land, or *soyurghals*. In 808/1405–6, for instance, he granted the region of Sarakhs to Sulaymānshāh.[51] In 908/1406, he bestowed the lands taken from the rebellious leader of Turshiz on Miḍrāb b. Chekü, who had been instrumental in Shāhrukh's victory over him.[52] In 810/1407–8, Shāhrukh granted several areas as *soyurghals*; he gave Damghan to Sayyid ᶜIzz al-Dīn of Hazar Jarib, Shaburqan to the prince Sayyidī Aḥmad b. ᶜUmar Shaykh, and Andkhud to his brother-in-law, Sayyid Aḥmad Tarkhan.[53] It seems likely moreover that many of Shāhrukh's emirs possessed *tiyüls*, lands distributed by the government; these are mentioned among the items which Ghiyāth al-Dīn Simnānī entered in his tax register when preparing to tax Shāhrukh's emirs.[54] The number of grants which Shāhrukh made in the first few years of his rule and the consistent use of the word *soyurghal* for this purpose suggest that these were indeed grants of land with tax immunity intended to provide income for the recipient. This was a means of support which was fairly rare under Temür, but became a major form of payment during Shāhrukh's reign.[55]

In discussing political events in Khorasan one should consider the role of the tribes of the Ulus Chaghatay two of which, the Arlat and the Apardï, had been centered at Shaburqan and Andkhud. Of the Apardï in this region there is no mention in contemporary histories, and I have not been able to trace them by indirect means. Their old headquarters at Shaburqan and Andkhud were used freely by Shāhrukh and his supporters, as well as by other people.[56] In 810/1407–8, as I have mentioned above, Shāhrukh granted both Andkhud and Shaburqan as *soyurghals* to his supporters. It is also unclear who led the Khorasan Apardï.[57]

The Arlat, who had been much less powerful at the time of Temür's rise to power, were more visible than the Apardï after Temür's death. They were led by Yādgārshāh Arlat, an emir of considerable prominence. Yādgārshāh had been with Khalīl Sulṭān in Tashkent and was among the emirs who raised him to the throne, but soon thereafter he switched his allegiance to Pīr Muḥammad b. Jahāngīr, and after Pīr Muḥammad's murder in 809/1407, went into Shāhrukh's service.[58] Yādgārshāh is mentioned twice at the head of Arlat troops, in 808/1406 and in 809/1407.[59] One cannot tell much from his career about the power or position of his tribe. It is notable that Yādgārshāh did not take part in the rebellions against either Pīr Muḥammad or Shāhrukh. He was indeed among the few prominent emirs who remained consistently loyal to the princes he served.

The political activity in Khorasan no longer included the tribes who had been such important actors at an earlier period. The men who now struggled to increase their own power or to resist that of Shāhrukh were those who under Temür had shown consistent loyalty and little independent political activity, namely the most favored of the local dynasties and the members of Temür's personal following.

Azerbaijan

Although Azerbaijan had been a favorite winter pasture for Temür and his army it was with Arab ᶜIraq the first province lost to the Timurids.[60] The political struggle in this region included all the groups I have discussed above – the members of Temür's dynasty and of his following, local rulers, and the nomad confederations of the area. It was the last of these, the Qaraqoyunlu Turkmens, who presented the greatest threat to Timurid control and who succeeded in taking over the province.

The history of these years shows clearly how difficult it was for the Timurid princes to keep the loyalty of their followers. Emirs migrated freely between Amīrānshāh's two sons, occasionally going over to serve other princes as well, and several of them resisted the princes they served. A further problem which confronted the princes was their lack of money; they quickly ran out of funds with which to pay their troops and had to reward them instead by permitting them to plunder their own province. The history of Azerbaijan therefore illustrates the weakest aspects of the system which Temür had constructed.

At Temür's death Azerbaijan was governed by Amīrānshāh's son ᶜUmar. The first threat to his sovereignty came from Jahānshāh b. Chekü, who had been one of Temür's closest followers and possibly his most powerful one, having inherited from his father Chekü Barlas both the Qara'unas troops and the position of *amīr al-umarā'*. Temür had appointed him as ᶜUmar's guardian when he made him governor of this province. Jahānshāh and ᶜUmar had apparently been increasingly estranged, as Jahānshāh, attempting to make ᶜUmar follow Temür's practice as he understood it, found ᶜUmar less and less willing to listen to him. About a month after Temür's death Jahānshāh rose against ᶜUmar; he came to the door of ᶜUmar's tent where ᶜUmar was conferring with several of his advisors, and killed some of those closest to the prince. However when Jahānshāh found himself outnumbered he fled, and was pursued and killed. The histories of the period all agree that this was an attempt to increase his own power and influence; according to one source he had felt himself ignored by ᶜUmar and so revenged himself on those more influential than he, according to others he already had great power and was aspiring to sovereignty.[61] Given his status he could well have thought himself in a position to rule Azerbaijan, whether through ᶜUmar or without him. He clearly felt himself equipped to interpret Temür's will.

The next challenge to ᶜUmar's rule came from his brother and his father, In 805/1403 Temür had divided western Iran among the sons of Amīrānshāh, placing Khalīl Sulṭān in Armenia and Georgia, ᶜUmar in Azerbaijan, and Abā Bakr in Arab ᶜIraq and Kurdistan. Amīrānshāh himself, having earlier been deprived of his governorship, had accompanied Abā Bakr to ᶜIraq.[62] Soon after Temür's death Abā Bakr lost ᶜIraq to Sulṭān Aḥmad Jalayir,[63] so Abā Bakr and Amīrānshāh joined ᶜUmar in Azerbaijan. Before long the princes began to disagree and ᶜUmar seized Abā Bakr, imprisoned him at Sultaniyya and plundered his army.[64]

Abā Bakr escaped with the help of his jailers, taking with him the contents of the treasury at Sultaniyya which he divided up among his soldiers. He set off to rejoin Amīrānshāh who had gone to Khorasan; this happened at the beginning of 808/1405.[65] Abā Bakr and Amīrānshāh then returned and captured Sultaniyya. Many of ᶜUmar's emirs deserted to Abā Bakr, including two who had just collected the taxes from Tabriz, and who now presented them to Abā Bakr instead of ᶜUmar. Nonetheless Abā Bakr put many of these people to death since some of them had been involved in his earlier capture.[66]

ᶜUmar, deserted by ever more emirs, retreated to Maragha, where he gathered around himself a new army consisting of Barlas, Suldus and Turkmen soldiers. He then headed for Tabriz thinking to fortify himself there and to collect money for his army. The population however had suffered too recently and too severely from the extortion of his officials and refused him entry. On hearing that Abā Bakr was approaching, ᶜUmar left for Fars, to solicit help from the sons of ᶜUmar Shaykh.[67] Together with them he fought Abā Bakr in Dhū'l-Qaᶜda 808/April 1406; Abā Bakr defeated the allies, and chased them back to Isfahan, whose region he plundered.[68] After this ᶜUmar fled to Shāhrukh in Khorasan, where he died at the end of 809/1407.[69]

Abā Bakr now took over Tabriz, but although he had no further competition from within the dynasty he encountered more formidable opponents among the local rulers and Turkmen tribes, particularly the Qaraqoyunlu. These groups had begun to cause trouble soon after Temür's death.[70] The Qaraqoyunlu leader Qara Yūsuf had found two local allies, Sayyidī Aḥmad whom Temür had confirmed as ruler of Shakki in 802/1399–1400, and Shaykh Ibrāhīm Shīrwānī who had been during Temür's life one of his staunchest and most active supporters, enjoying great personal favor.[71] Another threat to Azerbaijan was the Jalayirid dynasty of ᶜIraq, whose ruler, Sulṭān Aḥmad, took over Tabriz in 1406.[72] The Jalayir, like the Qaraqoyunlu, had survived intact under Temür's rule.

Abā Bakr succeeded in regaining both Tabriz and Sultaniyya for a time partly because of treachery within Sulṭān Aḥmad's following, but he soon lost the region again to Qara Yūsuf and his allies, who defeated him in Jumādā I 809/October 1406. In 810/1407–8, Abā Bakr and Amīrānshāh attempted to regain Azerbaijan but suffered a disastrous defeat in battle with Qara Yūsuf in Dhū'l-Qa^{c}da/April 1408. Amīrānshāh was killed and Abā Bakr took refuge first in Kerman and then in Sistan.[73] Azerbaijan was now lost to the Timurid dynasty.

The princes in Azerbaijan were defeated not only because of the strength of their opponents, but also because of the weakness of their own political and financial base. Part of the trouble and confusion in Azerbaijan was due to disagreement over the status of Temür's emirs after his death, and the kind of service which they owed to his descendants. Many emirs, and especially the most prominent ones, had begun as part of Amīrānshāh's army and had then passed into the service of his sons. They may well have felt that their loyalty lay with the whole family or with Amīrānshāh himself rather than with either one of his sons.[74] These emirs then were probably not rebelling but asserting their right to choose among the members of the family they served.

The history of Azerbaijan in these years is one of constant desertions and insubordination by the Chaghatay emirs, and harsh reprisals by the Timurid princes. When Abā Bakr and Amīrānshāh raided Sultaniyya in 808/1405 for instance many of ^{c}Umar's emirs left him to enter their service, including those who had just been collecting the taxes of Tabriz, as I have mentioned above. Even in times of relative success the princes could not count on their armies; as Abā Bakr turned back from ^{c}Iraq-i ^{c}Ajam where he had gone to confront ^{c}Umar and ^{c}Umar Shaykh's sons, several of his emirs deserted and went to Isfahan, some of them actually after he had defeated his opponents.[75]

In 809/1406–7 Buyan Qa'uchin who under Temür had been *darugha* first of Rayy and then of Tabriz, rose against Abā Bakr and suggested to ^{c}Umar that they undertake a joint attack against him. Abā Bakr defeated Buyan and put him to death with his relatives.[76] In 809 also, Abā Bakr faced resistance from a number of his most prominent emirs, many of them sons or relatives of Temür's personal followers. These emirs planned to overthrow Abā Bakr and install Amīrānshāh in his place; Abā Bakr soon discovered this, and killed several of the conspirators.[77]

The problems besetting the princes were exacerbated by their difficulty in finding sufficient funds to pay their armies. It is in this region that we see most clearly the financial problems of Temür's successors and the destructiveness of the measures they used to relieve them. The contents of the existing treasuries did not sustain the princes for long. When Abā Bakr escaped from Sultaniyya in early 808/1405, he took its treasure with him and divided it up among his followers. The treasury of Tabriz was also apparently soon emptied; early in 808 ^{c}Umar sent officials to extort wealth from the notables of Tabriz, and soon after tried to obtain yet more money from the population, in preparation for a campaign against Abā Bakr, but was refused admission into the city.[78]

When they had exhausted the resources to be obtained from the population by legal or quasi-legal means, the princes turned to plunder as a way to pay their armies. Thus when ᶜUmar headed to Sultaniyya against Abā Bakr in 808, his army raided herds of livestock along the way.[79] Abā Bakr, retreating after his defeat by Qara Yūsuf in 809/1406, allowed his army to sack Tabriz as a reward.[80] Later that year he sent part of his army to raid in Kurdistan, despite the help he had received from Malik ᶜIzz al-Dīn Kurd in fighting the Qaraqoyunlu.[81] He also plundered the regions of Maragha and Ardabil, both within his own region.[82]

In Azerbaijan therefore the measures Temür had taken to secure his personal power had indeed prevented the members of his own family from constructing a secure power base, but it had not destroyed the strength of the local nomad confederations nor shaken the position of the regional dynasties whom he had favored. Amīrānshāh, ᶜUmar and Abā Bakr, disagreeing among themselves and unsure of the loyalty of their followers, were ill-equipped to withstand the attacks of their local rivals for power.

The political situation in Temür's realm during the years after his death resembled in many ways that of the Ulus Chaghatay during his rise to power. Contestants for power spent their time on constant campaigns and those beneath them in almost constant rebellion. Power was very hard to hold, and emirs were quick to switch their allegiances when it seemed advantageous. Nonetheless under the surface the new situation was very different from the old. First of all the people who now held power and who took part in the political struggle were not those who had been most prominent in the earlier period. Only those who had been loyal to Temür throughout his life had remained strong enough to take part in the war of succession after his death. In the place of the tribal aristocracy, it was now the members of Temür's new elite – his descendants and the members of his following – who competed for control over his realm.

The other people who increased their own power at this period were the native rulers of the territories Temür had conquered. Here again a different set of people had risen to prominence through the personal favor of the sovereign. The strongest dynasties, which had posed a threat to Temür, had been weakened or destroyed while smaller ones were favored and given positions in the new army. It was these who now joined the struggle, trying to retain their independence or increase their holdings. Only one set of people succeeded both in opposing Temür during his reign and in retaining sufficient strength to challenge his descendants after his death. These were the nomad confederations of western Iran – the Jalayirids and the Qaraqoyunlu.

What had changed most during Temür's rule was the conduct of politics. Temür had come to power within a tribal political system which provided for those within it a common bond, a code of political behavior, and an absorbing occupation. This system however was not dependent on a central leader, and indeed the political dynamics of the Ulus Chaghatay had been detrimental to strong central leadership. In order to maintain power over the Ulus Chaghatay therefore, Temür had had not only to weaken the tribes but also to suppress the political system that centered around them.

In the new order that Temür set up, all political relationships focused on the sovereign; each of his subordinates was loyal directly to him. The relations among individuals and groups within the ruling elite remained undefined. This was true particularly of the relationship between the princes and the people attached to their provinces – both Chaghatay emirs and local rulers. In order to prevent the princes from gaining too much power, Temür had limited their mandates within the provinces they ruled; thus although the emirs and rulers who made up their armies provided service to the princes as governors, they still owed their primary loyalty and obedience to Temür.

When Temür died therefore he left behind a political order which could not function without him, and one which provided for his successors no clear political relationships or rules of conduct. It was partly this fact that made it so difficult for the Timurid princes to retain the cooperation of the Chaghatay emirs, and particularly of Temür's personal followers. As Temür's heirs, the princes attempted to act as sovereigns, but Temür's personal followers expected to be treated as allies and to hold a privileged position in the new order. They also wanted to enjoy some of the rights previously held by the tribal emirs – particularly the right to switch allegiance. Under these circumstances it was inevitable that Temür's emirs should disagree with their new masters. The will of the dead sovereign remained the paramount standard, but there was no agreement on who could best interpret it.

Temür's rule had changed both the rules of political activity and the incentives behind it. Within the Ulus Chaghatay men aspiring to rule had had little immediate material reward to offer their followers. Tribal emirs had attached themselves to one or another candidate for power for political reasons, hoping either to gain or to retain power over their own tribes. If they found that they had made the wrong choice, they changed their allegiance. This was a fluid political system but it was an established and accepted one, with rules understood by its participants. Supra-tribal leaders therefore accepted the frequent switching of allegiance as reasonable behavior, and only rarely punished it.

When Temür consolidated his power over the Ulus Chaghatay he substituted for these motivations a new set of rewards, and a new set of rules and relationships. Loyalty to the sovereign was now absolute and unchangeable.

The reward for service was no longer independent political advantage but the promise of booty and of advancement within a growing army and administration. After Temür's death, this system could not hold and his descendants had few attractive rewards to offer those who served them. Lacking the rules which had governed politics in the Ulus Chaghatay, they had to resort to a system of material reward and severe punishment. The succession struggle after Temür's death is notable both for its expense and for its violence. Since emirs gained no outside political advantage from their association with one or another prince, they now required greater and prompter material rewards to retain their loyalty. It is notable that the Timurid princes often rewarded their troops before campaigns, and often lavishly. In Azerbaijan therefore, ᶜUmar and Abā Bakr allowed their troops to plunder on their way to battle, or while preparing for a campaign. Khalīl Sulṭān likewise opened the doors of his treasuries before he set out to oppose Sulṭān Ḥusayn early in 808/1405 and before his expedition against Pīr Muḥammad later that year.

Even emirs planning to resist apparently needed money to do so. Sulaymānshāh, rebelling in Khorasan, used the funds which had been given him for a feast in order to bolster his own power.[83] According to Tāj al-Salmānī, Saᶜīd Khwāja likewise appropriated some funds from Shāhrukh's *dīwān* to use for his uprising.[84] Early rewards were the more necessary because the success of such expeditions was not assured. Thus in this new situation material rewards took the place of political ones, and advance payment replaced the expectation of booty at the end of a campaign.

Just as the Timurid princes had become lavish in their rewards, they had become quick to punish those who transgressed against them. After Temür's death his emirs, particularly the members of his personal following, who had been loyal exclusively to Temür, still felt free to switch allegiance, but the princes did not accept this, and frequently executed the emirs who deserted them. Thus for instance Abā Bakr killed most of the emirs who left ᶜUmar to join him. Shāhrukh likewise executed the emirs who led movements of opposition against him; both Saᶜīd Khwāja and Jahānmalik were killed, along with their closest associates.

The frequency of executions at this time shows also that the killing of Chaghatay emirs had become more acceptable and less risky than it had been earlier. Even after Temür came to power, during the first years of his reign, he had been hesitant to execute tribal emirs until they had rebelled several times. This caution was due partly to the fact that tribes were likely to take vengeance for the killing of one of their members. After Temür's death the emirs who were most active in politics were not tribal ones, nor apparently did they belong to any cohesive groups which could avenge their killing, or whose support would be lost through such an action. In the eyes of the dynasty moreover, they had become subjects rather than allies whose favor must be courted.

In the course of his reign Temür had succeeded in transforming the political world over which he had taken control, although he had done so without destroying most of the structures which had made it up. It was the Ulus Chaghatay that had been most completely changed. By the time of his death the tribes had been largely removed from political and even military activity. The people who were now fighting for power over Temür's realm were a new elite which possessed neither secure centers of power, nor clear political norms. The army of Transoxiana, with which Khalīl Sulṭān tried to maintain himself on the throne, was a primarily foreign one, made up of soldiers from the distant lands of Temür's dominions.

In the lands Temür conquered he had weakened or destroyed some dynasties and had elevated others, but those which remained functioned much as they had before. They operated therefore at an advantage while the members of the Ulus Chaghatay, threatened as much by their followers as their rivals, consumed the wealth of their realm in their struggle for control. Temür had given his dynasty sufficient power and charisma to maintain their rule, but when the question of succession was finally decided, the realm his successors inherited was a smaller and poorer one.

CHAPTER 8

Conclusion

Two relationships form central concerns in this study and pose the fundamental questions I have tried to answer. The first is the connection between institutions and the political dynamics they engender. I have tried to determine how and to what extent social, political and administrative structures determined the activities of the people within them, and conversely, how these people used the structures around them. The second relationship I have dealt with is that between politics and control. Tribal societies are often highly politicized and the practice of active and independent politics poses a clear threat to personal sovereignty. Much of this book is an examination of the way in which Temür suppressed political activity, and what this meant for the society he ruled.

The politics which threatened Temür's position were the tribal politics of the Ulus Chaghatay, the same politics he had practiced during his rise to power. It was the Turco-Mongolian tribes that provided the basic structure of the Ulus; they defined its membership, its territory and its identity. In many ways the tribes served as upholders of a stable order. Within their own regions they allocated grazing grounds to nomads and collected taxes from the settled population, and their territories together defined the boundaries of the Ulus. The tribes further helped to impose social and political order through the custom of tribal vengeance, which kept intertribal violence at an acceptably low level. At the same time, the close connection of the nomads to the settled population controlled violence against city and countryside.

The tribes likewise served as the main focus for politics within the Ulus, and here their role was much more complicated. For the politically active population of the Ulus Chaghatay – the tribal aristocracy – the tribe served as a framework for action; it was less a focus for loyalty than a tool to use or a prize to win. The politics of the Ulus Chaghatay was above all the politics of consent. The tribes within this confederation required chiefs, and their chiefs held at once a recognized position and considerable power. However chiefs could assume leadership only through the support of their followers and could retain it only with their continued backing. In this situation it is not surprising that the tribal chiefs often had rivals for leadership within the tribe. In their continuing struggle, both chief and rival sought allies among their fellow tribesmen, among members of other tribes, and even outside the Ulus Chaghatay. Thus while the tribes defined and motivated the political activities of their members, they did not limit them.

The question of leadership over the whole of the Ulus Chaghatay was an important one, and one even more difficult to resolve than that of leadership over the tribe. This too was an office which had to be gained and held with the consent of the population, and support was the more difficult to keep because a central leader was not necessary to the functioning of the Ulus. The idea of a central leader who would uphold the Chinggisid order and the honor of the Chaghadayid house was indeed a crucial part of the identity of the Ulus as a Mongol successor state and as heir to the traditions of the Mongol empire. Nonetheless the Ulus had been formed neither through conquest nor through attachment to an individual leader, but through a gradual gathering of tribes with common interests and common loyalties to the Chaghadayid house. Strong central leadership indeed was an inconvenience, since it was likely to limit the power of the tribes and circumscribe the activities of the tribal aristocracy. The members of the Ulus Chaghatay accorded recognition to the offices of central leadership – both khan and emir – but this did not make them obey the men who held the office. Central leaders who attempted to assert their authority might be deemed unfit and replaced without denying the validity of the office they held. We find that the Ulus Chaghatay rarely had strong central rule, but almost always had some supra-tribal ruler, or a contest for central leadership.

In the Ulus Chaghatay the structures and institutions – tribes, tribal and supratribal leaders – served less as instruments to limit and control the population than as a focus for political activity. This was a politics which allowed great latitude of individual choice, at least for those within the ruling class. What made it possible to sustain such a system was a strong set of common political norms, traditions and relationships shared by all the active members of the Ulus. These included the right to switch allegiance at will and to leave the Ulus and seek allies outside it, protected by the disapproval of internal violence. It was these relationships, even more than the formal structures, which determined the political system of the Ulus Chaghatay.

Although the Ulus Chaghatay provided Temür with both structural and ideological foundations useful to a central ruler these could not guarantee his rule, because they did not allow him to control relationships within the Ulus. He was able to exploit the ideal of central leadership to legitimate his sovereignty. Throughout his career he used and emphasized the legitimacy of the Chaghadayid house, and his followers continued throughout his life and beyond to identify themselves as Chaghatays. Nonetheless, since the loyalty owed to an office did not necessarily protect the person who held it, even a general acceptance of Temür's legitimation could not ensure his continuance in power. To remain in his position therefore, Temür had to attract the loyalty of the Ulus Chaghatay also to his own person. He had moreover to make this loyalty absolute and unchangeable, and it was here that the political traditions of the Ulus Chaghatay stood in his way. As ruler of the Ulus Temür faced a system which would either limit his power or, if he insisted on asserting control, would probably unseat him. In order to maintain his position and to become truly sovereign, he had to change this system radically. To gain and maintain personal sovereignty Temür needed a government dependent entirely on his person. Not only should the people within it depend directly upon him – so should the functions it fulfilled and the activity within it. This was the antithesis of the system which had existed in the Ulus Chaghatay in which power had been diffuse, and activity centered around the tribes.

In the place of the tribal aristocracy Temür now promoted a dependent elite, made up first of his personal following, and then of his own descendants. The administration which these men staffed did not function independently. It was a system of overlapping offices and responsibilities, in which Temür played people and groups off against each other. He used his senior followers to limit the power and independence of the princes whom he had appointed as governors, while using the different princely armies to scatter the families of these same followers. He settled Chaghatays outside of the original territory of the Ulus Chaghatay while deporting new populations to settle within it. Power of different kinds was carefully separated – the control of troops going to one set of people and the control of land to another. Most of this system was not new with Temür. It was typical of most non-bureaucratic governments and particularly of the Turco-Mongolian states whose tradition Temür inherited. It was also a highly successful system of personal control, and it was probably for this reason that it had become so widespread and so fully elaborated under Mongol rule. Temür had only to adopt it, and to change a few elements to enhance his own personal power.

What was most crucial to Temür and hardest for him to effect was the change in the conduct of politics, making all political movement dependent on himself. The most important element of this process was the suppression of tribal politics. After twelve years of patient effort, Temür was able to transfer the leadership of the Ulus to men personally loyal to him, but this in itself could not ensure the obedience of the Ulus tribes. It was not enough to put down tribal uprisings and to replace the tribal leadership; the internal politics of the tribes had also to be changed. There was no guarantee that the men Temür appointed to lead the tribes would be able to maintain their positions or that, as tribal chiefs, they could command the full loyalty of their tribesmen. Nor was it sufficient to weaken the tribes as centers of power; they had also to be constricted as centers of the political activity which brought with it a constant movement and shift of allegiances.

What made this process particularly difficult for Temür was the fact that he could afford to destroy almost none of the existing structures, and few of the people within them. Chinggis Khan, rising to power in a similarly fluid confederation, had inherited a culture with ingrained violence. He could kill those who opposed him, break up tribes by force, and massacre tribal populations. The Ulus Chaghatay, unlike Mongolia, was a society in balance and with a tradition which discouraged violence. Temür could not afford to flout this tradition. He had therefore to subvert, rather than to destroy, to balance rather than to build, and this may have been one reason for the insecurity which remained with him throughout his life.

What Temür did was to push the tribes outside of the central power structure, to suppress them as vehicles for individual power. Some of the methods he used were straightforward. He took from the tribes their control of land and regional manpower, leaving probably only the inherited troops of the tribe under the control of tribal chiefs. Moreover after his first years in power he removed the tribes from honorary positions within his realm. By denying the title of "Amīr" even to those of his followers who led tribes, he suppressed the tribes as vehicles for status or honor.

Temür's treatment of his own tribe, the Barlas, provides a good illustration of his policy. He came to power as chief of the Barlas, controlling among other resources the hereditary troops of the tribe. Nonetheless, once he had taken over the Ulus he did not choose to rule through the tribe, and indeed at some point he returned the hereditary troops – the *ulugh ming* – to two relatives of the former chief, neither of them particularly powerful emirs. Each of the five lineages of the Barlas was represented among Temür's *amīrs*, and a few Barlas emirs particularly close to Temür held hereditary governorships inside the territory of the Ulus Chaghatay. Neither Temür's own lineage nor that of the former chief held a preponderant position.

Temür turned the Barlas into a formal, immobile entity, a little apart from the center of power. An ambitious member of the Barlas tribe did not attain power through a position within the tribe but only through a direct relationship to Temür. The same was true, even more strongly, for the other tribes of the Ulus. There were powerful tribal emirs – Shaykh Nūr al-Dīn Jalayir and Jahānshāh Barlas for instance – but these men were not the chiefs of tribes. The leadership of a tribe no longer provided sufficient wealth, manpower or prestige to bring someone into the first ranks of Temür's government. It was therefore not a position worth fighting for. When the new order was in position, the tribes ceased to be a major focus of political activity, and much of the independent political activity of the Ulus disappeared.

Temür's management of his new elite shows an equal concern for the monopoly of movement. Temür determined the composition of this elite at the beginning of his career, promoting his personal followers, his sons and grandsons, and to a lesser extent, the *qa'uchin* emirs. In an active and expanding enterprise, one might expect continuing recruitment into the ruling group, but Temür's elite almost immediately became a closed class, increasing by natural reproduction rather than by the inclusion of new members from outside. Only a few tribal emirs and a small number of outsiders – primarily Khorasanians – were able to add themselves to the fringes of this group. Most of the offices held by Temür's elite were hereditary – with the choice among several candidates open to influence from Temür. Thus even within this class there was little room for advancement through personal maneuver. Positions which might have allowed independent or regional political influence, particularly governorships, were kept away from the most powerful members of the elite, and firmly under Temür's personal control.

Temür also guarded against the formation of strong personal relationships among the members of his elite, keeping all loyalties directed towards himself. The almost equal status he granted to the senior members of his following and his own family is an illustration of this. Although the princes held large armies, often from early in their careers, the emirs within the princely armies remained loyal primarily to Temür. In a state within which the primary standard was the will of the sovereign, princes of the blood could not claim much more authority than the personal followers who had formed the intimate circle of their leader from the early days of his career.

To govern as sovereign Temür did not dismantle and rebuild the political system, but subverted it. There were few new institutions within Temür's administration. He destroyed none of the structures of the Ulus Chaghatay and killed only a few of its people. The tribes and groups of the Ulus, the offices traditional to Turco-Mongolian states, and the individuals active before his rise, all remained in place. Nonetheless this was a true act of creation, and behind it lay an act of destruction. What Temür changed and changed radically was the meaning and function of structures. While he left individuals alive, he transformed their interrelationships and the rules which regulated their behavior. Temür achieved spectacular successes during his lifetime, and left a system which could not survive his death.

The fact of a breakdown should not surprise us. It is often remarked that power based on personal loyalties cannot be passed on intact. Moreover, within the Turco-Mongolian system, succession struggles were an accepted practice, useful for the maintenance of competent rule. The question we must address here then is why the struggle at Temür's death was exceptionally long, destructive and debilitating. Although his son Shāhrukh was eventually able to gain power and to reconstruct the Timurid realm, this task took him fifteen years, and the realm he eventually won was smaller and poorer than the one Temür had left. One should not ascribe the length of this struggle to Temür's failure to centralize his realm – to his creation of separate governorships under his sons. As I have shown, his government was on the contrary highly centralized; the problem he left behind him was not too many princes with power, but princes with too little power. None of Temür's descendants had a strong base from which to vie for power. It was

Temür's very success at monopolizing power which cost his descendants so dear at his death.

What made the Timurid succession so difficult was the absence of those political norms and relationships which had regulated earlier contests. When it became necessary once more to compete for power, there was no definite system to return to. The tribes, whose practice of vengeance had helped to regulate violence, were no longer at the center of politics. The main actors – Temür's descendants and his followers – had no clear political relationships beyond those which bound them to Temür. Temür's followers and their descendants wished to take on the rights and privileges earlier accorded to tribal emirs, and to enjoy the same freedom of action. The Timurid princes on the other hand wanted to practice a newer type of politics, and to demand from their subordinates the same absolute loyalty that Temür had commanded. Both groups tried to appeal to the one remaining standard, the will of the dead sovereign, each believing itself better qualified to know it. It was Temür's strength then, his success in dissolving old relationships and reordering them around himself, which made the political breakdown at his death so complete and so difficult to overcome. Had Temür been a lesser sovereign, his successors might have been greater ones.

Temür began his career within a tribal confederation which required no central leader to maintain its prosperity or its cohesion. Because the basis for rule in the Ulus Chaghatay was consent, he could maintain sovereign power only by making himself necessary. He spent his long life of conquest and maneuver doing just this, and by the end of his life he ruled a state dependent on his person, made up not of allies giving provisional loyalty, but of subjects owing it. Such a state could not survive its sovereign, but while it lasted it allowed its ruler spectacular successes, and a personal charisma which lasted well beyond his lifetime or that of his dynasty.

APPENDIX A

The powers of the Ulus Chaghatay

The Apardï

The Apardï were an important force in the Ulus Chaghatay in the mid-fourteenth century, and were active also in the politics of Khorasan. I have not found them mentioned however before this time. They are not among the tribes described or even mentioned in Rashīd al-Dīn or *The Secret History of the Mongols*.[1]

It seems likely that the Apardï, like the Borolday and the Yasa'urī, originated as the regiment of an individual leader. One of the senior Apardï emirs, Öljeytü, is once referred to as Öljeytü, son of Apardï.[2] The emirs of one branch of the Apardï at least – that at Shaburqan – were Naymans,[3] something which could more easily occur to a regiment than a tribe, and which recalls the Jawun-i Qurban, originally a garrison troop, whose emirs were Oyirat, as well as the Borolday whose emirs were of the Orona'ut clan. In all these cases, although the clan affiliation is mentioned in the sources, the emirs are most usually identified by the name of the group they lead.[4]

The Apardï seem to have been quite closely connected with the Qara'unas, and may indeed have been included within them. One of their centers was Arhang, very close to Sali Saray, the winter pasture of the Qara'unas emirs, and the Apardï emirs were among the most faithful supporters of both Qazaghan and Amīr Ḥusayn.[5] It is possible therefore that the Apardï, like the Borolday, originated as the personal troops of an emir of the Qara'unas. This would explain both their sudden appearance in Khorasan and their close connection with the Qara'unas.

The Apardï had two centers, one in northern Khorasan at Shaburqan and Andkhud, the other on the upper Oxus in Arhang and Khuttalan.[6] Each place had its own leader who passed his position on to his descendants; Muḥammad Khwāja Apardï ruled in Shaburqan until his death in 759/1358 when he was succeeded by his son Zinda Ḥasham, while the Apardï in Khuttalan were ruled by Öljeytü Apardï, who after his death in 776 or later was succeeded by his son, Khwāja Yūsuf.[7] In Khuttalan the Apardïs shared power with the Khuttalānī emirs. The two branches of the Apardï were related, and usually on friendly terms. They participated in many of the same campaigns, and were most often on the same side of quarrels within the Ulus.[8] It is likely that the Arhang Apardï were the senior branch.[9]

The two branches seem to have continued separate after Temür's takeover, but neither branch was very prominent during the latter part of his reign. Temür removed the control of Shaburqan from Zinda Ḥasham after his second rebellion in 772–3/1371–2 and gave it to a personal follower, Buyan Temür b. Aqbugha, also a Nayman. Nothing further is known of the Apardï under Buyan Temür. A *tümen* of Apardïs was sent with Temür's son ʿUmar Shaykh to Uzkand in 778–9/1376–8; it is not clear whether these were the Apardï of Shaburqan or those of Khuttalan. A few

Apardï emirs are mentioned later under ᶜUmar Shaykh.[10] The Apardï in Arhang and Khuttalan remained under their own leaders and are mentioned under Khwāja Yūsuf b. Öljeytü in 790/1388.[11] In 810 Arhang was held by Khwāja ᶜAlī Apardï, who was either Khwāja Yūsuf's son or his brother. He did not however take an active part in the struggles after Temür's death.[12]

There are not a great number of marriages recorded for the Apardï. When Qazaghan killed Qazan Khan he gave one of his wives to Muḥammad Khwāja Apardï, and Temür gave one of Amīr Ḥusayn's wives, Dilshād Agha, to Zinda Ḥasham.[13] Temür also married Khwāja Yūsuf's daughter, Beg Malik Agha, to his son ᶜUmar Shaykh.[14]

The Arlat

The position of the Arlat in the Ulus Chaghatay remains unclear. There are no Arlat listed among the emirs of Chaghadai, but Qaidu did have some in his following when he controlled the Chaghadayid khanate.[15] Mīrkhwānd states that Arlat emirs were established at Maymana and Faryab in Khorasan from the time of the Mongol conquest; since this is just the area where they were found in the mid-fourteenth century these are almost certainly the same people, who with the other tribes of northern Khorasan had switched their allegiance from the Ilkhans to the Chaghadayids.[16]

The Arlat at this time held Andkhud and Gurziwan.[17] Since Zinda Ḥasham Apardï is also mentioned as the holder of Andkhud and played a much more prominent part in Ulus affairs than any of the Arlat emirs, it is probable that the Arlat were subservient to the Apardï.[18] We know little about the leadership of the Arlat, except that Andkhud was held by Tilenchi Arlat at the time of Tughluq Temür's invasion.[19] Tilenchi was later killed by Zinda Ḥasham Apardï for his support of Temür at a time when Zinda Ḥasham was rebelling against him.[20] It seems possible that the leadership of the Arlat, like that of a number of other tribes, was divided geographically. While Tilenchi is mentioned in connection with Andkhud, another Arlat emir, Türken, had his territory at Gurziwan or Faryab.[21]

Although Ibn ᶜArabshāh mentions the Arlat as one of the four main tribes of the Ulus Chaghatay,[22] they did not figure prominently in the politics of the Ulus. Only one Arlat emir is mentioned frequently in all the sources; this is Temür's brother-in-law, Mu'ayyad Arlat. Mu'ayyad, however, was a member of Temür's personal following and owed his prominence to his closeness to Temür. He is not named as leader of the Arlat or in connection with the territory of the Arlat.[23]

Aside from Mu'ayyad and his sons there are relatively few mentions of Arlat emirs, either before or after Temür's takeover. The most prominent in the early years were Tilenchi and Türken, mentioned above, both more notable for their deaths than their lives.[24] Although the Arlat are mentioned together with the Apardï in their struggle against the kings of Herat in the 740s and 750s/1340s and 1350s, individual Arlat emirs are not mentioned, even in Qazaghan's campaign against Herat in 752/1351–2.[25]

At the end of Temür's reign however, and in the succession struggle after his death, the Arlat appear more prominently. They were led apparently by Yādgārshāh Arlat, who was a powerful emir at the end of Temür's life, later under Pīr Muḥammad b. Jahāngīr and after his death under Shāhrukh.

The Arlat had a number of important marriage alliances. The mother of Malik Muᶜizz al-Dīn Kart's second son, Malik Muḥammad, was an Arlat.[26] Temür's follower, Amīr Mu'ayyad Arlat, was married to Temür's sister, Shīrīn Beg Agha,[27] and Mu'ayyad's daughter by this union, Sevinch Qutluq, married Pīr Muḥammad

Kart, son of Malik Ghiyāth al-Dīn.[28] Later one of ᶜUmar Shaykh's daughters married Yādgārshāh Arlat.[29]

Badakhshan

The region of Badakhshan was ruled, throughout the Mongol and most of the Timurid period, by indigenous kings.[30] These were however hardly strong enough to remain independent from the larger powers surrounding them, and their allegiance apparently followed that of the region of northern and eastern Khorasan, of which they were a part. Badakhshan seems to have been the northernmost part of the appanage which the Ilkhans granted to the Chaghadayid prince Yasa'ur.[31]

By the middle of the fourteenth century in any case Badakhshan had become part of the Ulus Chaghatay. Its shahs took part in Qazaghan's campaign against Herat in 752/1351–2, and they are mentioned in the list of rulers who made up the Ulus in 760–1/1358–60.[32] The shahs, or more often simply the army of Badakhshan, made up part first of Amīr Ḥusayn's army, then of Temür's in his final campaign against Amīr Ḥusayn in 771/1370, and finally became part of Temür's army of conquest.[33]

Badakhshan retained its own leaders throughout this period. In 761–2/1360–1, its king was Shāh Bahā' al-Dīn, but later the control of Badakhshan was apparently shared between two leaders. Ibn ᶜArabshāh states that Badakhshan was ruled by two brothers, and the accounts of Temür's and Amīr Ḥusayn's campaign there in 770/1368–9 also mention two leaders: Shāh Shaykh Muḥammad and Shāh Shaykh ᶜAlī.[34] Two shahs of Badakhshan are mentioned on Temür's Indian campaign – Shāh Lashgar Shāh and Shāh Bahā' al-Dīn.[35] Although the Badakhshanis must be regarded as part of the Ulus Chaghatay, there are indications that they were not fully equal members; they did not play an active part in the internal politics of the Ulus, and they were identified as Tajiks or as mountain men – thus to some extent as foreign.[36] The dynasty of Badakhshan does not seem to have married into the families of Temür or Amīr Ḥusayn.

The Barlas

The Barlas controlled the region of Kish, which apparently constituted a *tümen*.[37] Its leading clan claimed descent from Qarachar Noyan Barlas, the emir of one of the thousands assigned by Chinggis Khan to Chaghadai, and the *Muᶜizz al-ansāb* contains an annotated genealogy of the clan beginning with Qarachar.[38] According to many Timurid histories, the Barlas emirs had from ancient times held a special position in regard to the Chinggisids and after Qarachar in the Chaghadayid khanate, as all powerful *amīr al-umarā'* to the Khan. This position was held supposedly by the emirs of Temür's lineage.[39] Unfortunately we have almost no other information on the standing of the Barlas from the time of Qarachar to that of Temür. Rashīd al-Dīn's discussion of the Barlas is not detailed; in his listing and description of tribes he gives them only a short paragraph, and he mentions few members of the tribe in the rest of his work.[40]

The interpretation of what evidence there is varies considerably. Bartol'd was sceptical about the importance of Qarachar and his descendants within the Chaghadayid realm, and dismissed as complete fabrication the claim that Qarachar's descendants held the post of *amīr al-umarā'* in the Chaghadayid khanate. To support his opinion he pointed out that none of the sons or grandsons of Qarachar (known to us through the *Muᶜizz al-ansāb*) are mentioned in Rashīd al-Dīn.[41]

A. Z. V. Togan was much more willing to give credence to the claims of Timurid historians and in his article "Tahqīq-i nasab-i Amīr-i Tīmūr" he tried to refute Bartol'd's arguments. He examined a very early manuscript of Rashīd al-Dīn's *Jāmiᶜ al-tawārīkh*, copied in Baghdad in 717/1317–18 (Revan Köşku 1518) and found two references to Qarachar's son Ijal ('YJL) who was Temür's ancestor and the supposed inheritor of Qarachar's position. Togan attributed Bartol'd's failure to find these references to the fact that in both these passages the manuscripts used by Berezin in the edition of *Jāmiᶜ al-tawārīkh* that Bartol'd read have blanks instead of the name of Ijal.[42]

The evidence which Togan gives however does not seem sufficient to prove that the Barlas were the most important tribe in the Chaghadayid khanate. Timurid histories in describing the events before Temür's rise give little information about the Barlas, although they could be expected to emphasize their importance. If the Barlas were paramount in the Ulus, moreover, one would expect them to intermarry with the Chaghadayid dynasty, but before the time of Temür no such marriages are recorded in the genealogy given by the *Muᶜizz al-ansāb*.[43]

The genealogy of the Barlas allows us to see something of the internal structure of the leading Barlas clan. The *Muᶜizz* lists the names of many sons of Qarachar, but gives detailed lineages from only five of these: Shirgha (SHYRGH'), Yesünte Möngke, Lala (L'L'), Ildiz(?) ('YLDR), and Ijal ('YJL). All of these lineages were important both before Temür's takeover and throughout his career.

These lineages do not seem to been separate political entities, nor did any one of them hold a monopoly on political and military power. At the time that the Barlas first appear in the sources, in 760/1358–9, their leader was Ḥājjī Beg, of the line of Yesünte Möngke.[44] When he died however, leadership passed not to his son, but to Temür, who was of the lineage of Ijal.[45] Later, the hereditary troops of the tribe were led again by Ḥājjī Beg's family.[46] Throughout the early part of Temür's life, Barlas emirs of all five lineages are mentioned, and most usually acting together.[47]

When Temür distributed land and power among the Barlas after his acquisition of power, he did not favor his own lineage, outside his immediate family. The best positions went to Temür's closest associate Chekü and passed on to his descendants, but other lineages were also rewarded.[48] All the lineages of the Barlas seem to have been associated with the region of Kish.

The lineages therefore seem not to have been separate political or territorial forces. Their importance is clearer in the matter of inheritance, which can be traced in the *Muᶜizz al-ansāb*, whose information covers also Shāhrukh's reign. It is clear that governorships and often the command of troops passed from one member of a lineage to another. There is no single pattern of inheritance; positions went with approximately equal frequency from father to son and uncle to nephew, and were sometimes divided between son and nephew.[49] At this time the Barlas were apparently not an exogamous tribe, since the genealogy records marriages within it such as that of Dawlat Geldi, daughter of Pāyanda Sulṭān Barlas, to Temür's son Amīrānshāh and even, later, marriages among the descendants of Temür.[50] Most marriages recorded however were outside the tribe.

The Barlas therefore were a long established tribe within the Ulus Chaghatay, controlling land close to the khan's seat within the Ulus, an area which produced enough soldiers to be styled a *tümen*. The leading clan claimed descent from one of Chaghadai's important emirs, and was divided into lineages which, while they did not function as distinct political or military units, were important as a vehicle for the apportionment and inheritance of land and offices within the tribe.

The Besüd

The Besüd tribe was centered near Kabul where indeed they are found to this day.[51] This was within the territory associated with the Qara'unas,[52] but there is so little information on the Besüd in the Timurid sources that it is difficult to judge whether they should really be considered part of the Ulus Chaghatay. They are mentioned twice: once in 769/1368 resisting Amīr Ḥusayn under the leadership of Aqbugha and Pūlād Besüd, and again rebelling against Temür in 790/1388 under Abū Saᶜīd Besüd. When Abū Saᶜīd rebelled his old enemy, Aqbugha, was taken out of captivity and reinstalled as leader – he was to report to Jahānshāh Barlas who was in charge of that region and of the Qara'unas.[53]

The Borolday

The Borolday *tümen* was formed by Borolday, emir of the Qara'unas under Tarmashirin Khan, and then fell under the control of the later emir of the Qara'unas, Qazaghan.[54] It remained a separate unit within the Qara'unas; it is mentioned in the armies of Amīr Ḥusayn, and after his death Temür gave it together with the armies of Qunduz and Baghlan to his follower Chekü Barlas.[55] Chekü's positions descended to his son Jahānshāh, under whom the Borolday are mentioned.[56] At the time of Shāhrukh, the Borolday *tümen* went to one of Jahānshāh's sons, and the command of Qunduz and Baghlan to another.[57] Although the command of the Borolday *tümen* was held by outsiders, some relatives of the late Borolday remained connected with it. Borolday's son Tughluq Temür murdered Qazaghan in 759/1357–8 because Qazaghan had refused to grant him (or return to him) control of the Borolday *ulus*.[58] During Temür's reign two of Borolday's nephews are mentioned, and they also rose against him with the Borolday troops, but later served Temür faithfully.[59]

The Jalayir

The Jalayir had a prominent place in the Ulus Chaghatay. They seem to have been part of it from the beginning; two of Chaghadai's emirs were Jalayirs, one of them at the head of one of the four thousands granted to Chaghadai by Chinggis Khan.[60] They are also listed by Ibn ᶜArabshāh as one of the four tribes of the Ulus Chaghatay.[61] Their territory was at Khujand on the northern edge of the Ulus, and they seem to have had good relations with the Moghuls.

We know of no major split in the tribe. At the time of the Moghul invasions of Transoxiana, the Jalayir *beg* was Bāyazīd, whom Tughluq Temür Khan killed shortly after his second invasion, in 762/1361.[62] For the next four years there seems to have been a power struggle between two main candidates, Bāyazīd's son ᶜAlī Darwīsh, and another emir, Bahrām. This is discussed in Chapter 3. In 766/1364–5 Bahrām Jalayir took control with Temür's help. He soon fled to Moghulistan, and he may have ruled his tribe from there.[63] He is last mentioned in 773/1371–2 and sometime before 776/1374–5 his son ᶜĀdilshāh inherited his place.[64] Temür executed ᶜĀdilshāh about 779/1377–8, and temporarily divided the Jalayir tribe. Two years later he reunited the tribe and put it under the leadership of Sarïbugha, a Jalayir emir who was a member of his following.[65] It seems likely that Sarïbugha's son Birdi Beg inherited the tribal troops. After Temür's death the tribe was apparently centered not at Khujand but in Utrar.[66]

The Jalayir had a number of prestigious marriage alliances. Bāyazīd Jalayir was married to a daughter of Tarmashirin Khan; she was the mother of his son ᶜAlī Darwīsh, and was taken over after Bāyazīd's death by Amīr Ḥusayn.[67] It is probable that this was Sevinch Qutluq, daughter of Tarmashirin, and wife of Amīr Ḥusayn, who was given after Amīr Ḥusayn's death to Bahrām Jalayir.[68] Bāyazīd's daughter Arzū Malik was married to Mūsā Taychi'ut.[69] ᶜUmar Shaykh b. Temür had two wives or concubines of the Jalayir tribe, and had children by both of them.[70]

The Khuttalānī emirs

The Khuttalānī emirs controlled the army of Khuttalan which constituted a *tümen* and they had considerable power within the Ulus Chaghatay. This army is mentioned quite frequently both before and after Temür's takeover, and usually in connection with these emirs.[71] The army of Khuttalan had probably originated as a regional army, but by the middle of the fourteenth century it functioned as a tribe. The provenance of its leaders is not entirely clear. Their use of a *niṣba*, rather than a tribal name, and the Persian names of several of them – Kaykhusraw, Kayqubād, and Shīr Bahrām – could suggest an Iranian origin.[72] On the other hand, there seems to be no distinction in political and military activity between them and the Turco-Mongolian tribes or troops who made up the Ulus, and when they had to flee the Ulus, they took refuge not in Khorasan, but in the Alay mountains or with the Moghul Khans.[73]

They were not the only rulers in Khuttalan. Shahr-i Mung, the summer capital of Qazaghan and Amīr Ḥusayn, was located in Khuttalan, as was one branch of the Apardï tribe, who were said to rule it jointly with the Khuttalānī emirs.[74] It seems that the Apardï were particularly connected with Arhang, and the Khuttalānī emirs may have been centered in Baljuwan, since Shīr Bahrām Khuttalānī went off there to join his people.[75]

Power over the *tümen* of Khuttalan alternated between two branches of the Khuttalānī family. In 761/1360 it was held by Kaykhusraw Khuttalānī, and when he deserted to the Moghuls in 762/1361, control seems to have gone to his relative, Shīr Bahrām, to return to Kaykhusraw after Shīr Bahrām had died and Kaykhusraw returned in 769/1368.[76] When Kaykhusraw was executed in 773–4/1372–3, Temür gave the *tümen* of Khuttalan to Shīr Bahrām's son Muḥammad Mīrkā.[77] He held it until he rebelled and was executed in 790/1388.[78] After this there is no mention of Khuttalānī emirs during Temür's life, but the army took part in the siege of Takrit in 796/1393.[79] After Temür's death Sulṭān Maḥmūd b. Kaykhusraw governed Khuttalan, but he did not take an active part in the succession struggles.[80] At some point during Shāhrukh's reign the region of Khuttalan was granted to Nūrmalik Barlas, and from him it passed to his son.[81]

The Khuttalānī emirs had marriage connections with both Temür and Amīr Ḥusayn. Kaykhusraw's niece ᶜĀdil Malik was married to Amīr Ḥusayn; after his death, Temür gave her to Chekü Barlas.[82] According to one account, Amīr Ḥusayn's wife Sevinch Qutluq, the daughter of Tarmashirin Khan, went to Kaykhusraw on Amīr Ḥusayn's death, although elsewhere it is stated that she went to Bahrām Jalayir.[83] Kaykhusraw married into the family of the Moghul khan during his stay in Moghulistan, and the daughter of this union was married to Temür's son Jahāngīr.[84] In the other branch of the family, Shīr Bahrām's son Muḥammad Mīrkā was married to Sulṭān Bakht Begüm, of Temür's family.[85]

The Qara'unas

More has been written on the Qara'unas than on any other group in the Ulus Chaghatay. Some of the scholarship should be summarized here, since the Qara'unas played a very important role in the Ulus during this period. Because the origin of the Qara'unas and their role in the Ilkhanid domains has been dealt with elsewhere,[86] I shall simply sketch it here.

In the early thirteenth century a fairly large contingent of Mongol troops was sent out to garrison the Indian and Kashmiri frontiers.[87] These were *tamma* troops sent by the rulers of several *uluses*: the Chaghadayid, Jochid, and Ögödeyid.[88] In about 1253 Möngke sent Sali Noyan Tatar to take over the sections of the army which had been sent out by Chaghadai and Ögödei. Sali was quartered in the region of Qunduz and Baghlan, which was to be a permanent garrison, and he was made subservient to Hülegü. The troops under Jochi's commander Negüder, who was still alive, seem to have remained independent of both Sali and Hülegü, and to have continued for some time to act on behalf of the Jochids.[89] Exactly when and how the term Qara'unas became attached to these troops is uncertain, and is a source of some controversy. Certainly they had become a distinct and recognized group within twenty years of Hülegü's conquests. They were not however a unified entity, and although one can trace the history of many of them, others remain obscure.

One *tümen* of Qara'unas was attached personally to the Ilkhans, and another was active in the Badghis area in Khorasan. The emirs of both these *tümens* were appointed by the khan, and their positions were not inherited.[90] The command over the garrison at Qunduz and Baghlan does seem to have been hereditary for some time; although Qunduz and Baghlan are not mentioned, we know that Sali Noyan's position passed to his son Uladu, and his in turn to his son Baktut.[91] Under Uladu furthermore the Qara'unas were to some extent reunited, since Ghazan Khan gave Uladu the command of the khan's personal Qara'unas *tümen*. As Uladu was active in Badghis and Juwayn, it seems likely that his command extended to the Qara'unas of that region as well.[92] The Negüderi probably were not included in the troops of Uladu. Throughout their history they seem to have kept a separate identity and to have retained their seat in the south. They are mentioned in Sistan, raiding in Kerman and Fars, and some of them serving in the armies of the kings of Herat.[93]

The transfer of Qara'unas allegiance from the Ilkhans to the Ulus Chaghatay has been discussed in Chapter 2, and need not be repeated here. What remains to be examined is the position of the Qara'unas within the Ulus. The emir of the Qara'unas under Tarmashirin Khan (1326–34) was Borolday, a very powerful and trusted man. He was of the Orona'ut tribe, and therefore not a descendant of Sali Noyan Tatar, whose son and grandson had ruled the Qara'unas of Qunduz and Baghlan up to 1320.[94] The next emir of the Qara'unas we know of was Qazaghan, and what we know of him concerns primarily the period after his takeover of the Ulus in 747/1346–7. He is described as one of the most powerful emirs of the Ulus Chaghatay, in control of the region of Khuttalan, and wintering in Sali Saray. It seems likely, given the coincidence of names, that this had been also the winter residence of the original Qara'unas emir, Sali Noyan.

We know little about Qazaghan's antecedents. His clan name is given as b'biyat, or t'biyat,[95] which connects him neither with Sali Noyan and his descendants, nor with Borolday. It is probable therefore that he had received his position by appointment, not inheritance. He did have a marriage connection with the family of Borolday since he and Borolday's son had married sisters, and he had managed to attach to himself the troops which had been Borolday's, referred to in the histories as the Borolday *tümen* or *ulus*.[96]

It is clear that the Qara'unas troops were still centered in Qunduz and Baghlan, but it is not easy to determine just whom one should include among them.[97] Since the term *Qara'unas* was a derogatory one, and was used as such by the Moghuls referring to the Chaghatays,[98] the court historians were understandably reluctant to use it. Both Yazdī and Shāmī avoided the term completely, except in their account of Temür's battles against the forces of Amīr Ḥusayn over Qarshi in 767–8/1366–8.[99] Before and after this one must look for the Qara'unas in the armies of Qunduz and Baghlan, which are often mentioned campaigning with Amīr Ḥusayn.[100] The *Muntakhab al-tawārīkh*, based on a different and more Turkish tradition, is somewhat more generous in its use of the term *Qara'unas*. It identifies Amīr Qazaghan as being "of the *qawm* of the Qara'unas" and in describing the Ulus Chaghatay in 761/

1360 mentions the Qara'unas as followers of Qazaghan's descendants; Ḥāfiẓ-i Abrū has incorporated this into his history.[101]

Among the Qara'unas one can certainly include the Negüderi who have traditionally been called Qara'unas, though they had their own leadership, and also the more recently formed Borolday *tümen*, which was directly under the control of the emir of the Qara'unas. It is not certain however whether or not other Khorasanian groups, such as the Apardï and the Arlat, should also be included. Jean Aubin refers to Muḥammad Khwāja Apardï and the Arlat emirs as Qara'unas, apparently following the contemporary Khorasanian historian Faryūmadī.[102] The *Muntakhab al-tawārīkh* once refers to Amīr Ḥusayn's follower Farhād Qara'unas; in Yazdī's *Ẓafarnāma* the same man is called Farhād Apardï.[103]

Some scholars have suggested that the Transoxanian tribes of the Ulus Chaghatay had become assimilated to the Qara'unas, and that this term applied equally to all of them.[104] The evidence of the Timurid sources does not seem to me to support such a conclusion. The use of the term Qara'unas in the histories, while not frequent, is consistent and always refers either to the personal troops attached to Qazaghan and his descendants, or to emirs based in the southern part of the Ulus Chaghatay – Khorasan and eastern Afghanistan – who were the close allies of that family. Temür's victory therefore represents a victory of the northern and older part of the Ulus Chaghatay over the southern coalition, led by the emirs of the Qara'unas, who had succeeded in gaining power over the Ulus with Qazaghan's victory in 747/1346–7.

After Temür's takeover, control over the Qara'unas (the armies of Qunduz and Baghlan) was given to his closest associate, Chekü Barlas. They were then passed on to his descendants, and remained in his family at least until 830.[105]

The Qa'uchin

This was a special class of military men important both before and after Temür's rise to power, making up part of his personal following in his early career and later part of his army. Their origin and their place in the Ulus Chaghatay have remained unclear, and it is impossible to determine with any certainty who and what they were. Here I shall present the evidence which is available and suggest some possible interpretations. The term *qa'uchin* has been defined in two ways. Doerfer, citing Niẓām al-Dīn Shāmī, defined it as "old, original" or "a guard regiment of experienced fighters." The definition given by Shāmī, who is the only contemporary writer to explain this term, is unfortunately very vague. He mentioned the "*qushūn-i būy wa qūshun-i khāṣṣa- yi aṣlī ki turkān qa'uchīn gūyand.*"[106]

The other definition is a somewhat later one, and is given by Mīrzā Muḥammad Ḥaydar. He wrote that the population of Kashghar was divided into four classes: *tümen*, the peasants; *qa'uchin*, the armies; *aymaq*, the nomads; and lastly the bureaucrats and the *ᶜulamā'*.[107] The same account of Kashghar and its classes is found in the Persian geography, *Haft Iqlīm*, here based on Mīrzā Muḥammad's work.[108] This definition is supported by Babur, who described one of Mīrzā ᶜUmar Shaykh's emirs, Qāsim Beg Qa'uchin, as being "of the ancient army *begs* of Andijan."[109] These two passages suggest that the *qa'uchin* may have been the commanders of a standing army quartered on the land. Unfortunately the sources do not provide sufficient information to allow us to choose with certainty between this description and that given by Shāmī, which indicates an army rather more personally attached to the khan. One can however discover from the histories something about the characteristics of the *qa'uchin* and their place in the Ulus Chaghatay.

It is clear that the *qa'uchin* were a recognized group or class of people, but they do not seem to have been attached to a specific region within Transoxiana, nor to have had any internal leadership. Although we know of one of them (Temüge) that his family was in the Kish region, for the others and for the group as a whole no geographical attachment is specified. Nor is there anywhere in the sources an indication either that one *qa'uchin* controlled the others, or that all of them were controlled by a leader outside their ranks either before or after Temür's takeover. Some of them at least had their own followings: Temüge Qa'uchin is mentioned joining Temür with fifteen men near Qarshi in 764/1363.[110] About the same Temüge it is stated that when he returned to this region to reconnoiter, he discovered that his family was camped nearby, which suggests that he was a nomad.[111]

It seems likely that the *qa'uchin* were a hereditary class, since of the seven or eight mentioned in Temür's early career, almost all are related to one or several of the others, and a number of those mentioned later are sons of these men.[112] On the other hand, not all men who were related to *qa'uchin* emirs were identified as *qa'uchin* themselves.[113] This probably indicates that while the position or title of *qa'uchin* was hereditary, it did not descend to all the sons of those who held it. Within the Ulus a position was usually inherited by one person, who could be a brother, son, nephew or even a cousin. Such a system could explain the use of the title *qa'uchin* to designate some, but not all, of a large number of related people.

Since a number of *qa'uchin* emirs were active before Temür's takeover, it is clear that they were not his creation. Of those mentioned during Temür's rise to power, all were his followers and remained faithful to him throughout this period, though none seem to have been among his closest associates or advisors.[114] Upon Temür's accession both these and a number of other *qa'uchin* emirs were appropriately rewarded; one was given Amīr Ḥusayn's daughter as wife, and four were given commands in the army.[115]

The fact that all the *qa'uchin* emirs mentioned at this period were attached to Temür might suggest that they were indeed a regiment or the descendants of such, over which Temür had succeeded in gaining control. On the other hand, the number of *qa'uchin* mentioned is small, and it is quite possible that if they were land troops dispersed throughout Transoxiana, the only ones identified would be those in Temür's own armies, about whom the sources had most information. Those in other regions would not be distinguished from the army as a whole.

After Temür's takeover the *qa'uchin* continued to be among his most reliable servitors, although as had been the case earlier, none were among the most important of his emirs. They continued also to be a definite group or class and were recognized as such. In accounts of Shāhrukh's appointment as governor of Khorasan in 799/1396–7, for instance, the emirs appointed with him are listed, with the *qa'uchin* emirs together, under a single heading ("*wa az qa'uchīnān*").[116] The *qa'uchin* are mentioned similarly at Temür's death: "the emirs, *khāṣṣagān*, and *qa'uchīnān* took the sashes off their turbans and threw themselves on the ground."[117] There are also two mentions of *qa'uchin* regiments.[118] On the whole however the *qa'uchin* seem to have been dispersed among the army. During the siege of Takrit in 796/1393–4 for example, six *qa'uchin* emirs are mentioned in the fighting, almost all of them in charge of different tunnels, and usually together with others not identified as *qa'uchin*.[119]

As I have stated above, the *qa'uchin* cannot be attached definitely to any one region of Transoxiana. They may however have been attached to Chaghadayid territories. The *Muᶜizz al-ansāb*, in listing the emirs attached to Shāhrukh after he came to power and was ruling at Herat, does not identify a single person as a *qa'uchin* although we know, as I have written above, that several were assigned to him by Temür when he became governor of Khorasan. On the other hand the list of the emirs of Ulugh Beg, who ruled in Transoxiana, identifies thirty people as *qa'uchin*.[120]

This is too large a difference to assign to chance. It seems possible that the emirs assigned to Shāhrukh, permanently settled outside of Transoxiana, had lost the title of *qa'uchin*, or had failed to inherit the position. This supposition gains support from a statement made by Ḥāfiẓ-i Abrū about Jahānmalik b. Mulkat, who was one of Shāhrukh's emirs. In describing the events in the years after Temür's death, Ḥāfiẓ-i Abrū identified Jahānmalik as a relative of Qumarī Qa'uchin, and wrote that his people (*qabīla*) were originally among the *qa'uchin* of Temür.[121]

What can one then say definitely about the *qa'uchin*? They were a hereditary military class or group, without internal leadership or control over a specific area within the Ulus Chaghatay, though probably attached to the Chaghadayid territories. Their non-tribal status is emphasized by their consistent loyalty to Temür, and by the fact that he used them often in positions of particular trust, such as military governorships, which could provide the holder with an individual power base and a chance to rebel.[122] It seems that they could either have originated as a special personal army loyal to the khan, which was probably at some point provided with land for its upkeep, or could simply be the standing army of the Ulus Chaghatay, also owing its loyalty directly to the khan, and given land perhaps during Kebeg's administrative reforms. There is in fact little difference between these two possibilities. I am inclined to think that they did have land both because of their attachment to the territory of the Chaghadayid khanate, and also because of their survival as a class, without internal leadership or attachment to the leadership of the Ulus after the downfall of the khans.

The Qipchaq

There are a fairly large number of Qipchaq emirs mentioned in the histories of Temür's career, but very little information is given about the Qipchaq tribe. It is not among those mentioned in the list of tribes and groups which controlled the territory in the Ulus in 761/1360.[123] Of the tribe as such there is almost no mention, although Qipchaq troops are twice referred to. Qipchaq forces fought under Sarïbugha Jalayir with Temür against the Moghuls in 766/1365, and made up part of the armies collected by Sarïbugha and ᶜĀdilshāh Jalayir during their rebellion against Temür in 777–1376–7. Later a Qipchaq *qoshun* is mentioned under ᶜUthmān Bahadur Qipchaq in 793/1390–1.[124] The presence of Qipchaqs in the Jalayir armies suggests that the Qipchaqs might have been a subject tribe to the Jalayirs. Some weight is given to this supposition by the fact that one of the Jalayir emirs under Temür is identified by Babur as being a "Turkistānī Qipchaq."[125]

The individual Qipchaq emirs mentioned in the histories seem to be connected not with the Jalayir but with Temür. The most prominent of these was ᶜAbbās Bahadur, a powerful member of Temür's following.[126] Another Qipchaq emir, Khitay Bahadur, is mentioned fairly frequently in Temür's early years and like ᶜAbbās was a personal follower.[127] Many relatives of these men, especially of ᶜAbbās Bahadur, are mentioned in the histories, and these account for all the Qipchaqs I have found.[128] Their standing therefore was probably due not to their tribal status but to their closeness to Temür. I would suggest therefore that the Qipchaq existed in the Ulus Chaghatay only as a subject tribe, without control over territory of its own, and that Qipchaq emirs found the best outlet for their ambitions in service to the ruler of the Ulus, rather than in the conduct of tribal affairs.

The Suldus

Of the four thousands assigned to Chaghadai by Chinggis Khan, one was headed by a Suldus emir, and another Suldus is listed among Chaghadai's emirs.[129] It seems likely that the Suldus of Temür's time were descended from these emirs. In the 750s/1350s and early 760s/1360s the main chief of the Suldus was Buyan Suldus, who held the regions of Shadman and Chaghaniyan.[130] Buyan is listed among the emirs participating in Qazaghan's campaign against Herat in 752/1351–2. In 760/1358–9, after ᶜAbd Allāh b. Qazaghan's move to Samarqand, Buyan went against him with Ḥājjī Beg Barlas, killed him and became emir of the Ulus himself, but he exerted little control over it.[131] He was executed by the Moghul Khan in 763/1362, and was succeeded as main chief of the Suldus by his son, Shaykh Muḥammad.[132]

The leadership of the Suldus was divided. While Buyan Suldus ruled from Shadman, Öljey Bugha Suldus "with his people (*qawm*)" had become independent in the region of Balkh.[133] After 761/1359–60 there is no mention of Öljey Bugha himself, but in 766/1364–5 the "*tümen* of Öljey Bugha Suldus" was located near Balkh.[134] At that time Mengli Bugha, based at the fortress of Ulaju, controlled or tried to control that region.[135] Mengli Bugha may well have been a brother or son of Öljey Bugha; he was in the same region, and had a similar name, which was common among members of one family. Temür and Amīr Ḥusayn took over most of the forces of Balkh but some time after Mengli Bugha's death Temür allowed his son, Pīr ᶜAlī Tāz, to inherit his *hazāra*. After Temür's death Pīr ᶜAlī held great power, as described in Chapter 7. During Temür's rise to power the histories mention also another emir of the Suldus apparently acting independently; this is Tughluq, who opposed Amīr Ḥusayn in 761–2/1360–1, and who is described as "*amīr* of a *qabīla*."[136]

Although one would expect a number of marriage alliances with a tribe as prominent as the Suldus, we know of only one; the daughter of Buyan Suldus was married to Amīr Ḥusayn and was taken over after his death by Temür.[137] Of the important tribes of the Ulus Chaghatay, the Suldus was the most harshly treated by Temür. In 777–8/1376–7, he executed Shaykh Muḥammad Suldus and gave control of the Suldus *tümen* to his follower, Aqtemür Bahadur.[138] This *tümen* later passed on to Aqtemür's son Shaykh Temür who is mentioned in 793/1390–1 leading several *hazāras* of Suldus troops.[139] In the later years of Temür's career, the sources mention an emir called Dawlat Temür Suldus, probably the son of Shaykh Temür.[140] Several Suldus emirs including the son of Mengli Bugha are mentioned in Temür's later years; some led their own *qoshuns* and were relatively prominent.[141] After Temür's death, Suldus emirs were still active in the region of Shadman.[142]

The Yasa'urī

The Yasa'urī had their origin in the personal troops of the Chaghadayid prince Yasa'ur. Yasa'ur had first rebelled against the Chaghadayids and appealed to the Ilkhans, who settled him in eastern Khorasan, then later he rebelled against the Ilkhans. He was killed in 1320 by the Chaghadayid khan Kebeg, to whom his *ulus* then transferred.[143] Yasa'ur's son, Qazan, was the last Chaghadayid khan to hold power over the Ulus Chaghatay.[144]

At Temür's time the Yasa'urī held the area of Samarqand and probably Bukhara as well.[145] They were led in the early 760s/1360s by Amīr Khiḍr Yasa'urī, but after he died in or before 766/1364–5, the leadership seems to have been shared. Three emirs are mentioned at the head of the Yasa'urī in 766/1364–5: Khiḍr's brother ᶜAlī, ᶜAlī's brother-in-law or son-in-law Ḥājjī Maḥmūdshāh, and Ilyās Yasa'urī.[146] It seems likely that many of the troops of the Yasa'urī were footmen, since in the account of the Yasa'urī defense of Bukhara against Amīr Ḥusayn in 768/1367 the footmen of Maḥmūdshāh are mentioned as the main defenders of Bukhara.[147]

The Yasa'urī land was very close to that of the Barlas, and the relationship between the two tribes seems to have been close, if not always cordial. There were in particular several marriages. Ḥājjī Maḥmūdshāh was the son of Temür's maternal uncle.[148] This would suggest that Temür's mother was a Yasa'urī. Temür's son Jahāngīr was married to Bakht Malik Agha, daughter of either Ilyās or Khiḍr Yasa'urī; she was the mother of his son Pīr Muḥammad.[149] Temür had also betrothed his daughter to ᶜAlī Yasa'urī, whom he executed.[150]

The Yasa'urī were not prominent after Temür's takeover of the Ulus Chaghatay. The only one who appears frequently in the histories after this is Temür's cousin Ḥājjī Maḥmūdshāh, who had been made a commander and *amīr dīwān* in 771.[151] His son is mentioned once, in 768/1395–6, and another Yasa'urī emir whose descent is not given, also once, in 804/1401–2.[152] Neither Yasa'urī emirs nor Yasa'urī troops are mentioned in accounts of the succession struggles after Temür's death.

APPENDIX B

Members of Temür's family

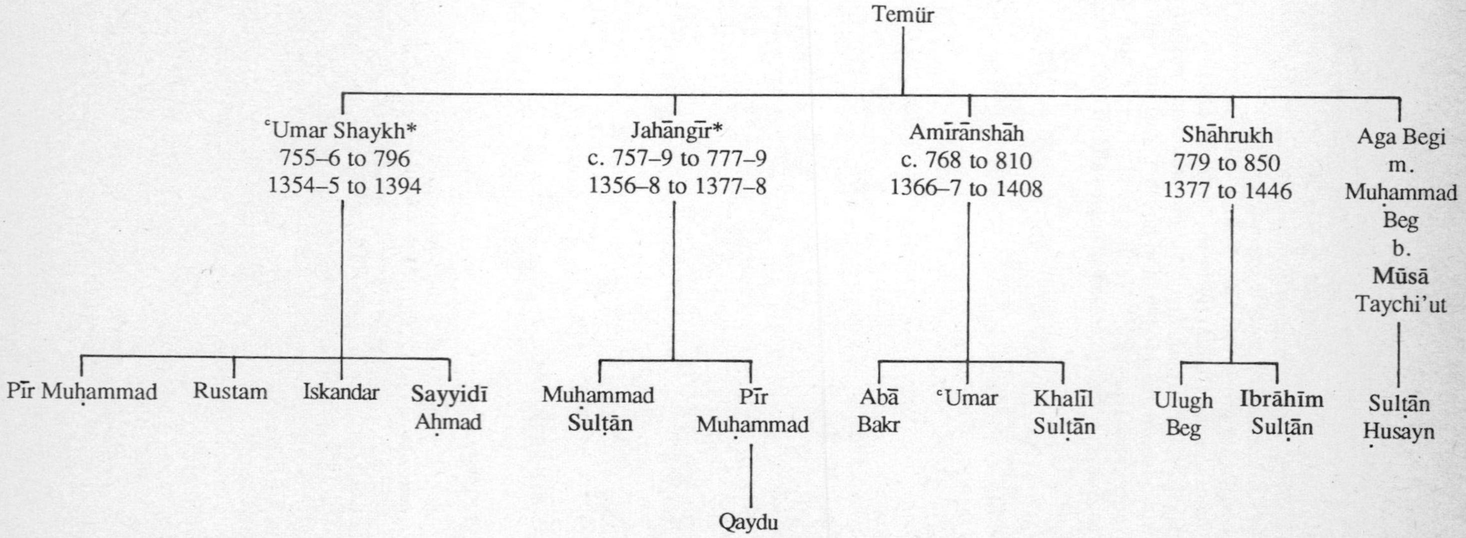

*It is not certain whether Temür's eldest son was ʿUmar Shaykh or Jahāngīr; although Jahāngīr is usually named as the eldest, there is also some evidence that suggests ʿUmar Shaykh may have been older than he.

APPENDIX C

The formal administrative structure

It is not easy to discern the organization of Temür's administration. The historical sources on his reign pay little attention to it, since they are largely concerned with his campaigns and unlike the histories of the Ilkhanids they were written by men outside his administration. For the period of Temür himself there seems to be no extant scribal handbook. We have an excellent one written under the Jalayirids, and one from the late Timurid period, but the considerable differences between the bureaucracies portrayed in these works makes it plain that one cannot extrapolate from them the structure of Temür's bureaucracy.[1] We do however have one very useful source which I have used extensively in this work. This is the *Mu^cizz al-ansāb*, an anonymous genealogy which, according to its preface, was commissioned by Shāhrukh in 830/1426–7. The *Mu^cizz* lists the princes of the Timurid house and after each one enumerates emirs and other office holders. This provides invaluable information on the offices and ranks which existed at the time and the identity of the people who held them. The recension which has come down to us however clearly originated from a later period, since it includes people and events from the second half of the ninth/fifteenth century.[2] It is possible therefore that the listing of offices and ranks here reflects a later and more articulated system. Much of the information it gives however agrees well with the accounts in contemporary histories.

The Persian administration

Under Temür, as under the Ilkhans and some other Middle Eastern dynasties, there was a central *dīwān* which moved with the sovereign on his campaigns, and also local *dīwāns* in the main cities of the realm.[3] The central *dīwān*, usually referred to as the *dīwān-i a^clā*, is much the best documented. The main duties of this *dīwān* were the collection of taxes, the registration of ransom money and money taken from treasuries in conquered cities, and the inspection of provincial *dīwāns*. In all of these activities, both Persians and Chaghatays were active. In the assessment and collection of taxes, the *dīwān* seems to have had quite broad powers, although it was open to interference from above. It was for instance the *dīwān-i a^clā* which determined the tribute to be paid by the ruler of Kashmir, but Temür decreased the sum.[4] Many of the people sent to the provinces to collect taxes were agents of the central *dīwān*.[5] Finally, the *dīwān-i a^clā* was active in the inspection of provincial *dīwāns*, and the rectification of local abuses, usually undertaken at Temür's instigation.

There is very little information in the histories of Temür's reign about the taxes which were being collected. Taxes are most usually referred to by the collective term *māl*.[6] It is probable that the taxes referred to included the agricultural tax (*kharāj*) and the commercial tax (*bāj*); the Georgians, on expressing their submission in 804/1401–2, offered to pay the *kharāj* and *bāj*.[7] There is evidence of commercial tolls collected possibly at the city gates.[8] We also know that Temür levied taxes in kind from many of the nomads within his army, but these may well have been collected by a different set of officials.[9]

Dīwān officials

The internal structure of the *dīwān* is difficult to discern.[10] I will discuss here several *dīwān* offices which appear in the sources, and attempt a description of their functions and relative power. The relations between these offices, and the structure of which they were a part, can however be sketched only in its barest outlines. Of the provincial *dīwāns* themselves we know very little except that they existed in many of the important cities, such as Shiraz, Isfahan, Yazd, Herat and Samarqand.[11] The heads of the provincial *dīwāns* were usually called *ṣāḥib dīwān*; this position was often given to a bureaucrat of local origin, as was done for instance in Kerman and Khorasan, though it might also be filled from the central *dīwān*.[12] About subordinate positions in the provincial *dīwāns* we know almost nothing. It is only in Herat that we know the names of some subordinate viziers, and also know of the existence of a *dīwān-i khāṣṣa*. What this was is not certain, though it might resemble the Seljukid *dīwān-i khāṣṣ*, which administered crown lands.[13]

Ṣāḥib dīwān: This seems to have been the highest official in the Persian *dīwān*.[14] It is difficult to be certain who was *ṣāḥib dīwān* during some periods of Temür's rule, and it is clear that this position was sometimes shared. The first chief of the *dīwān* whom we can identify was Khwāja Masᶜūd Simnānī who died in 803/1401; his position is not actually stated but implied by the fact that at his death management of the *dīwān* was entrusted to another scribe, Jalāl Islām.[15] Jalāl Islām's appointment however was temporary, and in 804/1401–2 the post of *ṣāḥib dīwān* was given to two men, Khwāja ᶜAlī Simnānī from Herat and Khwāja Sayf al-Dīn Tūnī from Sabzawar.[16] ᶜAlī Simnānī was later removed from his post and imprisoned.[17]

It seems likely that within the Persian bureaucracy the *ṣāḥib dīwān* was not very much more powerful than his fellow scribes. Khwāja Masᶜūd Simnānī is mentioned twice before his death; once discovering the evil designs of the messengers from the Mamluk sultan Faraj b. Barquq, and once collecting the ransom money at Damascus, along with several emirs and another scribe, Jalāl Islām.[18] It is possible indeed that Masᶜūd Simnānī and Jalāl Islām had equal status; Jalāl Islām is mentioned actually somewhat more often than Masᶜūd. He was among the scribes assessing the *māl-i amān* at Delhi; he was sent to Azerbaijan to straighten out Amīrānshāh's affairs, and at Damascus besides collecting ransom money he was charged with arranging the release of prisoners.[19] Despite his earlier prominence however, he is not mentioned during his brief term as head of the *dīwān*, and his successors, Khwāja ᶜAlī Simnānī and Khwāja Sayf al-Dīn Tūnī, appear in the histories only once during their term in office, calculating the *māl-i amān* at Bursa, in 804–5/1402.[20]

Vizier: The other frequently mentioned position within the *dīwān* is that of vizier. Under Temür this term seems to have referred not only to the head of the *dīwān*, but also to many of the people working within it.[21] All we know about the position of the people referred to as vizier is that they were scribes, working within the *dīwān*.

Ṣāḥib māl: This title is mentioned only once as far as I know. In the rebellion at Yazd in 798/1395–6 one of the three people killed was Sayyid Ṣadr al-Dīn, who was vizier and *ṣāḥib māl*.[22] It seems likely that he was chief of the *dīwān*. The term *māl* at this period is used to denote taxes or tax revenue, and sometimes apparently financial administration in general.[23]

Mufarrid: Several men are mentioned in this office, most of them sent to provincial cities to investigate cases of corruption. The most striking instance is that of Fakhr al-Dīn Aḥmad Ṭūsī and Aḥmad b. Shaykh Ḥasan whom Temür and Shāhrukh sent to Herat in 806–7/1404. These men extracted a large sum of money from the notables of Herat, tortured and ruined several scribes, and exiled many others to Moghulistan.[24]

Tax Collector: There were two ranks among tax collectors; those who were appointed to supervise the tax collection of a province or city, and the officials responsible for the actual collection, who were called *muḥaṣṣils*; these are discussed in the Chaghatay section. A number of people, both Chaghatay emirs and members of the settled bureaucracy, were sent to the provinces to organize the collection of taxes usually over a period of several years. Temür's follower Shaykh Nūr al-Dīn went to Shiraz to collect taxes in 798/1396, and returned to Temür's army in 800/1398, while Ghiyāth al-Dīn Sālār Simnānī was sent to collect the taxes of Yazd in 804/1401–2 and stayed there for the rest of Temür's reign.[25] These people seem to have enjoyed considerable power and standing. In Yazd Ghiyāth al-Dīn Sālār Simnānī erected on his own initiative but at *dīwān* expense a magnificent building to commemorate Temür's victory in Rum.[26] Since even Temür's own sons rarely undertook large building projects on their own, such an action suggests considerable stature and security. Two of these provincial tax collectors, Ghiyāth al-Dīn of Yazd and Aḥmad Dā'ūd from Kerman, are mentioned among those who came to Georgia in 806/1403–4 to pay their respects to Temür.[27] Their inclusion in a list consisting otherwise of governors, *darughas*, and the heads of provincial *dīwāns* confirms their high position.

The Chaghatay sphere

The Chaghatay *dīwān* was called the *dīwān-i buzurg*, and it is mentioned much less frequently than the *dīwān-i aᶜlā*. It seems to have served as a court of law for Chaghatay emirs and Timurid princes. In 773/1372 for instance when various tribal and settled emirs were caught plotting against Temür they were brought for judgement before the *dīwān-i buzurg*, and at a later date in 802/1399–1400 the *dīwān-i buzurg*, run by Shāhrukh and various (unnamed) emirs, examined and punished some of Amīrānshāh's emirs who had fled before the Georgians at the fortress of Alanjaq.[28] Two princes were brought for judgement before the *dīwān-i buzurg* – Pīr Muḥammad b. ᶜUmar Shaykh in 802–3/1400, and Iskandar b. ᶜUmar Shaykh in 804/1401–2. In both cases the *dīwān* sentenced them to beating.[29] It seems likely that the *dīwān-i buzurg* was a new name for the *yarghu* – the tribunal traditional in Turco-Mongolian states, which we know existed in the Ulus Chaghatay before Temür's rise to power.[30]

It is clear that there was an office or rank under Temür known as *amīr dīwān* or *dīwānī*.[31] On his takeover in 771/1370, Temür appointed several important emirs to this position, many of whom were prominent members of his following.[32] The meaning of this term is not explained in the histories and an examination of the activities of the *umarā' dīwān* after their appointment in 771/1370 yields little information on the nature of their position.[33] These emirs may have belonged to the *dīwān-i buzurg*, but they might also have been affiliated with the *dīwān-i aᶜlā*.[34] It is quite possible that during Temür's life the functions and membership of the Chaghatay *dīwān*, whether there were one or several of them, had not yet become fixed. It is I think wiser to proceed on this assumption than to try to make Temür's system fit into the mold of Ilkhanid or later Timurid administration, which were much more highly articulated.

In any case the Chaghatay *dīwān-i buzurg* does not seem to have been the defining institution of the Chaghatay government. Indeed there probably was no one central institution. What we find instead is a large collection of different offices, patterned on those of other Turco-Mongolian polities. I have divided these into four sets of positions: provincial offices, central government offices, court offices, and military offices.

Of the positions within the regional administration the most important was that of *darugha* or *ḥākim* – governor of a conquered city or town. Fortresses were held by less prestigious functionaries: *kotwāls*. Within the regions under the jurisdiction of the *darughas* there were separate officials to collect taxes, not always entirely under the control of the local *darugha*; these were usually called by the Arabic term *muḥaṣṣil*, and seem to have been Chaghatays. The tax on trade was collected by yet other functionaries – the *tamghachïs*. All these people owed obedience primarily to Temür, but they were also answerable to the provincial governors.

Chief among central government offices was the *muhrdār*, the keeper of the seal, a man very close to the sovereign. Under Temür this office was known by its Persian name; the Turkic term *tamghachï* which had traditionally been used for it was now applied to collectors of customs duties (*tamgha*). We hear also of judges, *yarghuchïs*, and of treasurers, *khazanchïs*. Within the court administration there were several offices which had originated in the royal household but had developed into positions of broader responsibility: the *qorchï* or bodyguard, the *akhtachï* or stablemaster, the *bökevül* or taster, the *bavurchï* or cook, and the *suchï* or steward. Military offices were naturally quite conspicuous in Temür's administration. They included the *amīr al-umarā'*, a term usually translated as "commander-in-chief," the *tovachï*; an inspector of troops who was in charge also of conscription, the *yurtchï* who found and organized the army camp, and the *yasavul*, a bodyguard of adjutant. Some of these positions existed also at the provincial level, under Temür's sons and grandsons.

Provincial offices

Darugha: Below the governors of provinces, who were princes, this was the most important of the provincial offices. Since I have discussed this office in detail elsewhere, I will give only an outline of its functions here.[35] The *darugha* was a governor, either over a region or over a city or town, governing sometimes in conjunction with a local native ruler. The *darugha* was usually the first Chaghatay official installed in a newly conquered area and he held varied responsibilities. *Darughas* were accompanied by a garrison of Chaghatay troops and commanded a local militia, with which they served to keep order and helped in the suppression of local disturbances. They were also involved in local administration, and were sometimes charged with the restoration of agriculture and city life in their regions. The provincial cities in Temür's realm had local *dīwāns*, staffed by a Persian bureaucracy. It is clear that the *darughas* were connected with these *dīwāns* but the extent to which they controlled them is unclear, and may have varied from one place to another. The responsibility for tax-collection was not among the tasks of Temür's *darughas*, and tax officials were not entirely under their control.[36]

Kotwāl: This term is used by the Persian historians of Temür's period for the guardian of a fortress or citadel; it would apply equally to the guardian installed by a local regime or to one of Temür's men.[37] Within a city, the position of *kotwāl* of the citadel might apparently be given either to the *darugha* of the city or to another person.[38] This seems not to have been a particularly high position. Few of those who held it are mentioned in the histories and most of those who do appear were not very prominent men.[39]

Muḥaṣṣil: The *muḥaṣṣils* were tax collectors, usually Chaghatay. This office seems to have been one of moderate prestige; we know the identity of only three men who held it, but all of these were of fairly high standing.[40] These *muḥaṣṣils* were the agents who actually undertook the collection of taxes. In Isfahan for instance the collection of ransom money (*māl-i amān*) was organized and supervised by some of Temür's emirs remaining apparently outside the gates, and *muḥaṣṣils* were sent into the city to collect the money.[14] *Muḥaṣṣils* are mentioned in many cities along with the *darugha* and his *nökers*, and were among the first officials to be killed when rebellions broke out.[42] The power and independence that the *muḥaṣṣils* could assume is shown by their actions in Lur-i Kuchik, where they murdered the *atabeg* in retaliation for the misbehavior of his son. In the account of this event there is no mention of the local *darughas*, although we know that some had been appointed to the area.[43] The colophon of an Armenian manuscript written in 1407 refers to the tax collectors who had subdued and enslaved many nations.[44]

Tamghachï: At Temür's time the *tamghachï* was a collector of commercial taxes, particularly customs duties. This office existed in the Golden Horde, in the Crimea, and under the Ilkhans. The *tamgha* tax which they collected was equivalent to the Persian *bāj*, and covered all taxes taken in cities from trade and industry.[45] There is little information on this office during Temür's period. It is not listed in the *Muʿizz al-ansāb*, and is mentioned only once in the histories; after capturing Ephesus in 805/1402, Temür imposed on it the *māl-i amān*, and appointed Naṣr Allāh Tamghachï to collect the tax.[46]

Central government offices

Muhrdār, Keeper of the Seal: This was one of the most prestigious posts within the central government. It was an office which existed in a great number of states and was usually of very high status, involving as it did close contact with the sovereign.[47] The only thing we know about this position under Temür is the identity of the people who held it. It was filled first by Temür's personal follower Eyegü Temür; at his death in 793/1391 the "*muhr-i khāṣṣ wa parwāna*" passed on to his relative Shāhmalik.[48] The office also belonged at some point to Eyegü Temür's son Shaykh Muḥammad.[49] Both Eyegü Temür and Shāhmalik were among Temür's most prominent emirs.

An examination of these men's careers fails to give information about the responsibilities of their position. Shāhmalik commanded some special court troops, and in the account of events in 807/1404–5, appears as one of several emirs particularly close to Temür and controlling access to him, but he did not always remain with him. It seems quite possible therefore that at this time, as under the Safawids, the office of *muhrdār* was in part an honorary one conferring prestige and perhaps a role in controlling access to the sovereign, but not entailing very definite responsibilities.

Khazanchï: The term *khazanchï* means "treasurer." This office is not attested, at least under this name, in the other nomad polities before and after Temür's time, although the Aqqoyunlu did have a treasurer (*khazīna-dār*) who was part of the supreme council; this position was held by Turks.[50] We know essentially nothing about the office under Temür except that it existed. Three emirs are characterized as *khazanchï*, but none of them are well known.[51] We cannot tell what treasuries or funds these men controlled.

Yarghuchï: The *yarghuchï* was a judge, an official of the Turco-Mongolian tribunal (*yarghu*), which probably existed in Temür's time as the *dīwān-i buzurg*.[52] This position is found under the great khans of the Mongolian empire, and also in the

Ilkhanid period.[53] The only evidence of the existence of the office of *yarghuchï* is the mention of Shaykh Arslan Yarghuchï in the siege of Takrit in 796/1393.[54] Apparently this is the same Shaykh Arslan who led the *tümen* of Kebeg Khan.

Court offices

Qorchï: The *qorchï* – quiverbearer – was a member of the guard or bodyguard of the sovereign. This is an office found in the *Secret History of the Mongols*, and in many Mongol successor states.[55] We know almost nothing of this office at Temür's period. The histories of Temür's rule mention only the title, appended after the name of one or two not very prominent emirs.[56] This position is not listed under Temür's name in the *Muᶜizz al-ansāb*, but does appear under several of his sons and grandsons.[57]

Qushchï: The *qushchï* was the falconer. This office existed in many Turkic and Mongolian states.[58] Under the later Timurids the *qushchï* was a military functionary but the office retained its original significance; the *qushchï* was in fact in charge of the royal falcons.[59] In the *Muᶜizz al-ansāb* this position is not listed under Temür, but it does appear in the lists of offices under several of his sons and grandsons, active already during his reign.[60] In the histories of Temür's period we have only the title, appended to the name of an emir mentioned once.[61]

Akhtachï: The *akhtachï* was the stablemaster. This official formed part of Chinggis Khan's *keshig*. The office existed in several Mongolian successor states and in later Timurid times under Babur.[62] It is not listed under Temür in the *Muᶜizz al-ansāb*, but does appear under a few of the princes who were active during his life.[63] During Temür's reign this title was held by Arghunshāh Akhtachï, a prominent emir, who may have been a Turkmen. His career was similar to those of Temür's followers.[64] We know also of an emir called ᶜĀdil Akhtachï, a member of Shāhrukh's special *qoshun*, who in the battle with Shāh Manṣūr stayed close to Shāhrukh and protected him.[65] Thus it seems that this position may have retained an element of personal service and closeness to the sovereign.

Bökevül: The *bökevül* was the royal taster, a military administrative officer.[66] This position also originated under Chinggis Khan and existed in the Mongol successor states. As it is described in the *Dastūr al-kātib*, written for the Jalayirids, the *bökevül* supervised the equipment and management of soldiers, transmitting to them the orders of the *dīwān*, and preventing disorder within the army. This description seems to fit the office as it existed in most other polities.[67] In the late Timurid period, the term *bökevül* is found in its original meaning, applied to the officials in charge of providing food for *madrasas*.[68]

The one mention of the office during Temür's reign could apply to either description. In 802/1399–1400, Shaykh Ibrāhīm of Shirwan provided so many horses and sheep for a feast that the cooks were unable to prepare them. The *tovachïs* therefore divided this task among the soldiers, and on the day of the feast, the *bökevüls* took charge of the food.[69] The *Muᶜizz al-ansāb* lists no *bökevüls* under Temür, but they are found under several of his sons and grandsons.[70]

Bavurchï: The *bavurchï* was a cook.[71] This office also originated under Chinggis Khan,[72] but does not seem to have become quite as important or widespread an office as that of *bökevül*.[73] The title *bavurchï* is attached to two emirs of Temür's period, one of whom, Tökel Bavurchï, was fairly prominent, served as a *darugha*, and is mentioned among those close to the sovereign.[74] The office is not among those listed in the *Muᶜizz al-ansāb*.

Suchï: The *suchï* was a cupbearer or steward.[75] This seems to have been a less common and prominent office than most of those I have described above. There is an emir under Temür called Cherkes Suchï. At the conquest of Baghdad in 795/1393 he, with the other *suchīs*, threw all the city's wine into the river at Temür's orders.[76] It seems likely therefore that this office had kept its original function. There are no *suchīs* listed under Temür in the *Muᶜizz al-ansāb*, but they do appear under several princes active during Temür's life.[77]

Military offices

Amīr al-umarā': This was the highest post in Temür's army and is usually translated as "commander-in-chief." The position existed elsewhere and could be one of very considerable power, particularly when the sovereign was weak.[78] In the Golden Horde in the fourteenth century, this title (in its Turkish form of *beglerbeg*) referred to the highest ranking of the four great Ulus emirs, often the most powerful person after the khan.[79]

The position of *amīr al-umarā'* is very little mentioned in the histories of Temür's period, although the *Muᶜizz al-ansāb* does inform us who filled it. The first to hold it was Chekü Barlas; from him it descended to his son Jahānshāh, and later to his other son Miḍrāb.[80] Clavijo, writing about Jahānshāh Barlas, describes him as commander-in-chief of the army and constable of the empire.[81] One other Barlas emir, Sulṭān Pīr Aḥmad, is also credited with this rank by the *Muᶜizz al-ansāb*, but he does not appear in the histories.[82] Both Chekü and Jahānshāh held great influence and power, but we cannot be sure that this was due to their position as *amīr al-umarā'*. Considering the silence of the sources about this post, it seems quite likely that they owed their strength as much to favor and to their command of the Qara'unas troops. Jahānshāh however did hold a position of responsibility within Temür's army; he was entrusted sometimes with important expeditions and was occasionally in charge of either the right or the left wing.[83]

There were also emirs appointed as *amīr al-umarā'* in the provinces of Temür's realm. This position was held in Khorasan by Aqbugha Nayman.[84] During the rebellion in 789–90/1387–8 while the governor Amīrānshāh was absent, Aqbugha took the initiative in restoring order, conscripting and commanding armies from large areas of Khorasan. He was also on hand to help Jahānshāh Barlas put down a rebellion in Kabul at about the same time.[85] It seems from Ḥāfiẓ-i Abrū's description that this position should have been the most powerful post in the province after that of governor, but that in fact Aqbugha was less powerful than another emir, Muḥammad Sulṭānshāh, who supervised financial affairs and was also a conspicuous military figure in the province.[86] This is all that the histories tell us about the office of *amīr al-umarā'*. It was clearly an office of great prestige, but we cannot ascertain the nature and extent of duties pertaining to it; they may well have been ill-defined, and have varied with the people who held the office.

Tovachī: The *tovachīs* were troop inspectors, who had as their task the supervision of the numbers, condition and equipment of the army, along with conscription for campaigns and the transmission of orders from the sovereign to the soldiers.[87] This office existed with very similar functions in other nomad polities.[88] There are numerous mentions of *tovachīs* in the histories of Temür's reign, which provide us with a good view of their activities. One of their most important tasks was the conscription of troops; sometimes the *tovachīs* seem to have done this directly, other times they ordered the emirs of the army to gather the troops under them.[89] In 807/1404–5 before Temür's campaign against China, the *tovachīs* had to determine the number of the army and to inform the foremost members of the Ulus what men and equipment they had to provide.[90]

Tovachīs were also often charged with the allocation of tasks among the emirs of the army. At the siege of Takrit in 796/1393 they organized the digging of tunnels, and when Temür's army was constructing a canal connecting the Aras River in Azerbaijan the *tovachïs* divided the work among emirs and soldiers.[91] They are mentioned singly or severally supervising the construction of buildings, dividing booty, organizing camping grounds, and helping with the arrangement of feasts.[92] This was an office which demanded competence and authority, and was held by appropriately powerful and prestigious men.

Yurtchï: The *yurtchï* was an official responsible for arranging the camp.[93] *Yurtchïs* and their tasks are mentioned several times in the histories of Temür's reign. They were sent to find a winter pasture in Georgia in 797/1394–5, and in Damascus in 803/1400 they informed Temür that the camp was overgrazed and found another suitable meadow for the army.[94] On the Indian campaign, they were sent to fetch the baggage train (*urugh*).[95] We know the identity of one *yurtchï*; this was Kepekchi, who was one of the emirs assigned to Shāhrukh, and was the brother of the *darugha* of Yazd, Temüge Qa'uchin.[96]

Yasavul: The *yasavul* was an adjutant, bailiff, or executor of royal decrees.[97] According to the *Dastūr al-kātib*, the *yasavul* was an important official who kept track of all military groups, and kept emirs and soldiers in their proper places and ranks.[98] In the histories of Temür's reign there are few mentions of this office. The *yasavuls* along with the *tovachïs* dispensed food and provision in the *khurïltay* before the Chinese campaign of 807/1404–5.[99] At the conquest of a Georgian fortress in 806/1403–4, it was one of Temür's *yasavuls* who sounded the trumpet before the attack of the army.[100] These examples, few though they are, do confirm the descriptions of the office given elsewhere. The holders of this position under Temür were not very prominent men, but they include both *qa'uchin* and Barlas emirs.[101]

Ranks under Temür: Amīr and Bahadur

In addition to specific offices the men who made up Temür's government held titles indicating an honorary rank. Most of the men mentioned in the histories, and essentially all Temür's important commanders, bore one of two titles – *amīr* or *bahadur*. For some people these titles were used interchangeably but Temür in distributing positions at his takeover distinguished between the two ranks, and the *Muᶜizz al-ansāb*, in enumerating the holders of ranks and offices, lists *amīrs* and *bahadurs* separately.

Amīr: In the histories of Temür's reign, the term *amīr* is most often used in place of the Turkic word *beg*: "chief" or "commander." This title applied to leadership at several different levels; the ruler of the Ulus Chaghatay – including Temür himself – was designated as *amīr*, so were tribal chiefs, and so were many men within the tribal aristocracy and within Temür's following, as well as the commanders of even small contingents in his army.[102] What we must determine here is whether one of the uses of this term was to designate men of a recognized rank, attainable only by birth or by appointment. Such was certainly the case in other similar polities, and under the later Timurids.[103]

For the period of Temür the only source which treats *amīrs* as the holders of a distinct rank is the *Muᶜizz al-ansāb*. The *Muᶜizz* lists them first under each prince, sometimes substituting for "*umarā*" the term "*dīwāniyān*," as I have mentioned above. The list of *amīrs* under Temür includes some but not all of any number of classes of people: members of Temür's following, Barlas, early tribal emirs, Khorasanians, one *qa'uchin*, and several emirs of unknown antecedents. Some of these *amīrs* were commanders of *tümens*, others apparently were not, and not all known commanders of *tümens* are on this list.[104] This rank could be inherited. With the exception of some of the early tribal *amīrs*, almost all *amīrs* who died during

Temür's lifetime passed their rank to a relative, and in some cases the inheritance is shown for three generations. The number of *amīrs* increased very little in this way, since the position passed usually to only one person at a time.[105]

Unfortunately one can discover little about the rank of *amīr* from the other sources on Temür's reign. The information given in the histories is much less clear than that in the *Mu^cizz*; here the ranks of *amīr* and *bahadur* seem almost interchangeable.[106] It is notable also that while even a cursory reading of later Timurid sources show that the title *beg* denoted a specific rank attainable only by inheritance or appointment,[107] the histories of Temür's reign give almost no information about it.

The *Mu^cizz al-ansāb*'s equation of *amīrs* with *dīwāniyān* could suggest that the rank of *amīr* was equivalent to that of *amīr dīwān*; these then would be the great emirs, possibly part of an advisory council, perhaps connected with either the *dīwan-i a^clā* or the *dīwān-i buzurg*. The *Tārīkh-i Ṭabaristān*, recounting Temür's conquest of Mazandaran in 794/1392, reports that the Mazandarani emir Iskandar Shaykhī encouraged the conquest of the area, talking in assemblies to the *umarā' dīwān* about its wealth and treasures.[108] This interpretation however can apply only to the *amīrs* listed in the *Mu^cizz al-ansāb*, not to the use of the title in historical writings, which is much broader. All we can state is that the rank of *amīr* was a hereditary position, which was not granted automatically even to the members of Temür's ruling elite.

Bahadur: After the list of *amīrs* in the *Mu^cizz al-ansāb* comes, under Temür and many of his descendants, a list of *bahadurs*. The meaning and significance of this rank cannot be elucidated. The term *bahadur* was a common one, often used as a title.[109] In the histories of Temür's reign the term *bahadur* is often appended to a personal name; it is found after the names of those listed in the *Mu^cizz al-ansāb* as *bahadur*, and also after the names of many princes. It is also occasionally used separately, to denote a class of people, though how definite a one is not clear. One can cite as an example the mention of "*amīrs* and *bahadurs* with their *tümens* and *hazāras* and *qoshuns*."[110]

Temür when taking over the Ulus Chaghatay appointed a number of men including several members of his following as *bahadur* and army commander; almost all of these people are listed as Temür's *bahadurs* in the *Mu^cizz al-ansāb*.[111] Though men of the rank of *amīr* sometimes had the title of *bahadur* attached to their names, the men listed as *bahadurs* were very rarely called *amīr*.[112] The people made *bahadur* were on the whole somewhat less prominent than Temür's *amīrs* and few of them belonged to the major Ulus tribes. A number however did command *tümens*.[113] Like the rank of *amīr*, that of *bahadur* was clearly hereditary.[114] It is probable that the positions of *amīr* and *bahadur* were ill-defined, and were primarily used as a means of rewarding Temür's followers.

Notes

1 Introduction

1 For a discussion of Temür's birthdate see B. A. F. Manz, "Tamerlane and the Symbolism of Sovereignty," *Iranian Studies*, vol. XXI, pp. 13–14 n.

2 For Chinggis Khan's career see Paul Ratchnevsky, *Činggis-khan, sein Leben und Wirken* (Wiesbaden, 1983).

3 Thomas T. Allsen, *Mongol Imperialism* (Berkeley; Los Angeles; London, 1987), throughout, Paul Buell, "Tribe, *Qan* and *Ulus* in Early Mongol China: some Prolegomena to Yüan History," Doctoral Dissertation, University of Washington, 1977, pp. 86-105, 123–6, 131–2, Rashīd al-Dīn, *The Successors of Genghis Khan*, trans. J. A. Boyle (New York; London, 1971), pp. 218–20.

4 Scholars have recently called into question the existence of the *yasa* as a written code, or even as a definite set of precepts; as an idea however its importance was undeniable. For a recent discussion see D. O. Morgan, "The 'Great *Yāsā* of Chingiz Khān' and Mongol law in the Īlkhānate," *Bulletin of the School of Oriental and African Studies*, vol. 49 # 1 (1986), pp. 163–76.

5 Buell, "Tribe, *Qan* and *Ulus*," pp. 125–30, 146–69, Allsen, *Mongol Imperialism*, pp. 100–8.

6 Buell, "Tribe, *Qan* and *Ulus*," p. 72, Peter Jackson, "The Dissolution of the Mongol Empire," *Central Asiatic Journal*, XXII # 3–4 (1978), pp. 191–2.

7 H. Franke, "From Tribal Chieftain to Universal Emperor and God: the Legitimation of the Yüan Dynasty," *Bayerische Akademie der Wissenschaften*, Phil.-hist. Klasse, Sitzungsberichte, 1978, H. 2, pp. 52–69.

8 A. Bausani, "Religion under the Mongols," *Cambridge History of Iran*, vol. 5 (Cambridge, 1968), pp. 541–3, B. D. Grekov and A. Iu. Iakubovskiĭ, *Zolotaia Orda i ee padenie* (Moscow: Leningrad, 1950), pp. 164–7, J. Spencer Trimingham, *The Sufi Orders in Islam* (Oxford, 1971), p. 91, René Grousset, *The Empire of the Steppes*, trans., N. Walford (New Brunswick, N.J., 1970), pp. 344–5, Mīrzā Muḥammad Ḥaydar Dughlat, *A History of the Moghuls of Central Asia, being the Tarikh-i Rashidi of Mirza Muhammad Haydar, Dughlát*, trans., E. Denison Ross, ed., N. Elias (London; New York, 1898, reprinted 1972), pp. 12–15.

9 We have evidence for instance that there were still Mongolian scribes and even singers in the courts of Iran in the second half of the fourteenth century but Mongolian documents surviving from this time suggest that their language was decadent, and its use essentially a formality. (Gottfried Hermann and Gerhardt Doerfer, "Ein persisch-mongolischer Erlass des Ǧalayeriden Šeyh Oveys," *Central Asiatic Journal*, XIX # 1–2, pp. 31, 56–7, Gerhard Doerfer, *Türkische und mongolische Elemente im Neupersischen, Akademie der*

Wissenschaften und der Literatur, Veröffentlichungen der orientalischen Kommission, vols. 16, 19–21 (1963, 1965, 1967, 1975), vol. I, pp. 16–17).

10 Bertold Spuler, *Die Goldene Horde* (2nd ed., Wiesbaden, 1965), pp. 285–90, Fedorov-Davydov, *Obshchestvennyĭ stroĭ Zolotoĭ Ordy* (Moscow, 1973), pp. 46–7, 66–7, A. P. Grigor'ev, "Ofitsial'nyĭ iazyk Zolotoĭ Ordy XIII–XIV vekov," *Tiurkologicheskiĭ sbornik* vol. 9 (1977), pp. 80–9.

11 Quotations in Turkic are reported from the last of the Ilkhans, Abū Saᶜīd (1316–35) and two Chaghadayid khans, Kebeg (1318–26) and Tarmashirin (1326–34). (B. Spuler, *Die Mongolen in Iran* (Berlin, 1985), p. 380, Ibn Baṭṭūṭa, *The Travels of Ibn Baṭṭūṭa*, trans., H. A. R. Gibb (Cambridge, 1958–71), vol. III, pp. 556–7.) Less is known about the eastern part of the Chaghadayid khanate; Mongolian was still used there for at least some official business into the late fourteenth century, but Turkic may well have been the spoken language of the ruling classes. Both Kebeg and Tarmashirin, who spoke Turkic, were khans of the whole Chaghadayid realm.

12 The exception to this is the Golden Horde where the Mongols chose the religion of the largely nomadic Turks of the steppe among whom they lived, rather than that of their Russian subjects whom they ruled from a distance.

13 D. O. Morgan, *The Mongols* (Oxford, 1986), p. 165, Karl Jahn, "Paper Currency in Iran," *Journal of Asian History*, vol. 4 # 2 (1970), pp. 120–6.

14 I. P. Petrushevsky, "The Socio-economic condition of Iran under the Īl-Khāns," *Cambridge History of Iran*, vol. v, p. 495. V. V. Bartol'd, *Dvenadtsat' lektsii po istorii turetskikh narodov Sredneĭ Azii*, in *Sochineniia*, vol. v (Moscow, 1968), p. 162, Fedorov-Davydov, *Obshchestvennyĭ stroĭ*, pp. 80–1.

15 Bartol'd, *Dvenadtsat' lektsii*, p. 162, M. G. Safargaliev, *Raspad Zolotoĭ Ordy* (Saransk, 1960), pp. 69–70.

16 Allsen, *Mongol Imperialism*, pp. 197–8, Karl Jahn, *Die Chinageschichte des Rašīd ad-Dīn* (Vienna, 1971), pp. 8, 11.

17 See Chapters 2 and 5.

18 Safargaliev, *Raspad*, pp. 120–1.

19 At this period, the term "Turkmen" applied to those western – or Oghuz – Turks in the Middle East who had been in the region before the Mongol invasion and had remained separate from the new Turco-Mongolian ruling class.

20 Sheila Blair, "The Mongol Capital of Sulṭāniyya 'the Imperial' " *Iran*, vol. 24 (1986), p. 147, D. Ayalon, "The great *yasa* of Chingiz Khan. A Reexamination," A, *Studia Islamica*, vol. XXXIII, p. 105.

21 John E. Woods, *The Aqquyunlu, Clan, Confederation, Empire: a Study in 15th/9th Century Turko-Iranian Politics* (Minneapolis; Chicago, 1976), pp. 4–5.

22 Charles J. Halperin, *Russia and the Golden Horde* (Bloomington, 1985), pp. 69, 98, 103.

23 Ruy Gonzalez de Clavijo, *Narrative of the Spanish Embassy to the Court of Timur at Samarkand in the years 1403–1406*, trans., Guy Le Strange (London, 1928), pp. 221, 282.

24 W. Fischel, *Ibn Khaldun and Tamerlane. Their historic Meeting in Damascus, 1401 A.D. (803 A.H.)* (Berkeley; Los Angeles, 1852) (hereafter Ibn Khaldūn, Fischel), p. 37, Jean of Sultaniyya, "Mémoire sur Tamerlan et sa cour par un Dominicain en 1403," ed. H. Moranvillé, *Bibliothèque de l'École des Chartes*, LV (Paris, 1894) (hereafter Jean of Sultaniyya), pp. 444–5.

25 I have discussed the problem of legitimation more fully in my article, "Tamerlane and the Symbolism of Sovereignty."

26 See Igor de Rachewiltz, "Some remarks on the Ideological Foundation of Chingis Khan's Empire," *Papers on Far Eastern History*, # 7 (March, 1973), pp. 21–36.

27 See for example A. K. S. Lambton, "The Internal Structure of the Saljuq Empire," *Cambridge History of Iran*, vol. 5, pp. 208–12.

28 Jean Aubin, "Comment Tamerlan prenait les villes," *Studia Islamica*, XIX (1963), pp. 109, 121–2.
29 Aubin, "Comment," pp. 86–7.
30 Clavijo, p. 221.
31 The fullest discussion of Temür's personality is H. R. Roemer's in his article "Tīmūr in Iran," *Cambridge History of Iran*, vol. VI (Cambridge, 1986), pp. 83–90.
32 Niẓām al-Dīn Shāmī, *Histoire des conquêtes de Tamerlan intitulée Ẓafarnāma, par Niẓāmuddīn Šāmī*, ed., F. Tauer (Prague, vol. I, 1937; vol. II, 1956) (hereafter ZNS) vol. II, pp. 192–3, 202.
33 Ibn Khaldūn, Fischel, pp. 37, 47.
34 Ibn Khaldūn, Fischel, p. 47.
35 Aubin, "Comment," p. 85.
36 Aubin, "Comment," pp. 88–90, J. Aubin, *Matériaux pour la biographie de Shah Niᶜmatullāh Walī Kermānī* (Paris; Tehran, 1956), pp. 11–13, 121–3.
37 Aubin, *Matériaux*, p. 11.
38 ZNS I, pp. 128, 198, 247, 279, 286.
39 Ḥāfiẓ-i Abrū, *Cinq opuscules de Ḥāfiẓ-i Abrū concernant l'histoire de l'Iran au temps de Tamerlan*, ed., F. Tauer (Prague, 1959), text, pp. 61–2, Jean Aubin, "Le khanat de Čagatai et le Khorasan (1334–1380)," *Turcica*, VIII # 2 (1976), pp. 52–3. There is some doubt about whether Temür actually succeeded in winning the approval of all local Sufi shaykhs (see cited passage in Aubin), but there can be none about his intentions.
40 V. V. Bartol'd, "O pogrebenii Timura," in *Sochineniia*, vol. II, pt. 2 (Moscow, 1964), pp. 424–37.
41 Two were particularly important, Amir Kulāl in Temür's earlier years, and Sayyid Baraka of Andkhud thereafter. (Aubin, *Matériaux*, pp. 11–13, 121–3, Ibn,ᶜArabshāh, *Tamerlane or Timur the Great Amir*, trans., J. H. Sanders (London, 1936, reprinted Lahore, 1976), pp. 5, 14.)
42 I have dealt with this trait elsewhere: see Manz, "Administration and the Delegation of Authority in Temür's Dominions," *Central Asiatic Journal*, XX # 3 (1976), pp. 191–207.
43 On Temür's reaction to deaths within his family see ZNS I, pp. 85–90, 149, 272–6, Sharaf al-Dīn ᶜAlī Yazdī, *Ẓafarnāma*, ed., Muḥammad ᶜAbbāsī (Tehran, sh. 1336/1957) (hereafter ZNY), vol. II, pp. 355–6. Outside observers attested to the size and richness of the Timurid princes' suites and in 1404 envoys were ordered to give obeisance to Temür's grandson Pīr Muḥammad whom he later named as his successor. (Clavijo, p. 254, Jean of Sultaniyya, p. 446.)
44 For an excellent discussion of the Timurid histories see John E. Woods, "The Rise of Tīmūrid Historiography," *Journal of Near Eastern Studies*, 46 # 2 (1987), pp. 81–108.

2 The Ulus Chaghatay in the mid fourteenth century

1 W. R. Rickmers, *The Duab of Turkestan* (Cambridge, 1913), pp. 36–9, 51–2, 59–62, 72–8, 164.
2 J. Humlum, *La géographie de l'Afghanestan* (Copenhagen; Stockholm; Oslo; Helsinki, 1959), pp. 106–7, 133, 281–4.
3 Rashīd al-Dīn, trans., L. A. Khetagurov, ed., A. A. Semenov, *Rashīd ad-Dīn: Sbornik letopiseĭ* (Moscow; Leningrad, 1952), vol. I, pt. 2, p. 69, V. V. Bartol'd, *Turkestan down to the Mongol Invasion*, trans., T. Minorsky (London, 1968), p. 393.
4 Jackson, "The Dissolution," pp. 186, 204–7, René Grousset, *L'Empire Mongol, 1re Phase* (Paris, 1941), pp. 325–32, Bartol'd, *Turkestan*, pp. 463, 468.
5 Bartol'd, *Turkestan*, pp. 465, 472–3, 483, 485.
6 Bartol'd, *Turkestan*, p. 488.

7 Bartol'd, *Istoriia Turkestana*, in *Sochineniia*, vol. II, pt. I (Moscow, 1963), p. 149, *Turkestan*, p. 483.
8 Bartol'd, *Istoriia Turkestana*, p. 149, *Turkestan*, pp. 491–3.
9 René Grousset, *The Empire of the Steppes*, p. 338.
10 Bartol'd, *Turkestan*, p. 493, *Istoriia Turkestana*, pp. 149–50.
11 See Chapter I.
12 V. V. Bartol'd, *Dvenadtsat' lektsii*, pp. 163, 169.
13 Bartol'd, *Dvenadtsat' lektsii*, p. 164, Zeki Velidi Togan, "Gazan-Han Halil ve Hoca Bahaeddin Nakşbend," in *Necâti Luğal Armagani* (Türk tarihi kurumu yayïnlarïndan VII seri sa. 50) (Ankara, 1968), pp. 775–6.
14 Aubin, "l'Ethnogénèse des Qaraunas," *Turcica*, I (1969), p. 82, Jackson, "The Dissolution," p. 243.
15 J. A. Boyle, "Dynastic and Political History of the Īl-Khāns," *The Cambridge History of Iran*, vol. V, pp. 356–60, 381–2, 405, 410, Bartol'd, *Dvenadtsat' lektsii*, p. 163, A. Urunbaev, ed., Sharaf al-Dīn ᶜAlī Yazdī, *Ẓafarnāme*, Tashkent, 1972 (hereafter ZNY, Urunbaev), *Muqaddima*, f. 80a.
16 Russell G. Kempiners, "The Struggle for Khurasan: Aspects of Political, Military and Socio-economic Interaction in the early 8th/14th Century," Doctoral Dissertation, University of Chicago, 1985, pp. 65–72.
17 Ḥāfiẓ-i Abrū, *Dhayl-i jāmiᶜ al-tawārīkh-i rashīdī*, ed., Kh. Bayānī (Tehran, sh. 1350/1972–3), p. 112.
18 Ḥāfiẓ-i Abrū, *Dhayl*, pp. 112, 114–15.
19 While Jean Aubin states that the Negüderi and perhaps some other Qara'unas were under Chaghadayid control by 1270, both Karl Jahn and Peter Jackson believe that this occurred only at the end of the thirteenth century. See Jean Aubin, "l'Ethnogénèse," pp. 82–4, and "Le Khanat," p. 17, Jackson, "The Dissolution," p. 243, Karl Jahn, "Zum Problem der mongolischen Eroberungen in Indien (13–14 Jahrhundert)," *Akten des vierund zwanzigsten internationalen Orientalisten-Kongresses, München, Aug.–Sept. 1957* (Wiesbaden, 1959), pp. 618–19. See also Kempiners, pp. 59–60.
20 Rashīd al-Dīn, *Jāmiᶜ al-tawārīkh*, ed. A. A. Ali-Zade (Baku, 1957), vol. III, p. 152, Aubin, "l'Ethnogénèse," pp. 82–4, K. Jahn, "Zum Problem," pp. 618–19, Jackson, "The Dissolution," p. 243. Here one is reminded of the influence wielded in Transoxiana by the officials of the Great Khan and of the house of Jochi in the early 13th century.
21 Ḥāfiẓ-i Abrū, *Dhayl*, p. 115.
22 They were killed together near Ghazna in 1320, while fighting the Chaghatay forces of Kebeg Khan. We do not know what happened to the troops of Baktut after this, but Ḥāfiẓ-i Abrū's *Dhayl-i jāmiᶜ al-tawārīkh* states that many of Yasa'ur's troops deserted to the Chaghadayids during their final confrontation. (Ḥāfiẓ-i Abrū, *Dhayl*, pp. 121, 136, 158–9).
23 Ibn Baṭṭūṭa, Gibb, vol. III, pp. 561, 585–6.
24 ZNY I, pp. 31–2, ZNS I, p. 15, II, pp. 11–12, Muᶜīn al-Dīn Naṭanzī, ed., J. Aubin, *Extraits du Muntakhab al tavārīkh-i Muᶜīnī* (Tehran, 1957) (hereafter *Muntakhab*), pp. 204–5. Most sources state that the Apardï were led by Muḥammad Khwāja Apardï, but he had in fact been killed shortly before this and succeeded by Zinda Ḥasham. (See *Cinq opuscules*, p. 47, notes, p. 29.)
25 ZNY I, p. 164, Ibn ᶜArabshāh, p. 4, *Cinq opuscules*, text, p. 38.
26 *Muᶜizz al-ansāb fī shajārat al-ansāb*, ms., Bibliothèque Nationale, Paris, 67 (hereafter *Muᶜizz*), ff. 28b, 81b–82a, Rashīd al-Dīn, *Shuᶜab-i panjgāna*, ms. Istanbul, Ahmet Salis 2937, f. 47b.
27 *Muᶜizz*, ff. 28b, 29a, RaD *Successors*, p. 145, *Shuᶜab-i panjgāna*, f. 117b, A. Z. V. Togan, "Taḥqīq-i nasab-i Amīr Tīmūr," in S. M. ᶜAbdullāh, ed., *Professor Muḥammad Shafīᶜ*

Presentation Volume (Lahore, 1955), p. 108, E. M. Quatremère, "Notice de l'ouvrage persan qui a pour titre: Matla-assaadein ou majma-albahrein, et qui contient l'histoire des deux sultans Schahrokh et Abou-Said," in *Notices et extraits des manuscrits de la Bibliothèque du Roi et autres bibliothèques*, vol. XIV, pt. I (1843), p. 280.

28 al-ᶜUmarī, *Das mongolische Weltreich: al-ᶜUmarīs Darstellung der mongolischen Reiche in seinem Werk Masālik al-abṣār fi mamālik al-amṣār*, ed. and trans., Klaus Lech (Wiesbaden, 1968), p. 123.

29 This is definitely the case with the Qara'unas and the Yasa'urī, and I believe that it is also true of the Apardï and the Khuttalānī emirs, as I have explained in Appendix A.

30 See for example ZNY I, pp. 114–15, 202, 339, ZNS I, p. 14, *Muᶜizz*, f. 101b, *Cinq opuscules*, text, p. 38.

31 It is used for instance for the Orona'ut, the Merkit and the Arlat, but not for the Barlas, Jalayir or Suldus. (ZNS I, pp. 15, 28, ZNY I, p. 547). For tribal sections see ZNY II, p. 38, ZNS II, p. 12, *Muntakhab*, p. 207.

32 E. E. Evans-Pritchard, *The Nuer* (Oxford, 1940), pp. 120–4, 148–50, Paul Kirchhoff, "The Principles of Clanship in Human Society," *Davidson Journal of Anthropology*, vol. I (1955), pp. 1–10.

33 Herbert S. Lewis, "Typology and Process in Political Evolution," in J. Helm, ed., *Essays on the Problem of Tribe: Proceedings of the 1967 Annual Spring Meeting of the American Ethnological Society* (Seattle, 1968), pp. 101–7.

34 See for example Rudi Linder, "What was a Nomadic Tribe?," *Comparative Studies in Society and History*, 24 # 4 (1982), pp. 698–701, Lois Beck, *The Qashqa'i of Iran* (New Haven; London, 1986), pp. 15–19.

35 Fredrik Barth, *Nomads of South Persia* (Oslo; London; New York, 1964), pp. 52, 84–6.

36 See for example B. Ia. Vladimirtsov, *Obshchestvennyĭ stroĭ mongolov: mongol'skiĭ kochevoĭ feodalizm* (Leningrad, 1934), pp. 59, 63, Omeljan Pritsak, "Stammesnamen und Titulaturen der altiaschen Völker," *Ural/Altaische Jahrbücher*, XXIV # 1–2, pp. 56–8.

37 Kirchhoff, "The Principles of Clanship," pp. 1–10.

38 ZNY I, pp. 106, 170, 194–6, ZNS I, pp. 64, 71, II, p. 30, *Muntakhab*, p. 297.

39 ZNY I, p. 363.

40 ZNY I, pp. 147, 149, 193, 196, 327, 364, 388, ZNS II, p. 37, *Muntakhab*, p. 235.

41 Also called the *ulugh tümen*: *Muᶜizz*, ff. 88b, 89b, ZNY I, pp. 36, 45.

42 The fact that the Jalayir and Suldus troops are identified by tribal name while the Barlas ones are not may be due to the nearness of the historians to the Barlas traditions; whereas the hereditary troops of the Barlas are identified by the name they held within the tribe, those of the Jalayir and Suldus, seen from a distance, are identified simply by the tribal name.

43 See for example Aqbugha and Temürtash Nayman, ZNY I, pp. 98, 100, 237 etc., Mūsā Taychi'ut, ZNY I, p. 100, Sayf al-Dīn Nüküz, pp. 48, 58, 67, *Muᶜizz*, f. 97a.

44 There is mention in the *Shams al-Ḥusn* of the "Chekene Barlas", but no indication of what this represented. (Tāj al-Salmānī, *Šams al-Ḥusn: eine Chronik vom Tode Timurs bis zum Jahre 1409 von Tağ as-Salmānī*, ed. and trans., Hans Robert Roemer (Wiesbaden, 1956), (hereafter *Shams*), f. 99b, p. 74).

45 ZNY I, pp. 106, 136, 170, *Muntakhab*, p. 240.

46 *Muntakhab*, p. 207.

47 ZNS II, p. 11, ZNY I, p. 30, *Muntakhab*, p. 262.

48 *Muntakhab*, p. 107.

49 ZNY. Urunbaev, *Muqaddima*, f. 80a.

50 ZNY I, p. 59.

51 Another example of such naming was the Jawun-i Qurban, or "three percent" of Khorasan, which originated as a garrison army stationed in Tus and Nishapur. (Aubin, "l'Ethnogénèse," p. 75.)

52 ZNY I, pp. 59, 147. This is reminiscent of the hereditary subject class (*unaghan boghol*) described among the early Mongols by Vladimirtsov. (*Obshchestvennyĭ stroĭ*, pp. 64–7.) See also for a more constricted definition C. E. Markov, *Kochevniki Azii* (Moscow, 1976), pp. 64–6. One may see a similar institution in the Ulus Chaghatay in the slaves or slave troops reportedly attached to the Chekene Barlas, mentioned by Tāj al-Salmānī, but their role remains obscure. (*Shams*, f. 99b, p. 74.)

53 ZNY I, pp. 36, 37, 66–7, ZNS I, p. 18, II, p. 14.

54 ZNY I, pp. 53, 59, 115, ZNS I, p. 44.

55 ZNY I, p. 147.

56 ZNY I, pp. 147, 181, 325, 334, *Muntakhab*, pp. 232, 258, 294–5.

57 Ibn ᶜArabshāh, p. 17.

58 A. K. Arends, A. B.Khalidov, O. D. Chekhovich, *Bukharskiĭ vaḳf* XIII *v.* (Moscow, 1979), pp. 14–15.

59 Allsen, *Mongol Imperialism*, pp. 193–4, 209–10.

60 B. Grekov and A. Iakubovskiĭ, *Zolotaia Orda*, pp. 108–10, Hsiao Ch'i-ch'ing, *The Military Establishment of the Yuan Dynasty* (Cambridge, Mass., 1978), pp. 18–25, A. I. Falina, "Reformy Gazan-Khana," *Uchenyi Zapiski Instituta Vostokovedeniia Akademii Nauk SSSR*, vol. XVII, pp. 69–71.

61 The conscription of local population by the Mongol successor states will be discussed in Chapter 5.

62 Clavijo, pp. 190–1, 210, Ibn ᶜArabshāh, p. 1.

63 ZNS II, p. 10, *Muntakhab*, p. 200.

64 *Muntakhab*, p. 222.

65 ZNY I, p. 32. For Bukhara as a winter pasture see ZNS I, p. 85, O. D. Chekhovich, *Bukharskie dokumenty* XIV *veka* (Tashkent, 1965), place names, pp. 46–50.

66 About the Qara'unas, whom I discussed above, we are specifically informed. The Suldus controlled the regions of Balkh and Chaghaniyan, contiguous across the Oxus; Balkh is relatively flat, Chaghaniyan mountainous. The Arlat were both at Andkhud, in the plain of Khorasan, and at Gurziwan, which while south of Andkhud is in a mountainous region.

67 ZNS I, p. 36, ZNY I, p. 110, *Muntakhab*, p. 235.

68 G. Le Strange, *The Lands of the Eastern Caliphate* (Cambridge, 1930) (Cambridge Geographical Series), pp. 426, 469–70.

69 ZNY I, pp. 106, 117, *Muntakhab*, p. 240.

70 ZNS II, p. 20.

71 Chekhovich, *Bukharskie dokumenty* XIV *veka*, pp. 53, 57, 59, 64–5.

72 ZNS I, p. 35.

73 ZNS I, pp. 42, 45, ZNY I, pp. 109, 116, 149, *Muntakhab*, pp. 242, 245–6, 284.

74 ZNY I, pp. 35–6, ZNS I, p. 16, *Muntakhab*, pp. 205–6.

75 ZNS I, pp. 19–20, ZNY I, pp. 47–9, 60, *Muntakhab*, pp. 210–11, 216. Similarly Bahrām Jalayir, leaving the Ulus in 767/1366, took with himself only his own followers and special troops. (ZNY I, p. 89, ZNS I, p. 35, Muntakhab, p. 235.)

76 The dependence of the standard histories – the two *Ẓafarnāma* of Shāmī and Yazdī, the *Mujmal-i Faṣīḥī*, and the *Majmaᶜ al-tawārīkh* of Ḥāfiẓ-i Abrū, on Chaghatay traditions rather than those of the local urban culture is shown by their reliance on the animal cycle for dates. This results in some disagreement over the chronology of events before the invasion of Khorasan. (See for example the murder of Qazaghan, dated by Yazdī as 759, by Ḥāfiẓ-i Abrū as 760 (ZNY I, p. 30, ZNS II, p. 11), the deposition and death of ᶜAbd Allāh b. Qazaghan, 760 in the *Mujmal-i Faṣīḥī*, 761 in Ḥāfiẓ-i Abrū (Faṣīḥ Khwāfī, *Mujmal-i Faṣīḥī*, ed. Muḥammad Farrukh (Mashhad, sh. 1339/1960–1), vol. III, p. 91, ZNS II, p. 11). This confusion continued through Temür's early career; Shāmī and Ḥāfiẓ-i Abrū date events consistently later than does Yazdī, while giving the same animal year. (See for example ZNY I, p. 182, ZNS I, p. 68, ZNY I, p. 188, ZNS I, p. 69.)

3 Temür's rise to power

1 See for example ZNY I, pp. 33, 38–41, 45, 60–2, 64–5, ZNS I, p. 23, *Muntakhab*, pp. 207, 209–10, 217–18.

2 ZNS II, p. 10, *Muntakhab*, p. 200.

3 I use the term "emir" to denote members of the ruling class outside the Timurid dynasty.

4 ZNS II, p. 10, P. Jackson, "The Mongols and the Delhi Sultanate in the Reign of Muhammad Tughluq (1325–1351)," *Central Asiatic Journal*, XIX # 1–2, p. 151.

5 ZNY I, p. 24, *Cinq opuscules*, text, p. 38, *Mujmal*, III, p. 69. Although the Arlat and Apardï had been fighting Malik Mu^cizz al-Dīn Kart for probably six years, the leadership of the Ulus had not come to their help before this. Jean Aubin suggests that the confusion within the Ulus may have caused this delay, or that the Karts attacked these tribes in order to help Qazan Khan in his troubles with his tribal emirs. (Aubin, "Khanat," pp. 27, 29–30, ZNY I, pp. 23–4, *Cinq opuscules*, text, pp. 37–8). However it is possible also that Qazan was simply less interested in Khorasan and less concerned about the Arlat and the Apardï than was Amīr Qazaghan.

6 He had with him his puppet Khan, Buyan Qulï Khan, Amīr Buyan Suldus, Muḥammad Khwāja Apardï of Shaburqan, Öljeytü Apardï of Khuttalan, Amīr Satïlmish, governor of Quhistan, Amīr ᶜAbd Allāh b. Tayghu, the shah of Badakhshan, and an Amīr Tümen, presumably Tümen Negüderī, leader of the Negüderī tribe. (ZNY I, pp. 25–8, *Cinq opuscules*, text, pp. 39–43.) ᶜAbd Allāh b. Tayghu is hard to identify, but since both he and his brothers are later mentioned as supporters of Amīr Ḥusayn, it seems that he was an ally of that family. Amīr Satïlmish Quhistānī was not normally a member of the Ulus, but he shared with the Arlat and Apardï a grudge against Malik Muᶜizz al-Dīn and had been forced to take refuge from him in Transoxiana. (*Cinq opuscules*, text, p. 45.)

7 ZNY I, pp. 29–30, ZNS I, p. 15, II, p. 11, *Muntakhab*, p. 262.

8 *Muntakhab*, p. 201.

9 ZNY I, pp. 30–2, ZNS I, p. 15, *Muntakhab*, p. 263.

10 ZNY I, pp. 33–6, ZNS I, pp. 15–16, II, pp. 11–12, *Muntakhab*, pp. 204, 206. For the period of Temür's rise to power I have chosen the dating of Yazdī's *Ẓafarnāma* over that of Ḥāfiẓ-i Abrū, which shows some inconsistencies.

11 ZNY I, p. 35, ZNS I, p. 16, *Muntakhab*, p. 117. The *Ẓafarnāma* of Sharaf al-Dīn ᶜAlī Yazdī mentions also as one reason for Temür's fears the recent death of his father, Amīr Taraghay, which suggests that his concern might have been the state of his personal inheritance as much as that of the whole tribe.

12 Clavijo, pp. 210–11, Ibn ᶜArabshāh, p. 2, Ibn ᶜArabshāh, Calcutta, p. 4.

13 Ibn ᶜArabshāh, p. 2, Ibn ᶜArabshāh, Calcutta, p. 4, Clavijo, p. 211.

14 ZNS I, p. 35. The importance of a personal following for a supratribal leader has long been recognized. The best known example is that of Chinggis Khan, whose personal following was crucial to him during his rise to power, and in the formation of his administration. More recently some scholars have described the importance which personal followers could have for tribal chiefs as well. (Halil Inalcik, "The Khan and the Tribal Aristocracy: the Crimean Khanate under Ṣāḥib Girey I," in *Eucharisterion: Essays Presented to Omeljan Pritsak on his Sixtieth Birthday by his Colleagues and Students*, pt. 1, pp. 450–2, 457, 462, also Woods, *Aqqoyunlu*, p. 8.)

15 ZNY I, p. 98, *Muᶜizz*, f. 95b.

16 ZNY I, p. 75. When in 776–7/1375–6 Temür was campaigning in Moghulistan, he stopped near At Bashi where he was entertained by the chief of that *hazāra* Mubārakshāh Merkit, who was an old friend of his. (ZNY I, p. 190.) The Merkit, with their land apparently in the T'ien Shan at the eastern end of Ferghana, seem to have had a position between the Chaghatays and the Moghuls.

17 ZNY I, p. 120, ZNS I, p. 46.

18 ZNY I, p. 36, ZNS, I, p. 16, *Muntakhab*, p. 206.
19 ZNY I, p. 37, ZNS I, p. 16, II, p. 13, *Muntakhab*, p. 206.
20 ZNY I, pp. 38–9, ZNS I, pp. 16–17, II, pp. 13–14, *Muntakhab*, p. 207. The *Muntakhab* is the only history which mentions Amīr Ḥusayn becoming leader of the whole of the Ulus at this time.
21 ZNY I, pp. 40–2, ZNS I, p. 17, II, p. 14, *Muntakhab*, pp. 207–8. It is possible that Temür did have some problem regaining his position within his tribe, though the sources ascribe objections against him to Bāyazīd Jalayir, rather than Ḥājjī Beg. We do not know Amīr Ḥusayn's actions at this time, but two of his closest allies, Zinda Ḥasham Apardï and ᶜAbd Allāh Tayghu, collected an army to oppose Ḥājjī Beg and Bāyazīd. No confrontation in fact resulted. (ZNS I, p. 18, II, p. 14, ZNY I, pp. 43–4.)
22 ZNS I, p. 18, II, pp. 14–15, ZNY I, pp. 44–5, *Muntakhab*, p. 209.
23 ZNY I, pp. 38, 45–6, ZNS I, pp. 18–19, II, p. 15, *Muntakhab*, pp. 209–10.
24 ZNY I, pp. 47, 49–52, ZNS I, pp. 19–21, II, pp. 15–17, *Muntakhab*, pp. 210–13.
25 ZNY I, pp. 53–6, ZNS I, pp. 21–2, *Muntakhab*, pp. 213–15. It is possible that this campaign was smaller, and undertaken without Amīr Ḥusayn. See Manz, "Sovereignty."
26 This will be discussed more fully below.
27 ZNY I, pp. 59–60, 67.
28 ZNY I, p. 58, *Muntakhab*, p. 216.
29 ZNY I, pp. 59–63, 67, ZNS I, pp. 22–4, II, p. 18, *Muntakhab*, pp. 215–17.
30 ZNY I, p. 63, ZNS I, p. 24. On the tensions of propinquity, see William Irons, *The Yomut Turkmen: A Study of Social Organization among a Central Asian Turkic-speaking Population* (Ann Arbor, 1975), pp. 63–4.
31 These were two men who should have been allies of Amīr Ḥusayn's: Abū Saᶜīd b. Tayghu and Ḥaydar Andkhūdī. The sons of Tayghu were usually supporters of the dynasty of Qazaghan with whom they had undertaken a number of campaigns. (ZNY I, pp. 25, 107.) Abū Saᶜīd however was also Mengli Bugha's brother-in-law, and this tie presumably overrode the other. Ḥaydar Andkhūdī is not clearly identified, but came under the jurisdiction of Zinda Ḥasham Apardï, an ally of Amīr Ḥusayn's. (ZNY I, p. 74.)
32 ZNY I, pp. 60–1, ZNS I, pp. 23–4, *Muntakhab*, p. 217.
33 ZNY I, pp. 64–72, ZNS I, pp. 25–6, *Muntakhab*, pp. 220–2.
34 ZNY I, pp. 72–5, ZNS I, p. 27, II, pp. 18–19, *Muntakhab*, pp. 221–2.
35 ZNY I, pp. 76–83, ZNS I, pp. 30–1, *Muntakhab*, pp. 226–7.
36 ZNY I, pp. 85–6, ZNS I, p. 32, II, p. 22, *Muntakhab*, pp. 232–3.
37 ZNY I, pp. 86–7, ZNS I, p. 33, *Muntakhab*, p. 234.
38 ZNY I, pp. 55, 67, *Muntakhab*, p. 214. The emirs were helped by ᶜAlī Darwīsh's grandmother, who was Amīr Ḥusayn's mother-in-law.
39 ZNY I, pp. 105, 172, *Muᶜizz*, f. 30b.
40 ZNY I, p. 87.
41 ZNY I, p. 89, ZNS I, p. 35, *Muntakhab*, pp. 235, 265.
42 ZNY I, pp. 90–5, ZNS I, pp. 35–7, II, p. 23, *Muntakhab*, pp. 236–7, 266.
43 ZNY I, pp. 95–106, ZNS I, pp. 38–41, II, p. 23, *Muntakhab*, pp. 237–40.
44 ZNY I, pp. 106–10, ZNS I, pp. 41–2, *Muntakhab*, pp. 240–2.
45 Jean Aubin believes that the two men did reach an accord and agree on joint action. This supposition is upheld by the fact that Temür's son, Jahāngīr, went to Herat accompanied by Mubārakshāh Sanjarī, and stayed there for the next few years; also Temür left his dependents in Makhan, apparently under the king's protection. (ZNY I, pp. 112–14, ZNS I, p. 44, Aubin, "Khanat," pp. 45–7, *Muntakhab*, p. 244.)
46 ZNY I, pp. 114–17, ZNS I, pp. 44–5, *Muntakhab*, pp. 244–5.
47 ZNY I, pp. 117–19, ZNS I, pp. 45–6.
48 ZNY I, pp. 119–20, ZNS I, pp. 46–7, *Muntakhab*, p. 247.
49 ZNY I, pp. 120–4, ZNS I, pp. 47–9, *Muntakhab*, pp. 247–50.

50 ZNY I, pp. 124–9, ZNS I, pp. 49–51, *Muntakhab*, pp. 250–3.
51 Jean Aubin suggests that this raid had been arranged previously with Temür to coincide with the arrival of the Moghul troops from the north, now called off. (ZNY I, pp. 129–30, ZNS I, p. 51, *Muntakhab*, p. 253, Aubin, "Khanat," p. 47.)
52 Bartol'd, *Dvenadtsat' lektsii*, pp. 173–4, B. G. Gafurov, *Istoriia tadzhikskogo naroda* (Moscow, 1963–5), vol. I, pt. I, pp. 128–30.
53 ZNY I, p. 131, ZNS I, p. 52.
54 Buyan, Tughluq and Mengli Bugha had all been inimical, and while Shaykh Muḥammad b. Buyan Suldus had sided with Amīr Ḥusayn against Temür in their recent confrontations, the sources all report that he had done so unenthusiastically.
55 ZNY I, pp. 137–40, ZNS I, pp. 54–5, II, p. 26, *Muntakhab*, pp. 258–60.
56 ZNY I, pp. 142–5, ZNS I, pp. 55–7, *Muntakhab*, pp. 260–1, 272, 181–2.
57 The *Muntakhab* suggests a reason for Sayyid Baraka's support; Temür was willing to present to him the *waqf* properties which Amīr Ḥusayn had refused him. (*Muntakhab*, p. 282.)
58 ZNY I, pp. 145–9, ZNS I, p. 57, *Muntakhab*, pp. 282–3.
59 ZNY I, pp. 149–53, ZNS I, pp. 57–60, *Muntakhab*, pp. 284–6.
60 ZNY I, pp. 153–4, ZNS I, p. 60, *Muntakhab*, pp. 286–7. Shāmī's *Ẓafarnāma*, written at Temür's command, states explicitly that this execution was done without Temür's knowledge or permission, and Sharaf al-Dīn ᶜAlī Yazdī repeats this account. The *Muntakhab*, written from a more independent viewpoint, also ascribes the initiative and the deed to Temür's emirs, but does not make it clear that Temür was ignorant of their intentions.
61 ZNY I, p. 155.
62 ZNY I, pp. 155–7. One should note that this account of Temür's acclamation is found only in Yazdī; other historians do not mention it.
63 ZNS I, p. 61, ZNY I, pp. 157–8. In the *Ẓafarnāma* of Sharaf al-Dīn ᶜAlī Yazdī, this event is portrayed as a direct affirmation of Temür's power, while in Shāmī's *Ẓafarnāma*, it is presented as the reaffirmation of Temür's puppet khan. As Professor John Woods has pointed out to me, Yazdī has systematically suppressed all mentions of the Chaghadayid khans whom Temür used to legitimize his rule.
64 ZNY I, pp. 161–2, *Muntakhab*, pp. 287–8.
65 ZNY I, p. 176.
66 ZNY I, pp. 163–5, ZNS I, p. 62, *Muntakhab*, pp. 291–3.
67 Öljeytü is mentioned as one of Qazaghan's greatest emirs in 752/1351–2, whereas Zinda Ḥasham first succeeded his father as head of the Apardï of Shaburqan in 759/1358. (*Cinq opuscules*, notes, p. 29, ZNY I, p. 25.)
68 ZNY I, pp. 165–6, ZNS I, pp. 62–3, *Muntakhab*, pp. 292–3.
69 ZNY I, pp. 166–9, ZNS I, p. 63, II, p. 29, *Muntakhab*, pp. 294–6.
70 It is not clear who and what Abū'l-Layth was. His name suggests a settled origin, and perhaps a religious, probably Sufi connection, but the evidence of names should not be considered conclusive.
71 ZNY I, pp. 171–3, ZNS I, p. 64, *Muntakhab*, p. 299.
72 ZNY I, pp. 173–6, ZNS I, p. 65, *Muntakhab*, pp. 301–2.
73 ZNY I, pp. 177–81, ZNS I, pp. 66–7, *Muntakhab*, pp. 302–3.
74 ZNY I, pp. 181–3, ZNS I, p. 68, *Muntakhab*, p. 303.
75 ZNY I, pp. 192–3, ZNS I, p. 70, II, p. 36, *Muntakhab*, p. 414.
76 ZNY I, p. 193, ZNS I, pp. 70–1, *Muntakhab*, pp. 414–15, *Mujmal*, vol. III, p. 108.
77 ZNY I, pp. 194–6, ZNS I, pp. 71–2, *Muntakhab*, p. 415.
78 ZNY I, pp. 197–9, 202, ZNS I, pp. 72–3, II, pp. 37–9, *Muntakhab*, pp. 416–17.
79 Anthropologists have noted that the practice of tribal vengeance often serves to keep order rather than to provoke violence. See for instance Ernest Gellner, *Muslim Society* (Cambridge, 1981), p. 97.

4 Temür's army of conquest

1 The range of dates presented in this account of Temür's early campaigns is due to the disagreement of the sources on how to translate the animal cycle into Ḥijra dates.
2 Safargaliev, *Raspad*, pp. 137–45.
3 Temür's Middle Eastern campaigns are well described in H. R. Roemer's chapter, "Tīmūr in Iran," pp. 42–97. In my account therefore I have footnoted only a few additional details.
4 *Muntakhab*, p. 311, *Cinq opuscules*, p. 40.
5 *Muntakhab*, pp. 312–14, *Cinq opuscules*, text, p. 66, notes, p. 41.
6 Khorezm may well have been under Tokhtamïsh's control at this period. See Safargaliev, *Raspad*, p. 142.
7 John Woods, "Turco-Iranica II: Notes on a Timurid Decree of 1396/798," *Journal of Near Eastern Studies*, 43 # 4 (1984), pp. 333–5.
8 ZNY II, p. 203.
9 ZNY II, p. 283.
10 In a few cases Ibn ᶜArabshāh gives the name of a son contemporary to himself rather than the father who actually served Temür before his rise to power, but this is easy to correct. (Ibn ᶜArabshāh, p. 2.)
11 An example of the first is Temür's expedition from the region of Marw against Qarshi in the winter of 768/1366–7. (ZNY I, pp. 114–18.) An example of the second is the list of Temür's emirs fined by Amīr Ḥusayn in 767/1366. (ZNY I, p. 86.)
12 Ḥusayn's provenance remains uncertain since he is not found in the genealogy of the Barlas, despite the later prominence of his son Khudāydād.
13 *Shams*, f. 108b, pp. 80–1.
14 The only post which was given to a tribal leader as well as to Temür's followers was that of *amīr dīwān*. This may have indicated membership on a judicial council, and will be discussed in Chapter 6. Even in this position the most important tribal emirs were not represented; the only one appointed was Ḥājjī Maḥmūdshāh Yasa'urī, who as Temür's maternal cousin also had personal ties to him. (ZNY I, pp. 161–2.)
15 ZNY I, pp. 106, 114, Clavijo, p. 211, T. I. Ter-Grigorian, trans., *Foma Metsopskii, Istoriia Timur-lanka* (Baku, 1957) (hereafter Thomas of Metsop), p. 55.
16 ZNY I, pp. 171, 176–9, 189, 194, ZNS I, pp. 64, 67, II, p. 34.
17 ZNY I, pp. 77, 196–7, 387; see also Appendix A: Qipchaq.
18 ZNY II, pp. 43, 125, ZNS I, p. 235, II, pp. 140, 161.
19 ZNY II, p. 80, ZNS I, pp. 188, 190.
20 ZNY I, p. 463, II, p. 100, ZNS I, p. 194, II, p. 66.
21 For slaves acquired as prisoners of war see *Shams*, f. 16b, p. 22.
22 ZNY I, pp. 251, 363, 366, 370, 389, ZNS I, p. 101, II, p. 48, *Muntakhab*, pp. 326–7, 347. In one other case, that of Buyan Temür b. Aqbugha, a *tümen* had been passed directly to the son of a follower, and from him to his son. (ZNY I, p. 366.) Of Temür's personal followers only one, Qumarï Ïnaq Qa'uchin, was alive at this time and did not as far as I know command a *tümen*. (ZNY I, pp. 225, 282, 290, 447 etc., ZNS I, p. 120, II, p. 78.)
23 Although troops and offices were usually inherited by only one person at a time, Temür often provided the sons or relatives of his personal followers with additional troops. Thus for instance the two sons of Sarïbugha Jalayir both commanded *tümens*; that of Shaykh Nūr al-Dīn consisted not of Jalayir tribesmen but of court troops. (ZNY I, p. 323, see also the discussion above.) While Temür's follower Aqbugha was still active, Temür gave the leadership of Apardï troops to his son, Buyan Temür.
24 It is not clear which was older; although Jahāngīr is usually named as the eldest, the birthdate suggested for ᶜUmar Shaykh is earlier. Jahāngīr died at age twenty in 777–8/1376–7, and ᶜUmar Shaykh at age forty in 796/1394. (ZNY I, pp. 199–201, 472–4.)

25 ZNY I, pp. 452, 463, 534, 535, 540, 542, 562, II, pp. 43, 97, 103, 122, 125, 129, 276, 320–1, 397–8, ZNS I, p. 235, II, pp. 130, 161.

26 Besides these twenty-two *tümens*, there were at various times two *tümens* led by emirs of the Barlas tribe who were personally close to Temür, two led by Chaghatay emirs without known tribal affiliation, five led by emirs from the territories Temür conquered, and one led by a Nayman emir of unknown descent: a total of ten, probably not all of which existed at any one time. (ZNY I, pp. 370, 463, 484, 485, II, pp. 25, 80, 103, 397–8, ZNS II, p. 111.)

27 The actual number of men in a *tümen* is impossible to determine. Where numbers are given in the histories, they usually include the troops of several men involved in an expedition, some of whom often are princes, some commanders of *tümens*, and some emirs of *qoshuns*. The numbers of troops specified in the histories are relatively modest, ranging from thirty to fifty thousand troops for large battles, to three thousand to fifteen thousand for most expeditions. The army gathered for Temür's final campaign to China was estimated at 200,000. (ZNY I, pp. 261, 333, 540, II, pp. 17, 56, 450, ZNS I, pp. 115, 176, 182, 250, II, pp. 118, 136, Ghiyāth al-Dīn ᶜAlī Yazdī, trans., A. A. Semenov, *Giyāsaddīn ᶜAlī, Dnevnik pokhoda Tīmūra v Indiiu* (Moscow, 1958) (hereafter *Rūznāma*), p. 94, *Mujmal*, III, p. 141, Īrāj Afshār, ed., Aḥmad b. Ḥusayn b. ᶜAlī Kātib, *Tārīkh-i jadīd-i Yazd* (Tehran, sh. 1345/1966), p. 90, *Muntakhab*, pp. 331, 342.)

28 Outside of the *tümens* mentioned here there were numerous troops, some of them from the regions newly conquered by Temür, and some personal regiments (*qoshuns*), not all of which apparently were organized into permanent *tümens*. While some *qoshuns* belonged in the *tümen* of a higher commander – particularly that of a prince – it seems likely that not all of them did. A number of fairly powerful commanders held their own regiments – examples are Allāhdād, Ītīlmīsh Qa'uchin, and La'l Barlas, none of whom apparently were affiliated with a prince or more powerful emir. (ZNY I, p. 341, II, p. 409.) When enumerating troops for a campaign the sources often list several emirs, characterizing them as "emirs of *qoshuns* and men attached to the court", "emirs of *tümens* and *qoshuns*," etc. (ZNY I, pp. 115, 352, 562, II, pp. 257, 268.) The membership of a *tümen* moreover was not entirely constant. There are indications that Temür could and did interfere in the makeup of *tümens* and even divide them. For instance when Temür was campaigning in Syria in 803/1400–1 he sent Jahānshāh and other emirs on a raid, and with them sent a group from every *tümen*. (ZNY II, p. 198.) Likewise when he appointed Shāhrukh to Khorasan in 799/1396–7, he appointed with him a large number of emirs, including some from every *tümen*. (ZNY I, p. 573.)

29 One can take as examples the Hsiung-nu, the Liao and the Mongols. (Omeljan Pritsak, "Die 24 Ta-ch'en," *Oriens Extremus*, I (1954), pp. 179–80, Karl A. Wittfogel and Feng Chia-sheng, *History of Chinese Society: Liao (907–1125)* (Philadelphia, 1949), pp. 191–2, 206, 434, Vladimirtsov, *Obshchestvennyĭ stroĭ*, p. 98.)

30 ZNY I, pp. 98, 350, *Muᶜizz*, ff. 100a, 116a.

31 Ḥājjī Sayf al-Dīn married one of his daughters first to Abā Bakr b. Amīrānshāh, and after his death to another of Amīrānshāh's sons, Ijal ('YJL), and married another daughter to Aḥmad b. ᶜUmar Shaykh. (*Muᶜizz*, ff. 108b, 109b, 110a, 123b, ZNY I, pp. 351, 402, ZNS II, p. 99.) Two of the descendants of ᶜAbbās Bahadur Qipchaq married into Temür's family. (ZNY I, p. 515, *Muᶜizz*, f. 125b.)

One other family married extensively into Temür's – that of Ghiyāth al-Dīn Tarkhan, whom I have mentioned above as someone who may well have been a follower of Temür's. Ghiyāth al-Dīn Tarkhan's ancestor, Kishiliq (Qishliq), had been made a *tarkhan* by Chinggis Khan, and had later been among Chaghadai's emirs. (ZNY I, p. 177, *Muᶜizz*, f. 29a, Bartol'd, *Turkestan*, p. 468.) This honor had descended in his family, and lent them considerable prestige. Three of Ghiyāth al-Dīn's daughters married sons or grandsons of Temür; one of these was Gawharshād, Shāhrukh's powerful and influential wife. (*Muᶜizz*, ff. 132b, 103b, 104b, 106b, ZNS II, p. 99.)

32 ZNY I, pp. 324–9, ZNS I, p. 110.
33 ZNY I, pp. 160, 327, II, p. 154.
34 Although the terms *tümen* and *hazāra* almost certainly do not represent exact numbers of troops, they do serve to give a relative estimation of troop size.
35 The families of Dādmalik Barlas and Aqtemür, then at the head of the Suldus were quartered there. (ZNY I, p. 325, ZNS II, p. 68.) For the period after Temür's death see Chapter 7.
36 ZNY I, pp. 161, 287, 516, 320, 463, II, pp. 272, 451, 503–4, ZNS II, p. 110, Ibn ᶜArabshāh, pp. 193–4.
37 See Chapter 7.
38 The area of Shaburqan, held by the western Apardï, seems still to have been under the control of Buyan Temür Nayman in 787–8/1385–6 as mentioned above, but after this there is no information on it during the course of Temür's life. After Temür's death it was apparently not under tribal control; Shāhrukh gave the governance of this region to one of his nephews. (*Muᶜizz*, f. 101b.) The Apardï of Khuttalan apparently retained their holdings; Öljeytü's grandson Khwāja ᶜAlī is mentioned as governor (*hākim*) of Sali Saray in 810/1407–8. (Ḥāfiẓ-i Abrū, *Majmaᶜ al-tawārīkh*, ms. Istanbul, Fatih 4371/1 (hereafter H.A. *Majmaᶜ*), f. 412a. As for the Arlat territories, we know only that in 790/1388 the governor of Herat, Aqbugha, collected soldiers from Gurziwan which had been one of the centers of Arlat power. This need not however necessarily mean that the Arlat were absent from the region. (ZNS II, pp. 78–9.)
39 Ibn ᶜArabshāh, pp. 193–4, 212–13.
40 ZNY I, p. 341, II, pp. 357, 409–10, 417, Ibn ᶜArabshāh, pp. 212–13, ZNS I, p. 285, II, p. 182.
41 See for example: Bartol'd, *Istoriia Turkestana*, p. 158.
42 Temür's second cousin, Taghay Bugha, governor of Balkh after Temür's takeover. (*Muᶜizz*, f. 94b, ZNY I, pp. 320, 463, ZNS II, p. 110.)
43 ZNY I, p. 441, *Muᶜizz*, f. 91b.
44 ZNY I, pp. 160, 183, 270, 275, 304, 327, 401, 467, *Muᶜizz*, ff. 83a, 86b.
45 According to the *Muᶜizz al-ansāb*, command of the *ulugh ming* went to Ḥājjī Beg's nephew Muḥammad Darwīsh but the *tümen-i kalān*, probably the same entity, is mentioned at the siege of Takrit in 796/1393 under the leadership of his grandson ᶜAlī Darwīsh. It is possible that it was jointly held, since Muḥammad Darwīsh was still active at this time. (*Muᶜizz*, f. 89b, ZNY I, pp. 239, 463.)
46 The emirs who commanded them did not play a particularly prominent part in Temür's campaigns. (ZNY I, pp. 239, 294, 467, II, pp. 82, 458, ZNS, I, pp. 144, 152, *Muntakhab*, p. 333.)
47 This was probably due to the pejorative connotations of the term Qara'unas. See Appendix A.
48 He is mentioned leading them in 790/1388. (ZNY I, pp. 327–9.) After this time the troops of Qunduz and Baghlan are not specifically mentioned in the histories, but we know from the *Muᶜizz al-ansāb* that their command continued within the family of Chekü, passing from Jahānshāh to his younger brother Miḍrāb, and then back to the sons of Jahānshāh. (*Muᶜizz*, ff. 92b, 93a.)
49 Clavijo, p. 213.
50 The areas of Qunduz and Baghlan are mentioned in the *Baburnāma*, in about 900/1494–5. They had by that time changed hands, and were under the control of a Qipchaq emir. The power that they lent their possessor however was still the same; their governor was one of the most powerful men in Transoxiana and Khorasan, with troops numbering twenty to thirty thousand. (*Baburnāma*, pp. 49–50, 57, 60, 194–6.) This description tallies strikingly with earlier ones of emirs of the Qara'unas, particularly Borolday and Qazaghan; even the numbers agree with the estimates of Qara'unas forces. (See Chapter 2 and Appendix A: Qara'unas.)

51 ZNY I, pp. 225, 234, 264, 315, 363, 436, 441, II, pp. 125, 268–9, etc., ZNS I, pp. 123, 137, II, pp. 136, 140, Clavijo, p. 220. Two of his sons, Birdi Beg and Shaykh Nūr al-Dīn, held very high positions, each commanding a *tümen* and serving as *darugha*. (ZNY I, pp. 363, 383, II, 43, 125, ZNS II, pp. 130, 136.)

52 There is no specific mention of the troops of Apardï or Shaburqan under Buyan Temür or his sons, but Buyan Temür was part of the Khorasanian army which went against Sultaniyya in 787–8/1385–6; since he had not apparently been appointed to serve in the garrison army of Khorasan, this suggests that he was then based in Shaburqan. (*Cinq opuscules*, text, p. 14, ZNS I, p. 185, II, p. 61, ZNY I, pp. 462, 538, II, pp. 34, 65–6, 213, 222, 257, 314, 367, 408, 449, *Mu*ᶜ*izz*, ff. 97a, 102b, Jaᶜfar b. Muḥammad al-Ḥusaynī (Jaᶜfarī), *Tārīkh-i Kabīr*, Leningrad, Publichnaia Biblioteka, ms. P.N.C. # 201 (hereafter Jaᶜfarī, Len.), f. 290a.)

53 See Chapter 7.

54 ZNY I, p. 462, II, p. 304. In 790/1388 Öljeytü Apardï's son Khwāja Yūsuf campaigned under Jahānshāh Barlas, at the head of the Apardï army collected in Arhang. (ZNY I, pp. 327–8.) Khwāja Yūsuf is not mentioned in the histories after this, and his son Khwāja ᶜAlī is mentioned only twice, in 796/1393 and 804/1402. (ZNY I, p. 462, II, p. 304.) After Temür's death Khwāja ᶜAlī was still in Khuttalan, but he took no part in the succession struggles. (H.A. *Majma*ᶜ, f. 412a.) Ḥāfiẓ-i Abrū identifies Khwāja ᶜAlī as Öljeytü's son, but as Yazdī is usually more exact in his recording of relationships, his identification of Khwāja ᶜAlī as Khwāja Yūsuf's son should probably be preferred.

55 ZNS I, p. 66, ZNY I, pp. 327, 462, II, p. 304.

56 ZNY I, pp. 162, 181, 280, 417, 445, ZNS I, p. 129, Jaᶜfarī, Len. f. 262a, *Mu*ᶜ*izz*, f. 107a.

57 Ḥājjī Maḥmūdshāh's son is mentioned once, in 798/1396, and two other emirs are mentioned once each, in 795/1393 and 805/1402. (ZNY I, pp. 434, 565, II, p. 325.)

58 After the execution of Kaykhusraw Khuttalānī in 773–4/1372–3, the *tümen* of Khuttalan was given to Muḥammad Mīrkā, the son of Shīr Bahrām who had held it earlier. Muḥammad Mīrkā's position was further strengthened by a marriage with Temür. (ZNY I, pp. 270, 324.) This connection did not however prevent him from rebelling in 790/1388 nor did it prevent Temür from executing him and his brother in retaliation. (ZNY I, pp. 324–6, ZNS I, p. 109, *Mujmal* III, p. 129, *Muntakhab*, pp. 340–1.) The army of Khuttalan nonetheless accompanied Temür on his campaign to the Dasht-i Qipchaq later in 790/1388. (ZNY I, p. 334.) The *tusqal* (guard) of the *tümen* of Khuttalan is mentioned at the siege of Takrit in 796/1393 together with the Barlas *tümen*; one of the emirs with it was Barlas, and two other emirs are mentioned without tribal affiliation. (ZNY I, p. 463, ZNS II, p. 110.)

59 ZNY I, pp. 327, 334, II, pp. 154, 450.

60 ZNY I, p. 462, II, p. 25, Jaᶜfarī, Len., f. 275a, ZNS I, p. 173.

61 Ratchnevsky, *Činggis-khan*, pp. 83–4, Bartol'd, *Turkestan*, pp. 382–6, *Secret History*, pp. 141–50, Thomas Barfield, *Inner Asia: A Study in Frontier History* (Draft manuscript for Foreign Cultures, 38, Harvard University, 1986), Chapt. VI, pp. 9–13.

62 As examples of this practice one can cite the Aqqoyunlu and some of the princes of medieval Rus', whose armies also contained tribal contingents. (Woods, *Aqquyulu*, pp. 9–11, D. S. Likhachev, B. A. Romanov, ed. and trans., *Povest' vremennykh let*, pt. I (Moscow; Leningrad, 1950), p. 300.)

63 While the histories of Chinggis Khan's career give more prominence to the tribal affiliations of his commanders and his troops than do the Timurid histories, it is clear that Chinggis' army, like Temür's, was not tribally organized. Many regiments indeed were made up of tribal troops, and some commanded by men from the same tribe, but control over these forces remained with Chinggis, and was granted in return for service rendered to him. (RaD, Khetagurov, vol. I, pt. 2, pp. 266–78, *Secret History*, pp. 141–61, Barfield, pp. 41–5.)

64 ZNS II, p. 93, ZNY II, pp. 447–8.
65 ZNY I, p. 196, ZNS II, p. 39.
66 ZNY I, pp. 218, 440–1.
67 Two of his later emirs were probably part of this group: Melesh Apardī and his son Bikesh. (ZNS II, pp. 37–8, ZNY I, pp. 352, 440–1.)
68 ZNY I, pp. 440–1. Although the lists of emirs attached to Temür's sons and grandsons are usually given on their appointments as governors, some at least of these emirs were attached to the princes before they became governors, notably ᶜUmar Shaykh and Shāhrukh. (ZNY I, pp. 436, 462–3.)
69 ZNY I, p. 225.
70 Another son of Mūsā Taychi'ut was appointed to accompany Pīr Muḥammad, and several *qa'uchin* emirs went with Shāhrukh to Khorasan. In addition the sons of Ghiyāth al-Dīn Tarkhan now began to appear; one of them was assigned to Pīr Muḥammad, and two to Shāhrukh. (ZNY I, pp. 401, 573.) The lists of emirs accompanying the princes appointed to governorship in Temür's later years are much shorter than most of the earlier lists, but they include approximately the same types of people. (ZNY II, pp. 368–9, 399, 402, Jaᶜfarī, Len., f. 291a.)
71 ZNY I, pp. 401, 573.
72 ZNY I, p. 573, II, p. 369.
73 ZNY I, pp. 401, 573, II, p. 153.
74 Woods, *Aqquyunlu*, p. 12.
75 Aubin, "l'Ethnogénèse," pp. 74–5.
76 Aqbugha was *amīr al-umarā'* of Khorasan and personally in charge of the defense of Herat until his death in 803/1400–1. (ZNY I, pp. 329, 565, II, p. 155, ZNS I, p. 110, II, p. 77. H.A. Geography, f. 315b, *Mujmal*, III, p. 145, *Baburnāma*, p. 24.) Sayf al-Dīn and ᶜUthmān seem to have held considerable local power; Sayf al-Dīn was closely involved with local administration, especially tax collection, and while ᶜUthmān's role is less clear, he was important and conspicuous enough to receive a letter from the powerful and influential *shaykh al-islām* Khwāja Yūsuf Jāmī. (ZNY I, pp. 225, 259, 262, 264, 282, 299, 302, ZNS II, p. 78, *Muntakhab*, p. 329, H.A. Geography, f. 318b, *Cinq opuscules*, text, p. 14, Hishmat Mu'ayyad, ed., Jalāl al-Dīn Yūsuf Ahl, *Farā'id-i Ghiyāthī* (Tehran, 2536/1977), vol. I, pp. 592–3.) After 1388, all except Aqbugha left Amīrānshāh's service, and are mentioned on campaign in a number of places with no reference to Amīrānshāh. (ZNY I, pp. 299, 316, 320, 334–6, 380–1, 400, 406–7, 434, 451–2, 500, 520, 551, 562, II, pp. 17, 153, *Muᶜizz*, f. 97a, Ibn ᶜArabshāh, p. 302.)
77 ZNY I, p. 441, II, pp. 368–9, ZNS II, pp. 127–30.
78 See Chapter 7.
79 ZNY II, pp. 44, 56, 103.
80 ZNY I, pp. 456, 462, 467.
81 See for instance one of Amīrānshāh's emirs, Muḥammad Sulṭānshāh in Tabriz in 788 and in Isfahan in 789–90 (ZNY I, pp. 289–90, *Mujmal* III, p. 126, H. A. Geography, f. 318b), Buhlūl, assigned to Pīr Muḥammad b. Jahāngīr, campaigning in Gilan with Shāhrukh in 805–6 (ZNY II, p. 397), and another of Pīr Muḥammad's emirs, Shams al-Dīn b. Üch Qara at Takrit in 796 (ZNY I, p. 462.)
82 I have discussed Temür's control over his descendants much more fully in an earlier paper ("Administration and the Delegation of Authority"), and so will not examine it further here.
83 ZNY II, pp. 250, 321.
84 ZNY II, pp. 386, 393, 399, Jaᶜfarī, Len., f. 291a.
85 ZNY I, p. 472, II, pp. 367, 399.
86 ZNY II, p. 449.
87 Temür did not appoint either of his surviving sons – Amīrānshāh and Shāhrukh – but

instead the children of his deceased son Jahāngīr; he first chose Muḥammad Sulṭān, who died in 805/1403, and then, on his deathbed, he appointed Muḥammad Sulṭān's brother, Pīr Muḥammad. (ZNS I, p. 192, ZNY II, p. 466.)

5 Temür's army of conquest: outsiders and conquered peoples

1 It is difficult in some cases to judge whether Temür was taking over direct control of an area, since the appointment of a governor (*ḥākim* or *darugha*) to a city did not necessarily mean the deposition of the local ruler; Temür's representatives were sometimes sent to govern in conjunction with a local ruler, taking responsibility for collection of tribute, and providing some garrison troops. (See for example ZNS I, pp. 93–4, II, p. 53, ZNY I, p. 321, Clavijo, p. 139, *Cinq opuscules*, notes, p. 46.) Some of the cities in which the local governor was deposed had been ruled by deputies of a larger power; Temür therefore was constricting the the area of a dynasty rather than destroying one. (See for example Manūchihr Sutūda, ed., Sayyid Ẓahīr al-Dīn Marᶜashī, *Tārīkh-i Gīlān wa Daylamistān* (Tehran 1347/1969–70), pp. 76–8, ZNS I, p. 131.

2 One can cite as examples Malik ᶜIzz al-Dīn Kurd and Amīr Ibrāhīmshāh in Kurdistan (ZNY I, p. 307, ZNS I, p. 130), Pīr Aḥmad Sāwa'ī in the area of Rayy, Hamadan, and Qum (ZNS II, p. 66), and Amīr Shaykh Ibrāhīm in Shirwan (ZNY I, p. 297).

3 Jean Aubin, "Comment," pp. 89–90.

4 For instance, when Temür ousted Amīr Walī from Mazandaran in 786–7/1384–5, he installed in his place a former pretender, Lughmān b. Taghaytemür, whom Amīr Walī had earlier chased out. (*Cinq opuscules*, text, pp. 10, 13–14, ZNS II, pp. 54, 66, *Mujmal* III, p. 123.)

5 ZNY I, pp. 410, 414, *Cinq opuscules*, text, p. 53, notes, p. 33, *Mujmal* III, p. 134, Felix Tauer ed., "Continuation du *Ẓafarnāma* de Niẓāmuddin Šāmī par Ḥāfiẓ-i Abrū," *Archiv Orientalni*, VI (hereafter H.A. Continuation), note, p. 441.

6 H.A. Continuation, p. 441, ZNS I, p. 127, ᶜAbbās Shāyān, ed., Sayyid Ẓahīr al-Dīn Marᶜashī, *Tārīkh-i Ṭabaristān wa Rūyān wa Māzandarān* (Tehran, sh. 1333/1955), (hereafter *Tārīkh-i Ṭabaristān*), pp., 308–9.

7 *Muntakhab*, pp. 49–51, Vladimir Minorsky, "Lur-i Buzurg," *Encyclopaedia of Islam*, (old ed.), vol. III, p. 48. Other similar examples of the captivity and return of rulers can be found in the cases of Malik ᶜIzz al-Dīn of Lur-i Kuchik, and Sulṭān ᶜĪsā of the Artuqi dynasty of Mardin. (*Muntakhab*, pp. 64–5, Ibn ᶜArabshāh, pp. 56–7, Vladimir Minorsky, "Lur-i Kūčik," *Encyclopaedia of Islam* (old ed.), vol. III, p. 49, ZNY I, pp. 471, 483, 561).

8 *Tārīkh-i Gīlān*, pp. 76–8.

9 H.A. Continuation, p. 441, ZNY II, p. 397.

10 The Great Khan Möngke for instance used very similar methods. See Allsen, *Mongol Imperialism*, pp. 63–76.

11 *Tārīkh-i Ṭabaristān*, pp. 299–301. There is some confusion in this account, since the author has dated Temür's second Iranian campaign as 792 rather than 794; this was when Sayyid Ghiyāth al-Dīn was sent to join Temür. The dates in this history however are frequently inaccurate, while the actual events described tally very well with other accounts of the same period.

12 ZNY I, pp. 540, 558, II, pp. 162–5, 304, 371, 378, 397.

13 *Tārīkh-i Ṭabaristān*, p. 300.

14 ZNY I, p. 162, II, pp. 397–8.

15 *Cinq opuscules*, text, p. 14. Similar examples can be found in the provinces of northwestern Iran. There was an expedition against Qara Yūsuf Qaraqoyunlu undertaken by Malik ᶜIzz al-Dīn Kurd with the help of the *darugha* of Basin. (Thomas of Metsop, p. 64.)

16 *Muᶜizz*, ff. 125b–126a.

17 ZNY I, p. 414, *Cinq opuscules*, notes, pp. 3–4, 33.

18 ZNY I, p. 414, *Tārīkh-i Ṭabaristān*, p. 301. Several rulers of Gilan and western

Mazandaran, Sayyid Ḥaydar Kiyā, Kiyā Malik-i Hazāraspī, and Khudāwand Muḥammad of Alamut, also joined Temür's suite when they lost their own regions in local upheavals. (*Tārīkh-i Gīlān*, pp. 62–5, 119–20, H. L. Rabino di Borgomale, "Les dynasties locales du Gilan et du Daylam," *Journal asiatique*, vol. 237, p. 317.) Yet another such person was Sārū ᶜĀdil, mentioned above, who had fled the Jalayirids to serve the Muzaffarids, and in 786–7/1384–5 came over to Temür and was given governance of Sultaniyya and Tabriz (ZNS I, p. 97, II, pp. 58–9.)

19 ZNY I, pp. 99, 207, *Muntakhab*, p. 424.

20 Both these men achieved distinguished careers in Temür's armies, and Mubashshir at least became the commander of a *tümen*. (ZNY I, pp. 249, 264, 278, 290, 370, 436, II, pp. 103, 138, 304, H.A. *Geography*, f. 318b.)

21 Ibn ᶜArabshāh, p. 161, ZNY II, pp. 490–1.

22 ZNS II, p. 56. *Qoshuns* ranged from fifty to five-hundred men.

23 *Muntakhab*, pp. 332–3, ZNS II, pp. 56–7, *Mujmal* III, p. 126, Thomas of Metsop, p. 57.

24 *Muntakhab*, pp. 64–7, V. Minorsky, "Lur-i Kučik," p. 49.

25 *Muntakhab*, p. 396.

26 Aubin, "Sarbadars," p. 112, Bartol'd, *Ulugbek i ego vremia*, p. 62.

27 Aubin, "Sarbadars," pp. 111–12, ZNS I, p. 99, *Mujmal* III, p. 125.

28 ZNY I, pp. 428, 463, 469, *Mujmal* III, p. 126, ZNS I, p. 145, II, p. 111.

29 *Cinq opuscules*, text, p. 26, ZNS II, pp. 79–83, H.A. Geography, ff. 124a, 316b, ZNY I, p. 468.

30 Several histories mention the damage done to Sunni shrines in Damascus by Shiᶜite emirs of Khorasan and Mazandaran who were campaigning in Temür's army. (*Mujmal* III, p. 143, *Muntakhab*, pp. 378–9, Ibn ᶜArabshāh, p. 158.) What damage they did, and how they managed it in the midst of a primarily Sunni army is not explained, but the fact that these histories, which come from different traditions, all mention the occurrence suggests that something of this sort must have happened.

31 ZNY I, p. 433, II, p. 262, ZNS II, p. 104. The *Mujmal-i Faṣīḥī* states that Qalᶜa-i Safid was given to Malik Shams al-Dīn b. Malik ᶜIzz al-Dīn Harāt Rūdī Ghurī (*Mujmal* III, p. 135); I have chosen the version of Yazdī and Ḥāfiẓ-i Abrū.

32 ZNS II, p. 66, *Mujmal* III, p. 134, H.A. Continuation, p. 441, note, *Tārīkh-i Ṭabaristān*, p. 317.

33 ZNY I, pp. 269–70, 559, II, pp. 222, 252, 304, ZNS I, pp. 228, 255, II, p. 177. According to Zambaur, Shāhshāhān did not come to the throne until 788, but the *Ẓafarnāma* of Yazdī specifically states that he was given the governance of Sistan in 785, and Shāmī, while he does not definitely state that Shāhshāhshān was installed then, does write that the former ruler, Quṭb al-Dīn, was captured and taken to Samarqand in that year. (Eduard von Zambaur, *Manuel de généalogie et de chronologie pour l'histoire de l'Islam* (Hanover, 1927), p. 200, ZNY I, pp. 269–70, ZNS I, pp. 92–3.) The rulers of Farah, having submitted to Temür on his campaign to the area in 785/1383, campaigned with Edigü Barlas in Kerman in 795–6/1393, and accompanied Temür on his Indian campaign; Shāh ᶜAlī Farāhī was given charge of a fortress on the Indian border, at the head of a thousand men. (ZNY I, p. 263, ZNS I, p. 177, II, p. 140, H.A. Geography, f. 169b.)

34 Temür also favored Amīr ᶜIzz al-Dīn, the son of ᶜImād al-Dīn of Simnan, just south of Mazandaran, who was given the rule of Simnan and Hazar Jarib. (ZNS I, p. 228, II, pp. 66, 160.)

35 Claude Cahen, "The Body Politic," in *Unity and Variety in Muslim Civilization*, ed. G. E. von Grunebaum (Chicago, 1955), pp. 144–6, C. E. Bosworth, "Ghaznevid Military Organization," *Der Islam*, 36, pp. 40–1, Marshall G. S. Hodgson, *The Venture of Islam* (Chicago; London, 1974), vol. II, p. 399, Daniel Pipes, *Slave Soldiers and Islam* (New Haven; London, 1981).

36 David Ayalon, "Aspects of the *Mamluk* Phenomenon," part I, *Der Islam* 53 (1976), pp. 211–12.

37 Claude Cahen, "l'Évolution de *l'iqṭā*ᶜ du IXe au XIIIe siècle," *Annales Economies, Sociétés, Civilisations*, VIII # 1, pp. 50–1, A. K. S. Lambton, *Landlord and Peasant in Persia* (2nd ed., Oxford, 1969), p. 90, and "Reflections on the *Iqṭā*ᶜ," in *Arabic and Islamic Studies in Honor of Hamilton A. R. Gibb*, ed., George Makdisi (Cambridge, Mass., 1965), pp. 372–3.

38 Examples are the Saffarid leader Yaᶜqūb b. Layth (A.D. 867–79) and the Ghaznevids. (C. E. Bosworth, "Recruitment, Muster and Review in Medieval Islamic Armies," in *War, Technology and Society in the Middle East*, ed. V. J. Parry and M. E. Yapp (London, 1975), pp. 67–8, Bosworth, "Ghaznevid Military Organization," pp. 55–60.)

39 D. O. Morgan, "The Mongol Armies in Persia," pp. 88–95, Falina, "Reformy Gazan-khana," pp. 69–71, Lambton, *Landlord and Peasant in Persia*, pp. 89–90, I. P. Petrushevskiĭ, *Zemledelie i agrarnye otnosheniia v Irane XII–XIV vekov* (Moscow; Leningrad, 1960), pp. 262–5, 399, John Masson Smith, "Mongol Manpower and Persian Population," *Journal of the Economic and Social History of the Orient*, XVIII # 3, p. 278. These scholars disagree among themselves on a number of issues: how great a change there was in real terms between the Seljukid and the Mongol *iqṭā*ᶜ, whether *iqṭā*ᶜs were granted only to Mongols or, as most scholars believe, both to Mongols and to local soldiers, and whether the *tümens* they established were military or merely administrative districts. They all however agree on the working of the *iqṭā*ᶜ in the Mongol period, and on the fact that local populations, as well as Mongols, were organized for conscription.

40 The number of soldiers actually levied was presumably less than these figures suggest. The one example given in the sources is that of Isfahan, a settled region of two *tümens*, which was required before Ghazan Khan to provide one thousand soldiers, and after him five-hundred. (Petrushevskiĭ, *Zemledelie*, p. 309, Lambton, *Landlord and Peasant in Persia*, p. 94.)

41 Morgan, "The Mongol Armies in Persia," p. 89.

42 Ch'i-ch'ing Hsiao, *The Military Establishment of the Yuan Dynasty*, pp. 18–24. The Golden Horde is much less well documented but it seems to have had a somewhat similar system. (Grekov and Yakubovskiĭ, *Zolotaia Orda*, pp. 109–11.) For a discussion of Mongol census taking and universal conscription, see Thomas T. Allsen, "Mongol Census Taking in Rus', 1245–1275," *Harvard Ukrainian Studies*, V # 1. PP. 32–53.

43 Smith, "Mongol Manpower and Persian Population," p. 292.

44 *Tārīkh-i Ṭabaristān*, p. 314, ZNY II, pp. 395, 404.

45 ZNS I, p. 128.

46 ZNY II, p. 47, Maḥmūd Kutubī, *Tārīkh-i āl-i Muẓaffar*, ed., ᶜAbd al-Ḥusayn Nawā'ī (Tehran, sh. 1335/1956), p. 123, *Rūznāma*, p. 86, ZNS I, p. 179.

47 ZNY II, pp. 165–6.

48 Allsen, *Mongol Imperialism*, pp. 192–3, Doerfer, *Türkische und mongolische Elemente*, vol. III, p. 65.

49 H.A. Geography, f. 127a, ZNY I, p. 560.

50 *Tārīkh-i Ṭabaristān*, p. 312.

51 N. Makhmudov, "Iz istorii zemel'nykh otnoshenii i nalogovoĭ politiki Timuridov," *Izvestiia Akademii Nauk Tadzhikskoĭ SSR, otdelenie obshchestvennykh nauk,* 32 # 1, pp. 21–33.

52 ZNY I, p. 440, ZNS I, p. 135, II, p. 106, H.A. Geography, f. 126a.

53 The Timurid histories often use the term Moghul to mean Turco-Mongolian, in this case used as a synonym for Chaghatay.

54 H.A. Geography, f. 170a.

55 ZNS I, pp. 176, 215, II, p. 66, ZNY II, pp. 38, 174, 378, 415, *Muntakhab*, p. 378, *Rūznāma*, p. 75, H.A. Continuation, p. 436.

56 ZNY II, p. 47, ZNS I, p. 179, *Rūznāma*, p. 86.

57 ZNY II, p. 299.

58 ZNS II, p. 172.

59 The Khalaj, found earlier both in Khorasan and in the region of Qum and Kashan, were nomads of Turkic language and customs, who had formed an important element in the armies of the Ghaznevids, Ghurids and other dynasties of eastern Iran. (C. E. Bosworth, "Khaladj," *Encyclopaedia of Islam*, N.E., vol. IV, p. 917, and *The Ghaznavids: Their Empire in Afghanistan and Eastern Iran 944:* 1040, (2nd ed., Beirut, 1973), p. 109.) I have been unable to identify the Saki, but the Feili are a well-known tribe of the Lur. (V. Minorsky, "Lur," *Encyclopaedia of Islam*, (old ed.) vol. III, pp. 42, 44.)

60 The emirs of Gharjistan had fought for the Samanids, and the Ghurs were in armies of the Ghazevids and several later dynasties. (Bartol'd, *Turkestan*, pp. 261, 406, Bosworth, *The Ghaznavids*, p. 114.) More recently both had been part of the armies of the Kartid kings of Herat. (*Cinq opuscules*, text, pp. 31–2.)

61 ZNY II, p. 405. Clavijo also mentions Kurds in Khorasan as part of Temür's forces. (Clavijo, p. 181.)

62 ZNY I, pp. 423, 469–70, 480, II, pp. 167, 250, 278, ZNS I, p. 146, II, pp. 165–7.

63 ZNY I, pp. 522, 543–7, II, pp. 197, 272, 327, 350, ZNS I, pp. 113, 158, II, p. 71.

64 See for instance ZNY I, pp. 303, 338, 347, 394, *Muntakhab*, p. 213, ZNS I, p. 214.

65 ZNY I, pp. 188, 338, 477–8, ZNS I, pp. 162, 214.

66 ZNY II, pp. 357, 407–10, 417, 450, ZNS I, p. 285, II, p. 182.

67 ZNY I, p. 341, II, p. 450. According to Clavijo Temür moved a large number of Aqqoyunlu to Samarqand, but since he mentions a rebellion at Damghan he has clearly confused them with the Qaratatars, who rebelled there. (Clavijo, pp. 134, 173.)

68 Moghul emirs would not be expected to use the *niṣba* so useful in placing the emirs of Iranian and Arab lands, and their tribal names are little help since so many of the same tribes existed also within the Ulus Chaghatay.

69 ZNY I, pp. 459, 463, 485–7, ZNS I, pp. 151–2. Another member of the Sufi dynasty, Bayrām Ṣūfī b. Yūsuf Ṣūfī, campaigned in Fars under Shāhrukh in 795. (ZNY I, p. 436.)

70 ZNY I, p. 441, II, pp. 159–61.

71 ZNY I, p. 462.

72 See Ibn ᶜArabshāh, pp. 117–18 (Arabic, p. 174), and for the probability that many were prisoners of war, the marriage portion of foreign households given to Ulugh Beg's bride in 807. (*Shams*, f. 16b, p. 22.)

73 There are a number of emirs in Temür's army bearing the title *oghlan* (son) which suggests Chinggisid descent. Some of these could have been Mongols or Jochids, but they might also have been Chinggisids from within the Ulus Chaghatay.

74 ZNY I, pp. 322, 392–4, 398.

75 ZNS I, pp. 138–40, II, p. 149, ZNY I, p. 283, 289, 469, II, pp. 167–8, 276, J. M. Smith, "Djalayir, Djalayirid," *Encyclopaedia of Islam*, N.E., vol. II, p. 401.

76 F. Sümer, "Ḳara-Ḳoyunlu," *Encyclopaedia of Islam*, N.E., vol. IV, pp. 585–6, ZNY I, pp. 303, 540, ZNS I, p. 103.

77 Sümer, "Ḳara-Ḳoyunlu," p. 586, ZNY II, p. 200, Thomas of Metsop, p. 64, Avedis K. Sanjian, ed. and trans., *Colophons of Armenian Manuscripts 1301–1480: A Source for Middle Eastern History* (Cambridge, Mass., 1969), pp. 115–16.

78 Sümer, "Ḳara-Ḳoyunlu," p. 586, ZNY II, pp. 369, 448–9.

79 Somewhat later Temür's supply train was attacked by a group of Aqqoyunlu princes, but since these were the sons of Qara ᶜUthmān's brothers, and were his rivals for power, this served merely to strengthen his position within the confederation. (Woods, *Aqquyunlu*, pp. 51–2.)

80 ZNY II, p. 450, *Shams*, f. 134b, p. 96.

81 Rudi Paul Lindner, *Nomads and Ottomans in Medieval Anatolia* (Bloomington, 1983), pp. 106–11. Woods, *Aqquyunlu*, pp. 7–8.

6 Structure and function in Temür's administration

1 The sources dealing most directly with administrative affairs are Ghiyāth al-Dīn Khwāndamīr's *Dastūr al-wuzarā'* (ed., Sa^cīd Nafīsī, Tehran, sh. 1317/1938–9) and the *Mu^cizz al-ansāb*.
2 *Muntakhab*, pp. 250, 301.
3 Dawlatshāh Samarqandī, ed. E. G. Browne, *The Tadhkiratu' sh-Shu^cara ("Memoirs of the Poets")* (London, 1901), pp. 108, 357.
4 ZNY II, p. 94, ZNY I, p. 204, *Tārīkh-i Gīlān*, pp. 119–20. The close involvement of Turkish emirs in most of the affairs of the *dīwān-i a^clā* suggests that this might refer to them, rather than to the honorary use of the title *amīr* by Persian scribes of high rank. This was sometimes done at least in the later Timurid periods; see Hans Robert Roemer, *Staatsschreiben der Timuridenzeit: Das Šaraf-nāma des ^cAbdallāh Marwārīd in kritischer Auswertung* (Wiesbaden, 1952), note, pp. 170–1, and Roger M. Savory, "The Development of the Early Safawid State under Ismā^cīl and Ṭahmāsp, as Studied in the 16th Century Persian Sources," Doctoral Dissertation, University of London, 1958, pp. 157, 168.
5 ZNY I, pp. 312, 316, II, pp. 59, 221, 327, *Muntakhab*, pp. 329–30.
6 ZNY II, p. 239. A similar situation is described at the taking of Delhi. (ZNY II, p. 94.)
7 ZNY I, p. 561, II, pp. 284, 397, Johann Schiltberger, *The Bondage and Travels of Johann Schiltberger, in Europe, Asia and Africa, 1396–1427*, trans. J. Buchan Telfer (London, 1879), pp. 26–7, Jean Aubin, "Un santon quhistani de l'époque timouride," *Revue des études islamiques*, XXXV, p. 209, *Mujmal* III, pp. 145–6, Ja^cfarī, Len., ff. 273b–74a.
8 H.A. Geography, f. 170b, Aubin, *Deux Sayyids de Bam au* XV *siècle* (Mainz, 1956), p. 396. We know also of one general inspection which Temür ordered in 806/1403–4. In this case Temür sent superintendents from his *dīwān* accompanied not by Chaghatays but by members of the religious classes. (ZNY II, pp. 387–8, ZNS I, pp. 287–8.)
9 ZNY II, p. 156. These were Temür Khwāja b. Aqbugha and Jalāl Islām.
10 ZNS II, p. 167.
11 ZNY II, pp. 396–7.
12 The term *nāyib* as used in the Timurid sources apparently means a deputy of agent – sometimes of a person, sometimes of the *dīwān*. As far as I can discover, it does not designate a specific office. (See for instance ZNS I, p. 228, II, pp. 130, 152, *Muntakhab*, p. 65.)
13 ZNY II, pp. 150, 369.
14 He had been preceded in this office by another emir, Ḥājjī Sayf al-Dīn. (H.A. Geography, f. 318b–19a.)
15 ZNS I, pp. 181–2. Khwāja Maḥmūd is later mentioned as one of the bureaucrats of Herat exiled in the purge by Fakhr al-Dīn Aḥmad. (*Mujmal* III, p. 150.)
16 ZNY II, pp. 63, 72, 92.
17 ZNY II, p. 261, *Dastūr al-wuzarā'*, p. 341.
18 ZNY II, pp. 29, 36, 134, 246, 270, 304, 345, ZNS II, pp. 171–2.
19 A. K. S. Lambton, "The Internal Structure of the Saljuq Empire," pp. 260–1.
20 Savory, "The Development of the Early Safawid State," pp. 195–6, 199, 239, 257–8, Vladimir Minorsky, "A Civil and Military Review in Fars 881/1476," *Bulletin of the School of Oriental and African Studies*, X # 1. p. 166. Minorsky suggested in the case of the Aqqoyunlu that these were guards to enhance the prestige of the departments, rather than troops which made up part of the army. In the light of the military activities of Persian bureaucrats under other nomadic dynasties however, it is conceivable that the followings of the Aqqoyunlu scribes could in fact have been active soldiers.
21 Eyegü Temür: ZNY I, pp. 234, 249, 272, 302, 323, 334, 338, 339, 377, ZNS I, p. 104, II, p. 62; Shāhmalik: ZNY I, pp. 380, 459, 463, 562, II, pp. 25, 36, 47, 68, 99, 107, 112, 322, 374–8, 454, 459, 466, Clavijo, p. 220, Ibn ^cArabshāh, p. 302; Shaykh Muḥammad b. Eyegū Temür: ZNY I, pp. 432, 463, II, pp. 27, 47, 56, 66, 122.

22 ZNY I, p. 559, Muḥammad-Mufīd Bāfqī, *Jāmi*[c]*-i Mufīdī*, ed. Irāj Afshār, vol. I (Tehran, sh. 1342/1963), pp. 161–2.
23 ZNY I, pp. 441, 463. Yādgār Barlas, while *darugha* of Balkh, campaigned in Iran and India with Temür, and Taghay Bugha Barlas, governor of Bukhara, continued to accompany Temür on his campaigns. (ZNY I, pp. 320, 327, 417, 463, 467, II, p. 66.)
24 ZNY I, p. 468, ZNS II, p. 77.
25 ZNY II, p. 36.
26 ZNY II, p. 450, ZNS II, p. 66.
27 ZNY II, pp. 395, 404–5. Neither of these emirs is listed in the *Mu*[c]*izz al-ansāb* as a *tovachï*. (*Mu*[c]*izz*, f. 97b–98a.)
28 H.A. Continuation, p. 436.
29 See for example E. Endicott-West, "Imperial Governance in Yüan Times," *Harvard Journal of Asiatic Studies*, vol. 46 # 2, pp. 542–4, and Thomas T. Allsen, *Mongol Imperialism*, pp. 112–13.
30 B. F. Manz, "Administration and the Delegation of Authority in Temür's Dominions."
31 *Dastūr al-wuzarā'*, pp. 340–5.
32 ZNY II, p. 405.
33 ZNY II, pp. 167–8, 228, Dawlatshāh, p. 330, ZNS II, pp. 152–3.
34 ZNS I, p. 204.
35 ZNS II, p. 153, H. A. Continuation, p. 443.
36 B. F. Manz, "The Office of *Darugha* under Tamerlane," *An Anniversary Volume in Honor of Francis Woodman Cleaves, Journal of Turkish Studies*, vol. 9, p. 64.
37 ZNS II, pp. 171–2, H.A. Continuation, p. 443.
38 See for example ZNS II, pp. 171–2, H.A. Continuation, pp. 443–4.
39 ZNY II, pp. 387–8.
40 ZNY II, pp. 393–4.
41 *Mujmal* III, pp. 148–50, H.A. Geography, f. 320b.
42 ZNY II, p. 421, H.A. Continuation, pp. 443–4.
43 ZNY II, p. 418.
44 Ibn [c]Arabshāh, p. 150.
45 ZNY II, pp. 33, 378–9. For the Mongols see Spuler, *Die Mongolen in Iran*, pp. 260–1.
46 ZNY II, pp. 393–4.
47 Spuler, *Die Mongolen in Iran*, pp. 260–3, A. A. Ali-zade, *Sotsial'no-ekonomicheskaia i politicheskaia istoriia Azarbaidzhana* XIII–XIV *vv*. (Baku, 1956), pp. 295–6, 300. The thesis advanced by Petrushevskiĭ that Persian bureaucrats espoused the cause of the population against the majority of the Mongol aristocracy who wished to exploit it mercilessly (Petrushevskiĭ, *Zemledelie*, pp. 46–53) applies primarily to a few upright viziers, chief among them Rashīd al-Dīn who, it will be noted, wrote his own history.
48 H.A. Geography, f. 177b, Māyil Harawī, ed., *Jughrāfiyā-i Ḥāfiẓ-i Abrū: qismat-i rub*[c]*-i Khurāsān Harāt* :Tehran, sh. 1349/1970–1), p. 34, Ibn [c]Arabshāh, pp. 47, 224–5, ZNY II, pp. 17, 31, Ja[c]farī, *Tārīkh-i Yazd*, ed., Īrāj Afshār (Tehran, sh. 1338/1960), p. 91, ZNS I, pp. 244–5, II, pp. 139, 197, *Mujmal* III, p. 143.
49 ZNY II, p. 36.
50 H.A. Continuation, pp. 443–4.
51 *Tārīkh-i Yazd*, pp. 74–160, *Tārīkh-i jadīd*, pp. 86–227, Renata Holod-Tretiak, "The Monuments of Yazd, 1300–1450: Architecture, Patronage and Setting," Doctoral Dissertation, Harvard University, 1972.
52 *Mujmal* III, pp. 145–6, *Tārīkh-i Yazd*, pp. 39–41, *Tārīkh-i jadīd*, pp. 92–3, *Dastūr al-wuzarā'*, p. 344, *Jāmi*[c]*-i mufīdī*, pp. 165–7, ZNY II, p. 321.
53 I can think of only one example of such activity; when Temür ordered the fortifications of Kerman destroyed, the head of the Kerman *dīwān*, Zayn al-Dīn Shahr-i Bābakī, appealed the decision, citing loss of revenue. This Temür accepted. (H.A. Geography, f. 170a, Aubin, *Deux sayyids*, p. 395.)

54 C. E. Bosworth, "The Political and Dynastic History of the Iranian World (A.D. 1000–1217)," in *The Cambridge History of Iran*, vol. v, pp. 22, 54, V. V. Bartol'd and J. A. Boyle, "Djuwaynī," *Encyclopaedia of Islam*, N.E., vol. II, pp. 606–7, Roger Savory, "The Development of the Early Safawid State," pp. 184, 193, 207–12. (Note that under the early Safavids, the position of *wakīl*, especially when held by a Persian, included in it many of the powers usually held by a vizier. See Savory, pp. 260–1.)

55 Lambton, "The Internal Structure of the Saljuq Empire," pp. 248, 267, Bosworth, "The Political and Dynastic History of the Iranian World," pp. 22, 45–6.

56 Bartol'd, Boyle, "Djuwaynī," pp. 606–7. Ali-zade, *Sotsial'no-ekonomicheskaia istoriia*, pp. 291–3.

57 Roger Savory, *Iran under the Safavids* (Cambridge, 1980), pp. 32, 34.

58 Savory, "The Development of the Early Safawid State," pp. 184–5, 193–5, 199, 207–12, 233, 240, 261.

59 Two other *amīrs* with tribal affiliations appear on the list – Tutak Nayman and Khwāja Yūsuf Merkit – neither of whom were prominent, or came from tribes that were powerful within the Ulus. (*Muᶜizz*, ff. 96b–97a.)

60 It is possible that this is a mistake, since Sarïbugha was appointed *amīr dīwān* at Temür's takeover in 771/1370. (ZNY I, p. 162.) This appointment was made however while Sarïbugha was simply one of Temür's followers, before he became chief of the Jalayir, and also before he and ᶜĀdilshāh rebelled against Temür, an incident which may have cancelled his appointment. Sarïbugha's son Shaykh Nūr al-Dīn Jalayir is included in the list. However, his troops consisted of men attached to the court (*khāna-bachagān-i khāṣṣ*); it was probably his brother Birdi Beg – not listed here – who inherited the tribal troops. (See Chapter 3.)

61 Aqbugha Nayman held the rank of *amīr* under Temür; this passed from him to his son Temür Khwāja, not to his other son Buyan Temür, who had been given control of the Apardï of Shaburqan.

62 The others are Ḥusayn and Khudāydād, who were Temür's personal followers, and an emir named Mīrak (or Pīrak), whose provenance I have been unable to ascertain. (*Muᶜizz*, ff. 96b–97a, also 83a, 86b, 87a, 90a, 92b, 94b.)

63 *Muᶜizz*, ff. 92b–93a.

64 The other followers or their relatives identified as *tovachï* in the *Muᶜizz* are Qumarï Ïnaq Qa'uchin, Ḥājjī Sayf al-Dīn, Dawlat Temür Suldus, who as I have shown above was probably Aqtemür's grandson, Yūsuf Jalīl b. Ḥasan Jāndār, a relative of Khitay Bahadur, and two emirs who may have been sons of Khitay – Jesike Khitay and Khudāydād Khitay. The largest other group found among the *tovachï* are the *qa'uchin* emirs, of which there were four, including Qumarï. (*Muᶜizz*, ff. 97a–98a.)

65 *Muᶜizz*, f. 97a, 98a.

66 ZNY I, pp. 161, 176, 287, 516, II, pp. 272–3, 451, Ibn ᶜArabshāh, pp. 193–4.

67 *Muntakhab*, p. 306. Shaykh ᶜAlī Bahadur is not mentioned in connection with Khorezm after his appointment there, but since the *darughas* of other regions also continued to campaign with Temür this is not conclusive evidence. What is more significant is the evidence of Tokhtamïsh's control; we have coins struck by him in Khorezm in 781. (Safargaliev, *Raspad*, p. 142.) Khorezm was reconquered in 790/1388, and in 793/1391 Mūsāka b. Changī Qa'uchin became *darugha* there. (ZNY I, p. 324, II, p. 266.)

68 Shaykh Nūr al-Din was sent to Shiraz with Muḥammad Sulṭān b. Jahāngīr in 798/1396 and left his post in 800/1398, while his brother Birdi Beg is mentioned in 798/1395–6 as *darugha* of Isfahan, and in 800/1397 left Fars to serve with Muḥammad Sulṭān in Moghulistan. (ZNS I, pp. 169–70, II, p. 130. *Rūznāma*, pp. 70–1, H.A. Geography, f. 127b, ZNY I, p. 562, II, p. 17.) There is some question also as to whether Shaykh Nūr al-Dīn should be considered a *darugha* in the usual sense; Shāmī's *Ẓafarnāma* and the *Rūznāma* both refer to him as *darugha*, but Ḥāfiẓ-i Abrū in his Geography states that he was sent to Shiraz with

Muḥammad Sulṭān to collect taxes. In addition to these men a young relative of Khitay Bahadur, Yūsuf Jalīl, served as *darugha* of Yazd for some time between 798/1395–6 and 806/1403–4. (*Tārīkh-i Yazd*, pp. 38, 125.)

69 Thomas T. Allsen, "Guard and Government in the Reign of the Grand Qan Möngke', 1251–59," *Harvard Journal of Asiatic Studies*, vol. 46 # 2, p. 518.

70 ZNY II, pp. 417, 250, 458; H.A. *Majma*ᶜ, f. 390b.

71 ZNY I, pp. 262, 441, 559, II, pp. 155, 266, 372, ZNS II, pp. 49, 170, *Cinq opuscules*, text, p. 68, notes, pp. 45–6.

72 Buyan Qa'uchin was *darugha* of Rayy for three or four years, and then apparently of Tabriz for about the same length of time. (ZNY II, pp. 150, 372, 417, *Majma*ᶜ, f. 380a.) Temüge Qa'uchin governed Yazd from 795/1392–3 at least past 798/1395–6, but left this post before 806/1403–4. Mūsāka b. Changī Qa'uchin on the other hand remained *darugha* of Khorezm for at least ten years. (ZNY I, p. 324, ZNS II, p. 170.) The only group which held the position of *darugha* for consistently long periods was the Barlas who held a number of governorships, especially within the territory of the Ulus Chaghatay. Sayfal Barlas was appointed to Qandahar on its conquest and remained there apparently throughout his career. (ZNY I, pp. 275, 329–30, II, p. 19.) Edigü Barlas was *darugha* of Sayram on the Turkistan frontier before his appointment to Kerman, and Nihawand was held by Mazīd Barlas. (ZNY I, pp. 160, 275, 320, 463, 560, II, pp. 154, 503, ZNS II, p. 110, *Mujmal*, III, p. 122, *Muntakhab*, p. 422.) The governorships of Balkh and Bukhara, held by Barlas emirs, were not only permanent but hereditary, as I shall explain below.

73 Manz, "Darugha," pp. 67–8, and n. p. 68.

74 Manz, "Darugha," p. 68, n.

75 Muḥammad Sulṭānshāh who administered Tabriz briefly after its conquest in 788/1386 was also a prominent emir but the size of his following is not known.

76 ZNY I, pp. 327, 463, II, p. 80, ZNS II, p. 111. See above, Chapter 4.

77 These were Sayfal in Qandahar, Mazīd in Nihawand, and Edigü when he was governor of Sayram. (ZNY I, pp. 204, 275, 329, 560, II, p. 19, ZNS II, p. 92, *Muntakhab*, p. 422.) Edigü, indeed, did lead large armies within Kerman after his appointment as governor there in 795/1393, but it is striking that unlike Temür's sons, he is rarely mentioned campaigning outside his own province.

78 See for instance: Endicott-West, "Regional and Local Government in Yüan China," Doctoral Dissertation, Princeton University, 1982, p. 30, RaD, Khetagurov, vol. I, pt. 2, pp. 268–9, Allsen, *Mongol Imperialism*, p. 223.

79 ZNY I, pp. 275, 380, ZNS I, p. 123.

80 ZNY I, pp. 441, 559, *Tārīkh-i Yazd*, p. 125, *Tārīkh-i jadīd*, p. 175.

81 ZNY II, pp. 155, 372.

82 Endicott-West, "Imperial Governance," p. 542.

83 Manz, "Darugha," p. 68.

7 The struggle for succession

1 ZNY II, pp. 458, 484, *Shams*, ff. 27b, 45a–b, pp. 25, 33–4.

2 ZNY II, pp. 489–505, *Shams*, ff. 47a–60a, pp. 35–43. Khalīl Sulṭān however installed a young prince of the senior line, Muḥammad Jahāngīr b. Muḥammad Sulṭān, as a puppet ruler.

3 *Shams*, ff. 47b–48a; 52b–60a, pp. 35–6, 39–43, ZNY II, pp. 488–90, 496–504, H.A. *Majma*ᶜ, ff. 364b–65a, 366a–67a.

4 ZNY II, p. 484, Ibn ᶜArabshāh, pp. 267, *Shams*, f. 138b, p. 100, H.A. *Majma*ᶜ, 387b.

5 *Shams*, ff. 44a–b, 77a–83a, pp. 32–3, 56–62, Ibn ᶜArabshāh, p. 261, H.A. *Majma*ᶜ, ff. 382a–83b, ZNY II, p. 482, Jaᶜfarī, Zaryab, pp. 33, 39.

6 *Shams*, f. 64a, pp. 45–6.

7 *Shams*, ff. 88b–97b, pp. 66–74, H.A. *Majma*[c], ff. 387a–88b, Ja[c]farī, Zaryab, pp. 39–41, Ibn [c]Arabshāh, pp. 266–68.
8 *Shams*, ff. 135a–36a, pp. 97–8, Ibn [c]Arabshāh, pp. 270–4, Ja[c]farī, Zaryab, p. 41, *Mujmal* III, p. 172, H.A. *Majma*[c], f. 398b–99a.
9 It is clear that Pīr [c]Alī Tāz and Pīr [c]Alī Suldus are the same person. Both names are used in Yazdī's *Ẓafarnāma*, and both applied to the governor of the fortress Banu on the Indian frontier. (ZNY II, p. 135.) The *Ẓafarnāma* identifies Pīr [c]Alī Suldus as the son of Mengli Bugha Suldus, while Tāj al-Salmānī identifies Pīr [c]Alī Tāz as the son of Mengli Temür, giving an account which strongly suggests that the same person is meant. (ZNY II, p. 458, *Shams*, f. 139a, p. 100.)
10 *Shams*, f. 139a, p. 100, see also Appendix A: Suldus.
11 ZNY I, pp. 327, 473, II, pp. 135, 276, 304, 405.
12 H. A. *Majma*[c], f. 367a, Ibn [c]Arabshāh, p. 266.
13 H.A. *Majma*[c], ff. 398b–99a.
14 *Shams*, ff. 135a–36a, pp. 96–8.
15 *Shams*, f. 167b, p. 122. See also Appendix A: Suldus.
16 *Shams*, f. 97a, pp. 72–3.
17 H.A. *Majma*[c], ff. 399a–b, *Shams*, ff. 139a–41a, pp. 100–1.
18 Ja[c]farī, Zaryab, p. 42, H.A. *Majma*[c], ff. 401b, 411a–13a, 418b, *Shams*, ff. 141a–42b, pp. 102–3.
19 ZNY I, p. 191, *Muntakhab*, p. 327. Since Khudāydād and his father are not listed in the genealogy of the Barlas given in the *Mu*[c]*izz al-ansāb* (except in a much later hand), it is possible that Khudāydād's father Ḥusayn came from outside the Ulus; there was also a Barlas tribe in the eastern Chaghadayid realm.
20 ZNY II, pp. 17, 321–2, Ibn [c]Arabshāh, pp. 243, 250–5.
21 *Shams*, ff. 68a, 132b, pp. 50, 94.
22 ZNY II, p. 17.
23 Shaykh Nūr al-Dīn had commanded court troops. (ZNY II, pp. 43–4, ZNS II, p. 140.)
24 *Shams*, ff. 131a–33a, 136a–37b, 152b–58a, pp. 93–4. 98, 110–14, Ibn [c]Arabshāh, pp. 275–6.
25 Ibn [c]Arabshāh, pp. 284–94, *Shams*, ff. 168a–76a, pp. 123–30, H.A. *Majma*[c], f. 435a–36b, 440b–41a.
26 *Shams*, f. 167b, p. 122.
27 H.A. *Majma*[c], f. 412a.
28 *Shams*, ff. 133a–35a, pp. 94–6, Ibn [c]Arabshāh, p. 275.
29 *Shams, ff.* 138b, 142a, pp. 100, 102–3, H.A. *Majma*[c], f. 421b.
30 Ja[c]farī, Zaryab, p. 39, Ibn [c]Arabshāh, pp. 267–8, *Shams*, ff. 61a–b, 79a–80a, pp. 44, 57–8, H.A. *Majma*[c], f. 387a–b.
31 *Shams*, ff. 166a–67b, pp. 121–2.
32 *Shams*, ff. 133a–34b, 168a, pp. 95–6, 123.
33 H.A. *Majma*[c], ff. 368a–69b, *Mujmal* III, pp. 155–6, 160, Ja[c]farī, Zaryab, p. 37, *Shams*, ff. 65a, 68a–69a, pp. 47, 50.
34 *Mujmal* III, pp. 168–70, H.A. *Majma*[c], ff. 392b–97a, *Shams*, ff. 108b–12b, pp. 81–2, Ja[c]farī, Zaryab, p. 43.
35 H.A. *Majma*[c], ff. 413b–414b, Ja[c]farī, Zaryab, pp. 44–5, *Shams*, ff. 142b–44a, pp. 103–4, *Mujmal* III, pp. 177, 180.
36 H.A. *Majma*[c], ff. 386a, 389a, *Mujmal* III, pp. 167–8.
37 H.A. *Majma*[c], ff. 399b–403a, *Mujmal* III, pp. 173–5.
38 H.A. *Majma*[c], ff. 429a–34b, *Shams*, ff. 158a–60b, pp. 115–16, *Mujmal* III, pp. 186–7.
39 R. M. Savory, "The Struggle for Supremacy in Persia after the Death of Tīmūr," *Der Islam*, XL # 1, p. 39.

40 ZNY I, p. 573, *Mujmal* III, p. 111.
41 H.A. *Majma*c, ff. 383b–85b, *Shams*, ff. 81a–88a, pp. 60–6, *Mujmal* III, pp. 161–2, 165–6.
42 H.A. *Majma*c, f. 389a, *Mujmal* III, p. 167, *Shams*, ff. 100a–102b, pp. 74–7.
43 Jacfarī, Zaryab, p. 37, *Mujmal* III, pp. 155–6, 160, *Shams*, ff. 68a–69a, p. 50, H.A. *Majma*c, ff. 366a, 385b. The name is sometimes given as Sayyid Khwāja. (*Mujmal* III, p. 155, *Majma*c, ff. 365b–66a.)
44 H.A. *Majma*c, ff. 389b–97a, 419b, *Shams*, ff. 99a–113b, pp. 74–83, *Mujmal* III, pp. 167–70, Jacfarī, Zaryab, pp. 43, 51.
45 H.A. *Majma*c, f. 416a.
46 ZNY I, pp. 462, 573, II, pp. 56, 103, 152, 276, 304, H.A. *Majma*c, ff. 367b, 375a, 385b, 386b, 396a, 404b, 411b, 412a–b.
47 *Dastūr al-wuzarā'*, pp. 344–5, H.A. *Majma*c, ff. 416b–17b.
48 Besides Jahānmalik the list includes Ḥasan Jāndār and his son Yūsuf Jalīl, who were relatives of Khitay and Sevinchek Bahadur. (ZNY I, p. 462, II, p. 167.) There were also three relatives of Aqbugha Nayman – his son Sulṭān Aḥmad, his grandson Shaykh Buhlūl b. Buyan Temür, and his nephew, Sacādat b. Temürtash, as well as Sulṭān Bāyazīd b. cUthmān, the grandson of Temür's follower cAbbās Bahadur. (ZNY II, pp. 408, 426, *Mu*c*izz*, f. 97a.)
49 H.A. *Majma*c, ff. 417a–418a, Jacfarī, Zaryab, p. 46, *Mujmal* III, p. 175, *Shams, ff.* 144b–48b, pp. 104–7.
50 *Shams*, f. 55b, pp. 41–2.
51 H.A. *Majma*c, f. 384a.
52 H.A. *Majma*c, f. 392b.
53 H.A. *Majma*c, ff. 412b, 415b, *Mujmal* III, p. 176. In 809/1406, he bestowed the lands taken from the rebellious leader of Turshiz on Miḍrāb b. Chekü, who had been instrumental in Shāhrukh's victory over him. (H.A. *Majma*c, f. 392b.) In 812, he granted Uzgand as *soyurghal* to Aḥmad b. cUmar Shaykh. (H.A. *Majma*c, f. 441a, *Mujmal* III, p. 193.)
54 *Dastūr al-wuzarā'*, p. 344, H. A. *Majma*c, f. 417a.
55 I. P. Petrushevskiĭ, "K istorii instituta soiurgala," *Sovetskoe vostokovedenie*, VI, pp. 228–30, A. Belenitskiĭ, "K istorii feodal'nogo zemlevladeniia v Sredneĭ Azii i Irane v timuridskuiu epokhu (XIV–XV vv.)," *Istorik-marksist*, 1941, # 4, pp. 46–52, Manz, "Administration and the Delegation of Authority," pp. 202–3.
56 Shāhrukh allowed Sulaymānshāh to remain there for some months in 807/1405 to restore his forces and later sent Ulugh Beg and Shāhmalik to govern the area. (H.A. *Majma*c, ff. 368a, 386a, 411a, *Mujmal*, p. 176.)
57 Temür had put the tribe under the charge of Buyan Temür b. Aqbugha; he is not in evidence at this period, and his son Shaykh Buhlūl is mentioned once once, participating in the rebellion of Jahānmalik b. Mulkat in 810/1408. Thus we cannot tell whether he was chief of the Apardï.
58 ZNY II, p. 458, *Shams*, f. 45a, 142b, pp. 33–4, 103, H. A. *Majma*c, ff. 388a, 411a–b, 412b, 415a, 418b.
59 H.A. *Majma*c, ff. 388b, 401a.
60 R. M. Savory, "The Struggle for Supremacy," p. 36.
61 Jacfarī, Zaryab, pp. 35–6, *Mujmal* III, p. 156, Clavijo, pp. 311–15, *Shams*, ff. 113b–15b, pp. 83–5, H.A. *Majma*c, ff. 370b–371a.
62 ZNY II, pp. 386, 393, 399, 406, Jacfarī, Len., f. 291a.
63 J. M. Smith, "D̲jalayir," p. 401, Jacfarī, Zaryab, p. 37.
64 H.A. *Majma*c, ff. 371b–372a, Jacfarī, Zaryab, p. 37, *Shams*, ff. 116b–17a, p. 86, *Mujmal* III, p. 156.
65 H.A. *Majma*c, f. 377a, Jacfarī, Zaryab, p. 37, *Shams*, ff. 118a–b, p. 87, Clavijo, pp. 324–6.
66 H.A. *Majma*c, ff. 377b–378b, *Shams*, ff. 118b–19a, p. 87, *Mujmal* III, pp. 162–3.

67 H.A. *Majma^c*, ff. 379a–80a, *Mujmal* III, pp. 163–4.
68 H.A. *Majma^c*, ff. 380b–82b, *Shams*, ff. 119b–22a, pp. 87–8, *Mujmal* III, pp. 164–5, Ja^{c}farī, Zaryab, pp. 38–40.
69 H.A. *Majma^c*, f. 404a, *Mujmal* III, p. 174.
70 Clavijo, pp. 328–31, H.A. *Majma^c*, f. 377b, *Mujmal* III, p. 162.
71 ZNY I, pp. 297, 558, II, pp. 92, 157–8, 162, 371, 384, 395.
72 H.A. *Majma^c*, ff. 405a–b, *Mujmal* III, p. 171.
73 H.A. *Majma^c*, ff. 406a–407b, 420b–423b, 428a–b, *Mujmal* III, pp. 171, 178–80, *Shams*, ff. 149a–52b, pp. 108–9, Ja^{c}farī, Zaryab, pp. 47–8.
74 This is true of Pīr Ḥusayn Barlas; Tökel b. Urus Bugha and ^{c}Umar Tābān were the sons of emirs assigned to Amīrānshāh. (ZNY I, p. 225.)
75 H.A. *Majma^c*, ff. 380b, 381b–382a.
76 H.A. *Majma^c*, f. 407a, *Mujmal* III, p. 171.
77 H.A. *Majma^c*, f. 407b, *Mujmal* III, p. 171.
78 H.A. *Majma^c*, f. 379a–b.
79 H.A. *Majma^c*, f. 378b.
80 H.A. *Majma^c*, ff. 406b–407a.
81 H.A. *Majma^c*, f. 407b.
82 H.A. *Majma^c*, f. 421b, *Mujmal* III, p. 178.
83 *Shams*, ff. 84b–85b, p. 63, H.A. *Majma^c*, f. 384a.
84 *Shams*, f. 107a, p. 79.

Appendix A

1 RaD, Khetagurov, vol. I, parts 1 and 2, RaD, ^{c}Ali-Zade, vol. III, Boyle, *Successors, The Secret History of the Mongols*, Muḥammad Zubayr as-Ṣiddīqī, ed. al-Harawī, *The Ta'rīkh Nāma-i Harāt* (Calcutta, 1944), H.A., *Dhayl*, Sayyid Muḥammad Kāẓim Ayām, ed., Mu^{c}īn al-Dīn Muḥammad Zamchī Isfizārī, *Rawḍāt al-jannāt fī awṣāf-i madīnat-i Harāt* (Tehran, sh. 1338/1959).
2 ZNY I, p. 121.
3 ZNY I, p. 32.
4 See for instance leaders of the Apardï, Jawun-i Qurban and Borolday. (ZNY I, p. 32, *Cinq opuscules*, text, pp. 27, 46–7, notes, pp. 28–9, Isfizārī, vol. II, p. 21.)
5 ZNY I, pp. 32, 328. Also, for example: ZNY I, pp. 25, 77, 120–1.
6 ZNY I, p. 32, ZNS I, p. 15, II, pp. 11–12, *Muntakhab*, p. 204.
7 *Cinq opuscules*, text, pp. 46–8, notes, p. 29, Aubin, "Khanat," pp. 41–2, ZNY I, pp. 164, 183, 276, 327.
8 Aubin, "Khanat," pp. 34–5, 39, *Cinq opuscules*, text, p. 39, ZNY I, pp. 25, 77, 147–9.
9 See Chapter 3.
10 ZNS II, p. 37, ZNY I, pp. 354, 441.
11 ZNY I, p. 327.
12 ZNY I, p. 462, H.A. *Majma^c*, f. 412a; see also Chapter 7.
13 ZNS II, p. 9, ZNY I, p. 155.
14 *Mu^{c}izz*, f. 101b.
15 *Shu^{c}ab-i panjgāna*, f. 47b, *Mu^{c}izz*, f. 29a, RaD, Khetagurov, vol. I, pt. 2, p. 275, Boyle, *Successors*, p. 314, ZNY, Urunbaev, *Muqaddima*, ff. 64b–65a.
16 Samarqandī, *Matla^c al-sa^{c}dayn*, p. 280, note.
17 Aubin, "Khanat," p. 18, ZNY I, pp. 117, 195.
18 *Cinq opuscules*, notes, p. 29, Aubin, "Khanat," p. 40.
19 *Muntakhab*, p. 117.
20 ZNY I, p. 164.

21 ZNY I, p. 195, *Muntakhab*, p. 415.
22 Ibn ᶜArabshāh, p. 4, Bartol'd, *Istoriia Turkestana*, p. 153.
23 ZNY I, pp. 65, 98, 100, 106, 142–4, 154,157, 179, 197, *Muntakhab*, pp. 223, 261, 272, 287, ZNS I, p. 41, *Cinq opuscules*, text, p. 59.
24 ZNY I, pp. 77, 79, 164, 192, 195, *Muntakhab*, pp. 117, 223, 414–15.
25 Aubin, "Khanat," pp. 27–9, ZNY I, pp. 25–8, *Cinq opuscules*, text, pp. 38–43.
26 Aubin, "Khanat," p. 49, *Cinq opuscules*, text, p. 49.
27 ZNY I, p. 98, *Muᶜizz*, f. 95b.
28 *Cinq opuscules*, text, p. 59.
29 *Muᶜizz*, f. 102a.
30 V. V. Bartol'd, "Badakhshān," in *Encyclopaedia of Islam*, N.E., vol. I, p. 852.
31 H.A., *Dhayl*, p. 112.
32 Aubin, "Khanat," pp. 34–5, *Cinq opuscules*, text, p. 39, ZNY I, pp. 25, 31–2.
33 ZNS II, pp. 22, 57, ZNY I, pp. 147, 249, 334, II, pp. 19, 450.
34 ZNY I, pp. 37–8, 134, *Muntakhab*, p. 256, Ibn ᶜArabshāh, pp. 9–10.
35 ZNY II, p. 19.
36 ZNS II, p. 53, *Muntakhab*, pp. 256–7.
37 ZNY I, pp. 31, 43–4, ZNS I, p. 18, *Muntakhab*, p. 205.
38 *Muᶜizz*, ff. 1b–2a, 28b, 81b–82a, Togan, "Nasab," pp. 106–7, *Shuᶜab-i panjgāna*, f. 47b.
39 ZNY, Urunbaev, *Muqaddima*, ff. 61b, 75b, 77a, 78a, 81a.
40 RaD, ᶜAli-zade, vol. I, pt. I, pp. 530–1, also vol. III and Boyle, *Successors*, *passim*.
41 Bartol'd, *Ulugbek i ego vremia*, in *Sochineniia*, vol. II, pt. 2 (Moscow, 1964), pp. 38–9, *Turkestan*, p. 53.
42 Togan, "Nasab," pp. 108–9.
43 *Muᶜizz*, ff. 28a–38a.
44 ZNY I, p. 60, *Muᶜizz*, f. 88b.
45 *Muᶜizz*, ff. 82b, 94b–96b, ZNY I, p. 36.
46 See Chapter 4.
47 *Muᶜizz*, ff. 86b, 88b, 90b, 94b–95b, ZNY I, pp. 48, 58, 60, 67, 72, 90, 92, 98, 101, 104, 143, 160, 320.
48 See for instance: ZNY I, pp. 160, 176, 239, 275, 320, 441, II, p. 504, *Muᶜizz*, ff. 88b, 92a.
49 See for example: *Muᶜizz*, ff. 91b, 92a, 133b.
50 *Muᶜizz*, ff. 90a, 197a, 108b.
51 Aubin, "Khanat," p. 18, E. Bacon, *Obok: a Study of Social Structure in Eurasia* (Viking Publications in Anthropology, # 25), New York, 1958, pp. 6–7.
52 Aubin, "Khanat," p. 18.
53 ZNY I, pp. 130, 329.
54 Ibn Baṭṭūṭa, vol. III, pp. 561, 585, Aubin, "Khanat," pp. 17–18, ZNS II, p. 11.
55 ZNY I, pp. 63, 176.
56 ZNY I, pp. 275, 327, II, p. 402.
57 *Muᶜizz*, f. 93a.
58 ZNY I, p. 29, *Muntakhab*, p. 262, ZNS II, p. 11.
59 ZNY I, p. 328, II, pp. 50, 70, 397, 403.
60 *Muᶜizz*, f. 28b, Boyle, *Successors*, p. 145, *Shuᶜab-i panjgāna*, f. 47b.
61 Ibn ᶜArabshāh, p. 4, Bartol'd, *Dvenadstat' lektsii*, p. 172.
62 See Chapter 3.
62 ZNY I, pp. 43–4, *Muntakhab*, p. 209.
63 ZNY I, pp. 89, 119–20, *Muntakhab*, pp. 235, 247–8, 265, ZNS I, pp. 45–6.
64 ZNY I, p. 189.
65 ZNY I, p. 202.
66 See Chapter 4.
67 ZNY I, p. 87.

68 ZNY I, p. 155, *Mu^c izz*, f. 32a. (According to the *Mu^c izz* she went first to Kaykhusraw Khuttalānī, and after his death to Bahrām.)
69 ZNY I, p. 104.
70 *Mu^c izz*, ff. 101b, 102a.
71 ZNY I, pp. 89, 137–8, 181, 324, *Muntakhab*, pp. 158, 235, 258, 265.
72 ZNY I, pp. 32, 38, 89.
73 ZNY I, pp. 119, 147, 181, 320, ZNS II, p. 15, *Muntakhab*, p. 283.
74 ZNY I, p. 32, *Muntakhab*, p. 200.
75 ZNY I, p. 63.
76 ZNY I, pp. 32, 45, 89, 137–8, ZNS II, p. 15, *Muntakhab*, pp. 158, 235, 258, 265.
77 ZNY I, p. 181.
78 ZNY I, pp. 324–6.
79 ZNY I, p. 463.
80 H.A., *Majma^c*, f. 412a.
81 *Mu^c izz*, ff. 92a, 133b.
82 ZNY I, p. 155.
83 ZNY I, p. 155, *Mu^c izz*, f. 32a.
84 ZNY I, p. 120, ZNS II, p. 40.
85 ZNY I, p. 324.
86 Samarqandī, *Matla^c al-Sa^c dayn*, note, pp. 282–4, Paul Pelliot, *Notes on Marco Polo* (Paris, 1959), vol. I, "Caraunas," pp. 183–96, Aubin, "l'Ethnogénèse des Qaraunas," pp. 65–94, Henry Yule, ed. and trans., *The Book of Ser Marco Polo the Venetian* (London, 1875), vol. I, pp. 102–9, Henry Howorth, *History of the Mongols from the 9th to the 19th Century* (London; New York, 1888), vol. III, pp. 388–9, Hirotoshi Shimo, "The Qaraunas in the Historical Materials of the Ilkhanate," in *Memoirs of the Research Department of the Toyo Bunko*, 35 (1977), pp. 131–81.
87 Aubin, "l'Ethnogénèse," pp. 69–73, Shimo, "The Qaraunas," pp. 162–70.
88 Aubin, "l'Ethnogénèse," pp. 69–75.
89 Aubin, "l'Ethnogénèse," pp. 79–81, Shimo, "The Qaraunas," pp. 163–70.
90 Aubin, "l'Ethnogénèse," pp. 74–5, 87, Shimo, "The Qaraunas," pp. 133–8, 141–53, 163, 171–5, 180.
91 Aubin, "l'Ethnogénèse," pp. 88, 90, Shimo, "The Qaraunas," pp. 163–70, 180.
92 Aubin, "l'Ethnogénèse," p. 88, Shimo, "The Qaraunas," pp. 163–70.
93 Aubin, "l'Ethnogénèse," pp. 83–6, 91, H.A., *Dhayl*, pp. 138–40.
94 ZNS I, p. 15, Aubin, "Khanat," pp. 17–18.
95 ZNY I, p. 21, Togan, "Nasab," p. 112.
96 ZNS II, p. 11, ZNY I, p. 29.
97 *Muntakhab*, pp. 123, 197, 204.
98 Bartol'd, *Dvenadstat' lektsii*, p. 170.
99 ZNY I, pp. 96–128, ZNS I, pp. 38–50.
100 See for example: ZNY I, pp. 57, 63, 133, *Muntakhab*, pp. 123, 125–6, 209–10, 215, 232, 254.
101 *Muntakhab*, pp. 123, 197, 204, ZNS II, p. 12.
102 Aubin, "Khanat," pp. 29, 39.
103 *Muntakhab*, p. 223, ZNY I, pp. 77, 79.
104 Aubin, "Khanat," pp. 18–19, ZNS II, p. 292 (index), Roemer, "Timur," pp. 43–4.
105 ZNY I, p. 176, *Mu^c izz*, f. 93a.
106 G. Doerfer, *Türkische und mongolische Elemente im Neupersischen*, vol. I, p. 423, ZNS I, p. 134.
107 *Tārīkh-i Rashīdī*, p. 301.
108 E. Quatremère ed., "Haft Iqlīm," in notes to "Matla-assaadein," *Notices et Extraits*,

vol. xiv, pt. 1, pp.475–6, V. V. Bartol'd, review of Charles Schefer, *Description topographique et historique de Boukhara par Mohammed Nerchakhy, suivie de textes relatifs à la Transoxiane*, in *Sochineniia*, vol. viii, p. 20.

109 *Baburnāma*, p. 26.

110 ZNY i, p. 53.

111 ZNY i, p. 59.

112 *Mu*^c^*izz*, ff. 97b, 98a, ZNY i, pp. 53, 155, 161, 163, 225, 324, 441, 463, ii, pp. 227, 412, ZNS ii, p. 49.

113 Temür's follower Aqtemür for instance is not identified as *qa'uchin*, although he was related to both Qumarï Qa'uchin and Temüge Qa'uchin (ZNY i, pp. 208, 225, 441); likewise, neither Eyegü Temür nor his relative and successor Shāhmalik were called *qa'uchin*, although they were related to Tābān Bahadur Qa'uchin, and Eyegü Temür's son Shaykh Muḥammad is identified as *qa'uchin*. (ZNY i, p. 380, ii, p. 412, ZNS i, p. 122, ii, p. 96, *Shams*, ff. 91b–92a, p. 69, *Mu*^c^*izz*, f. 98a.)

114 See for example: ZNY i, pp. 53, 59, 76–8, 86, 135.

115 ZNY i, pp. 155, 161–2.

116 ZNY i, p. 573.

117 ZNY ii, p. 474.

118 ZNY i, p. 436, ii, p. 100, ZNS i, p. 194.

119 ZNY i, pp. 462–3.

120 *Mu*^c^*izz*, ff. 132b–137a, 137b–139a.

121 H.A., *Majma*^c^, f. 416a.

122 *Mu*^c^*izz*, ff. 97b, 98a, ZNY i, pp. 324, 441, ii, 155, 200, 334, 372, ZNS i, p. 91, ii, p. 49.

123 ZNY i, pp. 31–2, ZNS i, p. 15, ii, pp. 11–12, *Muntakhab*, p. 204.

124 ZNY i, pp. 77, 196–7, 387.

125 *Baburnāma*, p. 19.

126 Ibn ^c^Arabshāh, p. 2.

127 *Mu*^c^*izz*, f. 98a, ZNY i, pp. 111, 127, 131, 162, 167, 170, 196–7, etc.

128 ZNY i, pp. 225, 234, 266, 312, 388, 401, 441, 462, ii, pp. 150, 166, 167, 290, 304, 361, *Mu*^c^*izz*, f. 97b, 98a.

129 Togan, "Nasab," p. 108, *Shu*^c^*ab-i panjgāna*, f. 47b, *Mu*^c^*izz*, f. 29a.

130 ZNY i, pp. 25, 31, *Muntakhab*, p. 117.

131 See Chapter 2.

132 ZNY i, pp. 45, 67, ZNS i, p. 19, *Mujmal*, iii, p. 95, *Muntakhab*, p. 258.

133 ZNY i, p. 32.

134 ZNY i, p. 83, ZNS i, p. 30.

135 ZNY i, pp. 59–60, 83, *Muntakhab*, p. 217.

136 ZNY i, p. 39, ZNS i, p. 17, *Muntakhab*, p. 207.

137 ZNY i, p. 155.

138 ZNY i, p. 193, *Muntakhab*, p. 415, *Mujmal*, iii, p. 107.

139 ZNY i, p. 364.

140 ZNY i, p. 467, ii, pp. 25, 53, 250, 304, 322, 426, *Mu*^c^*izz*, ff. 98a, 127a. ZNY i, pp. 364, 368, ZNS ii, p. 98. There is no mention after 793/1391 of the Suldus *tümen*. About 800/1397–8 however the histories begin to mention a new and powerful emir – Dawlat Temür Tovachï, identified in the *Mu*^c^*izz al-ansāb* as a Suldus. This might very well be the son of Shaykh Temür, now known by the name of the tribe he led. (ZNY i, p. 467, ii, pp. 25, 53, 250, 304, 322, 426, *Mu*^c^*izz*, ff. 98a, 127a.) The similarity of names is an argument for this supposition; it was common to pass on part of a name to the next generation, as indeed Aqtemür had done in naming his son Shaykh Temür. Shaykh Temür is last mentioned in 796/1393 while Dawlat Temür first appears in 800/1397–8, remaining active throughout the rest of Temür's life and after his death; thus he was clearly of a younger generation. The

identification of an outside leader by the name of the tribe he led was not uncommon; the examples of the Jawun-i Qurban and the Apardï emirs have been cited earlier to illustrate this practice.

141 For example: Pīr ᶜAlī Suldus b. Mengli Bugha, ZNY I, p. 473, II, pp. 40, 135, 304, 321, 405, 458, also Dawlat Temür Tovachï Suldus, *Muᶜizz*, f. 98a, ZNY II, pp. 83, 250, 291, 322, 426.
142 See Chapter 7.
143 Bartol'd, *Dvenadtsat' lektsii*, p. 172, Aubin, "Khanat," p. 27, H.A., *Dhayl*, pp. 106–58, *passim*.
144 Bartol'd, *Dvenadtsat' lektsii*, p. 164.
145 ZNY I, pp. 32, 106, 109, *Muntakhab*, pp. 117, 240, Aubin, "Khanat," p. 27.
146 ZNY I, p. 90.
147 ZNY I, p. 109, *Muntakhab*, pp. 240–1.
148 *Muᶜizz*, f. 97a.
149 ZNS II, p. 40, ZNY I, p. 201.
150 *Muntakhab*, p. 281.
151 ZNY I, pp. 162, 280, 340, 417, 445.
152 ZNY I, p. 565, II, p. 326.

Appendix C

1 For the Jalayirids we have Nakchiwānī's *Dastūr al-kātib*, (Muḥammad b. Hindushāh Nakhchiwānī, *Dastūr al-kātib fī taᶜyīn al-marātib*, ed. A. A. Ali-zade (Moscow, 1971–6), which although written under the Jalayirids also reflects Ilkhanid practice, and for the late Timurid period the *Sharafnāma* of ᶜAbd Allāh Marwārīd. (ᶜAbd Allāh Marwārīd, H. R. Roemer, ed., *Staatsschreiben der Timuridenzeit: Das Šaraf-nāmä des ᶜAbdallāh Marwārīd in kritischer Auswertung* (Wiesbaden, 1952).
2 The *Muᶜizz* mentions ᶜUmar Shaykh Mirza b. Abu Saᶜīd born in 860/1456, but not his son Babur, born in 888/1483. The numerous titles accorded to Sulṭān Ḥusayn Bayqara and the large number of emirs listed under him suggest that this recension was written after his conquest of Herat in 1469. (*Muᶜizz*, ff. 155a, 156b–159b.)
3 Ali-zade, *Sotsial'no-ekonomicheskaia istoriia*, p. 290, Bosworth, *The Ghaznavids*, pp. 82–5.
4 ZNY II, p. 122, ZNS I, p. 204.
5 These people sometimes remained for several years in the regions to which they were assigned. (Jean Aubin, "Un santon quhistānī," p. 209, *Mujmal*, III, pp. 145–6, ZNY II, pp. 321, 378–9.
6 See for example ZNY II, pp. 321, 396–7, ZNS II, pp. 294–5.
7 ZNS I, p. 243.
8 Jean Aubin, *Deux Sayyids*, p. 395, Clavijo, p. 205.
9 Clavijo, pp. 181, 186, 195.
10 Actually despite frequent mention of the *dīwān-i aᶜlā*, no one person is definitely identified as belonging to it; scribes are simply mentioned as members of the "*dīwān*." We do know of Persians who were members of a central *dīwān*, and know some of those who headed it. This *dīwān* could be identical with the *dīwān-i aᶜlā*, or could simply be part of it.
11 ZNY II, pp. 378–9, 396–7, H.A. Geography, f. 318b, Jaᶜfarī, Len., ff. 273b–74a, H.A. Continuation, p. 443. One should note that the *dīwān* in Samarqand was not the central *dīwān*, which traveled with the sovereign, but was essentially a provincial *dīwān*, though one which possessed greater power and prestige than most others.
12 H.A. Geography, f. 318b, H.A. Continuation, p. 443, Jaᶜfarī, Len., ff. 273b–74a, *Jāmiᶜ-i mufīdī*, I, p. 162, Aubin, *Deux sayyids*, p. 395.
13 A. K. S. Lambton, "Dīwān"–"Iran", *Encyclopaedia of Islam*, N.E., vol. II, p. 333.

14 This term was used under the Ilkhanids. Ali-zade, *Sotsial'no-ekonomicheskaia istoriia*, pp. 290–1, ZNY II, p. 270, H.A. Continuation, pp. 443–4, H.A. Geography, f. 318b.
15 ZNY II, pp. 226, 239, 261, ZNS II, p. 171, *Dastūr al-wuzarā'*, p. 341.
16 ZNY II, p. 270, ZNS II, p. 171, *Dastūr al-wuzarā'*, p. 341.
17 H.A. Continuation, p. 444.
18 ZNY II, pp. 226, 239, ZNS II, p. 236.
19 ZNY II, pp. 94, 156, 239, 246.
20 ZNY II, p. 325.
21 In the few clear references to a vizier as head of the *dīwān*, it is coupled with another title such as *ṣāḥib dīwān* or *ṣāḥib māl*. (Jaᶜfarī, Len., f. 274a, *Dastūr al-wuzarā'*, pp. 341, 343, 345–8.)
22 Jaᶜfarī, Len., f. 274a.
23 For the use of the term *māl*, see also M. Minovi and V. Minorsky, "Naṣīr al-Dīn Ṭūsī on Finance," BSOAS, x # 3 (1940), pp. 758, 761, 762, 763, 771, 773, 775, 788, and Heribert Busse, *Untersuchungen zum islamischen Kanzleiwesen an Hand turkmenischer und safawidischer Urkunden* (Cairo, 1959), pp. 150, 152, 159, 165, 183. See for Temür's time: *Muntakhab*, pp. 65–6, ZNY II, p. 321, ZNY II, pp. 284–5. 394, Jaᶜfarī, Len., f. 286a.
24 ZNY I, p. 565, II, pp. 284–5, ZNS II, p. 129, H.A. Continuation, p. 442, H.A. Geography, f. 320b, *Mujmal* III, pp. 148–50.
25 H.A. Geography, f. 127a, *Dastūr al-wuzarā'*, pp. 343–5, *Mujmal* III, p. 145, *Jāmiᶜ-i mufīdī*, p. 167, ZNY II, pp. 278–9. See also Sayyid Ḥasan Khwārazmī. (Aubin, "Un santon," p. 209.)
26 *Dastūr al-wuzarā'*, pp. 343–4, *Mujmal* III, pp. 145–6, *Tārīkh-i Yazd*, pp. 39–41, *Tārīkh-i jadīd*, pp. 92–3.
27 ZNY II, pp. 378–9.
28 *Muntakhab*, p. 411, ZNY II, pp. 165–6.
29 ZNY II, pp. 191, 275.
30 A. A. Ali-zade, *Sotsial'no-ekonomicheskaia istoriia*, p. 269, ZNY II, pp. 165–6.
31 In the *Muᶜizz al-ansāb* under many princes the first people to be listed are the "*dīwāniyān*", who were Chaghatay emirs. These might well be the same as the *amīr dīwān*, since these lists correspond to the lists of "*umarā'*" given under other princes. (*Muᶜizz*, ff. 96b, 102b, 104b, 107b, 108b–109a, 110b, 117b, 119b, 125b–126a, 141b, 151b–152a.)
32 ZNY I, pp. 161–2.
33 One other *amīr dīwān* was Aqbugha's grandson, Luṭf Allāh, who was given this post on his appointment to Fars in 805/1402–3. (ZNY II, p. 367.) The fact that he was the grandson of one of Temür's *umarā' dīwān* suggests that this office was hereditary.
34 See Chapter 6.
35 Manz, "Darugha."
36 See Manz, "Darugha," pp. 60–6.
37 See for example *Muntakhab*, p. 311, *Tārīkh-i āl-i Muẓaffar*, p. 123, ZNS I, p. 177.
38 *Tārīkh-i āl-i Muẓaffar*, p. 123, ZNS II, p. 185.
39 See ZNS I, p. 177, II, pp. 104, 140, H.A. Continuation, p. 438.
40 ZNY II, pp. 334, 379.
41 ZNY I, p. 312.
42 ZNS II, pp. 55, 126, ZNY I, p. 259, Jaᶜfarī, Len., f. 264a.
43 *Muntakhab*, pp. 65–6.
44 Sanjian, *Colophons of Armenian Manuscripts 1301–1480*, p. 130.
45 Doerfer, *Türkische und mongolische Elemente*, vol. II, pp. 565–8, Bartol'd, "Persidskaia nadpis' na stene Anniĭskoĭ mecheti," in *Sochineniia*, vol. IV, pp. 332–3, Allsen, *Mongol Imperialism*, pp. 158–62.
46 ZNY II, p. 335.

47 V. Minorsky, "A Civil and Military Review in Fars in 881/1476," pp. 153, 157, 170–1, Bartol'd, *Mir Ali-Shir i politicheskaia Zhizn'* in *Sochineniia*, vol. II, pt. 2, p. 232, Woods, *Aqquyunlu*, p. 11, V. Minorsky, ed. and trans., *Tadhkirat al-mulūk: A Manual of Ṣafavid Administration (c. 1137/1725)* (Cambridge, 1943), pp. 62, 132–3.
48 *Muʿizz*, f. 98a, ZNS I, p. 122, II, p. 96, ZNY I, p. 123.
49 It was also held by an emir called ʿAbd Allāh, whose identity is unclear. (*Muʿizz*, f. 98a.)
50 Woods, *Aqqoyunlu*, p. 11.
51 ZNY I, p. 463, II, pp. 153–4.
52 Doerfer, *Türkische und mongolische Elemente*, vol. IV, pp. 64–6.
53 Bartol'd, *Turkestan, Sochineniia* vol. I, p. 559, Ali-zade, *Sotsial'no-ekonomicheksaia istoriia*, p. 269, *Dastūr al-kātib*, pp. 29–30, Allsen, *Mongol Imperialism*, pp. 94–5.
54 ZNS II, p. 110, ZNY I, p. 462.
55 Doerfer, *Türkische und mongolische Elemente*, vol. I, pp. 429–32, *Baburnāma*, p. 188, Minorsky, *Tadhkirat al-mulūk*, pp. 15, 44, 113–15.
56 ZNY II, p. 25, ZNS II, p. 111.
57 *Muʿizz*, ff. 103a, 105a, 120a, 127a, 139a.
58 Doerfer, *Türkische und mongolische Elemente*, vol. III, pp. 548–9, Fedorov-Davydov, *Obshchestvennyĭ stroĭ*, pp. 96–7.
59 Roemer, *Staatsschreiben der Timuridenzeit*, pp. 172–3.
60 *Muʿizz*, ff. 103a, 105a, 108a, 120a, 127b.
61 ZNY I, p. 462, ZNS II, p. 110.
62 Doerfer, *Türkische und mongolische Elemente*, vol. I, pp. 117–18, Bartol'd, *Turkestan, Sochineniia*, vol. I, p. 448, *Secret History*, pp. 56–7, Allsen, "Guard and Government," p. 509.
63 *Muʿizz*, ff. 103a, 120a, 128a.
64 ZNY I, pp. 261, 294, 496, 562, 577, II, 153, 419, 451, 483, 489–90, Ibn ʿArabshāh, pp. 193–4.
65 ZNS I, pp. 133–4, *Tārīkh-i āl-Muẓaffar*, p. 125.
66 Doerfer, *Türkische und Mongolische Elemente*, vol. II, pp. 301–7.
67 Bartol'd, *Turkestan, Sochineniia*, vol. I, p. 447, *Secret History*, p. 55, *Dastūr al-kātib*, vol. II, pp. 53–4, Fedorov-Davydov, *Obshchestvennyĭ Stroĭ*, pp. 96–7, Minorsky, *Tadhkirat al-mulūk*, p. 15, Minorsky, "A Civil and Military Review," p. 71, Minorsky, "The Aq-qoyunlu and Land Reforms," *Bulletin of the School of Oriental and African Studies*, XVII, p. 453, Woods, *Aqquyunlu*, p. 11.
68 Roemer, *Staatsschreiben*, pp. 155–6.
69 ZNY II, p. 158.
70 *Muʿizz*, ff. 103a, 108a, 120a, 127a, 134b.
71 Doerfer, *Türkische und mongolische Elemente*, vol. I, pp. 202–5.
72 Bartol'd, *Turkestan, Sochineniia*, vol. I, p. 447.
73 Doerfer, *Türkische und mongolische Elemente*, vol. I, pp. 202–5.
74 ZNY I, pp. 321, 354, 436, 462, 533, II, 227, 280–1, 301, 416.
75 Doerfer, *Türkische und mongolische Elemente*, vol. 20, pp. 285–6.
76 ZNY I, pp. 457, 462.
77 *Muʿizz*, ff. 103a, 108a, 120a, 127b, 134b.
78 Woods, *Aqqoyunlu*, p. 11, Ali-zade, *Sotsial'no-ekonomicheskaia istoriia*, pp. 268, 291.
79 Fedorov-Davydov, *Obshchestvennyĭ stroĭ*, p. 90.
80 *Muʿizz*, ff. 91b, 92b.
81 Clavijo, p. 213.
82 *Muʿizz*, f. 88b.
83 ZNY I, pp. 327–9, 342, 563, II, pp. 69, 102, 118, 358–9, ZNS I, p. 200.
84 H.A. Geography, f. 315a.
85 ZNY I, pp. 329–30, 337, ZNS II, pp. 77–9.

86 H.A. Geography, f. 318b, *Muntakhab*, p. 319, *Cinq opuscules*, notes, p. 45.
87 Doerfer, *Türkische und mongolische Elemente*, vol. I, pp. 260–2.
88 ZNY I, p. 25, Minorsky, "A Civil and Military Review," pp. 152, 163, Woods, *Aqquyunlu*, p. 11, Akhmedov, *Gosudarstvo kochevykh Uzbekov* (Moscow, 1965), p. 104.
89 *Muntakhab*, p. 292, ZNS II, pp. 70, 93, ZNY I, p. 487, II, p. 152.
90 ZNY II, pp. 447–8.
91 ZNS II, p. 109, ZNY II, pp. 282–3.
92 *Mujmal*, III, p. 143, ZNY I, pp. 466, 530, 552, II, pp. 157, 265, H.A. Continuation, p. 446.
93 Doerfer, *Türkische und mongolische Elemente*, vol. IV, pp. 216–17, Bartol'd, *Turkestan*, *Sochineniia*, vol. I, pp. 447–8, Shīrīn Bayānī, *Tārīkh-i āl-i Jalāyir* (Tehran, sh. 1345/1967), p. 179, *Dastūr al-kātib*, pp. 62–7.
94 ZNY I, p. 522 II, p. 230.
95 ZNS I, pp. 199–200, ZNY II, p. 113. For another mention see *Muntakhab*, p. 311.
96 ZNY I, pp. 441, 463, 573, ZNS II, p. 111.
97 Doerfer, *Türkische und mongolische Elemente*, vol. IV, pp. 166–72.
98 *Dastūr al-kātib*, pp. 57–8, see also Minorsky, *Tadhkirat al-mulūk*, text, p. 64, commentary, p. 33, Minorsky, "A Civil and Military Review," p. 171, Woods, *Aqquyunlu*, p. 11, Akhmedov, *Gosudarstvo kochevykh Uzbekov*, p. 102.
99 H.A. Continuation, p. 446.
100 ZNY II, p. 376, ZNS I, pp. 280–3.
101 *Muᶜizz*, f. 98b, *Rūznāma*, p. 52, ZNY I, pp. 467, 533, II, pp. 25, 122, 299.
102 *Muntakhab*, p. 221, *Muᶜizz*, ff. 88b, 96b–97a, H.A. Continuation, p. 434, *Rūznāma*, p. 136.
103 In the Golden Horde, the word *beg* was a recognized title and denoted either a member of the tribal aristocracy of fairly high rank, or a leader in government. (G. A. Fedorov-Davydov, *Obshchestvennyĭ stroĭ*, pp. 46–7, 90.) For the later Timurid period see Roemer, *Staatsschreiben*, pp. 170–1, 173. The exact nature of this hereditary rank however seems to have remained uncertain, as is shown by the disagreement over whether Mīr ᶜAlī Shīr Nawā'ī, born into the high service aristocracy, did or did not inherit the title of *beg*. (Bartol'd, *Mir Ali-Shir*, p. 212, Maria Eva Subtelny, "The Poetic Circle at the Court of the Timurid, Sulṭān Ḥusain Baiqara, and its Political Significance," Doctoral Dissertation, Harvard University, 1979, p. 100.)
104 *Muᶜizz*, ff. 96b–97a. One cannot on the other hand assume that its listing of *amīrs* is complete, or that such a listing in itself proves the existence of a definite and limited number of *amīrs*.
105 Even when *amīrs* had several sons, only one usually appears on the list, and that if the father died during Temür's lifetime. There are some exceptions to this, for example the descendants and relatives of Aqbugha Nayman, of which several are listed, and also the listing of Tökel Barlas, whose father Yādgār Barlas probably did not die before Temür. (*Muᶜizz*, ff. 96b–97a, ZNY II, pp. 286, 426, 449, 458 (for Saᶜādat Nayman), ZNY II, p. 367 (for Luṭf Allāh Nayman), ZNY II, p. 426 (for Yādgār Barlas).
106 See ZNS, vol. II, index, ZNY, ed., Urunbaev, index, ZNY I, pp. 441, 475, ZNS II, p. 61, *Cinq opuscules*, text, p. 14.
107 *Baburnāma*, pp. 272, 273, 278, *Tārīkh-i Rashīdī*, pp. 305–9, 459.
108 *Tārīkh-i Ṭabaristān*, p. 301.
109 Doerfer, *Türkische und mongolische Elemente*, vol. II, pp. 366–7. Mirza Ḥaydar, distinguishing the *bahadurs* from the *amīrs*, wrote that they were a different set of people, who fought alone without a following, but had distinguished themselves in past battles. (*Tārīkh-i Rashīdī*, p. 301.)
110 ZNS II, p. 38.
111 ZNY I, p. 162, *Muᶜizz*, ff. 98a–98b.
112 ZNS II, index, ZNY, ed., Urunbaev, index, and as examples: Aqtemür, ZNY I, pp. 179,

193, 197, 203, 207–8, 449, 264, 267, 325; Elchi Bugha, ZNY I, pp. 194, 196, 202, 207, 219, 261; Khitay Bahadur, ZNY I, pp. 167, 170, 179, 197, 202, 207; Sevinchek Bahadur, ZNY I, pp. 234, 270, 278, 323, 335, 354, 375, 381, 417.

113 The list includes Shaykh Temür, who in 793/1391 is mentioned as emir of a *tümen*. (ZNY I, pp. 193, 389.) Shaykh ᶜAlī Bahadur and Sevinchek Bahadur also both commanded *tümens*. (ZNY I, p. 251, II, pp. 320–1, ZNS II, p. 48.)

114 We find listed several sets of fathers and sons, or older and younger relatives: Aqtemür (d. 788) and his son Shaykh Temür, Shaykh ᶜAlī Bahadur (last mentioned in 801) and his son Sayyid ᶜAlī, Khitay Bahadur (d. 780) and his brother Sevinchek. (*Muᶜizz*, ff. 98a–b, ZNY I, pp. 207, 288, II, p. 27.)

Bibliography

Primary sources

Aḥmad b. Ḥusayn b. ᶜAlī Kātib, *Tārīkh-i jadīd-i Yazd*, ed. Īrāj Afshār, Tehran, sh. 1345/1966.

Arends, A. K., Khalidov, A. B., Chekhovich, O. D., *Bukharskiĭ vaqf* XIII *v.*, Moscow, 1979.

Aubin, Jean, ed., *Matériaux pour la biographie de Shāh Niᶜmatullāh Walī Kermānī*, Paris; Tehran, 1956.

Babur, Ẓahīr al-Dīn Muḥammad, *The Bābur-Nāma in English (Memoirs of Bābur)*, trans., A. S. Beveridge, London, 1922 (reprinted, 1969).

Baburnāma: see Babur, Ẓahīr al-Dīn Muḥammad.

Bāfqī, Muḥammad-Mufīd Mustawfī, *Jāmiᶜ-i mufīdī*, ed., Īrāj Afshār, Tehran, vol. I, sh. 1342/1963, vol. III, sh. 1340/1961.

Boyle, *Successors*: see Rashīd al-Dīn.

Chekhovich, O. D., *Bukharskie dokumenty* XIV *veka*, Tashkent, 1965.

Cinq opuscules: see Ḥāfiẓ-i Abrū.

Clavijo, Ruy González de, *Narrative of the Spanish Embassy to the Court of Timur at Samarkand in the years 1403–1406*, trans., Guy Le Strange, London, 1928 (Broadway Travellers Series).

Dastūr al-Kātib: see Nakhchiwānī, Muḥammad b. Hindushāh.

Dastūr al-wuzarā': see Khwāndamīr, Ghiyāth al-Dīn.

Dawlatshāh Samarqandī, *The Tadhkiratu' sh-Shuᶜara* ("*Memoirs of the Poets*"), ed., E. G. Browne, London, 1901.

Faṣīḥ Khwāfī, Aḥmad b. Jalāl al-Dīn, *Mujmal-i faṣīhī*, ed., Muḥammad Farrukh, 3 vols., Mashhad, sh. 1339/1960–1.

Foma Metsopskiĭ, *Istoriia Timur-lanka*, trans., T. I. Ter-Grigorian, Baku, 1957.

H.A.: see Ḥāfiẓ-i Abrū.

H.A. *Majmaᶜ*: see Ḥāfiẓ-i Abrū, *Majmaᶜ*.

Ḥāfiẓ-i Abrū, *Dhayl-i jāmiᶜ al-tawārīkh-i rashīdī*, ed., Kh. Bayānī, Tehran, sh. 1350/1972–3.

Cinq opuscules de Ḥāfiẓ-i Abrū concernant l'histoire de l'Iran au temps de Tamerlan, ed., F. Tauer, Prague, 1959.

"Continuation du *Ẓafarnāma* de Niẓāmuddīn Šāmī par Ḥāfiẓ-i Abrū," ed., F. Tauer, *Archiv Orientální*, VI (1934), pp. 429–66.

Majmaᶜ al-tawārīkh (also called *Zubdat al-tawārīkh*) MS. Instanbul, Fatih 4371/1.

Geography MS. London, British Library, Or. 1577.

Jughrāfiyā-i Ḥāfiẓ-i Abrū: qismat-i rubᶜ-i Khurāsān, Harāt, ed., Māyil Harawī, Tehran, sh. 1349/1971–2.

Haft iqlīm, trans., E. M. Quatremère, *Notices et extraits des manuscrits de la Bibliothèque du Roi et autres bibliothèques*, vol. XIV, pt. I (Paris, 1843).

al-Harawī, Sayf ibn Muḥammad ibn Ya^c^qūb, *The Ta'rīkh Nāma-i Harāt*, ed., Muḥammad Zubayr al-Ṣiddīqī, Calcutta, 1944.

Ibn ^c^Arabshāh, Aḥmad, *Tamerlane or Timur the Great Amir*, trans. J. H. Sanders, London, 1936 (reprinted, Lahore, 1976). (Where not otherwise indicated, citations from Ibn ^c^Arabshāh refer to this edition.)

The Timurnamah, or Ajayabul magfur fi akhbar-i Timur, ed., H. S. Jarrett, Calcutta, 1882.

Ibn Baṭṭūṭa, Shams al-Dīn, *The Travels of Ibn Baṭṭūṭa*, trans, H. A. R. Gibb, 3 vols., Cambridge, 1958–71 (Hakluyt Society).

Ibn Khaldūn, *Ibn Khaldun and Tamerlane*, ed. and trans. Walter Fischel (Berkeley; Los Angeles, 1952).

Isfizārī, Mu^c^īn al-Dīn Muḥammad Zamchī, *Rawḍāt al-jannāt fī awṣāf-i madīnat-i Harāt*, ed., Sayyid Muḥammad Kāẓim Ayām, 2 vols., Tehran, sh. 1338/1959.

Ja^c^farī, Ja^c^far b. Muḥammad al-Ḥusaynī, "Der Bericht über die Nachfolger Timurs aus dem Tāriḫ-i Kabīr des Ca^c^far ibn Muḥammad al-Ḥusaynī," trans., Abbas Zaryab, Doctoral Dissertation, Mainz, 1960.

Tārīkh-i Kabīr, MS. Leningrad, Publichnaia Biblioteka, P.N.C. 201.

Tārīkh-i Yazd, ed., Īrāj Afshār, Tehran, sh. 1338/1960.

Jāmi^c^-i mufīdī: see Bāfqī, Muḥammad-Mufīd Mustawfī.

Jean of Sultaniyya, "Mémoire sur Tamerlan et sa cour par un Dominicain, en 1403," ed., H. Moranvillé, *Bibliothèque de l'École des Chartes*, vol. 55 (Paris, 1894), pp. 433–64.

Khwāndamīr, Ghiyāth al-Dīn b. Humām al-Dīn, *Dastūr al-wuzarā'*, ed., Sa^c^īd Nafīsī, Tehran, sh. 1317/1938–9.

Kutubī, Maḥmūd, *Tārīkh-i āl-i Muẓaffar*, ed. ^c^Abd al-Ḥusayn Nawā'ī, Tehran, sh. 1335/1956.

Mar^c^ashī, Sayyid Ẓahīr al-Dīn, *Tārīkh-i Gīlān wa Daylamistān*, ed., Manūchihr Sutūda, Tehran, sh. 1347/1969–70.

Tārīkh-i Tabaristān wa Rūyān wa Māzandarān, ed., ^c^Abbās Shāyān, Tehran, sh. 1333/1955.

Marco Polo, *The Book of Ser Marco Polo, the Venetian*, ed. and trans., Henry Yule, 2 vols., London, 1875.

Marwārīd, ^c^Abd Allāh, *Staatsschrieben der Timuridenzeit: Das Šaraf-nāmä des ^c^Abdallāh Marwārīd in kritischer Auswertung*, ed. and trans., Hans Robert Roemer, Wiesbaden, 1952 (Akademie der Wissenschaften und der Literatur, Veröffentlichungen der orientalischen Kommission, III).

Mīrzā Muḥammad Ḥaydar Dughlat, *A History of the Moghuls of Central Asia, being the Tarikh-i Rashidi of Mirza Muhammad Haydar, Dughlát*, trans., E. Denison Ross, ed., N. Elias, London; New York, 1898 (reprinted, 1972).

Mu^c^izz al-ansāb fī shajārat al-ansāb, MS. Paris, Bibliothèque Nationale 67.

Mujmal: see Faṣīḥ Khwāfī, Jalāl al-Dīn Muḥammad.

Muntakhab: see Naṭanzī, Mu^c^īn al-Dīn.

Nakhchiwānī, Muḥammad b. Hindushāh, *Dastūr al-kātib fī ta^c^yīn al-marātib*, ed., A. A. Ali-zade, 2 vols., Moscow, 1964–76 (Pamiatniki literatury narodov vostoka, IX).

Naṭanzī, Mu^c^īn al-Dīn, *Extraits du Muntakhab al-tavārīkh-i Mu^c^īnī (Anonym d'Iskandar)*, ed. Jean Aubin, Tehran, sh. 1336/1957.

Nawā'ī, ^c^Abd al-Ḥusayn, ed., *Asnād wa makātibāt-i tārīkhī-i Īrān*, Tehran, 2536/1977.

Povest' vremennykh let, ed., D. S. Likhachev, trans., B. A. Romanov, pt. 1, Moscow; Leningrad, 1950.
RaD: see Rashīd al-Dīn.
Rashīd al-Dīn, Faḍl Allāh, *Jāmiᶜ al-tawārīkh*, ed., A. A. Ali-zade, 3 vols., Baku, 1957.
Rashīd ad-Dīn, Sbornik letopiseĭ, ed., A. A. Semenov, trans., L. A. Khetagurov, vol. 1, pts. 1 and 2, Moscow; Leningrad, 1952.
Shuᶜab-i panjgāna, MS. Istanbul, Ahmet Salis 2937.
The Successors of Genghis Khan, translated from the Persian of Rashīd al-Dīn, trans., J. A. Boyle, New York; London, 1971 (Persian Heritage Series).
Rūznāma: see Yazdī, Ghiyāth al-Dīn ᶜAlī, *Dnevnik*.
Samarqandī, ᶜAbd al-Razzāq, "Notice de l'ouvrage persan qui a pour titre: Matla-assaadein ou majma-albahrein, et qui contient l'histoire des deux sultans Schahrokh et Abou-Said," trans., E. M. Quatremère, *Notices et extraits des manuscrits de la Bibliothèque du Roi et autres bibliothèques*, XIV, pt. 1 (Paris, 1843).
Sanjian, Avedis, K., ed. and trans., *Colophons of Armenian Manuscripts 1301–1480. A Source for Middle Eastern History*, Cambridge, Mass., 1969.
Schiltberger, Johann, *The Bondage and Travels of Johann Schiltberger, in Europe, Asia and Africa, 1396–1427*, trans., J. Buchan Telfer, London, 1879 (Hakluyt Society).
The Secret History of the Mongols, trans., Frances W. Cleaves, vol. 1 (translation), Cambridge, Mass.; London, 1982 (Harvard-Yenching Institute).
Shāmī, Niẓām al-Dīn, *Histoire des conquêtes de Tamerlan intitulée Ẓafarnāma, par Niẓāmuddīn Šāmī*, ed. F. Tauer, Prague, vol. 1, 1937, vol. II, 1956. (Volume II contains additions made by Ḥāfiẓ-i Abrū.)
Shams: see Tāj al-Salmānī.
Shuᶜab-i panjgāna: see Rashīd al-Dīn.
Tadhkirat al-mulūk: A Manual of Ṣafavid Administration (c. 1137/1725), trans., V. Minorsky, Cambridge, 1943 (E. J. W. Gibb Memorial Series, N.S. XVI).
Tāj al-Salmānī, *Šams al-Ḥusn: eine Chronik vom Tode Timurs bis zum Jahre 1409 von Tağ al-Salmānī*, ed. and trans., Hans Robert Roemer, Wiesbaden, 1956 (Akademie der Wissenschaften und der Literatur. Veröffentlichungen der orientalischen Kommission, VIII).
Tārīkh-i Gīlān: see Marᶜashī, Sayyid Ẓahīr al-Dīn.
Tārīkh-i jadīd: see Aḥmad b. Ḥusayn b. ᶜAlī.
Tārīkh-i Rashīdī: see Mīrzā Muḥammad Ḥaydar Dughlat.
Tārīkh-i Ṭabaristān: see Marᶜashī, Sayyid Ẓahīr al-Dīn.
Tārīkh-i Yazd: see Jaᶜfarī, Jaᶜfar b. Muḥammad al-Ḥusaynī.
Thomas of Metsop: see Foma Metsopskii.
Tisengausen, V., ed. and trans., *Sbornik materialov, otnosiashchikhsa k istorii Zolotoĭ Ordy*, vol. 1, St. Petersburg, 1884.
al-ᶜUmarī, *Das mongolische Weltreich: al-ᶜUmarīs Darstellung der mongolischen Reiche in seinem Werk Masālik al-abṣār fī mamālik al-amṣār*, ed. and trans., Klaus Lech, Wiesbaden, 1968.
Yazdī, Ghiyāth al-Dīn ᶜAlī, *Ģiyāsaddīn ᶜAlī, Dvenik pokhoda Tīmūra v Indiiu*, trans., A. A. Semenov, Moscow, 1958.
Yazdī, Sharaf al-Dīn ᶜAlī, *Ẓafarnāma*, ed., Muḥammad ᶜAbbāsī, 2 vols., Tehran, sh. 1336/1957.
Ẓafarnāme, ed., Urunbaev, Tashkent, 1972.
Yūsuf Ahl, Jalāl al-Dīn, *Farā'id-i Ghiyāthī*, ed., Ḥishmat Mu'ayyad, vol. 1, Tehran, 2536/1977.

ZNS: see Shāmī, Niẓām al-Dīn, *Ẓafarnāma*.
ZNY: see Yazdī, Sharaf al-Dīn, *Ẓafarnāma*, ed. ᶜAbbāsī.

Secondary works

Akhmedov, B. A., *Gosudarstvo kochevykh Uzbekov*, Moscow, 1965.

Ali-zade, A. A. *Sotsial'no-ekonomicheskaia i politicheskaia istoriia Azarbaidzhana XIII–XIV* vv., Baku, 1956.

Allsen, Thomas T., "Guard and government in the Reign of the Grand Qan Möngke, 1251–59," *Harvard Journal of Asiatic Studies*, vol. 46, # 2 (1986), pp. 495–521.

"Mongol Census Taking in Rus', 1245–1275," *Harvard Ukrainian Studies*, V # 1 (1981), pp. 32–53.

Mongol Imperialism, Berkeley; Los Angeles; London, 1987.

Aubin, Jean, "Comment Tamerlan prenait les villes," *Studia Islamica*, XIX (1963), pp. 83–122.

Deux sayyids de Bam au xv. siècle; contribution à l'histoire de l'Iran timouride, Wiesbaden, 1956. (Akademie der Wissenschaften und der Literatur, *Abhandlungen der Geistes- und sozialwissenschaftlichen Klasse*, 1956 # 7).

"La fin de l'état Sarbadâr du Khorasan," *Journal asiatique*, 262 (1974), pp. 95–117.

"Le Khanat de Čaġatai et le Khorasan (1334–1380)," *Turcica*, VIII # 2 (1976), pp. 16–60.

"l'Ethnogénèse des Qaraunas," *Turcica* I (1969), pp. 65–94.

"Un santon quhistānī de l'époque timouride," *Revue des études islamiques*, XXXV (1967).

Ayalon, David, "Aspects of the *Mamluk* Phenomenon," *Der Islam*, vol. 53 (1976), pp. 196–255, vol. 54 (1977), pp. 1–32.

"The Great *Yāsa* of Chingiz Khān. A Reexamination," A, *Studia Islamica*, vol. XXXIII (1971), pp. 97–140.

Bacon, Elizabeth, *Obok: a Study of Social Structure in Eurasia*, New York, 1958 (Viking Fund Publications in Anthropology, # 25).

Barfield, Thomas, *Inner Asia: A Study in Frontier History*, Draft manuscript for Foreign Cultures 38, Harvard University, 1986.

Barth, Fredrik, *Nomads of South Persia*, Oslo; London; New York, 1964.

Bartol'd, V. V., "Badakhshān," in *Encyclopaedia of Islam*, N.E. vol. I, pp. 851–5 (revised by A. Bennigsen and H. Carrère-d'Encausse).

"Djuwaynī, ᶜAlā al-Dīn ᶜAtā-Malik," in *Encyclopaedia of Islam*, N.E., vol. II, pp. 606–7 (revised by J. A. Boyle).

Dvenadtsat' lektsii po istorii turetskikh narodov Sredneĭ Azii, in *Sochineniia*, vol. V, Moscow, 1968, pp. 16–192.

Istoriia Turkestana, in *Sochineniia*, vol. II, pt. 1, Moscow, 1963, pp. 109–66.

Mir Ali-Shir i politicheskaia zhizn', in *Sochineniia*, vol. II, pt. 2, Moscow, 1964.

"O pogrebenii Timura," *Sochineniia*, vol. II, pt. 2 (Moscow, 1964), pp. 423–54.

"Persidskaia nadpis' na stene Anniĭskoĭ mecheti," in *Sochineniia*, vol. IV (1966), pp. 332–3.

Review of Charles Schefer, "Description topographique et historique et Boukhara par Mohammed Nerchakhy, suivie de textes relatifs à la Transoxiane," in *Sochineniia*, vol. VIII, Moscow, 1973, pp. 17–20.

Turkestan down to the Mongol Invasion, trans., T. Minorsky (3rd edition), London, 1968.

Turkestan v epokhu mongol'skogo nashestviia, in *Sochineniia*, vol. I, Moscow, 1963.
Ulugbek i ego vremia, in *Sochineniia*, vol. II, pt. 2, Moscow, 1964.
Bausani, A., "Religion under the Mongols" in *Cambridge History of Iran*, vol. 5, Cambridge, 1968, pp. 538–49.
Bayānī, Shīrīn, *Tārīkh-i āl-i Jalāyir*, Tehran, sh. 1345/1967.
Beck, Lois, *The Qashqa'i of Iran*, New Haven; London, 1986.
Belenitskiĭ, A., "K istorii feodal'nogo zemlevladeniia v Sredneĭ Azii i Irane v timuridskuiu epokhu (XIV–XV vv.)," *Istorik-marksist*, 1941 # 4, pp. 43–58.
Blair, Sheila, "The Mongol Capital of Sulṭāniyya, 'The Imperial'," *Iran*, vol. 24 (1986) pp. 139–51.
Bosworth, C. E., "Ghaznevid Military Organization," *Der Islam*, 36 (1960), pp. 37–77.
The Ghaznavids: Their Empire in Afghanistan and Eastern Iran 944–1040 (2nd edition) Beirut, 1973.
"Khaladj," in *Encyclopaedia of Islam*, N.E., vol. IV, pp. 917–18.
"The Political and Dynastic History of the Iranian World (A.D. 1000–1217)," in *The Cambridge History of Iran*, vol. v, Cambridge, 1968, pp. 1–102.
"Recruitment, Muster and Review in Medieval Islamic Armies," in V. J. Parry and M. E. Yapp, eds., *War, Technology and Society in the Middle East*, London, 1975, pp. 59–77.
Boyle, J. A., "Dynastic and Political History of the Īl-khāns," in *The Cambridge History of Iran*, vol. v, Cambridge, 1968, pp. 303–422.
Buell, Paul D., "Tribe, *Qan* and *Ulus* in Early Mongol China: some Prolegomena to Yüan History," Doctoral Dissertation, University of Washington, 1977.
Busse, Heribert, *Untersuchungen zum islamischen Kanzleiwesen an Hand turkmenischer und safawidischer Urkunden* (Abhandlungen des deutschen archäologischen Instituts Kairo, Islamische Reihe I) Cairo, 1959.
Cahen, Claude, "The Body Politic," in G. E. Von Grunebaum, ed., *Unity and Variety in Muslim Civilization*, Chicago, 1955, pp. 132–63.
"l'Evolution de *l'iqṭāᶜ* du IXe au XIIIe siècle," *Annales Economies, sociétés, civilizations*, VIII # 1 (1953), pp. 25–52.
Doerfer, Gerhard, *Türkische und mongolische Elemente in Neupersischen*, Band I: *Mongolische Elemente im Neupersischen*, Band II–IV: *Türkische Elemente im Neupersischen*, in *Akademie der Wissenschaften und der Literatur, Veröffentlichungen der orientalischen Kommission*, vols. 16 (Band I) 1963, 19–21 (Band II–IV), 1965, 1967, 1975.
Endicott-West, Elizabeth, "Regional and Local Government in Yüan China," Doctoral Dissertation, Princeton University, 1982.
"Imperial Governance in Yüan Times," *Harvard Journal of Asiatic Studies*, vol. 46 # 2 (1986), pp. 523–49.
Evans-Pritchard, E. E., *The Nuer*, Oxford, 1940.
Falina, A. I., "Reformy Gazan–Khana," *Uchenye zapiski Instituta Vostokovedeniia Akademii Nauk SSSR*, XVII (1959), pp. 51–71.
Fedorov-Davydov, G. A., *Obshchestvennyĭ stroĭ Zolotoĭ Ordy*, Moscow, 1973.
Fletcher, Joseph, "Turco-Mongolian Monarchic Tradition in the Ottoman Empire," in *Eucharisterion: Essays Presented to Omeljan Pritsak on his Sixtieth Birthday by his Colleagues and Students*, in *Harvard Ukrainian Studies* III–IV (1979–80) pt. 1, pp. 236–51.
"The Mongols: Ecological and Social Perspectives," *Harvard Journal of Asiatic Studies*, vol. 46 # 1 (1986), pp. 11–50.
Franke, Herbert, "From Tribal Chieftain to Universal Emperor and God: the

Legitimation of the Yüan Dynasty," *Bayerische Akademie der Wissenschaften*, Phil.-hist. Klasse, Sitzungsberichte, 1978, H. 2 (Munich, 1978).
Gellner, Ernest, *Muslim Society*, Cambridge, 1981.
Gafurov, B. G., ed., *Istoriia tadzhikskogo naroda*, 2 vols., Moscow, 1963–5.
Grekov, B. and Iakubovskiĭ, A., *Zolotaia Orda i ee padenie*, Moscow; Leningrad, 1950.
Grivor'ev, A. P., "Ofitsial'nyĭ iazyk Zolotoĭ Ordy XIII–XIV vekov," *Tiurkologicheskiĭ sbornik*, vol. 9 (1977).
Grousset, René, *l'Empire Mongol (1re phase)*, Paris, 1941.
The Empire of the Steppes, trans., N. Walford, New Brunswick, N.J., 1970.
Halperin, Charles J., *Russia and the Golden Horde*, Bloomington, 1985.
Herrmann, Gottfried and Doerfer, Gerhard, "Ein persisch-mongolischer Erlass des Ǧalāyeriden Šeyḫ Oveys," *Central Asiatic Journal*, vol. XIX # 1–2 (1975), pp. 1–84.
Hodgson, Marshall G. S., *The Venture of Islam*, 3 vols., Chicago; London, 1974.
Holod-Tretiak, Renata, "The Monuments of Yazd, 1300–1450: Architecture, Patronage and Setting," Doctoral Dissertation, Harvard University, 1972.
Howorth, Henry H., *History of the Mongols from the 9th to the 19th Century*, Part III: The Mongols in Persia, London, 1888.
Hsiao, Ch'i-ch'ing, *The Military Establishment of the Yuan Dynasty*, Cambridge, Mass., 1978 (Harvard East Asian Monographs # 77).
Humlum, Johannes, *La géographie de l'Afghanistan*, Copenhagen; Stockholm; Oslo; Helsinki, 1959.
Inalcik, Halil, "The Khan and the Tribal Aristocracy: the Crimean Khanate under Ṣāḥib Giray I," in *Eucharisterion: Essays Presented to Omeljan Pritsak on his Sixtieth Birthday by his Colleagues and Students*, in *Harvard Ukrainian Studies*, III–IV, 1979–80, pp. 445–66.
Irons, William G., *The Yomut Turkmen: A Study of Social Organization among a Central Asian Turkic-speaking Population*, Ann Arbor, 1975 (Anthropological Paper # 58, University of Michigan Museum of Anthropology) 1969.
Jackson, Peter, "The Dissolution of the Mongol Empire," *Central Asiatic Journal*, XXII # 3–4 (1978), pp. 186–244.
"The Mongols and the Delhi Sultanate in the Reign of Muhammad Tughluq (1325–1351)," *Central Asiatic Journal*, XIX # 1–2 (1975), pp. 118–56.
Jahn, Karl, *Die Chinageschichte des Rašīd ad-Dīn* (Österreichische Akademie der Wissenschaften, Phil.-hist. Klasse, Denkschriften 105, Vienna, 1971).
"Paper Currency in Iran," *Journal of Asian History*, vol. 4 # 2 (1970), pp. 101–35.
"Zum Problem der mongolischen Eroberungen in Indien (13–14 Jahrhundert)," *Akten des vierundzwanzigsten internationalen Orientalisten-Kongresses, München, Aug.–Sept. 1957*, Wiesbaden, 1959, pp. 617–19.
Kempiners, Russell G., "The Struggle for Khurāsān: Aspects of Political, Military and Socio-economic Interaction in the Early 8th/14th Century," Doctoral Dissertation, University of Chicago, 1985.
Kirchhoff, Paul, "The Principles of Clanship in Human Society," *Davidson Journal of Anthropology* I (1955) pp. 1–10.
Lambton, A. K. S., "Dīwān," pt. iii: "Iran," *Encyclopaedia of Islam*, N.E., vol. II, pp. 332–6.
"The Internal Structure of the Saljuq Empire," in *The Cambridge History of Iran*, vol. V, Cambridge, 1968, pp. 203–83.
Landlord and Peasant in Persia (2nd printing) London, 1969 (1st edition, 1953).
"Reflections on the *Iqṭāᶜ*," in George Makdisi, ed., *Arabic and Islamic Studies in honor of Hamilton A. R. Gibb*, Cambridge, Mass., 1965, pp. 358–76.

Le Strange, Guy, *The Lands of the Eastern Caliphate*, Cambridge, 1930 (Cambridge Geographical Series).

Lewis, Herbert S., "Typology and Process in Political Evolution," in June Helm, ed., *Essays on the Problem of Tribe: Proceedings of the 1967 Annual Spring Meeting of the American Ethnological Society*, Seattle, 1968, pp. 101–10.

Lindner, Rudi Paul, *Nomads and Ottomans in Medieval Anatolia* (Indiana University Uralic and Altaic Series, vol. 144), Bloomington, 1983.

"What Was a Nomadic Tribe?," *Comparative Studies in Society and History*, 24 # 4 (1982), pp. 689–711.

Makhmudov, N., "Iz istorii zemel'nykh otnosheniĭ i nalogovoĭ politiki Timuridov," in *Izvestiia Akademii Nauk Tadzh. SSR*, otd. obshchestvennykh nauk, 32 # 1 (1963), pp. 21–33.

Manz, Beatrice Forbes, "Administration and the Delegation of Authority in Temür's Dominions," *Central Asiatic Journal*, xx # 3 (1976), pp. 191–207.

"The Office of *Darugha* under Tamerlane," *An Anniversary Volume in Honor of Francis Woodman Cleaves, Journal of Turkish Studies*, vol. 9 (1965), pp. 59–69.

"Tamerlane and the Symbolism of Sovereignty," *Iranian Studies*, vol. xxi # 1–2, pp. 105–22.

Markov, G. E., *Kochevniki Azii*, Moscow, 1976.

Minorsky, Vladimir, "The Aq-qoyunlu and Land Reforms," *Bulletin of the School of Oriental and African Studies*, xvii # 3 (1955), pp. 449–62.

"A Civil and Military Review in Fars in 881/1476," *Bulletin of the School of Oriental and African Studies*, x # 1 (1939), pp. 141–78.

"Lur," in *Encyclopaedia of Islam* (old ed.), vol. iii, pp. 41–6.

"Lur-i Buzurg," in *Encyclopaedia of Islam* (old ed.), vol. iii, pp. 46–8.

"Lur-i Kūčik," in *Encyclopaedia of Islam* (old ed.), vol. iii, pp. 48–50.

and M. Minovi, "Naṣīr al-Dīn Ṭūsī on Finance," *Bulletin of the School of Oriental and African Studies*, x # 3 (1940), pp. 755–89.

Morgan, D. O., "The Mongol Armies in Persia," *Der Islam*, 56 # 1 (1979), pp. 81–96.

The Mongols, Oxford, 1986.

"The 'Great *Yāsā* of Chingiz Khān' and Mongol Law in the Īlkhānate," *Bulletin of the School of Oriental and African Studies*, vol. 49 # 1 (1986), pp. 163–76.

Pelliot, Paul, *Notes on Marco Polo*, 3 vols., Paris, 1959.

Notes sur l'histoire de la Horde d'Or, Paris, 1950.

Petrushevskiĭ, I. P., "K istorii instituta *soĭurgala*," *Sovetskoe vostokovedenie*, vi (1949), pp. 227–46.

Zemledelie i agrarnye otnosheniia v Irane xiii–xiv vekov, Moscow; Leningrad, 1960.

"The Socio-economic Condition of Iran under the Īl-Khāns," *Cambridge History of Iran*, vol. v, Cambridge, 1968, pp. 483–537.

Pipes, Daniel, *Slave Soldiers and Islam: The Genesis of a Military System*, New Haven; London, 1981.

Pritsak, Omeljan, "Die 24 Ta-ch'en," *Oriens Extremus*, 1 (1954), pp. 178–201.

"Stammesnamen und Titulaturen der altaischen Völker," *Ural-Altaische Jahrbücher*, xxiv # 1–2 (1952), pp. 49–104.

Rabino di Borgomale, H. L., "Les dynasties locales du Gîlân et du Daylam," *Journal asiatique*, 237 (1949), pp. 301–50.

Rachewiltz, Igor de, "Some Remarks on the Ideological Foundations of Chingis Khan's Empire," *Papers on Far Eastern History*, # 7 (1973), pp. 21–36.

Ratchnevsky, Paul, *Činggis-khan: sein Leben und Wirken*, Wiesbaden, 1983.

Richard, Jean, "La conversion de Berke et les débuts de l'islamisation de la Horde d'Or," *Revue des études islamiques*, vol. 35 (1967), pp. 173–84.
Rickmers, W. Rickmer, *The Duab of Turkestan*, Cambridge, 1913.
Roemer, H. R., "Tīmūr in Iran," in *Cambridge History of Iran*, vol. 6, Cambridge, 1986, pp. 42–97.
Safargaliev, M. G., *Raspad Zolotoĭ Ordy*, Saransk, 1960.
Savory, Roger Mervyn, "The Development of the Early Ṣafawid State under Ismāᶜīl and Taḥmāsp, as studied in the 16th Century Persian Sources," Doctoral Dissertation, University of London, 1958.
Iran under the Safavids, Cambridge, 1980.
"The Struggle for Supremacy in Persia after the Death of Tīmūr," *Der Islam*, XL (1964), pp. 35–65.
Shimo, Hirotoshi, "The Qaraunas in the Historical Materials of the Ilkhanate," *Memoirs of the Research Department of the Toyo Bunko*, 35 (1977), pp. 131–81.
Smith, John M., "D̲j̲alāyir, D̲j̲alāyirids," in *Encyclopaedia of Islam*, N.E., vol. II, pp. 401–2.
"Mongol Manpower and Persian Population," *Journal of the Economic and Social History of the Orient*, XVIII, pt. 3 (1975), pp. 271–99.
Spuler, Bertold, *Die Goldene Horde*, 2nd ed., Wiesbaden, 1965.
Die Mongolen in Iran: Politik, Verwaltung und Kultur der Ilkhanzeit 1220–1350, Berlin, 1985.
Subtelny, Maria Eva, "The Poetic Circle at the Court of the Timurid, Sulṭān Ḥusain Baiqara, and its Political Significance," Doctoral Dissertation, Harvard University, 1979.
Sümer, Farük, "Ḳara-Ḳoyunlu," *Encyclopaedia of Islam*, N.E., vol.IV, pp. 584–8.
Togan, Aḥmad Zeki Velidi, "Qazan-han Halil ve Hoca Bahaeddin Naksbend," *Necati Lugal Armagani*, (Türk tarihi kurumu yayïnlarïndan vii seri Sa. 50), Ankara, 1968.
"Taḥqīq-i nasab-i Amīr Tīmūr," in S. M. ᶜAbdullah, ed. *Professor Muḥammad Shafīᶜ Presentation Volume*, Lahore, 1955.
Tolstov, S. P., ed., *Istoriia Uzbekskoĭ SSR*, 2 vols., Tashkent, 1955.
Trimingham, J. Spencer, *The Sufi Orders in Islam*, Oxford, 1971.
Vladimirtsov, B. Ia, *Obshchestvennyĭ stroĭ mongolov; mongol'skiĭ kochevoĭ feodalizm*, Leningrad, 1934.
Wittfogel, Karl A., and Feng Chia-sheng, *History of Chinese Society: Liao (907–1125)*, Philadelphia, 1949 (Transactions of the American Philosophical Society.)
Woods, John E., *The Aqquyunlu, Clan, Confederation, Empire: a Study in 15th/9th Century Turko-Iranian Politics*, Minneapolis; Chicago, 1976.
"The rise of Tīmūrīd Historiography," *Journal of Near Eastern Studies*, vol. 46 # 2 (1987), pp. 81–108.
"Turco-Iranica II: Notes on a Timurid Decree of 1396/798," *Journal of Near Eastern Studies*, vol. 43 # 4 (1984), pp. 331–7.
Zambaur, Eduard von, *Manuel de généalogie et de chronologie pour l'histoire de l'Islam*, Hanover, 1927.

Index

Abā Bakr b. Amīrānshāh, 77, 85–7, 131, 138, 142–4, 146, 186 n. 31
Abarquh, 112, 122
ᶜAbbās Qipchaq, Bahadur, 46, 74, 76, 78, 121, 163, 186 n. 131, 199 n. 48
ᶜAbd al-Jabbār Khwārazmī, 17
ᶜAbd Allāh b. Qazaghan, of Qara'unas, 34, 44, 47, 55, 58, 64, 164, 181 n. 76, 206 n. 49
ᶜAbd Allāh b. Tayghu, 182 n. 6, 183 n. 21
ᶜAbd al-Raḥmān, tovachï, 100, 124
ᶜAbd al-Raḥmān Qorchï, 124
Abū Isḥāq, 60, 61
Abū Saᶜīd, Ilkhan, 177 n. 11
Abū Saᶜīd b. Tayghu, 183 n. 31
Abū Saᶜīd Besüd, 158
Abū'l-Layth Samarqandī, 60
Abū'l-Maᶜālī, Khāndzāda, of Tirmidh, 60
ᶜĀdil Akhtachï, 172
ᶜĀdil Malik bt. Kayqubād Khuttalānī, 57, 159
ᶜĀdilshāh Jalayir, 61, 62, 64, 75, 119, 158, 163, 196 n. 60
Afrāsiyāb, of Lur-i Buzurg, 92
Agha Begi bt. Temür, 132
Aḥmad, Atabeg of Lur-i Buzurg (Pīr Aḥmad), 92, 94, 101
Aḥmad b. ᶜUmar Shaykh, 140, 186 n. 31, 199 n. 53
Aḥmad Jalayir, Sulṭān, 70–3, 101, 103, 142–3, 199 n. 53
Aḥmad b. Shaykh Ḥasan, 169
Aḥmad Dā'ūd, 169
Aḥmad Yasawī, Shaykh, 17
Ajodhan, 111
akhtachï, 170, 172
Alamut, 191
Alanjak, 95
Aleppo, 73
ᶜAlī Darwīsh Jalayir, 51–2, 57, 61, 63, 158, 183 n. 38
ᶜAlī Darwīsh Barlas, 187 n. 45
ᶜAlī Farāhī, Shāh, 191 n. 33
ᶜAlī Kiyā, Sayyid, 92
ᶜAlī Mu'ayyad Sabzawārī, Khwāja (Sarbadār), 95
ᶜAlī Shīr Nawā'ī, 207 n. 103
ᶜAlī Simnānī, Khwāja, 168
ᶜAlī Sulṭān Tovachï, 100
ᶜAlī Yasa'urī, 52, 53, 56, 164, 165
Allāhdād, Bahadur, 76, 110, 186 n. 28
Alughu Khan, Chaghadayid, 23
amīr, 14, 43, 57; in Temür's administration, 110, 119–20, 123, 126, 151, 164, 174–5, 194 n. 4, 207 nn. 104, 105, 109; *amīr al-umarā'*, 121, 123–4, 141, 156, 170, 173, 189 n. 76; *amīr dīwān* (see also *dīwānī, dīwāniyān*), 165, 169, 175, 185 n. 14, 196 n. 60, 205 nn. 31, 33
Amīr Kulāl, 178 n. 41
Amīr Walī; *see* Walī, Amīr
Amīrānshāh b. Temür, 77, 93, 98, 102, 157, 168, 169, 173, 189 n. 81, 200 n. 74; appointed governor of Khorasan, 70, 85, 189 nn. 76, 87; appointed governor of W. Iran, 72; attempted rebellion, 72–3, 110–11, 114; sons, 87–8, 131, 138, 186 n. 31; after Temür's death, 141–4
Amul, 17, 92–5
Anatolia, 1, 10, 11, 72–3, 80, 90, 93, 103
Andkhud, 17, 27, 31, 51, 56, 132, 140, 154–5, 178 n. 41, 181 n. 66
Andijan, 62, 85, 87, 134, 161
Angren River, 23
Ankara, 73
Anūshīrwān b. Aqbugha, 85
Apardï tribe, 154–5, 187 n. 38, 200 n. 4, 203–4 n. 140; origins, 28, 180 n. 29; within the Ulus Chaghatay, 27–8, 31, 35, 43–4, 159, 161, 179 n. 24, 182 nn. 5, 6; during Temür's rise, 51, 56–7; during Temür's reign, 59–60, 62, 75–6, 79, 82–3, 85, 88, 119, 184 n. 67, 185 n. 23, 188 nn. 52, 54, 196 n. 61; after Temür's death, 136, 140, 199 n. 57
Aqbugha Besüd, 158